Lecture Notes in Computer Science 2712

Edited by G. Goos, J. Hartmanis, and J. van Leeuwen

W0225733

Springer
Berlin
Heidelberg
New York
Hong Kong
London
Milan
Paris
Tokyo

Anne James   Brian Lings
Muhammad Younas (Eds.)

New Horizons in
Information Management

20th British National Conference on Databases, BNCOD 20
Coventry, UK, July 15-17, 2003
Proceedings

 Springer

Series Editors

Gerhard Goos, Karlsruhe University, Germany
Juris Hartmanis, Cornell University, NY, USA
Jan van Leeuwen, Utrecht University, The Netherlands

Volume Editors

Anne James
Muhammad Younas
Coventry University, School of Mathematical and Information Sciences
Priory Street, Coventry CV1 5FB, UK
E-mail: {A.James,M.Younas}@coventry.ac.uk

Brian Lings
University of Exeter, Department of Computer Science
Prince of Wales Road, Exeter EX4 4PT, UK
E-mail: B.J.Lings@exeter.ac.uk

Cataloging-in-Publication Data applied for

Bibliographic information published by Die Deutsche Bibliothek
 Die Deutsche Bibliothek lists this publication in the Deutsche Nationalbibliografie;

detailed bibliographic data is available in the Internet at <http://dnb.ddb.de>.

CR Subject Classification (1998): H.2-4

ISSN 0302-9743
ISBN 3-540-40536-4 Springer-Verlag Berlin Heidelberg New York

Springer-Verlag Berlin Heidelberg New York
a member of BertelsmannSpringer Science+Business Media GmbH

http://www.springer.de

© Springer-Verlag Berlin Heidelberg 2003
Printed in Germany

Typesetting: Camera-ready by author, data conversion by PTP-Berlin GmbH
Printed on acid-free paper   SPIN: 10928776   06/3142   5 4 3 2 1 0

Preface

The British National Conference on Databases (BNCOD) was established in 1980 as a forum for research into the theory and practice of databases. The 20th in the series (BNCOD 20) was held at Coventry University in July 2003. This volume contains the BNCOD 20 proceedings. It was a delight to welcome researchers from all over the world to BNCOD 20. A strong response to our call for research papers together with the thoughtful work of the programme committee led to an excellent technical programme covering many fascinating challenges facing the database world today.

The theme of BNCOD 20 was "New Horizons in Information Management". Over the last decades database technology has become embedded in most of the information systems we use in commerce and industry and has been proven to be an essential tool in information management. Advances in database technology have enabled new methods of working with information. Similarly, new requirements of information systems have led to extensions of database technology. Novel application areas demand further development and integration of database theory within emerging fields. BNCOD 20 called for papers on new directions in information management and how database techniques are being adapted to support these. The global technological infrastructure is considered to be particularly pertinent. Thus areas such as the Semantic Web, the Hidden Web, information systems integration, information retrieval, co-operative working and Web-based agents, as they relate to databases, were of considerable interest.

BNCOD 20 had great pleasure in receiving two eminent invited speakers: Prof. Malcolm Atkinson from the Universities of Glasgow and Edinburgh, Scotland, UK and Director of the National e-Science Centre, Scotland, UK and Prof. Hector Garcia-Molina from Stanford University, USA. Both considered the challenges and opportunities afforded by the new technological environment.

Malcolm Atkinson has a long track record of contributions to research in large and long-lived systems. He is currently working on GridNet, a project to establish a UK Network of Excellence in Grid Computing and e-Science. He is also working on the auto-optimization of highly scalable index frameworks for large collections of reference data and developing techniques and software to support management and monitoring of user actions in distributed systems. In this invited presentation Malcolm explores the Grid and e-Science. He raises the question of how DBMS will fit into the "global computing machine" and considers the extent to which current database solutions fit the new Grid operation model.

Hector Garcia-Molina is the Leonard Bosack and Sandra Lerner Professor in the Departments of Computer Science and Electrical Engineering at Stanford University, Stanford, USA. He is the current chairman of the Computer Science Department and was the recipient of the 1999 ACM SIGMOD Innovations Award. His research interests include distributed computing systems, digital libraries and database systems. Hector is currently involved in developing improved methods for searching the Web and also techniques for managing peer-to-peer networks. In his presentation he addressed the area of Web crawling. Web crawlers can consume significant resources. Hector discusses how efficient crawlers can be built and how the Hidden Web can be accessed.

The refereed papers are presented in five sessions. The first refereed paper session is on XML and Semistructured Data and contains two full and two short papers. The first paper by Vincent et al. defines multivalued dependencies in XML (XMVDs). It shows that, for a very general class of mappings from relations to XML, a relation satisfies an MVD if and only if the corresponding XML document satisfies the corresponding XMVD. Thus they consider their definition of XMVD in XML documents to be a natural extension of the definition of MVD in relations. Moon et al. investigate the problem of processing an XML path expression using an XML cache maintained as materialized views. They propose algorithms to rewrite the given XML path expression using its relevant materialized view, and also provide implementation details of their approach. The paper by Pandrangi et al. describes WebVigil, a system for detecting changes in Web pages based on user profiles. Although this approach is discussed in the context of HTML and XML it can be generalized to other technologies. The session ends with two short papers, which are related to ontologies. The first paper by Bi et al. describes a query paradigm based on ontologies, aggregate table-driven querying, and expansion of QBE. The authors claim two novel features: visually specifying aggregate table queries and table layout in a single process and providing users with an ontology guide in composing complex analysis tasks as queries. The final short paper by Volz considers the requirements for a new level of data independence for ontology-based applications. For example, customization for other agents may be required. It proposes a solution based on the idea of integrative external ontologies.

The second refereed paper session is on Performance in Searching and Mining and contains three full and one short paper. The first paper by Garcia-Arellano et al. evaluates the relative performance of the IQ-tree and the A-tree in similarity search in high-dimensional data spaces. They introduce the Clustered IQ-tree, which is an indexing strategy that combines the best features of the IQ tree and the A-tree leading to a seemingly better and more stable performance over different types of data set. The paper by Mishra et al. concentrates on the K-way join approach, a technique for mining data irrespective of stored format. The authors look at various optimization methods for the K-way join and evaluate them. This work aims at feeding the results into an optimizer for data mining. The paper by Yiannis et al. explores the effects of compression on the cost of external sorting. Whilst compression can often be useful, on-the-fly compression can be slow and some compression techniques do not allow random access to individual records. Yiannis et al. look at these issues for various techniques and develop improved solutions. They show that incorporation of compression can significantly accelerate query processing. The final paper of the session is a short paper by Srikumar et al. In the paper the authors present MaxDomino, an algorithm for mining maximal frequent sets using the novel concept of the dominancy factor of a transaction.

Transformation, integration and extension were the topics of the third refereed paper session. This session contained three full and two short papers. Engstrom et al. consider maintenance policies for externally materialized multi-source views. They consider various methods and show that in all situations it is more efficient to use auxiliary views than policies which require consistency-preserving algorithms. Tong considers transformation optimization techniques within the automed database integration system. A new representation of schema transformations is presented.

These are claimed to facilitate the verification of well-formedness and the optimization of the transformation sequences. The paper by Scallehn et al. raises the issue of dealing with discrepancies in data integration. The authors present similarity-based variants of grouping and join operations as a solution to this problem of attributes that are similar but not equal. The first of the two short papers in this session is by Green et al. They describe ProSQL, a prototyping tool to support the development of extensions to SQL. The system was developed by building a wrapper around an existing DBMS and providing a collection of interfaces through which a designer can define extensions to the basic relational database. The final short paper by Al-Mourad et al. addresses the problem of integrating object-oriented schemas with multiple behaviour requirements. The Multiple Views supporting the Multiple Behaviours System (MVMBS) is described.

The fourth refereed paper session was on events and transactions and included two full and two short papers. Hinze tackles the problem of rapid notification of composite events. Currently the detection of composite events requires a second filtering step after the identification of the primitive components. Hinze proposes a single-step method for the filtering of composite events, and presents results which show improvement in performance for event filtering. Ray investigates an interesting issue of multi-level secure (MLS) active database systems by defining MLS rules and assigning them security levels. Ray also determines the impact of MLS rules on the execution models of existing active database systems. The short paper by Howard et al. describes a Compliant Systems Architecture (CSA) and shows how it can deliver flexibility within a two-phase commit protocol of distributed transactions. CSA aims at providing strict separation of policy and mechanism. Lim et al. present a new concurrent B^{link}-tree algorithm that provides a concurrent tree restructuring mechanism for handling underflow nodes as well as overflow nodes.

Two short papers are delivered in the final refereed paper session, which is on Personalisation and the Web. Dempster et al. discuss a framework for personalisation and an initial prototype toolkit. Cooper et al. propose an approach to information extraction from e-mail text, which involves creating sentence structures from metadata, pattern-matching, and generating update statements.

Once again BNCOD yielded an excellent range of papers. This was through the industry and interest of our international research community and this is much appreciated. The pivotal role of databases in information systems continues to interest, challenge and provide opportunities for the development of new and improved systems.

Acknowledgements

We would like to thank the programme committee for their excellent work in reviewing and providing comments on the many papers submitted to the conference. Once again their dedication and commitment helped to produce another inspiring and technical programme of the high standard expected of the BNCOD series. Thanks go also to Alex Gray for inviting us to organize BNCOD20 and for providing useful advice and enthusiasm throughout. Thanks also to Mary Garvey and Mike Jackson for help with the organization and sharing of ideas. The administrative support of Serena Morgan and Rachel Carter was most appreciated and likewise the help provided at the conference by Yih-Ling Hedley, Rahat Iqbal and Mofed Salem.

April 2003   Anne James, Brian Lings, Muhammad Younas

Conference Committees

Programme Committee

Brian Lings (Chair)	University of Exeter
David Bell	University of Ulster
Peter Buneman	University of Edinburgh
Barry Eaglestone	University of Sheffield
Suzanne Embury	University of Manchester
Alex Gray	University of Wales, Cardiff
Peter Gray	University of Aberdeen
Mike Jackson	University of Wolverhampton
Anne James	Coventry University
Keith Jeffery	CLRC Rutherford Appleton
Jessie Kennedy	Napier University
Nigel Martin	Birkbeck College, University of London
Peter McBrien	Imperial College, University of London
Ken Moody	University of Cambridge
Werner Nutt,	Heriot-Watt University
Norman Paton	University of Manchester
Alexandra Poulovassilis	Birkbeck College, University of London
Brian Read	London Metropolitan University
Howard Williams	Heriot-Watt University
Muhammad Younas	Coventry University

Organizing Committee

Anne James (Chair)	Coventry University
Mary Garvey	University of Wolverhampton
Alex Gray	University of Wales, Cardiff
Mike Jackson (Prizes Chair)	University of Wolverhampton
Muhammad Younas	Coventry University

Steering Committee

Alex Gray (Chair)	University of Wales, Cardiff
Carole Goble	University of Manchester
Barry Eaglestone	University of Sheffield
Keith Jeffery	CLRC Rutherford Appleton
Roger Johnson	Birkbeck College, University of London
Brian Lings	University of Exeter

Table of Contents

Transformation, Integration, and Extension

Events and Transactions

Personalisation and the Web

Author Index

Databases and the Grid: Who Challenges Whom?

Extended Abstract

Malcolm P. Atkinson

National e-Science Centre, 15 South College Street
Edinburgh, EH8 9AA, UK
mpa@dcs.gla.ac.uk

Abstract. An overview of e-Science and its data requirements exposes a number of challenges and opportunities. The Grid is an attempt to build a virtual abstract operating system, over an arbitrarily large globally distributed collection of heterogeneous resources. The Grid models of authentification, authorisation and accounting, aspire to delivering a single sign-on mechanism for access to this global computer. These models also support dynamic sharing and virtual organisations. The emerging model of composition is based on web services.

Has the database research community done this already? Does the DBMS we have today already fit as components in this 'global' machine? Those DBMS contain many of the resources scientists use, and the scientists want more of them, with even more data. There are more research questions than answers so far, and this talk will seek to engage the Database community in addressing them.

Digital data are now fundamental to all branches of science and engineering; they play a major role in medical research and diagnosis, and underpin business and governmental decision processes. Increasingly these data are organised as shared and structured collections, which are held in databases, in structured documents and in structured assemblies of binary files. The advent of ubiquitous Internet computing and the scale of modern challenges, such as deciphering the function of all the genes in a large number of species, from bacteria to crops, farm animals and humans, has led to widespread collaboration in the creation, curation, publication, management and exploitation of these structured collections. Although individual collections are typically specialized to hold data of interest to particular communities, substantial advances can be achieved by combining information from multiple data resources. For example, astronomers are building virtual observatories, where data collected at different frequencies, X-ray, radio, optical, infrared, etc., and at different times, can be conveniently combined to discover new properties of the universe. Similarly, functional genomics requires comparison between species, integration with protein biochemistry and crystallography databases, laboratory phenotypical data and population studies. Almost every application involves the execution of computational models or computationally demanding analyses using data from diverse sources.

These diverse structured collections are geographically distributed, hosted on a variety of platforms and administered independently according to differing policies. As they increase in scale and number it becomes impractical to arrange their integration by taking local copies or by constructing ad hoc

A. James, B. Lings, M. Younas (Eds.): BNCOD 2003, LNCS 2712, pp. 1–2, 2003.

integration schemes. The Grid provides a platform that potentially enables a systematic approach to this integration. It can support authentication and authorisation, resource discovery, data transmission, process creation and scheduling, and dynamic binding across heterogeneous platforms. These facilities could form a consistent foundation for systematic data access and integration that would be a significant advance over current practice, where each environmental requirement of an integration scheme has to be handled separately on each platform.

The Grid's designers and implementers need to consider data access and integration as a primary application target for two reasons. Firstly, a great many of the applications of the Grid include a significant data access and integration requirement. Virtually every scientific, engineering, medical and decision-support application depends on accessing distributed heterogeneous collections of structured data. Secondly, the Grid itself uses many structured data collections for its own operation and administration. As Grid technology becomes more sophisticated and autonomic, the number, volume and diversity of these collections will increase. It is therefore imperative that Grid designers and developers support and use systematic data access and integration methods.

Challenges in Crawling the Web

Hector Garcia-Molina

Computer Science Department, Stanford University

Abstract. The World Wide Web, or simply the Web, is rapidly becoming the world's collective information store, containing everything from news, to entertainment, to personal communications, to product descriptions. This world information store is distributed across millions of computers, but it is often important to gather significant parts of it at a single site. One reason is to build content indices, such as Google. Another reason is to mine the cached Web, looking for trends or data correlations. A third reason for gathering a Web copy is to create a historical record for Web sites that are ephemeral or changing.

The system that explores the Web and makes copies of discovered pages is called a *crawler*. Crawlers consume significant network and computing resources, both at the visited web servers and at the site(s) collecting the pages, and thus it is critical to make them efficient and well behaved. Furthermore, often pages of interest are in the so-called "hidden-web," reachable only via query interfaces. In this talk I will discuss how to build an effective crawler, addressing questions such as:

 - How can a crawler gather "important" pages only?
 - How can a crawler efficiently maintain its collection "fresh"?
 - How can a crawler be parallelized?
 - How can we access pages from the hidden web?

This is joint work with Junghoo Cho, Taher H. Haveliwala, Wang Lam, Andreas Paepcke, and Sriram Raghavan. Additional information and papers related to this talk can be found at
http://www-diglib.stanford.edu/~testbed/doc2/WebBase/
(or by searching for "Stanford WebBase" at Google).

A. James, B. Lings, M. Younas (Eds.): BNCOD 2003, LNCS 2712, p. 3, 2003.

Multivalued Dependencies in XML

Millist W. Vincent and Jixue Liu

School of Computer and Information Science
University of South Australia
{millist.vincent, jixue.liu }@unisa.edu.au

Abstract. Functional dependencies (FDs) and multivalued dependencies (MVDs) play a fundamental role in relational databases where they provide semantics for the data and at the same time are the foundation for database design. Since XML documents are closely coupled with relational databases in that XML documents are typically exported and imported from relational databases, the study of FDs and MVDs in XML is of fundamental significance in XML research. In this paper we investigate the issue of defining multivalued dependencies in XML, a topic which to the best of our knowledge has not been previously investigated. We define multivalued dependencies in XML (XMVDs) and justify our definition by proving that, for a very general class of mappings from relations to XML, a relation satisfies an MVD if and only if the corresponding XML document satisfies the corresponding XMVD. Thus our definition of a XMVD in a XML document is a natural extension of the definition of a MVD in relations.

1 Introduction

XML has recently emerged as a standard for data representation and interchange on the Internet [18,1]. While providing syntactic flexibility, XML provides little semantic content and as a result several papers have addressed the topic of how to improve the semantic expressiveness of XML. Among the most important of these approaches has been that of defining integrity constraints in XML [5]. Several different classes of integrity constraints for XML have been defined including key constraints [5,6], path constraints [8], and inclusion constraints [9] and properties such as axiomatization and satisfiability have been investigated for these constraints. However, one topic that has been identified as an open problem in XML research [18] and which has been little investigated is how to extended the traditional integrity constraints in relational databases, namely *functional dependencies* (FDs) and *multivalued dependencies* (MVDs), to XML and then how to develop a normalisation theory for XML. This problem is not of just theoretical interest. The theory of normalisation forms the cornerstone of practical relational database design and the development of a similar theory for XML will similarly lay the foundation for understanding how to design XML documents. In addition, the study of FDs and MVDs in XML is important because of the close connection between XML and relational databases. With current technology, the source of XML data is typically a relational database [1] and relational

A. James, B. Lings, M. Younas (Eds.): BNCOD 2003, LNCS 2712, pp. 4–18, 2003.

databases are also normally used to store XML data [12]. Hence, given that FDs and MVDs are the most important constraints in relational databases, the study of these constraints in XML assumes heightened importance over other types of constraints which are unique to XML [7]. The only papers that have specifically addressed the problem of FDs in XML are the recent papers [2,15,16]. Before presenting the contributions of [2,15,16], we briefly outline the approaches to defining FD satisfaction in incomplete relational databases.

There are two approaches, the first called the *weak satisfaction* approach and the other called the *strong satisfaction* approach [3]. In the weak satisfaction approach, a relation is defined to weakly satisfy a FD if there exists *at least one* completion of the relation, obtained by replacing all occurrences of nulls by data values, which satisfies the FD. A relation is said to strongly satisfy a FD if *every* completion of the relation satisfies the FD. Both approaches have their advantages and disadvantages (a more complete discussion of this issue can be found in [15]). The weak satisfaction approach has the advantage of allowing a high degree of uncertainty to be represented in a database but at the expense of making maintenance of integrity constraints much more difficult. In contrast, the strong satisfaction approach restricts the amount of uncertainty that can be represented in a database but makes the maintenance of integrity constraints much easier. However, as argued in [11], both approaches have their place in real world applications and should be viewed as complementary rather than competing approaches. Also, it is possible to combine the two approaches by having some FDs in a relation strongly satisfied and others weakly satisfied [10].

The contribution of [2] was, for the first time, to define FDs in XML (what we call XFDs) and then to define a normal form for a XML document based on the definition of a XFD. However, there are some difficulties with the definition of a XFD given in [2]. The most fundamental problem is that although it is explicitly recognised in the definitions that XML documents have missing information, the definitions in [2], while having some elements of the weak instance approach, are not a strict extension of this approach since there are XFDs that are violated according to the definition in [2] yet there are completions of the tree that satisfy the XFDs (see [15] for an example). As a result of this it is not clear that there is any correspondence between FDs in relations and XFDs in XML documents.

In [15,16] a different and more straightforward approach was taken to defining XFDs which overcomes the difficulties just discussed with the approach adopted in [2]. The definition in [15,16] is based on extending the strong satisfaction approach to XML. The definition of a XFD given in [15] was justified formally by two main results. The first result showed that for a very general class of mappings from an incomplete relation into a XML document, a relation strongly satisfies a unary FD (only one attribute on the l.h.s. of the FD) if and only if the corresponding XML document strongly satisfies the corresponding XFD. The second result showed that a XML document strongly satisfies a XFD if and only if every completion of the XML document also satisfies the XFD. The other contributions in [15] were firstly to define a set of axioms for reasoning about the implication of XFDs and show that the axioms are sound for arbitrary XFDs.

The final contribution was to define a normal form, based on a modification of the one proposed in [2], and prove that it is a necessary and sufficient condition for the elimination of redundancy in a XML document.

In this paper we extend the work in [15] and investigate the issue of multi-valued dependencies in XML, a topic which to the best of our knowledge has not been investigated previously. We firstly give a definition of MVDs in XML (what we call XMVDs) using an extension of the approach used in [15]. We then formally justify the definition by proving that, for a very general class of mappings from relations to XML, a relation satisfies a MVD if and only if the corresponding XML document satisfies the corresponding XMVD. Thus our definition of a XMVD in a XML document is a natural extension of the definition of a MVD in relations. Finally, we note that in contrast to [15], in the present paper we assume that XML documents do not have missing information and leave the problem of how to extend the approach to the case of missing information for future research.

The rest of this paper is organised as follows. Section 2 contains some preliminary definitions. In Section 3 we present the definition of a XMVD. Section 4 contains the main result of the paper on the correspondence between MVDs in relations and XMVDs in XML documents. Finally, Section 5 contains some concluding comments.

2   Preliminary Definitions

In this section we present some preliminary definitions that we need before defining XFDs. We model an XML document as a tree as follows.

Definition 1. *Assume a countably infinite set* $\mathbf{E}$ *of element labels (tags), a countable infinite set* $\mathbf{A}$ *of attribute names and a symbol* $\mathcal{S}$ *indicating text. An XML tree is defined to be* $T = (V, lab, ele, att, val, v_r)$ *where* V *is a finite set of nodes in* T *; lab is a function from* V *to* $\mathbf{E} \cup \mathbf{A} \cup \{\mathcal{S}\}$ *; ele is a partial function from* V *to a sequence of* V *nodes such that for any* $v \in V$ *, if* $ele(v)$ *is defined then* $lab(v) \in \mathbf{E}$ *; att is a partial function from* $V \times \mathbf{A}$ *to* V *such that for any* $v \in V$ *and* $l \in \mathbf{A}$ *, if* $att(v, l) = v_1$ *then* $lab(v) \in \mathbf{E}$ *and* $lab(v_1) = l$ *; val is a function such that for any node in* $v \in V, val(v) = v$ *if* $lab(v) \in \mathbf{E}$ *and* $val(v)$ *is a string if either* $lab(v) = \mathcal{S}$ *or* $lab(v) \in \mathbf{A}$ *;* v_r *is a distinguished node in* V *called the root of* T *and we define* $lab(v_r) = root$ *. Since node identifiers are unique, a consequence of the definition of val is that if* $v_1 \in \mathbf{E}$ *and* $v_2 \in \mathbf{E}$ *and* $v_1 \neq v_2$ *then* $val(v_1) \neq val(v_2)$ *. We also extend the definition of val to sets of nodes and if* $V_1 \subseteq V$ *, then* $val(V_1)$ *is the set defined by* $val(V_1) = \{val(v) | v \in V_1\}$ *.*

For any $v \in V$ *, if* $ele(v)$ *is defined then the nodes in* $ele(v)$ *are called* subelements *of* v *. For any* $l \in \mathbf{A}$ *, if* $att(v, l) = v_1$ *then* v_1 *is called an* attribute *of* v *. Note that an XML tree* T *must be a tree. Since* T *is a tree the set of ancestors of a node* v *, is denoted by* $Ancestor(v)$ *. The children of a node* v *are also defined as in Definition 1 and we denote the parent of a node* v *by* $Parent(v)$ *.*

We note that our definition of *val* differs slightly from that in [6] since we have extended the definition of the *val* function so that it is also defined on element nodes. The reason for this is that we want to include in our definition paths that do not end at leaf nodes, and when we do this we want to compare element nodes by node identity, i.e. node equality, but when we compare attribute or text nodes we want to compare them by their contents, i.e. value equality. This point will become clearer in the examples and definitions that follow.

We now give some preliminary definitions related to paths.

Definition 2. *A* path *is an expression of the form* $l_1. \cdots . l_n$, $n \geq 1$, *where* $l_i \in \mathbf{E} \cup \mathbf{A} \cup \{S\}$ *for all* $i, 1 \leq i \leq n$ *and* $l_1 = root$. *If* p *is the path* $l_1. \cdots . l_n$ *then* $Last(p) = l_n$.

For instance, if $\mathbf{E} = \{\texttt{root}, \texttt{Division}, \texttt{Employee}\}$ and $\mathbf{A} = \{\texttt{D\#}, \texttt{Emp\#}\}$ then `root`, `root.Division`, `root.Division.D#`,
`root.Division.Employee.Emp#.S` are all paths.

Definition 3. *Let* p *denote the path* $l_1. \cdots . l_n$. *The function* $Parnt(p)$ *is the path* $l_1. \cdots . l_{n-1}$. *Let* p *denote the path* $l_1. \cdots . l_n$ *and let* q *denote the path* $q_1. \cdots . q_m$. *The path* p *is said to be a* prefix *of the path* q, *denoted by* $p \subseteq q$, *if* $n \leq m$ *and* $l_1 = q_1, \ldots, l_n = q_n$. *Two paths* p *and* q *are equal, denoted by* $p = q$, *if* p *is a prefix of* q *and* q *is a prefix of* p. *The path* p *is said to be a* strict prefix *of* q, *denoted by* $p \subset q$, *if* p *is a prefix of* q *and* $p \neq q$. *We also define the intersection of two paths* p_1 *and* p_2, *denoted but* $p_1 \cap p_2$, *to be the maximal common prefix of both paths. It is clear that the intersection of two paths is also a path.*

For example, if $\mathbf{E} = \{\texttt{root}, \texttt{Division}, \texttt{Employee}\}$ and $\mathbf{A} = \{\texttt{D\#}, \texttt{Emp\#}\}$ then `root.Division` is a strict prefix of `root.Division.Employee` and
`root.Division.D#` $\cap$ `root.Division.Employee.Emp#.S` $=$ `root.Division`.

Definition 4. *A path instance in an XML tree* T *is a sequence* $\bar{v}_1. \cdots . \bar{v}_n$ *such that* $\bar{v}_1 = v_r$ *and for all* $\bar{v}_i, 1 < i \leq n, v_i \in V$ *and* $\bar{v}_i$ *is a child of* $\bar{v}_{i-1}$. *A path instance* $\bar{v}_1. \cdots . \bar{v}_n$ *is said to be defined over the path* $l_1. \cdots . l_n$ *if for all* $\bar{v}_i, 1 \leq i \leq n$, $lab(\bar{v}_i) = l_i$. *Two path instances* $\bar{v}_1. \cdots . \bar{v}_n$ *and* $\bar{v}'_1. \cdots . \bar{v}'_n$ *are said to be distinct if* $v_i \neq v'_i$ *for some* $i, 1 \leq i \leq n$. *The path instance* $\bar{v}_1. \cdots . \bar{v}_n$ *is said to be a* prefix *of* $\bar{v}'_1. \cdots . \bar{v}'_m$ *if* $n \leq m$ *and* $\bar{v}_i = \bar{v}'_i$ *for all* $i, 1 \leq i \leq n$. *The path instance* $\bar{v}_1. \cdots . \bar{v}_n$ *is said to be a* strict prefix *of* $\bar{v}'_1. \cdots . \bar{v}'_m$ *if* $n < m$ *and* $\bar{v}_i = \bar{v}'_i$ *for all* $i, 1 \leq i \leq n$. *The set of path instances over a path* p *in a tree* T *is denoted by* $Paths(p)$

For example, in Figure 1, $v_r.v_1.v_3$ is a path instance defined over the path `root.Dept.Section` and $v_r.v_1.v_3$ is a strict prefix of $v_r.v_1.v_3.v_4$

We now assume the existence of a set of legal paths P for an XML application. Essentially, P defines the semantics of an XML application in the same way that a set of relational schema define the semantics of a relational application. P may be derived from the DTD, if one exists, or P be derived from some other source which understands the semantics of the application if no DTD exists. The advantage of assuming the existence of a set of paths, rather than a DTD, is that it allows for a greater degree of generality since having an XML tree conforming to a set of paths is much less restrictive than having it conform to a DTD. Firstly we place the following restriction on the set of paths.

Definition 5. *A set P of paths is* consistent *if for any path $p \in P$, if $p_1 \subset p$ then $p_1 \in P$.*

This is natural restriction on the set of paths and any set of paths that is generated from a DTD will be consistent.

We now define the notion of an XML tree conforming to a set of paths P.

Definition 6. *Let P be a consistent set of paths and let T be an XML tree. Then T is said to* conform *to P if every path instance in T is a path instance over some path in P.*

The next issue that arises in developing the machinery to define XFDs is the issue is that of missing information. This is addressed in [15] but in this we take the simplifying assumption that there is no missing information in XML trees. More formally, we have the following definition.

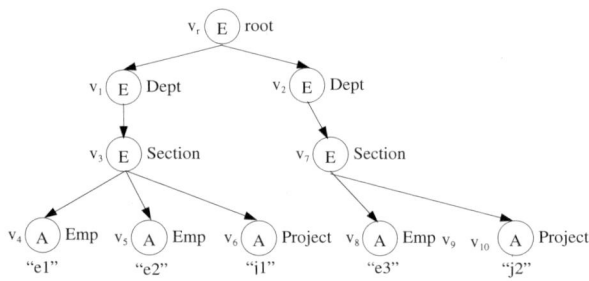

Fig. 1. A complete XML tree.

Definition 7. *Let P be a consistent set of paths, let T be an XML that conforms to P. Then T is defined to be* complete *if whenever there exist paths p_1 and p_2 in P such that $p_1 \subset p_2$ and there exists a path instance $\bar{v}_1.\cdots.\bar{v}_n$ defined over p_1, in T, then there exists a path instance $\bar{v}'_1.\cdots.\bar{v}'_m$ defined over p_2 in T such that $\bar{v}_1.\cdots.\bar{v}_n$ is a prefix of the instance $\bar{v}'_1.\cdots.\bar{v}'_m$.*

For example, if we take P to be {root, root.Dept, root.Dept.Section, root.Dept.Section.Emp, root.Dept.Section.Project} then the tree in Figure 1 conforms to P and is complete.

The next function returns all the final nodes of the path instances of a path p in T.

Definition 8. *Let P be a consistent set of paths, let T be an XML tree that conforms to P. The function $N(p)$, where $p \in P$, is the set of nodes defined by $N(p) = \{\bar{v} | \bar{v}_1.\cdots.\bar{v}_n \in Paths(p) \wedge \bar{v} = \bar{v}_n\}$.*

For example, in Figure 1, $N(\texttt{root.Dept}) = \{v_1, v_2\}$.
We now need to define a function that returns a node and its ancestors.

Definition 9. *Let P be a consistent set of paths, let T be an XML tree that conforms to P. The function $AAncestor(v)$, where $v \in V \cup \mathbf{N}$, is the set of nodes in T defined by $AAncestor(v) = v \cup Ancestor(v)$.*

For example in Figure 1, $AAncestor(v_3) = \{v_r, v_1, v_3\}$. The next function returns all nodes that are the final nodes of path instances of p and are descendants of v.

Definition 10. *Let P be a consistent set of paths, let T be an XML tree that conforms to P. The function $Nodes(v, p)$, where $v \in V \cup \mathbf{N}$ and $p \in P$, is the set of nodes in T defined by $Nodes(v, p) = \{x | x \in N(p) \wedge v \in AAncestor(x)\}$*

For example, in Figure 1 , $Nodes(v_1, \texttt{root.Dept.Section.Emp}) = \{v_4, v_5\}$. We also define a partial ordering on the set of nodes as follows.

Definition 11. *The partial ordering $>$ on the set of nodes V in an XML tree T is defined by $v_1 > v_2$ iff $v_2 \in Ancestor(v_1)$.*

3   XMVDs in XML

Before presenting the main definition of the paper, we present an example to illustrate the thinking behind the definition. Consider the relation shown in Figure 2. It satisfies the MVD $\texttt{Course} \twoheadrightarrow \texttt{Teacher} | \texttt{Text}$. The XML tree shown in Figure 3 is then a XML representation of the data in Figure 2. The tree has the following property. There exists two path instances of $\texttt{root.Id.Id.Id.Text}$, namely $v_r.v_{13}.v_{17}.v_{21}.v_9$ and $v_r.v_{16}.v_{20}.v_{24}.v_{12}$ such that $val(v_9) \neq val(v_{12})$. Also, these two paths have the property that for the closest $\texttt{Teacher}$ node to v_9, namely v_5, and the closest $\texttt{Teacher}$ node to v_{12}, namely v_8, then $val(v_5) \neq val(v_8)$ and for the closest $\texttt{Course}$ node to both v_9 and v_5, namely v_1, and for the closest $\texttt{Course}$ node to both v_{12} and v_8, namely v_4, we have that $val(v_1) = val(v_4)$. Then the existence of the two path instances $v_r.v_{13}.v_{17}.v_{21}.v_9$ and $v_r.v_{16}.v_{20}.v_{24}.v_{12}$ with these properties and the fact that $\texttt{Course} \twoheadrightarrow \texttt{Teacher} | \texttt{Text}$ is satisfied in the relation in Figure 2 implies that there exists two path instances of $\texttt{root.Id.Id.Id.Text}$, namely $v_r.v_{15}.v_{19}.v_{23}.v_{11}$ and $v_r.v_{14}.v_{18}.v_{22}.v_{10}$, with the following properties. $val(v_{11}) = val(v_9)$ and for the closest $\texttt{Teacher}$ node to v_{11}, v_7, $val(v_7) = val(v_8)$ and for the closest $\texttt{Course}$ node to v_{11} and v_7, namely v_3, $val(v_3) = val(v_1)$. Also, $val(v_{10}) = val(v_{12})$ and the closest $\texttt{Teacher}$ node to v_{10}, v_6, $val(v_6) = val(v_5)$ and for the closest $\texttt{Course}$ node to v_{10} and v_6, namely v_2, $val(v_2) = val(v_4)$. This type of constraint is a XMVD. We note however that there are many other ways that the relation in Figure 2 could be represented in a XML tree. For instance we could also represent the relation by Figure 4 and this XML tree also satisfies the XMVD. In comparing the two representations, it is clear that the representation in Figure 4 is a more compact representation than that in Figure 3. This issue is investigated in more detail in [17] where it

Course	Teacher	Text
Algorithms	Fred	Text A
Algorithms	Mary	Text B
Algorithms	Fred	Text B
Algorithms	Mary	Text A

Fig. 2. A flat relation satisfying a MVD.

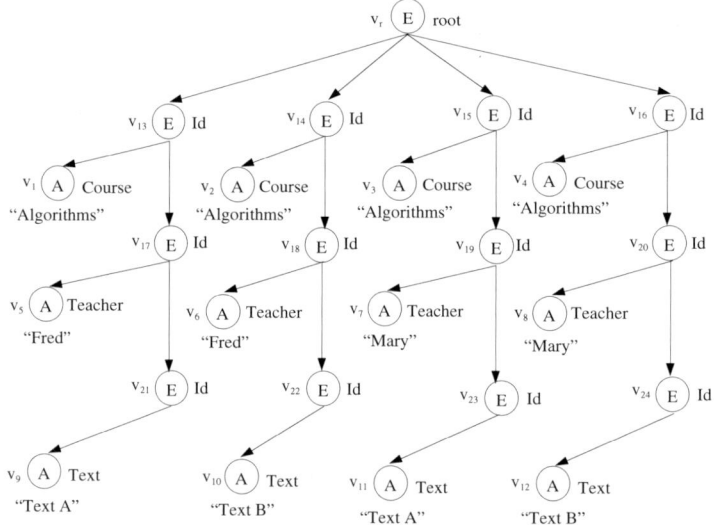

Fig. 3. A XML tree

is shown that the XML tree in Figure 3 is not normalised whereas the one in Figure 4 is normalised.

This leads us to the main definition of our paper. In this paper we consider the simplest case where there are only single paths on the l.h.s. and r.h.s. of the XMVD and all paths end in an attribute or text node.

Definition 12. *Let P be a consistent set of paths and let T be a XML tree that conforms to P and is complete. A XMVD is a statement of the form $p \rightarrow\rightarrow q|r$ where p, q and r are paths in P. T satisfies $p \rightarrow\rightarrow q|r$ if whenever there exists two distinct paths path instances $\bar{v}_1.\cdots.\bar{v}_n$ and $\bar{w}_1.\cdots.\bar{w}_n$ in $Paths(q)$ such that:*

(i) $val(\bar{v}_n) \neq val(\bar{w}_n)$;

(ii) there exists two nodes z_1, z_2, where $z_1 \in Nodes(x_{1_1}, r)$ and $z_2 \in Nodes(y_{1_1}, r)$ such that $val(z_1) \neq val(z_2)$;

(iii) there exists two nodes z_3 and z_4, where $z_3 \in Nodes(x_{1_1}, p)$ and $z_4 \in Nodes(y_{1_1}, p)$, such that $val(z_3) = val(z_4)$;

then:

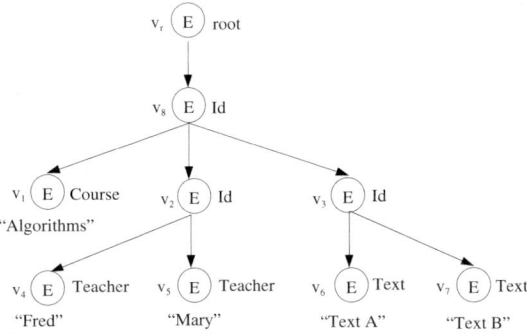

Fig. 4. A XML tree

(a) there exists a path $\bar{v}'_1. \cdots .\bar{v}'_n$ in $Paths(q)$ such that $val(\bar{v}'_n) = val(\bar{v}_n)$ and there exists a node z'_1 in $Nodes(x'_{1_1}, r)$ such that $val(z'_1) = val(z_2)$ and there exists a node z'_3 in $Nodes(x'_{1_1}, p)$ such that $val(z'_3) = val(z_3)$;

(b) there exists a path $\bar{w}'_1. \cdots .\bar{w}'_n$ in $Paths(q)$ such that $val(\bar{w}'_n) = val(\bar{w}_n)$ and there exists a node z'_2 in $Nodes(x'_{1_1}, r)$ such that $val(z'_2) = val(z_1)$ and there exists a node z'_4 in $Nodes(x'_{1_1}, p_l)$ such that $val(z'_4) = val(z_4)$;

where $x_{1_1} = \{v | v \in \{\bar{v}_1, \cdots, \bar{v}_n\} \wedge v \in N(r \cap q)\}$ and $y_{1_1} = \{v | v \in \{\bar{w}_1, \cdots, \bar{v}_n\} \wedge v \in N(r \cap q)\}$ and $x_{1_{1_1}} = \{v | v \in \{\bar{v}_1, \cdots, \bar{v}_n\} \wedge v \in N(p \cap r \cap q)\}$ and $y_{1_{1_1}} = \{v | v \in \{\bar{w}_1, \cdots, \bar{w}_n\} \wedge v \in N(p \cap r \cap q)\}$

$x'_{1_1} = \{v | v \in \{\bar{v}'_1, \cdots, \bar{v}'_n\} \wedge v \in N(r \cap q)\}$ and $y'_{1_1} = \{v | v \in \{\bar{w}'_1, \cdots, \bar{v}'_n\} \wedge v \in N(r \cap q)\}$ and $x'_{1_{1_1}} = \{v | v \in \{\bar{v}'_1, \cdots, \bar{v}'_n\} \wedge v \in N(p \cap r \cap q)\}$ and $y'_{1_{1_1}} = \{v | v \in \{\bar{w}'_1, \cdots, \bar{w}'_n\} \wedge v \in N(p \cap r \cap q)\}$.

We note that since the path $r \cap q$ is a prefix of q, there exists only one node in $\bar{v}_1. \cdots .\bar{v}_n$ that is also in $N(r \cap q)$ and so x_1 is always defined and is a single node. Similarly for $y_1, x_{1_{1_1}}, y_{1_{1_1}}, x'_{1_1}, y'_{1_1}, x'_{1_{1_1}}, y'_{1_{1_1}}$. We now illustrate the definition by some examples.

Example 1. Consider the XML tree shown in Figure 4 and the XMVD
root.Id.Course $\rightarrow\rightarrow$ root.Id.Id.Teacher|root.Id.Id.Text. Let $\bar{v}_1. \cdots .\bar{v}_n$ be the path instance $v_r.v_8.v_2.v_4$ and let $\bar{w}_1. \cdots .\bar{w}_n$ be the path instance $v_r.v_8.v_2.v_5$. Both path instances are in $Paths(\text{root.Id.Id.Teacher})$ and $val(v_4) \neq val(v_5)$. Moreover, $x_{1_1} = v_8$, $y_{1_1} = v_8$, $x_{1_{1_1}} = v_8$ and $y_{1_{1_1}} = v_8$. So if we let $z_1 = v_6$ and $z_2 = v_7$ then $z_1 \in Nodes(x_{1_1}, \text{root.Id.Id.Text})$ and $z_2 \in Nodes(y_{1_1}, \text{root.Id.Id.Text})$. Also if we let $z_3 = v_8$ and $z_4 = v_8$ then $z_3 \in Nodes(x_{1_{1_1}}, \text{root.Id.Course})$ and $z_4 \in Nodes(y_{1_{1_1}}, \text{root.Id.Course})$ then $val(z_3) = val(z_4)$. Hence conditions (i), (ii) and (iii) of the definition of a XMVD are satisfied.

If we let $\bar{v}'^i_1. \cdots .\bar{v}'^i_n$ be the path $v_r.v_8.v_2.v_4$ we firstly have that $val(\bar{v}'^i_n) = val(\bar{v}^i_n)$ as required. Also, since the path instances are the same we have that $x_{1_1} = x'_{1_1}$ and $x_{1_{1_1}} = x'_{1_{1_1}}$. So if we let $z'_1 = v_7$ then

$z'_1 \in Nodes(x'_{1_1}, \texttt{root.Id.Id.Text})$ and $val(z'_1) = val(z_2)$ and if we let $z'_3 = v_8$ then

$z'_3 \in Nodes(x'_{1_1}, \texttt{root.Id.Course})$ and $val(z'_3) = val(z_3)$. So part (a) of the definition of an XMVD is satisfied. Next if we let $\bar{w}'^i_1 . \cdots . \bar{w}'^i_n$ be the path $v_r.v_8.v_2.v_5$ then we firstly have that $val(\bar{w}'^i_n) = val(\bar{w}^i_n)$ since the paths are the same . Also, since the paths are the same we have that $y_{1_1} = y'_{1_1}$ and $y_{1_{1_1}} = y'_{1_{1_1}}$. So if we let $z'_2 = v_6$ then $z'_2 \in Nodes(y'_{1_1}, \texttt{root.Id.Id.Text})$ and $val(z'_2) = val(z_1)$ and if we let $z'_4 = v_8$ then $z'_4 \in Nodes(x'_{1_1}, \texttt{root.Id.Course})$ and $val(z'_4) = val(z_4)$. Hence part (b) on the definition of a XMVD is satisfied and so T satisfies $\texttt{root.Id.Course} \rightarrow\rightarrow \texttt{root.Id.Id.Teacher}|\texttt{root.Id.Id.Text}$.

As explained earlier, the tree in Figure 4 also satisfies

$\texttt{root.Id.Course} \rightarrow\rightarrow \texttt{root.Id.Id.Teacher}|\texttt{root.Id.Id.Text}$.

Example 2. Consider the XML tree shown in Figure 5 and the XMVD $\texttt{root.Project.P\#} \rightarrow\rightarrow \texttt{Root.Project.Person.Name}|\texttt{root.Project.Part.Pid}$. For the path instances $v_r.v_1.v_5.v_{13}$ and $v_r.v_2.v_8.v_{16}$ in

$Paths(\texttt{Root.Project.Person.Name})$ we have that $val(v_{13}) \neq val(v_{16})$. Moreover, $x_{1_1} = v_1$, $y_{1_1} = v_2$, $x_{1_{1_1}} = v_1$ and $y_{1_{1_1}} = v_1$. So if we let $z_1 = v_{17}$ and $z_2 = v_{18}$ then

$z_1 \in Nodes(x_{1_1}, \texttt{root.Project.Part.Pid})$ and

$z_2 \in Nodes(y_{1_1}, \texttt{root.Project.Part.Pid})$. Also if we let $z_3 = v_4$ and $z_4 = v_7$ then $z_3 \in Nodes(x_{1_1}, \texttt{root.Project.P\#})$ and

$z_4 \in Nodes(y_{1_1}, \texttt{root.Project.P\#})$ and $val(z_3) = val(z_4)$. Hence conditions (i), (ii) and (iii) of the definition of a XMVD are satisfied. However, for the only other path in

$Paths(\texttt{Root.Project.Person.Name})$, namely $v_r.v_3.v_{11}.v_{19}$ we have that $x'_{1_1} = v_3$ and so $Nodes(x'_{1_1}, \texttt{root.Project.part.Pid}) = v_{21}$ and since $val(v_{21}) \neq val(z_2)$ and so it does not satisfy condition (a) and thus $\texttt{root.Project.P\#} \rightarrow\rightarrow \texttt{Root.Project.Person.Name}|\texttt{root.Project.part.Pid}$ is violated in T.

Consider then the XMVD XMVD $\texttt{root.Project.Person.Name}$

$\rightarrow\rightarrow \texttt{Root.Project.Person.Skill}|\texttt{root.Project.P\#}$ in the same XML tree. For the path instances $v_r.v_1.v_5.v_{14}$ and $v_r.v_3.v_{11}.v_{20}$ in

$Paths(\texttt{Root.Project.Person.Skill})$ we have that $val(v_{14}) \neq val(v_{20})$. Moreover, $x_{1_1} = v_1$, $y_{1_1} = v_3$, $x_{1_{1_1}} = v_{13}$ and $y_{1_{1_1}} = v_{19}$. So if we let $z_1 = v_4$ and $z_2 = v_{10}$ then $z_1 \in Nodes(x_{1_1}, \texttt{root.Project.P\#})$ and $z_2 \in Nodes(y_{1_1}, \texttt{root.Project.P\#})$. Also if we let $z_3 = v_{13}$ and $z_4 = v_{19}$ then $z_3 \in Nodes(x_{1_{1_1}}, \texttt{root.Project.Person.Name})$ and

$z_4 \in Nodes(y_{1_{1_1}}, \texttt{root.Project.Person.Name})$ and $val(z_3) = val(z_4)$. Hence the conditions of (i), (ii) and (iii) of the definition of a XMVD are satisfied. However there does not exist another path instance in $Paths(\texttt{Root.Project.Person.Skill})$ such that val of the last node in the path is equal to val of node v_{14} and so part (a) of the definition of a XMVD is violated.

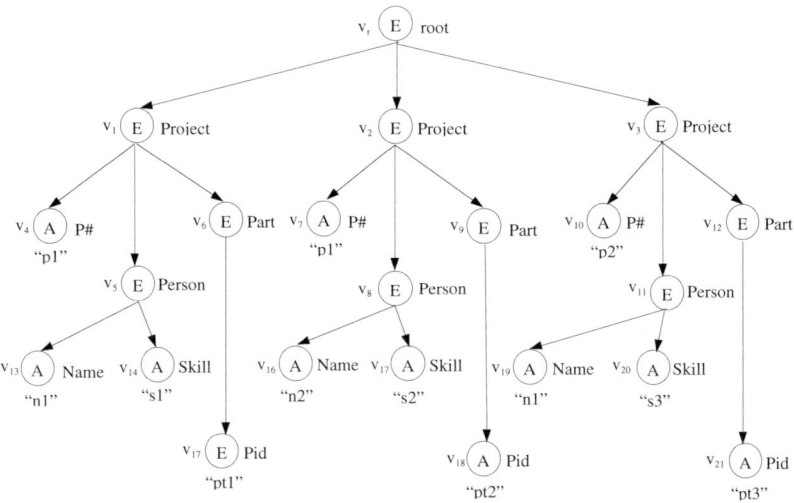

Fig. 5. A XML tree

4   XMVDs in XML and MVDs in Relations

In this section we provide a formal justification for the definition of a XMVD given in the previous section. We prove that for a very general class of mappings of a relation into a XML document, a relation satisfies a MVD if and only if the XML document also satisfies the equivalent XMVD. As our technique for mapping relations to XML trees is done via nested relations, we firstly present the definitions for nested relations adapted from the definitions given in [14].

Definition 13. *Let U be a fixed countable set of atomic attribute names. Associated with each attribute name $A \in U$ is a countably infinite set of values denoted by $DOM(A)$ and the set **DOM** is defined by **DOM** $= \cup DOM(A_i)$ for all $A_i \in U$. We assume that $DOM(A_i) \cap DOM(A_j) = \phi$ if $i \neq j$. A scheme tree is a tree containing at least one node and whose nodes are labelled with nonempty sets of attributes that form a partition of a finite subset of U. If n denotes a node in a scheme tree S then:*

  - $ATT(n)$ is the set of attributes associated with n;
  - $A(n)$ is the union of $ATT(n_1)$ for all $n_1 \in Ancestor(n)$.

Figure 6 illustrates an example scheme tree defined over the set of attributes {Name, Sid, Major, Class, Exam, Project}.

Definition 14. *A nested relation scheme (NRS) for a scheme tree S, denoted by $N(S)$, is the set defined recursively by:*

  (i) If S consists of a single node n then $N(S) = ATT(n)$;
  (ii) If $A = ATT(ROOT(S))$ and $S_1, \cdots, S_k, k \geq 1$, are the principal subtrees of S then $N(S) = A \cup \{N(S_1)\} \cdots \{N(S_k)\}$.

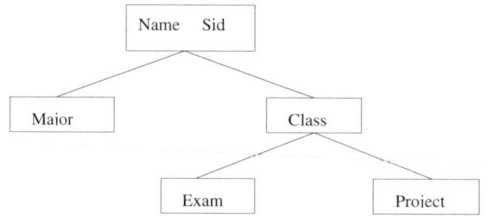

Fig. 6. A scheme tree

For example, for the scheme tree S shown in Figure 6, $N(S)$ = {Name, Sid, {Major},

{Class, {Exam}, {Project}}}. We now recursively define the domain of a scheme tree S, denoted by $DOM(N(S))$.

Definition 15. *(i) If S consists of a single node n with $ATT(n) = \{A_1, \cdots, A_n\}$ then $DOM(N(S)) = DOM(A_1) \times \cdots \times DOM(A_n)$;*

(ii) If $A = ATT(ROOT(S))$ and $S_1, \cdots, S_k$ are the principal subtrees of S, then $DOM(N(S) = DOM(A) \times P(DOM(N(S_1))) \times \cdots \times P(DOM(N(S_k)))$ where $P(Y)$ denotes the set of all nonempty, finite subsets of a set Y.

The set of *atomic attributes* in $N(S)$, denoted by $Z(N(S))$, is defined by $Z(N(S)) = N(S) \cap U$. The set of higher order attributes in $N(S)$, denoted by $H(N(S))$, is defined by $H(N(S)) = N(S) - Z(N(S))$. For instance, for the example shown in Figure 6, $Z(N(S)) = \{$Name, Sid$\}$ and $H(N(S)) = \{\{$Major$\}, \{$Class, $\{$Exam$\}$, $\{$Project$\}\}\}$.

Finally we define a nested relation over a nested relation scheme $N(S)$, denoted by $r^*(N(S))$, or often simply by r^* when $N(S)$ is understood, to be a finite nonempty set of elements from $DOM(N(S))$. If t is a tuple in r^* and Y is a nonempty subset of $N(S)$, then $t[Y]$ denotes the restriction of t to Y and the restriction of r^* to Y is then the nested relation defined by $r^*[Y] = \{t[Y]|t \in r\}$. An example of a nested relation over the scheme tree of Figure 6 is shown in Figure 7.

A tuple t_1 is said to be a *subtuple* of a tuple t in r^* if there exists $Y \in H(N(S))$ such that $t_1 \in t[Y]$ or there exists a tuple t_2, defined over some NRS N_1, such that t_2 is a subtuple of t and there exists $Y_1 \in H(N_1)$ such that $t_1 \in t_2[Y_1]$. For example in the relation shown in Figure 7 the tuples

< CS100, {mid-year, final}, {Project A, Project B, Project C} > and < Project A > are both subtuples of

< Anna, Sid1, {Maths, Computing}, {CS100, {mid-year, final}, {Project A, Project B, Project C}} >.

We now introduce the nest and unnest operators for nested relations as defined in [13].

Name	Sid	{Major}	{Class	{Exam}	{Project}}
Anna	Sid1	Maths	CS100	Mid-year	Project A
		Computing		Final	Project B
					Project C
Bill	Sid2	Physics	P100	Final	Prac 1
					Prac 2
		Chemistry	CH200	Test A	Experiment 1
				Test B	Experiment 2 1

Fig. 7. A nested relation.

Definition 16. *Let Y be a nonempty proper subset of $N(S)$. Then the operation of nesting a relation r^* on Y, denoted by $\nu_Y(r^*)$, is defined to be a nested relation over the scheme $(N(S) - Y) \cup \{Y\}$ and a tuple $t \in \nu_Y(r^*)$ iff:*
(i) there exists $t_1 \in r^*$ such that $t[N(S) - Y] = t_1[N(S) - Y]$ and
(ii) $t[\{Y\}] = \{t_2[Y] | t_2 \in r^*$ and $t_2[N(S) - Y] = t[N(S) - Y]\}$.

Definition 17. *Let $r^*(N(S))$ be a relation and $\{Y\}$ an element of $H(N(S))$. Then the unnesting of r^* on $\{Y\}$, denoted by $\mu_{\{Y\}}(r^*)$, is a relation over the nested scheme $(N(S) - \{Y\}) \cup Y$ and a tuple $t \in \mu_{\{Y\}}(r^*)$ iff there exists $t_1 \in r^*$ such that $t_1[N(S) - \{Y\}] = t[N(S) - \{Y\}]$ and $t[Y] \in t_1[\{Y\}]$.*

More generally, one can define the *total unnest* of a nested relation r^*, denoted by $\mu^*(r^*)$, as the flat relation defined as follows.

Definition 18. *(i) if r^* is a flat relation then $\mu^*(r^*) = r^*$;*
(ii) otherwise $\mu^*(r^*) = \mu^*((\mu_{\{Y\}}(r^*)))$ where $\{Y\}$ is a higher order attribute in the NRS for r^*.

It can be shown [13] that the order of unnesting is immaterial and so $\mu^*(r)$ is uniquely defined. Also, we need the following result from [13]. Let us denote the NRS of nested relation r^* by $N(r^*)$.

Lemma 1. *For any nested relation r^* and any $Y \subseteq N(r^*)$, $\mu_{\{Y\}}(\nu_Y(r^*)) = r^*$.*

We note the well known result [13] that the converse of the above lemma does not hold, i.e. there are nested relations such that $\nu_Y(\mu_{\{Y\}}(r^*)) \neq r^*$.

4.1   Mapping from Relations to XML

The translation of a relation into a XML tree consists of two phases. In the first we map the relation to a nested relation whose nesting structure is arbitrary and then we map the nested relation to a XML tree.

In the first step we let the nested relation r^* be defined by $r_i = \nu_{Y_{i-1}}(r_{i-1}), r_0 = r, r^* = r_n, 1 \leq i \leq n$ where r represents the initial (flat) relation and r^* represents the final nested relation. The Y_i are allowed to be arbitrary apart from the obvious restriction that Y_i is an element of the NRS for r_i.

In the second step of the mapping procedure we take the nested relation and convert it to a XML tree as follows. We start with an initially empty tree. For each tuple t in r^* we first create an element node of type Id and then for each $A \in Z(N(r^*))$ we insert a single attribute node with a value $t[A]$. We then repeat recursively the procedure for each subtuple of t. We now illustrate these steps by an example.

Example 3. Consider the flat relation shown in Figure 8.

Name	Sid	Major	Class	Exam	Project
Anna	Sid1	Maths	CS100	Mid-year	Project A
Anna	Sid1	Maths	CS100	Mid-year	Project B
Anna	Sid1	Maths	CS100	Final	Project A
Anna	Sid1	Maths	CS100	Final	Project B
Anna	Sid1	Physics	CS100	Mid-year	Project A
Anna	Sid1	Physics	CS100	Mid-year	Project B
Anna	Sid1	Physics	CS100	Final	Project A
Anna	Sid1	Physics	CS100	Final	Project B
Bill	Sid2	Chemistry	CH200	Test A	Prac 1
Bill	Sid2	Chemistry	CH200	Test B	Prac 1
Bill	Sid2	Chemistry	CH200	Test A	Prac 2
Bill	Sid2	Chemistry	CH200	Test B	Prac 2

Fig. 8. A flat relation.

If we then transform the relation r in Figure 8 by the sequence of nestings $r_1 = \nu_{PROJECT}(r)$, $r_2 = \nu_{EXAM}(r_1)$, $r_3 = \nu_{CLASS,\{EXAM\},\{PROJECT\}}(r_2)$, $r^* = \nu_{MAJOR}(r_3)$ then the relation r^* is shown in Figure 9. We then transform the nested relation in Figure 9 to the XML tree shown in Figure 10.

Name	Sid	{Major}	{Class	{Exam}	{Project}}
Anna	Sid1	Maths	CS100	Mid-year	Project A
		Physics		Final	Project B
Bill	Sid2	Chemistry	CH200	Test A	Prac 1
				Test B	Prac 2

Fig. 9. A nested relation derived from a flat relation.

This now leads to the main result of this section which establishes the correspondence between satisfaction of MVDs in relations and satisfaction of XMVDs in XML. We denote by T_{r^*} the XML tree derived from r^*.

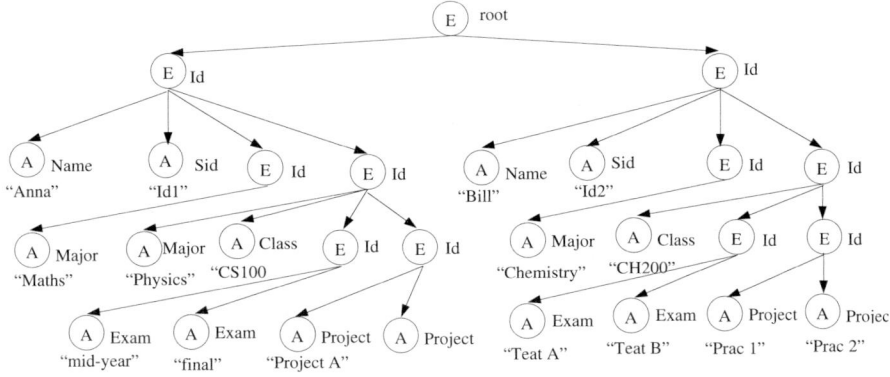

Fig. 10. A XML tree derived from a nested relation.

Theorem 1. *Let r be a flat relation and let $A \rightarrow B|C$ be a MVD defined over r. Then T_{r^*} satisfies $p_A \rightarrow q_B|r_C$, where p_A denotes the path in T_{r^*} to reach A and q_B denotes the path to reach B and r_C denotes the path to reach C, iff r satisfies $A \rightarrow B|C$.*

5   Conclusions

In this paper we have extended the work in [15] and investigated the issue of multivalued dependencies in XML, a topic which to the best of our knowledge has not been investigated previously. Multivalued dependencies (MVDs) play a fundamental role in relational databases where they provide semantics for the data and at the same time are the foundation for database design. Since XML documents are closely coupled with relational databases in that XML documents are typically exported and imported from relational databases, the study of MVDs in XML is of fundamental significance in XML research. We firstly gave a definition of MVDs in XML (what we call XMVDs) using an extension of the approach used in [15]. We then formally justified the definition by proving that, for a very general class of mappings from relations to XML, a relation satisfies a MVD if and only if the corresponding XML document satisfies the corresponding XMVD. Thus our definition of a XMVD in a XML document is a natural extension of the definition of a MVD in relations.

There are several other topics related to the one addressed in this paper that we intend to pursue in the future. The first is the relationship between XMVDs and normalisation. Some important first steps have already been made in [17] where a 4NF for XML documents is defined and shown to be a necessary and sufficient condition for the elimination of redundancy. However algorithms and techniques for converting unnormalised documents to normalised were not covered in [17] and this topic warrants further investigation. Also, in [15], an axiom system was provided for XFDs. Similarly, an axiom system needs to be developed for XMVDs. Thirdly, we have assumed in this paper that XML documents do not contain missing information and so our definitions and results need to be extended to the more typical case where XML documents contain missing information. Finally, it is expected that XMVDs and XFDs interact in the same fashion that FDs and MVDs interact [4] and so this topic warrants further investigation.

References

1. S. Abiteboul, P. Buneman, and D. Suciu. *Data on the Web*. Morgan Kauffman, 2000.
2. M. Arenas and L. Libkin. A normal form for xml documents. In *Proc. ACM PODS Conference*, pages 85–96, 2002.
3. P. Atzeni and V. DeAntonellis. *Foundations of databases*. Benjamin Cummings, 1993.
4. C. Beeri, R. Fagin, and J.H. Howard. A complete exiomatization for functional and multivalued dependencies. In *ACM SIGMOD Conference*, pages 47–61, 1977.
5. P. Buneman, S. Davidson, W. Fan, and C. Hara. Reasoning about keys for xml. In *International Workshop on Database Programming Languages*, 2001.
6. P. Buneman, S. Davidson, W. Fan, C. Hara, and W. Tan. Keys for xml. *Computer Networks*, 39(5):473–487, 2002.
7. P. Buneman, W. Fan, J. Simeon, and S. Weinstein. Constraints for semistructured data and xml. *ACM SIGMOD Record*, 30(1):45–47, 2001.
8. P. Buneman, W. Fan, and S. Weinstein. Path constraints on structured and semistructured data. In *Proc. ACM PODS Conference*, pages 129–138, 1998.
9. W. Fan and J. Simeon. Integrity constraints for xml. In *Proc. ACM PODS Conference*, pages 23–34, 2000.
10. M. Levene and G. Loizu. Axiomatization of functional dependencies in incomplete relations. *Theoretical Computer Science*, 206:283–300, 1998.
11. M. Levene and G. Loizu. *A guided tour of relational databases and beyond*. Springer, 1999.
12. J. Shanmugasundaram, K. Tufte, C. Zhang, G. He, D. J. DeWitt, and J. F. Naughton:. Relational databases for querying xml documents: Limitations and opportunities. In *VLDB Conference*, pages 302–314, 1999.
13. S.J. Thomas and P.C. Fischer. Nested relational structures. In P. Kanellakis, editor, *The theory of databases*, pages 269 –307. JAI Press, 1986.
14. M. W. Vincent and M. Levene. Restructuring partitioned normal relations without information loss. *SIAM Journal on Computing*, 39(5):1550–1567, 2000.
15. M.W. Vincent and J. Liu. Strong functional dependencies and a redundancy free normal form for xml. Submitted for publication, 2002.
16. M.W. Vincent and J. Liu. Functional dependencies for xml. In *Fifth Asian Pacific Web Conference*, 2003.
17. M.W. Vincent and J. Liu. Multivalued dependencies and a 4nf for xml. In *15th CAISE Conference*, 2003.
18. J. Widom. Data management for xml - research directions. *IEEE data Engineering Bulletin*, 22(3):44–52, 1999.

Processing XML Path Expressions Using XML Materialised Views[*]

ChanHo Moon, SooHee Kim[**], and Hyunchul Kang

Dept. of Computer Science and Engineering, Chung-Ang University,
Seoul, 156-756, Korea
{moonch,shkim}@dblab.cse.cau.ac.kr, hckang@cau.ac.kr

Abstract. Recently, semantic caching for the database-backed web applications has received much attention. The results of frequent queries could be cached for repeated reuse or for efficient processing of the relevant queries. Since the emergence of XML as a standard for data exchange on the web, today's web applications are to retrieve information from the remote XML sources across the network, and thus, it is desirable to maintain the XML query results in the cache for the web applications. In this paper, we investigate the problem of processing an XML path expression, which is one of the core features of XML query languages, using the XML cache maintained as materialised views. Algorithms to rewrite the given XML path expression using its relevant materialised view are proposed. Also provided are the implementation details of how an XML path expression is processed with its relevant XML materialised view when a relational DBMS is employed for storing XML base documents as well as their materialised views. The preliminary experimental results show that our scheme is feasible and promising.

Keywords: XML, path expression, query rewriting, materialised view, semantic caching, database-backed web application

1 Introduction

Caching of frequently queried portion of databases lends itself to efficient query processing in the database-backed web applications [19][22][23]. With proper management of the cache such as cache replacement and cache refresh against the updates to the underlying data, for the repeated queries, their results would be directly available from the cache, and for the relevant queries, they could be rewritten against the cached results. As such, the workload on the database system, which might be the performance bottleneck, could be alleviated, and the communication overhead across the network, which might be sometimes huge, could be reduced.

---

[*] This work was supported by the Strategic Research Program of Information and Telecommunication Research Institute, Chung-Ang University in 2003.

[**] Current address: CDMA Handsets Lab, S/W Development Dept., LG Electronics Inc., Seoul, 153-023, Korea

A. James, B. Lings, M. Younas (Eds.): BNCOD 2003, LNCS 2712, pp. 19–37, 2003.

Fig. 1 shows the popular 3-tier architecture for the database-backed web applications. The web server sends the queries embedded in the web pages to the data server usually by way of the middleware layer, the application server. It is often the application server where the cache is maintained and subsequent query processing with it is handled.

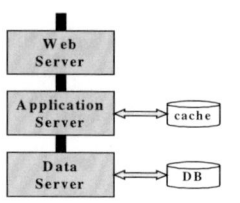

Fig. 1. 3-tier Architecture for Database-backed Web Applications

Since XML is the de facto standard for data exchange on the web, efficient XML query processing that capitalizes on XML cache is desirable for the XML database-backed web applications, and recently the problem has started to receive attention [16][8][9][24]. In this paper, we investigate the problem of processing XML path expressions using XML cache. The path expression is one of the core features of XML query languages like XQuery [4], XPath [3], XQL [27], and so on. As for XML caching, we consider semantic caching which is view-based query caching [10][28] whereby the result of an XML path expression against the base XML documents in the underlying XML data source is cached and maintained as a materialised view.

In order to capitalize on the materialised views in processing XML queries in path expression, given a query, it should be possible to compute the whole or part of its result from the relevant materialised view, and to rewrite the original path expression against the base XML documents into the one against the materialised view.

The containment relationships between the query result and the relevant materialised view are classified into five types as shown in Fig. 2 [20]. Fig. 2(a) shows the case where the materialised view and the query result are in complete match. Fig. 2(b) and (c) show the cases where the materialised view contains the query result, and vice versa, respectively. Fig. 2(d) shows the case where the materialised view and the query result only partially match. Finally, Fig. 2(e) shows the case where there is no match between the two.

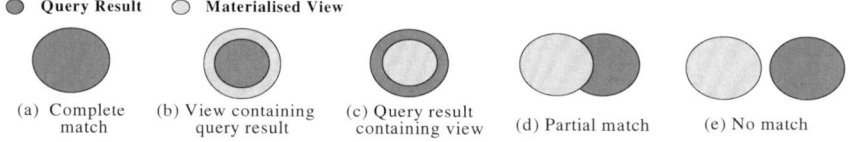

Fig. 2. Relationship between Materialised View and Query Result

As such, there could be three types of XML query processing with the materialised views as shown in Fig. 3. The first type called *MV (Materialised View Only)* could be employed for the cases of Fig. 2(a) and (b) if query rewriting is possible. The second type called *BD+MV (Both Base Documents and Materialised View)* could be employed for the cases of Fig. 2(c) and (d). Here, the query rewriting is more complicated than that of MV. The original query is decomposed into two subqueries, one against the materialised view and the other against the base documents. The third type called *BD (Base Documents Only)* is left for the cases of Fig. 2(e) or for the cases where query rewriting is impossible.

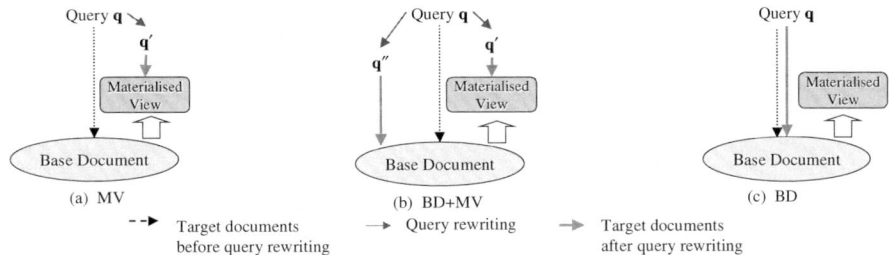

Fig. 3. Types of XML Query Processing Using Materialised Views

In this paper, we propose two algorithms required for rewriting an XML path expression with an XML materialised view. The first one determines the type of query processing given two XML path expressions q and v where q is against the base XML documents and v is the one that has defined the XML materialised view out of them. The second one rewrites q into q′ (for MV) or q into q′ and q″ (for BD+MV) where q′ is against the materialised view whereas q″ is against the base documents.

We also provide the implementation details of how an XML path expression is processed with its relevant XML materialised view when a *relational DBMS* is employed for storing base XML documents as well as their materialised views. Since the relational DBMSs are in dominantly wide use, storing and querying XML documents with them is of pragmatic importance and is attracting much attention [31][11][13][14][29]. The results of preliminary performance experiments are also reported.

The rest of this paper is organized as follows. Section 2 surveys the related work. Section 3 deals with problem of rewriting XML path expressions with the XML materialised views. Section 4 presents the implementation issues and the preliminary experimental results on performance. Finally, Section 5 gives some concluding remarks.

2 Related Work

Query rewriting with views or with the materialised views has received much attention in the context of the relational database [21] and also of the semistructured data model [25][6][12]. However, only recently the problem has started to be addressed with the XML query languages [16][8][9][24].

In [16], a system for semantic caching of XML databases for a subset of XQuery, called XCacher, is presented. The XQuery query dealt with consists of an extract (FOR-WHERE clauses) and a construct part (RETURN clause), and the extract part is cached by XCacher. The cache is organized using a modification of the incomplete tree [2]. XCacher is located at the application server. It intercepts the XML query that is sent from the web server to the XML data server, rewrites it into the refinement query against the cache and the remainder queries against the XML database, and merges the partial results of the rewritten queries.

In [8][9], the query containment mapping and rewriting algorithms for a subset of XQuery are proposed. Implementation of a semantic XML caching system called ACE-XQ is described, which performs query containment mapping and rewriting using the pattern variables in the two XQuery queries, one in the query and the other in the view.

In [24], a formal model of cache answerability for XPath queries is presented. Three types of query rewriting, equivalent, weak equivalent, and partial equivalent, are defined. The presented model is a formal one. Thus, for it to be implemented some functionality such as the storage and retrieval mechanism for XML data, the sequential evaluation of XPath subqueries, and the storage structure of cache contents needs to be specifically provided.

For query processing with materialised views to be possible, consistency maintenance of the materialised views needs to be efficiently supported. Usually it is desirable to incrementally refresh them by reflecting only the relevant updates done to their underlying data. This problem has also received much attention in the context of the relational database [15] and also of the semistructured data model [1][32][30]. The same problem with XML data has been recently investigated [26][7][17][18].

In [26][7], incremental refresh of the materialised views over the XML data is investigated. The XML sources are stored in the binary form of persistent DOMs, and the views are defined in a subset of XQL. The updates considered are the insertion/deletion of a segment of an XML tree and modification on the value of a leaf node of the XML tree. An auxiliary information structure called the aggregate path index(APIX) which holds the collection of qualified data objects with respect to the query pattern [7] is used to check the update's relevance to the view. The APIX is generated when the view is initially computed and maintained against the subsequent updates on the XML sources.

In [17], deferred incremental refresh of XML materialised views is investigated. A model of the XML materialised view derived from a collection of XML documents conforming to some schema is presented, and the problem is dealt with for the case where XML documents as well as their materialised views are stored in the object-relational DBMS and the update log is employed for deferred refresh of the views.

In [18], the XML view index(XVI), which contains the identifiers of the view's underlying XML elements as well as the information on the view out of its definition in XQuery expression, is investigated. Since XVI stores just the identifiers of the XML elements not the elements themselves, when the view is to be retrieved, its XVI should be materialised against its underlying XML documents. The algorithms to efficiently materialise an XVI and to incrementally maintain its consistency given a update to the underlying XML documents are proposed.

3   Rewriting XML Path Expressions

In this section, we propose two algorithms required for rewriting an XML query in path expression to capitalize on the materialised view relevant to the query.

3.1   Examples

Before describing our algorithms, let us consider some of the cases where query rewriting with the materialised view is possible and the ones where it is not. Fig. 4 shows a DTD and its XML document instance for the running example of the paper. It is on the bookstore which sells books and magazines. Some path expressions in the following examples are without filter operators whereby predicate conditions are given whereas some are with them and may be tricky (refer to Fig. 5).

```
<!ELEMENT bookstore (book*, magazine*)>

<!ELEMENT book (title, author*, price)>
<!ELEMENT author (first-name, last-name, award)>
<!ELEMENT first-name (#PCDATA)>
<!ELEMENT last-name (#PCDATA)>
<!ELEMENT award (#PCDATA)>

<!ELEMENT magazine (title, price, subscription)>
<!ELEMENT title (#PCDATA)>
<!ELEMENT price (#PCDATA)>
<!ELEMENT subscription (per)>
<!ELEMENT per (#PCDATA)>
```

(a) DTD

```
<bookstore>
    <book>
        <title>Seven</title>
        <author>
            <first-name>Joe</first-name>
            <last-name>Bob</last-name>
            <award>Review</award>
        </author>
        <price>12</price>
    </book>

    <magazine>
        <title>Tracking Trenton</title>
        <price>2.50</price>
        <subscription>
            <per>year</per>
        </subscription>
    </magazine>
    ........
</bookstore>
```

(b) XML Document Instance

Fig. 4. DTD and XML Document Instance

Example 3.1
Suppose there exists a materialised view defined as *bookstore/magazine* which stores a set of subtrees (of the base XML documents) each of which is rooted at the magazine element, and an XML query *bookstore/magazine/subscription* which is to retrieve a set of subtrees each of which is rooted at the subscription element, is given. Then, the query result could be retrieved from the materialised view since the query is to retrieve the subtrees of the materialised view.   □

Example 3.2
Suppose there exists a materialised view defined as *bookstore/book/author* and an XML query *bookstore/book* is given. Then, the query result could be obtained by merging the entire materialised view and the elements retrieved from the base documents. To be exact, the query result is a set of subtrees each of which is rooted at the book element with three subelements: title, author, and price in that order. Title and

price are leaf elements, whereas author forms a subtree that constitutes the materialised view.   ☐

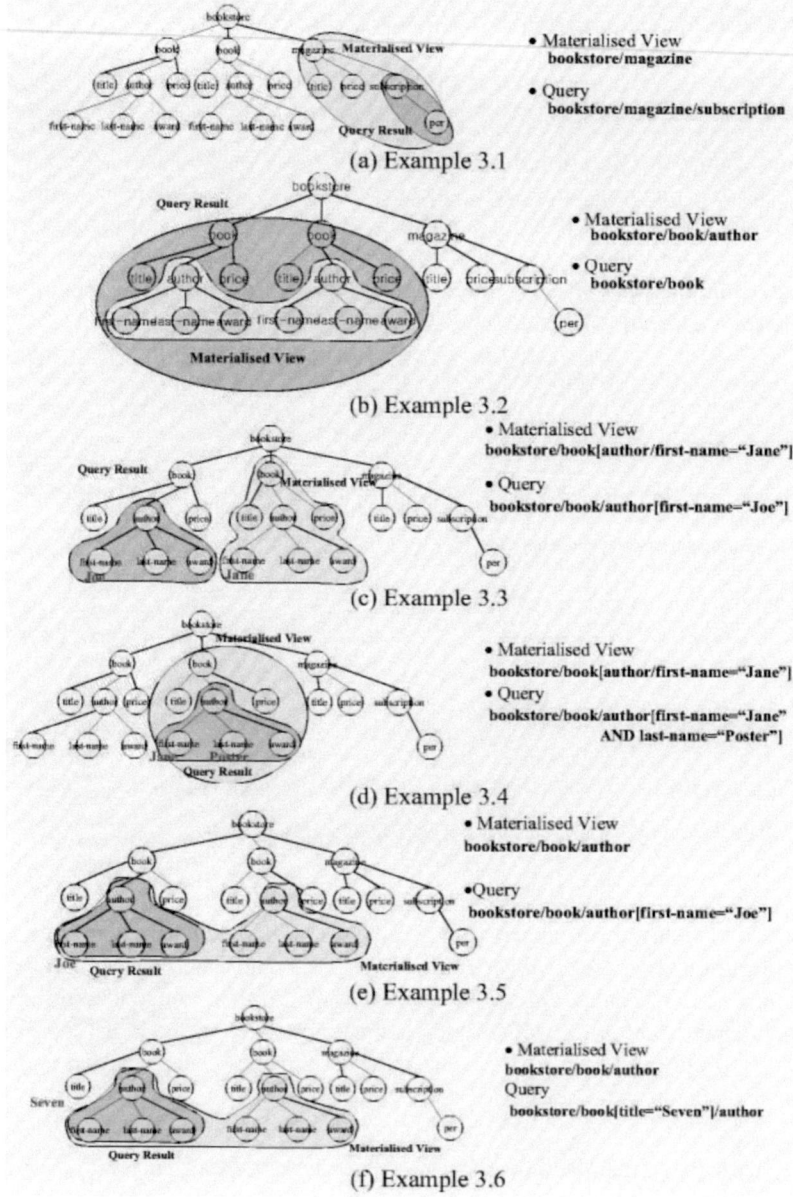

Fig. 5. Examples of Relationship between Materialised View and Query Result

Example 3.3

The above two examples have shown the XML queries and views without filter operators.

Suppose there exists a materialised view defined as *bookstore/book[author/first-name= "Jane"]* and an XML query *bookstore/book/author[first-name="Joe"]* is given. The tree structure of the materialised view subsumes that of the query result, i.e., the subtree rooted at the book element contains the subtree rooted at the author element. However, the two path expressions designate different author subtrees. As such, the materialised view is of no use for the query at hand unless Joe is a co-author of the book authored by Jane. □

Example 3.4

Suppose there exists a materialised view defined as *bookstore/book[author/first-name="Jane"]* and an XML query *bookstore/book/author[first-name="Jane" AND last-name="Poster"]* is given. Since the tree structure of the materialised view subsumes that of the query result and the condition with the query is more restrictive than that of the materialised view, the query result could be obtained from the materialised view. □

Example 3.5

Now let us consider the case where the view is defined without filter operators whereas the query is with them.

Suppose there exists a materialised view defined as *bookstore/book/author* and an XML query *bookstore/book/author[first-name="Joe"]* is given. For the same reason as in Example 3.4, the query result could be obtained from the view. □

We note that one of the representative cases where query rewriting with the materialised view is simple and effective is when the materialised view and the query result have the same path, and the condition in the filter operator with the query is more restrictive than that of the view (which may not be given, i.e., vacuous TRUE as in Example 3.5). However, in such a case and even in the case where the materialised view is containing the query result completely, query rewriting may be impossible. The next example shows the case.

Example 3.6

Suppose there exists a materialised view defined as *bookstore/book/author* and an XML query *bookstore/book[title="Seven"]/author* is given. Although the materialised view does contain the query result, the query result cannot be retrieved from the materialised view because the materialised view does not store the title element on which the query's condition is specified. □

3.2 Model of XML View

We consider the XML query in path expression against *a collection of* XML documents that conform to some DTD, rather than against a single XML document. The result of a path expression against a single XML document is a subtree rooted at the last element in the path excluding the filter operator. We call that element as the *target element* of the query. For example, for path expression *bookstore/book[author/first-name="Jane"]*, the target element is book.

An XML view is a forest of subtrees each of which is rooted at the target element of the view's path expression. In this paper, an XML view defined by a path expression is modelled as an XML document. To form a single document with all the subtrees retrieved from all the source documents, a root element named *mv*, which stands for materialised view, is used [17].

3.3 Determining Query Processing Type

From the examples in Section 3.1, we note that to see whether or not the existing materialised view can be capitalized on in processing a given query, both the paths and conditions of the view and of the query need to be compared with each other.

Suppose that query q and materialised view v are given. Let *q.path* and *v.path* denote the *target element path* of q and v, respectively, which is the path expression in q and v, respectively excluding the conditions on the target element or on its subelements, if any. For example, Table 1 shows q.path's and v.path's of q's and v's in Example 3.1 through Example 3.6.

Table 1. Examples of Target Element Path

q	q.path	v	v.path
bookstore/magazine/ subscription	bookstore/magazine/ subscription	bookstore/magazine	bookstore/magazine
bookstore/book	bookstore/book	bookstore/book/author	bookstore/book/author
bookstore/book/ author[first-name="Joe"]	bookstore/book/ author	bookstore/book [author/first-name="Jane"]	bookstore/book
bookstore/book/author[first-name="Jane" AND last-name="Poster"]	bookstore/book/author	Bookstore/book [author/first-name="Jane"]	bookstore/book
bookstore/book/author [first-name="Joe"]	bookstore/book/author	bookstore/book/author	bookstore/book/author
bookstore/book [title="Seven"]/author	bookstore/book [title="Seven"]/author	bookstore/book/author	bookstore/book/author

In some cases, the type of processing q with v could be determined just by comparing q.path with v.path. Given two target element path P_1 and P_2 of XML document D, let us define operator $<_p$ between the two as follows: $P_1 <_p P_2$ iff $P_1 \neq P_2$ and P_1 is a prefix of P_2. That is, $P_1 <_p P_2$ when P_2 designates a proper subtree of the subtree designated by P_1 with respect to D. For example, in Example 3.3, q.path = *bookstore/book/author* and v.path = *bookstore/book*, and as such, v.path $<_p$ q.path. What this means is that q could be entirely processed with v (i.e., MV type) since q is to retrieve a proper subtree of v's materialisation and both q and v do not include any condition.

In Example 3.2, on the other hand, q.path $<_p$ v.path because q.path = *bookstore/book* and v.path = *bookstore/book/author*. Since both q and v do not include any

Table 2. Examples of Target Element Condition

q	q.con	v	v.con
bookstore/magazine/subscription	{ }	bookstore/magazine	{ }
bookstore/book	{ }	bookstore/book/author	{ }
bookstore/book/author [first-name="Joe"]	{bookstore/book/author/ first-name="Joe"}	bookstore/book[author/ first-name="Jane"]	{bookstore/book/author/ first-name="Jane"}
bookstore/book/author [first-name="Jane" AND last-name ="Poster"]	{bookstore/book/author/ first-name="Jane", bookstore/book/author/ last-name="Poster" }	bookstore/book[author/ first-name="Jane"]	{bookstore/book/author /first-name="Jane"}
bookstore/book/author [first-name="Joe"]	{bookstore/book/author/ first-name="Joe"}	bookstore/book/author	{ }
bookstore/book [title="Seven"]/author	{ }	bookstore/book/author	{ }

condition, in this case, q could be only partially answered with v. The complete answer should be obtained by accessing the base documents as well (i.e., BD+MV type).

When there are some conditions specified on the target element or on its subelements in q and/or v, not just the target element paths of q and v but their conditions also need to be compared in determining the type of processing q with v. Let us assume that these conditions are specified in conjunctive normal form p_1 AND … AND p_n in a filter operator, where p_i is a predicate condition on an element ($i = 1, …, n$). Let *q.con* and *v.con* denote the *target element condition* of q and v, respectively, which is formulated as a set of predicates $\{P_1, …, P_n\}$ where P_i is obtained from p_i as follows: For the element involved in the condition p_i, P_i is the full path to that element within the XML document ($i = 1, …, n$). For example, in Example 3.4, the condition in q and v is *[first-name="Jane" AND last-name="Poster"]* and *[author/first-name="Jane"]*, respectively. Therefore, q.con = *{bookstore/book/author/first-name="Jane", bookstore/book/author/last-name="Poster"}* and v.con = *{bookstore/book/author/first-name="Jane"}*. If q or v does not include any filter operator, q.con or v.con is an empty set. Table 2 shows q.con's and v.con's of q's and v's in Example 3.1 through Example 3.6.

Since q.con and v.con are sets, one may be a subset of the other. If v.con $\subset$ q.con, it means that q has more restrictive condition than v in retrieving XML documents and that q could be processed with v as long as v.path = q.path or v.path $<_p$ q.path.

In all, Table 3 summarizes how the type of query processing with a materialised view is determined in terms of the target element paths and conditions. The BD+MV types are further categorized into BD+MV1, BD+MV2, and BD+MV3 because their query rewritings are different.

Table 3. Determining Type of XML Query Processing with Materialised View

Condition \ Path		v.path = q.path	v.path $<_p$ q.path	q.path $<_p$ v.path	Otherwise
Conditions Not Given	-	MV	MV	BD+MV1	BD
Conditions Given	v.con = q.con	MV	MV	BD+MV1	BD
	v.con $\subset$ q.con	MV	MV	BD+MV1	BD
	v.con $\supset$ q.con	BD+MV2	BD+MV3	BD	BD
	otherwise	BD	BD	BD	BD

Fig. 6 is the algorithmic description of Table 3 in a C-like pseudo code (algorithm *Check_Containment*). Given query q and materialised view v both in XML path expression, Check_Containment identifies the applicable type of query processing, returning one of five values: MV, BD+MV1, BD+MV2, and BD+MV3, and BD.[1]

```
Check_Containment(q, v)
{    /* q : XML path expression
        v : definition of XML materialised view in path expression
    */

if ((v.path = q.path OR v.path <ₚ q.path) AND v.con ⊆ q.con) return(MV);
if (q.path <ₚ v.path AND v.con ⊆ q.con) return(BD+MV1);
if (q.path = v.path AND q.con ⊂ v.con) return(BD+MV2);
if (v.path <ₚ q.path AND q.con ⊂ v.con) return(BD+MV3);
return(BD);
}
```

Fig. 6. Algorithm for Checking Containment Relationship between Query and View

3.4   Rewriting of Path Expression

From the examples in Section 3.1, we note that to see whether or not the existing materialised view can be capitalized on in processing a given query, both the paths and conditions of the view and of the query need to be compared with each other. Fig. 7 shows the C-like pseudo code of the algorithm *Rewrite_Path* for rewriting an XML query in path expression with its relevant materialised view. Given query q, materialised view v, and q's processing type using v which was determined by algorithm Check_Containment, Rewrite_Path rewrites q into q' and q" which are against v and against the base documents, respectively. For BD+MV, there are three different patterns of rewriting. For BD, query rewriting is vacuously done. For MV, q" is set to NULL, whereas for BD, q' is set to NULL and q is copied to q".

Rewriting of a path expression is done with manipulating the substrings of the path expressions in q and v. To describe Rewrite_Path, we need to define some further notations.

Given path expression p, let *p.elem* denote the target element of p, and let *p.len* denote the length of p, which is defined to be the number of elements from the first element up to the target element along p. When p = *bookstore/book[title=“Seven”] /author[first-name=“Joe”]*, for example, p.elem = *author* and p.len = 3.

Given path expression p and integer i, let *d_path(p,i)* denote the *descendent path* of p which is defined to be the suffix of p starting from the character after the i-th element of p and also after its filter operator as well, if any. When p = *bookstore/book[title=“Seven”]/author[first-name=“Joe”]*, for example, d_path(p,2) = */author[first-name=“Joe”]*, and d_path(p,3) = NULL.

Another notation we need to pay attention to is the backslash(\) used to generate q" in the case of BD+MV1. In XML path expressions, the slash(/) is used as the path operator, denoting parent-child relationship among elements. We introduce the *ex cluding operator*, and use the backslash(\) to denote it. What it does is to specify the subelement of the target element *not* to be retrieved. For example, path expres-

---

[1] Given a query, algorithm Check_Containment is supposed to be repeatedly called for each view available in the cache. The process of determining the type of query processing is subsumed by that of selecting the materialised view to be capitalized on (see the implementation issue described in Section 4.2).

sionbookstore/book\author is to retrieve the book element with all its subelements except author.

For path expression p, what function *refine_path(p)* does is to trim the redundant prefixes off the full path expressions in the filter operators of p. For example, */author[bookstore/ book/author/first-name = "Joe"]* is refined to */author[first-name = "Joe"]*. (This is necessary because the path expressions in the filter

Table 4. Notations

notation	description
x + y	concatenation of string x and y
and(*con*)	if *con* = { }, returns NULL if *con* = {P}, returns "P" if *con* = {P$_1$, ..., P$_n$}, returns "P$_1$ AND ... AND P$_n$"
not(*con*)	returns "NOT(*con*)"
filter(*con*)	if *con* = NULL, returns NULL otherwise, returns "[*con*]"

operators were transformed into their full path version when q.con and v.con are obtained.) It also replaces any occurrence of the backslash immediately followed by a slash (i.e., '\'/') in p with a backslash. (Such a sequence can occur because the descendent path obtained with path decomposition may start with a slash.)

Finally, other notations for character string manipulation, +, and(), not(), filter(), are given in Table 4.

3.5 Examples of Query Rewriting

As we explained in Section 3.1, Example 3.1, Example 3.4, and Example 3.5 are all the cases where MV type query rewriting is possible. For each of these three examples, Table 5 shows the values of various notations used in Rewrite_Path en route to obtaining the rewritten path expression (refined q'). We can confirm that in all three examples, query rewriting done by Rewrite_Path is correct.

As for BD+MV type query rewriting, Table 6 shows five different examples, one for each case of BD+MV types in Table 3, and their correspond-

```
Rewrite_Path(v, q, type, q', q")
{
/*  v : definition of XML materialised view in path expression
    q : XML path expression
    q' : XML path expression against v
    q" : XML path expression against the base XML documents
    type : type of processing q with v determined by algorithm
           Check_Containment
*/
switch(type) {
  case MV :
      q' = "mv/"+v.elem+d_path(q, v.len).path+filter(and(q.con – v.con));
      q" := NULL;
      break;
  case BD+MV1 :
      q' := "mv/" + v.elem + filter(and(q.con – v.con));
      q" := q + "\" + d_path(v, q.len).path + filter(and(q.con));
      break;
  case BD+MV2 :
      q' := "mv/" + v.elem
      q" := q.path + filter(and( q.con ∪ { not(and(v.con – q.con)) } ));
      break;
  case BD+MV3 :
      q' := "mv/" + v.elem + d_path(q, v.len).path + filter(and(q.con));
      q" := v.path + filter(not(and(v.con))) + d_path(q, v.len);
      break;
  case BD :
      q' := NULL;
      q" := q;
      break;
} /* end of switch */

q' := refine_path(q');
q" := refine_path(q");
}
```

Fig. 7. Algorithm for Rewriting XML Path Expression Using XML Materialised View

ing rewritten q's and q"s generated by Rewrite_Path. We can confirm that in all five examples, query rewriting done by Rewrite_Path is correct.[2]

4 Implementation

We have developed a prototype XML storage system that supports the materialised views on top of an object-relational DBMS [17]. It was implemented in Java with Oracle 8*i*, and runs on Windows 2000 Server. It is now being extended to incorporate our proposal described in the previous section so that it may process XML path expressions with the materialised views defined also in path expression. In this section, we present the implementation details and some preliminary performance results.

Table 5. Examples of XML Query Rewriting: MV

example ⟍ notation	Example 3.1	Example 3.4	Example 3.5
q	bookstore/ magazine/ subscription	bookstore/book/author [first-name="Jane" AND last-name= "Poster"]	bookstore/book/ author [first-name="Joe"]
v	bookstore/ magazine	bookstore/book[author/ first-name="Jane"]	bookstore/book/ author
v.elem	magazine	book	author
v.len	2	2	3
d_path(q, v.len)	/subscription	/author[first-name="Jane" AND last-name="Poster"]	NULL
d_path(q, v.len).path	/subscription	/author	NULL
q.con	{ }	{bookstore/book/author/ first-name="Jane", bookstore/book/author/ last-name="Poster"}	{bookstore/book/ author/ first-name="Joe"}
v.con	{ }	{bookstore/book/author/ first-name="Jane"}	{ }
q.con − v.con	{ }	{bookstore/book/author/ last-name="Poster"}	{bookstore/book/author/ first-name="Joe"}
and(q.con−v.con)	NULL	bookstore/book/author/ last-name="Poster"	bookstore/book/author/ first-name="Joe"
filter(and(q.con−v.con))	NULL	[bookstore/book/author/ last-name="Poster"]	[bookstore/book/author/ first-name="Joe"]
initial q'	mv/magazine/ subscription	mv/book/author [bookstore/book/author/ last-name="Poster"],	mv/author [bookstore/book/ author/ first-name="Joe"]
refined q'	mv/magazine/ subscription	mv/book/author [last-name="Poster"]	mv/author [first-name="Joe"]

---

[2] Note that the books can be co-authored in our example DTD. As such, the filter operators on the author element after the excluding operator are explicitly required though they might look redundant.

4.1 Table Schema

There are five categories of tables. They are for storing DTD information, view definitions, base documents, the information for deferred incremental view refresh, and
materialised views. The tables in the first two categories are duplicated both at the
XML source site and at the cache site. The ones in the next two categories are stored
at the source site whereas the ones in the last category are stored at the cache site.

As for storing the base documents, among others, there are two tables used: *Ele-
ment_Info* table and *Element_Content* table.[3] The former stores the information on
each element which is mapped to a tuple, and includes *DTDid, Did, Eid, Ename,
Epath,* and *ParentEid* columns. Did and DTDid store the identifier of the base XML
document and its DTD, respectively. The indices on DTDid are provided for selective
access only to those documents conforming to a given DTD. Eid and Ename store the
identifier and name of the element, respectively. Eid is not just the unique identifier of
the element but carries information on the order of the elements in a document. When
an XML document is decomposed into elements to be stored in the above two tables,
Eid values are assigned in a monotonically increasing way from the root element to its
subelements in the DFS(Depth First Search) order. This order information is very
useful in XML tagging (see Section 4.4). Epath stores the path from the root of the
document to that element. For the author element, for example, Epath = *book-
store/book/author.* ParentEid stores the parent-child relationship among the elements.

Element_Content table stores the parsed character data of the leaf elements, and includes DTDid, Did, Eid, Epath, and *Content* columns. Since our XML view is modelled as an XML document (see Section 3.2), the schema of the tables for the materialised views (i.e., *View_Element_Info* and *View_Element_Content* tables) are the same
as their base document counterparts except that they have the view identifier column
(i.e., *Vid*) and some information on element mapping between the base documents and
the view, which is used in the process of incremental view refresh [17]. The indices on
Vid are provided for selective access only to those tuples for a given view.

4.2 View Selection and Query Rewriting

When an XML query in path expression is received, first its corresponding DTD information is retrieved from the DTD information table. Then, all the tuples storing the
information on the views defined with respect to the same DTD are retrieved from the
view definition table. For each of those views, its definition in path expression and the
query's path expression are given to algorithm Check_Containment which examines
the containment relationship between the two and determines the query processing
type as one of MV, BD+MV1, BD+MV2, and BD+MV3, and BD.

If more than one view can be used for query rewriting, the view which allows MV
type processing with the closest containment is selected. If none makes MV type proc-

---

[3] In our previous implementation [17], the *edge-inlining* approach described in [13] was
adopted for table schema design. Now, we are employing the *edge-separate table* approach
[13].

Table 6. Examples of XML Query Rewriting: BD+MV

expr type	q	v	q'	q"
BD+MV1	bookstore/book	bookstore/book/author	mv/author	bookstore/book\author
BD+MV1	bookstore/book [author/ first-name= "Michael"]	bookstore/book/ author [first-name= "Michael"]	mv/author	bookstore/book [author/first-name="Michael"] \author [first-name= "Michael"]
BD+MV1	bookstore/book [author/first-name= "Michael" AND author/ last-name= "Kay"]	bookstore/book/author [first-name= "Michael"]	mv/author [last-name= "Kay"]	bookstore/book [author/first-name="Michael" AND author/last-name="Kay"] \author[first-name="Michael" AND last-name = "Kay"]
BD+MV2	bookstore/book/ author[first-name= "Michael"]	bookstore/book/author [first-name="Michael" AND last-name= "Kay"]	mv/author	bookstore/book/author [first-name="Michael" AND NOT (last-name = "Kay")]
BD+MV3	bookstore/book/ author[first-name= "Michael"]	book- store/book[author/ first-name="Michael" AND author/ last-name= "Kay"]	mv/book/ author [first-name ="Michael"]	bookstore/book [NOT (author/first-name = "Michael" AND author/ last-name ="Kay")]/ author[first-name="Michael"]

essing possible, the one for BD+MV type processing with the closest containment is selected. Once the processing type and the view to be capitalized on are determined, the original query is rewritten into subqueries which are also in path expression.

4.3   XML Path Expression to SQL Mapping

For MV, the rewritten subquery in XML path expression is mapped into SQL expressions against the materialised view tables whereas for BD+MV, the two subqueries are mapped to SQL, one against the materialised view tables and the other against the base document tables. In this XML-to-SQL mapping, DTD information is consulted to generate the list of elements to be included in the query result. While this is done, the information for XML tagging [14][29] is also produced.

Suppose that we are given an XML path expression, a/b/c, against a materialised view whose Vid = v and that element c has elements d and e as its subelements, which are leaf elements. Then, the SQL statement generated for it against View_Element_Info table is:

```
SELECT  Did, Eid, Ename, Epath, ParentEid
FROM   View_Element_Info
WHERE  Vid = v AND
       ((Ename = 'c' AND Epath = 'a/b/c') OR
        (Ename = 'd' AND Epath = 'a/b/c/d') OR
        (Ename = 'e' AND Epath = 'a/b/c/e'))
ORDER BY  Did  Eid
```

The order by clause is necessary for efficient XML tagging to be performed next with the produced tuple stream (see Section 4.4). The SQL statement against View_Element_Content table for leaf elements is similarly generated.

Meanwhile, for the path expression with a filter operator, say, a/b/c[d='x'], against the base documents whose DTDid = n, the SQL statement generated against Element_Info table is:

```
SELECT *
FROM  Element_Info
WHERE DTDid = n AND
           ((Ename = 'c' AND Epath = 'a/b/c') OR
           (Ename = 'd' AND Epath = 'a/b/c/d') OR
           (Ename = 'e' AND Epath = 'a/b/c/e'))
           AND Did IN (SELECT Did
                  FROM Element_Content
                  WHERE DTDid = n
                      AND Epath = 'a/b/c/d/#PCDATA'
                      AND Content = 'x')
ORDER BY Did Eid
```

Suppose that element c can occur more than once as subelements of b in a document. Then, there can be the case that some of them is with d = 'x' and some with d ≠ 'x'. The above SQL statement does not exclude the latter c subtrees. As such, the original tuple stream produced undergoes further screening. It is conducted on a document basis as the original stream is produced.

For the excluding operator (e.g., a/b\c) we introduced for BD+MV type processing, the WHERE clause needs some adjustment. For element c, for example, that belongs to the subtree to be excluded, the predicate condition (Ename = 'c' AND Epath = 'a/b/c') is omitted.

4.4 XML Tagging

As the tuple streams are produced, they are fed into the tagging process which generates the final query result that consists of the retrieved XML subtrees. For MV or BD type processing, there are two tuple streams produced, one from the element information table and the other from the element content table. Due to the order by clause in the SQL statements generated (i.e., ORDER BY Did Eid), the tuples in these tuple streams are produced as sorted on the document identifier and on the element identifier within a document, which is the DFS order as explained in Section 4.1. This ordering makes it possible for each subtree of the query result out of a document to be generated in a pipelined way as the two tuple streams are produced. As such, with the tagging information generated when the DTD information is analyzed for the query, the pair of tuple streams can be straightforwardly transformed into XML.

For BD+MV type processing, on the other hand, there are four tuple streams involved. They are merged into two streams before starting to be fed into the tagging process. The original two out of the element information tables for the base documents and for the materialised views, and also the two out of the content tables are merged into one, respectively. Since each of the original tuple streams is produced as sorted on the document identifier and on the element identifier within a document, their merge which maintains the same sort order is simple. In all, the entire process is performed in a pipelined way. As the four tuple streams involved are produced, they are fed into the merge process whose output streams are then fed into the tagging process.

The XML tagging for BD+MV type processing is always performed at the XML cache site. As such, the tuple streams out of the XML source site are sent to the cache site as they are produced. For BD type processing, however, it depends on whether or not the tuple streams produced are to be cached (i.e., stored in the corresponding materialised view tables at the cache site). If not to be cached, XML tagging takes places at the source site and the query result in XML is sent.

4.5   Preliminary Performance Evaluation

In this section, we report some preliminary performance experimental results. Two types of base XML documents were used in the experiments. One is the extended version of the bookstore documents used for the running example of the paper which is of small size consisting of about 25 elements per document on the average. The other is the plays of Shakespeare [5] whose average number of elements per document is about 8,500.

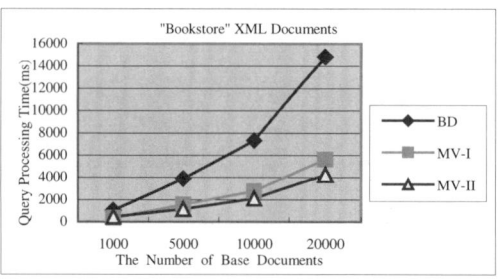

Fig. 8. Time for Processing XML Path Expressions Using Materialised Views

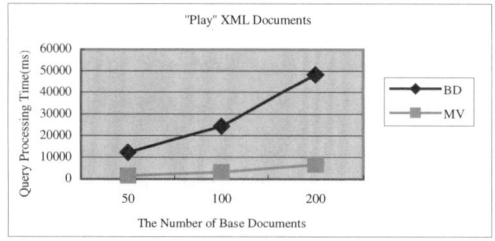

Fig. 9. Time for Processing XML Path Expressions Using Materialised Views

Since our system has not yet been ported to the web environment and is running in a centralized environment only, the performance of the MV type processing to that of the BD type processing where the communication cost is ignored were compared. The experiments were conducted on a Pentium III (550MHz Dual) PC with 1024 MB main memory running Windows 2000 Server. Fig. 8 and Fig. 9 compare the query processing times by these two methods as the number of base document (D) increases.

In Fig. 8, which is out of the experiments against the bookstore documents, query q was *bookstore/book/author/first-name*, and for MV, there were two materialised views available. One is v1 defined by *bookstore/book/author*, and the other is v2 defined by *bookstore/book/author/first-name*. The times it took to process q with v1 and with v2 were both measured. Since v2 is the smaller view containing the result of q (in fact, q and v2 are in exact match), processing q with it took the least time (curve MV-II). Processing q with v1 (curve MV-I) took a little longer. The performance improvement by MV over BD is significant even when the cost for transmitting the retrieved XML result to the query site in the web environment is not counted for BD. The times it took for BD without communication are 2.31, 3.42, 3.47, and 3.48 times as long as those for MV capitalizing on v2 when D = 1000, 5000, 10000, and 20000, respectively. In Fig. 9, which is out of the experiments against the large play documents, the ratios increased to 7.82, 7.77, and 7.18 when D = 50, 100, and 200, respectively.

5 Concluding Remarks

In this paper, processing the XML query in path expression with the XML materialised view defined also in path expression was investigated. Such a technique can be employed for efficient support of XML database-backed web applications.

Given two XML path expressions, one for the query and the other for the materialised view maintained as a result of semantic caching of XML source, we proposed algorithms *Check_Containment* and *Rewrite_Path* that checks the containment relationship between the query result and the materialised view, and performs the appropriate query rewriting using the materialised view, respectively. In doing so, we also introduced the *excluding operator* for XML path expression.

Our proposal is now being implemented with the prototype XML storage system that supports XML view materialisation previously developed by us in Java with Oracle 8i on Windows 2000 Server [17]. A *relational DBMS* is employed as the XML storage because of its pragmatic importance. We thus described some details of the implementation issues such as table schema, view selection and query rewriting, XML path expression to SQL mapping, and XML tagging. Some preliminary experimental results on performance were also presented, showing that our scheme is feasible and promising.

The path expression is one of the core features of XML query languages, and employing a relational DBMS as the XML store is regarded as a very practical approach. As further research, we plan to consider several different table schemas like those examined in [31][29][14] and also their variations for storing not just the base XML documents but their materialised views defined in path expressions, and compare them in terms of the performance tradeoffs in processing XML path expressions using the XML materialised views in the web application context.

References

1. S. Abiteboul et al., "Incremental Maintenance for Materialized Views over Semistructured Data," Proc. Int'l Conf. on VLDB, 1998, pp. 38–49.
2. S. Abiteboul et al., "Representing and Querying XML with Incomplete Information," Proc. Int'l Symp. on PODS, 2001.
3. A. Berglund et al., "XML Path Language (XPath) 2.0," http://www.w3.org/TR/xpath20/, Nov. 2002.

4. S. Boag et al., "XQuery 1.0: An XML Query Language," http://www.w3.org/TR/xquery/, 2002.
5. J. Bosak, "The Plays of Shakespeare," http://www.ibiblio.org/bosak/, 1999.
6. D. Calvanese et al., "Answering Regular Path Queries Using Views," Proc. Int'l Conf. on Data Eng., pp. 389–398, 2000.
7. L. Chen and E. Rundensteiner, "Aggregate Path Index for Incremental Web View Mainte-nance," Proc. 2nd Int'l Workshop on Advanced Issues of E-Commerce and Web-based In-formation Systems, 2000.
8. L. Chen and E. Rundensteiner, "ACE-XQ: A CachE-aware XQuery Answering System," Proc. Workshop on the Web and Databases, 2002.
9. L. Chen et al., "XCache – A Semantic Caching System for XML Queries," Proc. ACM SIGMOD Int'l Conf. on Management of Data, 2002.
10. S. Dar et al., "Semantic Data Caching and Replacement," Proc. Int'l Conf. on VLDB, 1996, pp. 330–341.
11. A. Deutsch et al., "Storing Semistructured Data with STORED," Proc. ACM SIGMOD Int'l Conf. on Management of Data, 1999, pp. 431–442
12. D. Florescu et al., "Query Containment for Conjunctive Queries with Regular Expres-sions," Proc. Int'l Symp. on PODS, 1998, pp. 139–148.
13. D. Florescu and D. Kossmann, "Storing and Querying XML Data Using an RDBMS," IEEE Data Eng. Bulletin, Vol. 22, No. 3, Sep. 1999, pp. 27–34.
14. D. Florescu and D. Kossmann, "A Performance Evaluation of Alternative Mapping Schemes for Storing XML Data in a Relational Database," Tech. Rep., INRIA, France, 1999.
15. A. Gupta and I. Mumick, "Materialized Views: Techniques, Implementations, and Appli-cations," 1999, MIT Press.
16. V. Hristidis and M. Petropoulos, "Semantic Caching of XML Databases," Proc. Workshop on the Web and Databases, 2002.
17. H. Kang et al., "Deferred Incremental Refresh of XML Materialized Views: Algorithms and Performance Evaluation," Proc. the 14-th Australasian Database Conf., Feb. 2003, pp. 217–226.
18. Y. Kim, C. Moon, and H. Kang, "XML View Indexing: Issues and Solutions," Proc. Int'l Conf. on Information and Knowledge Engineering, Jun. 2002, pp. 327–333.
19. A. Labrinidis and N. Roussopoulos, "Web View Materialization," Proc. ACM SIGMOD Int'l Conf. on Management of Data, 2000, pp. 367–378.
20. D. Lee and W. Chu, "A Semantic Caching Scheme for Wrappers in Web Databases," Tech. Rep. TR-990004, UCLA, Feb. 1999.
21. A. Levy et al., "Answering Queries Using Views," Proc. of ACM Int'l Symp. on PODS, 1995.
22. Q. Luo and J. Naughton, "Form-Based Proxy Caching for Database-Backed Web Sites," VLDB J. 2001, pp. 191–200.
23. Q. Luo et al., "Active Query Caching for Database Web Servers," Proc. WebDB, 2000, pp. 29–34.
24. P. Marron and G. Lausen, "Efficient Cache Answerability for XPath Queries," Proc. the 2nd Int'l Workshop on Data Integration over the Web, 2002, pp. 35–45.
25. Y. Papakonstantinou and V. Vassalos, "Query Rewriting for Semistructured Data," SIGMOD Proc. Int'l Conf. on Management of Data, pp. 455–466, 1999.
26. L. Quan et al., "Argos: Efficient Refresh in an XQL-Based Web Caching System," Proc. Workshop on the Web and Databases, 2000, pp. 23–28.

27. J. Robie et al., "XML Query Language (XQL)," http://www.w3.org/TandS/QL/ QL98/pp/xql.html, 1998.
28. N. Roussopoulos and H. Kang, "Principles and Techniques in the Design of ADMS±," IEEE Computer, Vol. 19, No. 12, Dec. 1986, pp. 19–25.
29. J. Shanmugasundaram et al., "Relational Databases for Querying XML Documents: Limitations and Opportunities," Proc. Int'l Conf. on VLDB, 1999, pp. 302–314.
30. D. Suciu, "Query Decomposition and View Maintenance for Query Languages for Unstructured Data," Proc. Int'l Conf. on VLDB, 1996, pp. 227–238.
31. F. Tian et al., "The Design and Performance Evaluation of Alternative XML Storage Strategies," ACM SIGMOD Record, Vol. 31, No. 1, Mar. 2002, pp. 5–10.
32. Y. Zhuge and H. Garcia-Molina, "Graph Structured Views and Their Incremental Maintenance," Proc. Int'l Conf. on Data Engineering, 1998, pp. 116–125.

WebVigiL: User Profile-Based Change Detection for HTML/XML Documents[1]

N. Pandrangi, J. Jacob, A. Sanka, and S. Chakravarthy

Information Technology Laboratory and
Computer Science and Engineering Department
The University of Texas at Arlington, Arlington, TX 76019
{pandrang,jacob,asanka,sharma}@cse.uta.edu

Abstract. With the exponential increase of information on the web, the emphasis has shifted from mere viewing of information to efficient retrieval and notification of selective information. Currently, users have to poll the pages manually to check for changes of interest, resulting in waste of resources and associated high cost. Hence, an efficient and effective change detection and notification mechanism is needed. WebVigiL, a general-purpose, active capability-based information monitoring and notification system, handles specification, management, and propagation of customized changes as requested by a user. The emphasis of change detection in WebVigiL is to detect customized changes on the document, based on user intent. In this paper, we propose two different algorithms to handle change detection to contents of semi-structured and unstructured documents. Though the approach taken is general, we will explain the change detection in the context of HTML (unstructured) and XML (semi-structured) documents. We also provide a simple change presentation scheme to display the changes computed. We highlight the change detection in the context of WebVigiL and briefly describe the rest of the system.

1 Introduction

The Internet is evolving as a repository of information, and the user's interest has expanded from querying information to monitoring evolution of the pages. The emphasis is on selective change detection, as the users are typically not interested in changes to the entire page but to a particular portion or section. The need to monitor changes to documents of interest is not only true for the Internet but also for other large heterogeneous repositories. Different users may be interested in knowing changes to specific web pages (or even combinations there-of), and want to know when those changes take place. Some examples are: students want to know when the

---
[1] This work was supported, in part, by the Office of Naval Research & the SPAWAR System Center–San Diego & by the Rome Laboratory grant F30602-01-2-05430, and by NSF grants IIS-0123730 and ITR 0121297.

A. James, B. Lings, M. Younas (Eds.): BNCOD 2003, LNCS 2712, pp. 38–57, 2003.
© Springer-Verlag Berlin Heidelberg 2003

web contents of the courses (they have registered for) change; users may want to know when news items are posted in a specific context (appearance of key words, phrases etc.) they are interested in. In general, the ability to specify changes to arbitrary documents and get notified according to user-preferred ways in a timely manner will be useful for reducing/avoiding the wasteful navigation of web and its associated cost in this information age.

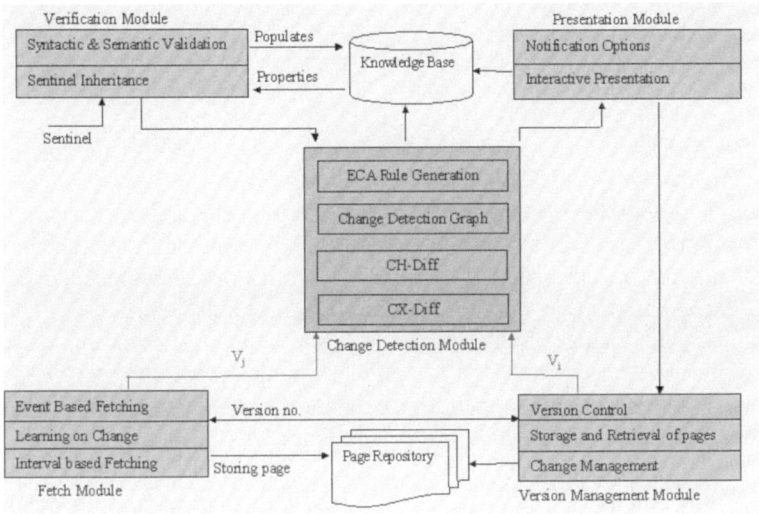

Fig. 1. WebVigiL Architecture, with the emphasis given to the modules presented in this paper

WebVigiL [1-3] provides a powerful way to disseminate information efficiently without sending unnecessary or irrelevant information. The emphasis in WebVigiL is to detect changes and notify the users based on user defined profiles. The change detection approach taken by WebVigiL is general but will be explained in this paper in context of the Hyper Text Markup Language (HTML) and eXtensible Markup Language (XML), which constitute a major portion of the web documents on the Internet. Fig. 1 shows the overall system architecture of WebVigiL. User-defined sentinels (profiles indicating the user intent on which pages to monitor, how to monitor, what changes to compute, and how to present and notify) are verified both syntactically and semantically prior to persisting their details in the knowledge base. Once a sentinel is validated, the change detector module generates the ECA rules for the run time management of that sentinel. The fetch module fetches pages for all active (or enabled) sentinels, forwards them to the version management module for adding them to the page repository and notifies the change detection module. The change detection module detects the changes according to the specification and notifies the presentation module. WebVigiL allows the user to specify the type of change of interest. Based on these documents, either the HTML or the XML change detection mechanism is called. The changes are detected and stored in the change repository. The presentation module takes these changes and presents it in a user-friendly manner. The main contributions of the paper are: a) CH-Diff, a change generating mechanism for detecting customized changes to HTML documents and b) CX-Diff, an approach for detecting customized changes to ordered labeled XML documents. The remainder of the paper is organized as follows. Section 2 discusses various tools developed for detecting changes to HTML and XML pages. Section 3 gives the problem overview. Sections 4 and 5 discuss, respectively, the algorithms proposed for change detection to HTML and XML documents. Section 6 discusses the various presentation modules and Section 7 provides current status and conclusions.

2 Related Work

Many research groups have been working on detecting changes to various types of documents. WordPerfect has a "mark changes" facility that can detect changes based on how documents are compared (on either a word, phrase, sentence, or paragraph basis). Most previous work in change detection has dealt only with flat-files [4] and in [5, 6] authors, detect changes between strings using the longest common subsequence [7] algorithm and considers insertion and deletion operations. AIDE [8] uses HTMLdiff to graphically present differences using heuristics to determine additions and deletions between versions of a page. A weighted LCS algorithm [7] is used by HTMLdiff to determine changes. WebBeholder [9] aims at tracking and viewing changes on web using a service provider agent and a number of mobile agents representing users. The service provider agent is responsible for retrieving and comparing HTML documents. A Difference Engine is used to compare and summarize change information. The authors present an algorithm called Longest Common Tag Sequence (LOGTAGS) for finding the right places for context comparison within a pair of HTML documents. In situations where the user is interested in change to a particular phrase, above-mentioned approaches will end up computing change to the whole page, resulting in excessive computational overhead. Considerable work [10, 11] has been done investigating methods and techniques for detecting duplicated portions of code or portions of similar code in procedural software systems. In [12], the authors suggest websites to be good candidates for clone proliferation, and propose an approach for clone analysis for websites based on Levenstein distance [13]. This method is computationally expensive as Levenstein distance involves evaluation of all possible alignments between strings before an optimal alignment is determined.

Many algorithms have been proposed for tree-tree comparison taking some tree features into consideration [14-16]. Chawathe et. al. [16] proposed an algorithm for hierarchical structured data wherein a minimum cost edit script is generated which transforms tree T1 to T2. The matching nodes are detected by satisfying a pre-defined function equal(x,y) where $x \hat{I}$ T1 and $y \hat{I}$ T2 and the longest common subsequence (LCS) method is used to reduce the number of moves for aligning the nodes. This algorithm works for semi-structured documents such as latex. But the assumptions do not hold good for XML documents as they contain duplicate nodes and subtrees. X-diff [17] detects changes on parsed unordered labeled tree of XML. X-diff finds the equivalent second level subtrees and compares the nodes using the structural information denoted as signature In order to detect move operations i.e. if a node is moved from position i in old tree to position j in the new tree, an unordered tree cannot be considered. In [18], the authors formulated a change detection algorithm called diff to detect changes between two given ordered XML trees T1 and T2. XMLTreeDiff [19], a tool developed by IBM, is a set of JavaBeans and does ordered tree to tree comparison to detect changes between XML documents. WebCiao [20] a website visualization and tracking system focuses on the structural changes on a HTML page i.e. change in the links of a given page. Most of the given algorithms do not support customized changes to the nodes (i.e. change to part of a node or spanning multiple nodes) and hence these algorithms cannot be mapped directly to satisfy the monitoring requirements of WebVigiL.

3 Problem Overview

The World Wide Web (the Web) has become a universal repository of information and continues to grow at an astounding pace. Hyper Text Markup Language (HTML) has been used as a universal format for publishing documents on the web since 1990. In 1998, the W3C approved eXtensible Markup Language (XML), which combined the power of SGML with the simplicity of HTML, was introduced. Over the coming years XML is likely to replace HTML as the standard web publishing language but until then both will coexist. In this section, we will highlight the differences between semi-structured (XML) and unstructured (HTML) documents. We will also introduce the problems associated with detecting changes using examples, and then present the need to have different change detection approaches for each type of document.

3.1 What Is a Change

It is useful to be able to know of changes to a document of interest on the web. Combinations of changes detected in content (data/text) and structure can flag a change to the page. We flag a change to a page only when a change in the content is detected ignoring the structural changes. From a user point of view, structural changes to a page do not seem to be important. Further more, we assume the structure of the page to be relatively stable. A web page can be viewed as a set of markup tags and data. In an XML page, combination of the content and the tags define the nature of the content whereas in HTML they define the presentation aspects of the content. Hence, as the format and representation of both HTML and XML differ, separate approaches need to be adopted for change detection for these documents. The change detection tools for HTML pages discussed in the previous section take into account the tags of the page along with the content for detecting change, resulting in consumption of significant computational and memory resources. Unlike HTML, tags in XML pages define the content of a page. Hence the structural information of the tags can be exploited to detect changes to the content.

3.2   Importance of User Intent

The web user's interest has extended from mere viewing of information to monitoring evolution of selective information on the pages. Hence, the change detection tool should be capable of detecting preferred change, such as the appearance/disappearance of keywords, update to a phrase, etc. Consider the scenario: A student wants to monitor the college schedule of classes for a particular course name (keyword). In such cases, detecting changes to the complete page results in excessive computation and dissemination of irrelevant information. Hence, there is a need to support detecting changes based on user's intent.

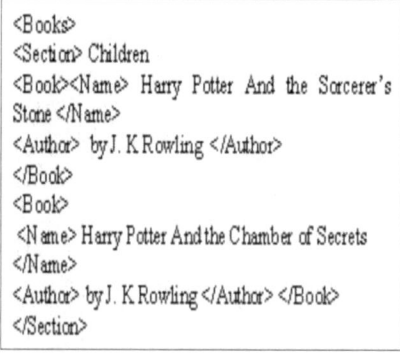

Fig. 2. XML Document

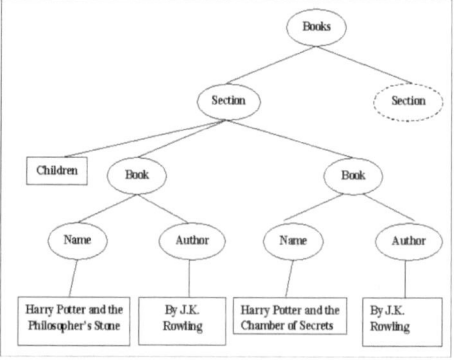

Fig. 3. Ordered Labeled XML tree

3.3   XML Problem Overview

As shown in Fig. 2, an XML document contains user-defined tags, denoted as elements. Each element consists of attributes and text nodes. As XML was defined for semi-structured documents containing ordered elements [21, 22], such documents can be mapped into an ordered labeled tree. The ordered tree for the XML document in Fig. 2 is shown in Fig. 3. Change detection for semi-structured, ordered XML trees is complex because of the following issues:

1. XML contains duplicate nodes. By duplicate nodes, we mean similar leaf nodes containing the same context. As shown in Fig. 3, the node 'J K Rowling' appears twice in the tree for the same context i.e. 'Books-Section-Book-Author'. Duplicate sub trees defined for the same context are also possible in XML. Order becomes very critical for such duplicate nodes as a node n, existing at position pi in the old tree should be compared to the node existing in the equivalent ith position in the new tree with respect to their siblings.
2. Two XML documents may contain the same content having the same structure but the nodes may be realigned in different subtrees or with respect to the siblings. For

example, for a tree T1 rooted at R with children pi to pm, a node along with its structural information can be moved from j where i £ j £ m in T1 to position k in T2 where j ≠ k, when considered with respect to the siblings. The change mechanism developed should be capable of detecting such move operations.

3. WebVigiL supports customized change detection to the contents, such as phrase and keyword change. Keywords and phrases can be part of the node or can span multiple nodes. Hence the algorithm should be capable of extracting the required content of interest and detect changes.

The change detection tools discussed earlier for XML documents do not handle customized changes. The proposed algorithms for HTML are for unordered trees. Hence, an algorithm is proposed, taking into consideration an ordered, labeled XML tree and the position of occurrence of the node with respect to its sibling.

4 HTML Change Detection

In this section we formally define change in a page, different types of changes identified and approaches for detecting these changes. In the later part of the section, we will present a generalized approach termed CH-Diff for detecting customized changes to HTML documents.

Change Type	Synopsis
Links	Insertion of new links or deletion of old links
Images	Insertion of new images or deletion of old images
Keyword(s)	Insertion or deletion of selected words
Phrase(s)	Insertion/deletion/update to selected text phrase
All Words	Any change to words in the page
Any Change	Any change to words or links or images in page

Fig. 4. Types of changes supported

4.1 Changes of Interest in a Page

A HTML document can be viewed as a document containing raw text along with formatting and presentation markups and certain content-defining markups. As explained in the earlier section, by a change we mean change to the raw text but not to the structure of the page. In addition to detecting changes to the data between the markups, we also detect changes to certain content-defining markups, such as (<IMG src ="."">) and (A href ="." >). We view a page as a sequence of words and certain content-defining markups while ignoring other markups (presentation markups). Users may be interested in appearance or disappearance of certain words or a section of contiguous words or links/images in the page. Thus the contents of a page can be classified, based on the user intent, into keywords, phrases, all-words, links and images.

1. Keywords: A set of unique words from the page, with no upper bound on the number of words.
2. Phrase: Contiguous words from the page, with no upper bound on the number of words.
3. All-Words: All the words in the page constitute this set; which also encompasses all keywords and phrases.
4. Links: A set of hypertext references extracted from the hypertext tag (<A href=".">).
5. Images: A set of image references extracted from the image source tag (IMG src=".">).

Since the words in phrase and keywords are a subset of the all words, we filter out the page into all-words and content-based (links, images) sets. We treat the context and content-tag sequence separately while keeping the processing order in the right sequence. A simple HTML parser [23] is used to parse the page and for filtering the page accordingly. Fig. 4 shows the classification of the contents of a page based on user intent.

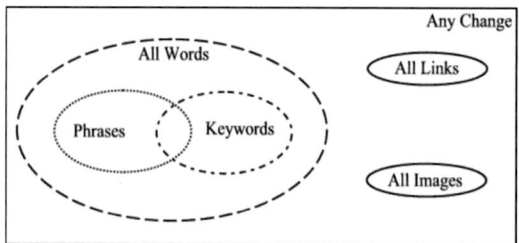

Fig. 5. Classification of contents of a page

A user may wish to track changes at the page level or at an object level. From the user point of view, by an object level change we mean change to the object of interest to the user, such as change to a particular phrase or keyword. Hence if t is the object of interest, then set T is defined as a set of all objects of type t extracted from the page. A page level change is any change to the page (i.e. words, links or images). For detecting changes to phrases and keywords we need to extract them from the all-words set. Object identification and extraction techniques are discussed in the following section. At the object level

a change is categorized as an appearance or disappearance of an object from the page. A move of an object in the page is taken as a sequence of disappearance and appearance. In the rest of the paper, we refer to disappearance and appearance as delete and insert respectively. In section 4.3 we will discuss more about each change type (insert/delete/update) for the objects in a page and approaches taken for the detection of change. In general, the change detection and change presentation is achieved through three phases namely, 1) Object identification and extraction 2) Change detection 3) Change presentation.

4.2   Object Identification and Extraction

Identification and extraction of objects (links, images and keywords) from a page is straightforward whereas the task for extracting objects of type "phrase" is complicated. Consider the scenario where the phrase has been partially modified; in such a case a direct string matching will fail to locate the phrase. In order to extract the modified phrase we need additional information like the location of the phrase in the previous version. To address this problem we assign a signature to each occurrence of the phrase. The words before and after the phrase constitute the signature of the phrase. In the current prototype, we assume that the selected words surrounding the object are relatively stable. Currently, ten words (or less) before and after the phrase constitute its signature. WebCQ [24] also uses the concept of a bounding box to tackle this problem. Issues like the dynamic configuration of signature length based on the nature of the page (static/dynamic), change to signature in combination with change to phrase are being investigated.

4.3   Detecting Changes to Objects

As discussed in section 4.1 the changes of interest are links, images, keywords, phrase, all words and anychange. Fig. 5 shows when a change is flagged for each of the supported change types. By anychange we mean change to "all-words" in the page and/or changes to links/images. For detecting changes to "all-words" we could use LCS. The existing tools use LCS (with several speed optimizations) to compare HTML pages at page level. But for scenarios where the user is only interested in a change to a particular object in a page, using LCS approach will be computationally expensive. Let t be the object type, which is of interest in a page, S(A) be the set of objects of type t extracted from version Vi and S(B) be the set of objects extracted from version Vi+1. Here S(A) – S(B) gives the objects that are absent in S(B) indicating deletion of those objects between versions Vi and Vi+1. Similarly S(B) – S(A) gives the new objects that have been inserted or added into version Vi+1. We will improve upon this idea by introducing the concept of window-based change detection.

4.3.1 CH-Diff: A Customized Change Detection Algorithm for HTML

We define a set s{(o1,c1),(o2,c2),(o3,c3),…,(on,cn)} where o1,o2,o3.. on are objects of type t with c1,c2,..cn being the corresponding number of occurrences (> 0) of each object in a version Vi. For detecting changes to objects of type t in version Vi, we need to compare the set obtained from Vi, with the old set obtained from version Vi-1. Increase or decrease in the number of instances of an object, is taken as an insert or delete. As the name of the approach indicates we form a window of objects which are ordered based on their hash codes. In java 1.3, for every string object a hash code [25] is generated (since every object is of type string in our case we use this hash code). The hash code of the first and last object in the re-ordered old set defines the bounds of the window.

1. **Phase-I:** Every object in new set with a hash code greater than the upper bound or lower than the lowerbound is flagged as an insert. Objects that have their hash code within [lowerbound, upperbound] are searched for occurrence in the objects defining this range (in re-ordered old set). If found, the occurrence count is compared and accordingly an insert or delete is flagged. If not found then the object in the new set is flagged as insert.
2. **Phase-II:** All objects in re-ordered old set that have not participated in the previous phase are flagged as deletes.

Since the objects are extracted from the page and change is deduced from the occurrence count, knowing exactly which instance of this object changed in the page requires additional computation. We do the additional computation based on the user preferences at the presentation phase. The signature of each instance of the keywords is used to detect the exact instance that was deleted. For phrases, in addition to insert and delete, an update to a phrase is also detected. Here, for phrases, the objects in the extracted set denote the signature of each instance (occurrence) of the phrase. The process involved in change detection of a phrase is as follows: Initially during the object extraction phase, Knuth-Morris-Pratt (KMP) string-matching algorithm is used for matching of the phrase with the words extracted from the page (words object). For every hit, the corresponding signature (bounding box) is extracted. Thus the set of objects extracted from the new and old version of a page for phrase detection is the signature of each instance of the phrase in the corresponding version. The window-based approach results in indicating inserts and deletes to the objects considered. Delete to the object here has two possibilities: either the phrase was completely deleted from the new version or the phrase is partially updated but is not caught by KMP. Here we use a heuristic approach for determining an update to a phrase. The object that was flagged as deleted in the old set (i.e., signature of that instance of a phrase) is used against the new page to get the words wrapped by this signature. LCS is now run on the words thus extracted and the phrase, and if the length of the resulting longest common subsequence is greater than a given percentage (the percentage can be adjusted on the fly based on past history) of the length of the phrase we take it as an update else a delete is flagged.

Consider the example where a user is interested in monitoring changes to objects {a, b, c, d, e} and let the set of these objects extracted from an old and a new version of a page be {(d,2),(b,2),(c,2)} and {(a,1), (c,2),(b,2),(e,1)} respectively. By analyzing these sets it is obvious that objects "a" and "e" have been inserted in the page and both the instances of object "d" are deleted from the old page. Fig. 6 shows the phases of the change detection algorithm along with the changes detected at each pass. The change computed is used in change presentation phase for presenting the changes. In section 6 we will discuss about presentation schemes and point out the type of scheme taken for each change type. In the following section we will present approaches for detecting customized changes for XML pages where the approach taken is different from HTML pages as explained in the problem overview.

		Re-ordered Old Set	Object in New Set	Insert set	Delete set	No change set
Phase-I	1.	{(b,2), (c,2),(d,2)}	(a,1)	{}	{}	{}
	2.	{(b,2), (c,2),(d,2)}	(a,1)	{(a,1)}	{}	{}
	3.	{(b,2), (c,2),(d,2)}	(c,2)	{(a,1)}	{}	{(c,2)}
	4.	{(b,2), (c,2),(d,2)}	(b,2)	{(a,1)}	{}	{(c,2),(b,2)}
	5.	{(b,2), (c,2),(d,2)}	(e,1)	{(a,1),(e,1)}	{}	{(c,2),(b,2)}

		Re-ordered Old Set	New Set	Insert set	Delete set	No change set
Phase-II	1.	{(b,2), (c,2),(d,2)}	{(a,1), (c,2),(b,2),(e,1)}	{(a,1),(e,1)}	{(d,2)}	{(c,2),(b,2)}

Fig. 6. Operations in Phase I and II

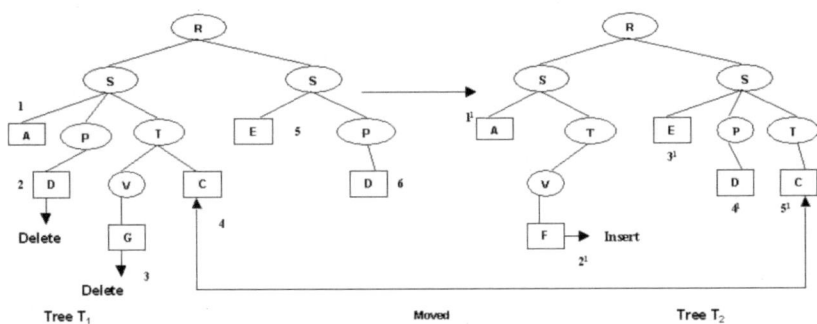

Fig. 7. Change Operations on trees T1 and T2

5   Change Detection for XML

An XML document consists of nodes that represent elements, text, attributes etc. and can be represented as an ordered labeled tree. The structural information, such as the element and sibling information can be utilized efficiently to detect changes in XML. The structural information denoted as path or signature is defined as:

Signature: The ancestral path of a leaf node from the parent to the root, denoted by path(x) for node x. For attributes, the label of the attribute also becomes a part of the signature. In Fig. 3, the path for the node "Harry Potter and the Chamber of Secrets" is Books-Section-Book-Name.

CX-Diff detects customized changes on XML documents like keywords and phrases (defined in section 4.1). These changes are word-based changes on the content of the page. In an XML tree, the leaf nodes represent the content. Hence changes to the leaf nodes are of interest. The structure is only taken into consideration for efficient change detection to the content. Keyword can be part of the leaf node or be the node itself. For example, in Fig. 3, keyword 'Harry' is part of the entire node 'Harry Potter and the Chamber of Secrets'. Similarly for a phrase change, the given phrase could be part of the node, the node itself or can span more than one node. Detecting changes to contents constituting part of the node or spanning several nodes complicates the extraction of the content and change detection. For XML, the attributes of an element are considered unordered [22]. But as the changes are detected considering the content to be ordered, the attributes are assumed to be ordered for the proposed change detection algorithm. Attributes defining ID and IDREFS are also considered as simple ordered attributes. In addition, we only consider well-formed XML documents and don't process DTD, CData, Entity and Processing Instructions nodes. The changes are detected by identifying the change operations, which transform a tree T1 to tree T2.

5.1   Change Operation

Given two ordered XML trees T1 and T2, consider the change operations from the set E = {insert, delete, move} which when applied to T1 transforms it into a new tree T2. To detect the change operations, the structure is also taken into consideration. The content of a leaf node is defined as its value and is denoted as $v(x)$ where x is a leaf node. The operations can be defined as follows:

1. Insert: Insertion of a new leaf node at the ith position is denoted by insert $(v(x),i)$. If n1...nm are the leaf nodes in T1 and for 1< k< m, if n1....nk-1,x,nk....nm are the leaf nodes in T2, then the node x is considered inserted. As structure defines the context for the content in XML, a node of the same value but different signature is considered inserted. Insert of a keyword is defined as the appearance of a keyword k in the ith leaf node x of the tree T1, denoted by insert_keyword (k,x,i) where the keyword can be part of the leaf node x or the node itself. Insert of a phrase is defined as appearance of a complete phrase at position i in the tree T1, denoted by (p,i).

2. Delete: The deletion of an old leaf node at the ith position is denoted by delete $(v(x),i)$. A leaf node x having the value $v(x)$ is deleted from the ith position in tree T1 rooted at root R. Given two ordered XML trees T1 and T2, T1 will be same as T2 except that it will not contain x. Delete of a keyword is defined as the disappearance of the keyword k in the ith leaf node x of the tree T1, denoted by delete_keyword (k,x,i). Delete of a phrase is defined as disappearance of a phrase p at ith position in the tree T1, denoted by (p,i).

3. Move: For the tree T1 , containing leaf nodes from n1 to nm, a leaf node x containing signature s is shifted from position j in T1 to position k in the new tree T2 where $1<=j<=m$ and $j \neq k$ with respect to the siblings. Move is denoted as move (x,j,k) where x is the leaf node moved from position j to position k. Move is only applicable to a complete node. Keyword and phrase changes are changes detected to part of the node or on the contents of more than one node. Hence, move is not applicable to keyword and phrase change but only for any change on the leaf nodes.

As shown in Fig. 7, leaf nodes having value 'D' and 'G' are deleted in tree T1 in position 2 and 3 respectively and   leaf node with value 'F' is inserted in tree T2. Leaf node 'C' is moved from position 4 in Tree T1 to position 5 in T2.

5.2   CX-Diff: Customized Change Detection for Ordered Documents

For customized change detection based on user intent, extraction of the objects of interest like keywords and phrases is necessary to detect changes to a page. Signature is computed for each extracted leaf node. To detect change operations between given trees T1 and T2, the unique inserts/deletes are filtered and matching nodes and signatures are extracted. The common order subsequence is detected on the extracted matching nodes to detect move and insert/deletes to duplicate nodes. The algorithm consists of following steps: i) object extraction and signature computation, ii) filtering of unique inserts/deletes and iii) finding the common order subsequence between the leaf nodes of the given trees. For reducing the computational time for detecting changes, an optimization is also proposed.

5.2.1   Object Extraction and Signature Computation

Based on the user intent, the object of interest needs to be extracted from the contents of the XML document and the structural information derived by computing the signature. To access the content and extract the structure of the XML document, it is first transformed into a Document Object Model (DOM) [26]. The Xerces-J 1.4.4 java parser [27] for XML is used for this purpose. The tree is traversed top down and the leaf node consisting of text and attribute nodes are extracted. The signature of each node is also computed from the extracted element information.

1. For keyword extraction, if $v(x)$ is the value(content) of leaf node x, the value is divided into its respective words $w1$ to wn where n is the number of words in v. A string compare is carried for each word w and the given keyword k. If a word wi equal to the keyword k is found, the order of occurrence of the keyword in the node, value of the leaf node $v(x)$ and its signature is extracted.

2. For phrase extraction, value of all the leaf nodes are divided into words and extracted in the order of occurrence. The Knuth-Morris-Pratt (KMP) string-matching algorithm is run against the sequence of words and all exact matches to the given phrase are extracted along with its associated signature. If a phrase is part of a node or spans more than one node, the part of the node (s) containing the phrase is extracted and inserted as a separate phrase node in its correct order of occurrence and the tree is realigned.

For the given tree T1 and T2 in Fig. 7, the tree is traversed and the leaf nodes and their associated signatures are extracted and added to the T1set and T2set respectively as shown in Fig. 8.

5.2.2   Filtering Unique Inserts/Deletes

In a given tree T, a node x containing value $v(x)$ can be distinct or can have multiple occurrences. Insertion/Deletion of distinct nodes can result in unique insert/delete unless they are moved, and can be detected on an unordered tree. Similarly, leaf nodes containing non-matching signature can also be considered as unique inserts/deletes as the signature define the context. To reduce the computation cost of finding the common order subsequence between two ordered trees, by considering all the leaf nodes, the unique inserts/deletes are filtered out and matching nodes extracted by the defined functions totalMatch and signatureMatch. The functions are defined as:

Total Match: For each extracted node, the function totalMatch(old_tree, new_tree) extracts the set of best matches denoted as M such that for the given trees T1 and T2 and leaf node x in T1 and leaf node y in T2, $(x, y) \hat{I} M$ if $v(x) = v(y)$ and $path(x) = path(y)$.

The value v of the node along with the signature is mapped to the java-generated hash code [25]. The nodes with the associated signature are sorted on the hash code. Every element in T2Set with a hash code greater than the upper bound or lower than the lowerbound of T1Set is flagged as an 'insert'. Elements that have their hash code within [lowerbound, upperbound] are searched for occurrence for similar elements in the T1Set. If not found, these elements are flagged as 'insert'. Similarly, the nodes with their associated signatures not matched in T1Set are flagged as 'delete'. For phrase change, the associated phrase for each node is also marked as 'insert/delete'.

Signature Match: All the matching signatures in the old and new tree, containing non-matching leaf nodes are included in the set M. For leaf node x in tree T1 and y in tree T2, if $path(x) = path(y)$ and $v(x) \neq v(y)$, then $path(x)$ and $path(y)$ are included in the match set M.

For keyword change detection, the instances of keyword may not have changed in a leaf node though the value of the node may have changed. The algorithm should capture such instances of keywords, which have not changed. In addition, as XML is well-defined document, it can be assumed that the structure is generally stable. Hence, many times, though the contents change, the structure remains the same and this information can be included for optimal detection of common order subsequence between two trees. The non-matching nodes of Total Match are given to the function signatureMatch, to extract common signatures. For keyword change, the associated keywords are also extracted. The distinct leaf node having value 'G' in Tree T1 and node having value 'F' in Tree T2 in Fig. 7 are detected as deleted and inserted after computation of the function totalMatch as shown in Fig. 8. Though value of leaf nodes 'G' in T1and 'F' in T2 do not match but path(G)=path(F). Hence, for efficient computation of common order subsequence, the common signature information is extracted by the function signatureMatch and included as elements in the matchedT1set and matchedT2set. As shown in Fig. 8, at the end of phase I, all unique inserts i.e. 'F' and unique deletes i.e. 'G' are detected and common structural information of such unique inserts/deletes are extracted. For keywords and phrase change, if all the extracted keywords and phrases result in unique insert/delete, then the computation can be considered complete at this stage.

5.2.3 Finding the Common Order Subsequence

For change detection to multiple occurrences of a node with common signatures and for moved nodes, it is necessary to consider an ordered tree. Due to realignment of the node and inserts and deletes, the order of occurrence needs to be considered with respect to the sibling. Hence, the common order subsequence is computed by running the Longest Common Subsequence (LCS) algorithm [7] between the matched nodes of both the trees. All the matched nodes are aligned in the order of occurrence. For keyword change, the extracted keywords, which are part of the leaf node, are also aligned with its matching parent leaf node and signature. It is observed that though the content may change the keyword in the content may not change. To avoid missing detection of such keywords, if the signature of the extracted keyword matches and extracted by the function signatureMatch, the associated keyword is also aligned for LCS. As explained in section 5.2.1, the phrase is inserted as a text node and hence is treated as a complete leaf node. For detecting LCS, each node is mapped into its equivalent hash code and the nodes resulting in the common order subsequence are extracted. The nodes, which do not constitute the common order subsequence between the given two trees, are differentiated as inserts, deletes or moves. At the end of this phase, all the moved nodes and the duplicate inserts/deletes will be detected. For example, in Fig. 3, if "J.K Rowling" at 3rd position is deleted, the delete will be detected for correct position. Similarly, at the end of the LCS computation on the matched nodes in Fig. 8, the deletion of the node 'D' at position 2 in T1 as well as the move of node 'C' from position 4 in T1 to position 5 in T2 can be detected. Hence, this algorithm detects effectively customized changes like keywords, phrases etc based on user intent. In addition, changes to duplicate leaf nodes containing common structural information and moves are accurately detected.

	Elements in T_1 Set	Elements in T_2 Set	Delete set	Insert set	
Phase-I:	(A,path(A))	(A,path(A))			
Filter Unique Inserts/Deletes	(D,path(D))	(F,path(F))		(F,2)	
	(G,path(G))	(E,path(E))	(G,3)		
	(C,path(C))	(D,path(D))			
	(E,path(E))	(C,path(C))			
	(D,path(D))				

	Elements in Matched T_1 Set	Elements in Matched T_2 Set	Delete set	Insert set	Move set
Phase-II:	(A,path(A))	(A,path(A))	(D,2)	(F,2)	(C,4,5)
Common Order Subsequence	(D,path(D))	(path(F))	(G,3)		
	(path(G))	(E,path(E))			
	(C,path(C))	(D,path(D))			
	(E,path(E))	(C,path(C))			
	(D,path(D))				

Fig. 8. Phases of CX-Diff algorithm

5.2.4 Optimization

To improve the time taken by the above algorithm, an additional phase of eliminating common second level subtree is introduced. Subtrees are computed at the second level as the second level defines the main context of the contents in the document. For given trees T1 and T2, the second level element node is denoted as l(s) where l is the label of node s. if l(s1) is the second level node of T1 and its equivalent node in T2 is l(s2), the subtrees of T1 and T2 are considered matched if l(s1) = l(s2) and all the leaf nodes along with the signature in T1 is equal to the leaf nodes and their associated signature in T2 in the same order of occurrence. All the nodes of the matched subtrees are removed from the matched set M. Hence, the size of M for LCS is reduced and the cost of computation is improved. But accurate results cannot be achieved if the sibling information is lost. Hence this optimization trades computation time to accuracy. Our experience has indicated that doing LCS at the 2nd level does not affect the accuracy of change detection except in very rare cases. Furthermore, WebVigiL allows the user to decide whether accuracy of change detection or time is important. Based on the user policy, the decision to utilize the optimization technique is made.

6   Change Presentation

Change presentation is the last phase of web monitoring where the detected changes, as outlined in the previous sections, are presented to the user. For meaningful interpretation of the presented changes, we have investigated three ways to present it to the user:

1. **Only Change Approach:** Showing only the changes and omitting the common objects of the two pages is advantageous for pages of large size but will make interpretation intricate. This approach can be meaningful for hand-held devises to conserve the amount of data transmitted over a limited bandwidth.
2. **Single Frame Approach:** Produce a single document by merging the two documents summarizing all inserted, deleted and common objects. The advantage lies in displaying the common objects just once, but with the draw back of possibly changing the page structure.
3. **Dual Frame Approach:** Showing both the documents side-by-side in different frames and highlighting the changes between the documents has the advantage of uncomplicated interpretation of the changes presented. When the number of changes to be presented is large, this approach may make it difficult to interpret the changes. This can be remedied by presenting parts of the pages at a time to limit the number of changes displayed in each installment.

In WebVigiL we intend to use all of the three presentation schemes summarized above in a selected combination depending upon the type of change type being presented. For example we plan on testing the Dual Frame Approach for presenting changes to phrases and keywords. For displaying changes to image we plan on using the Single Frame approach (showing both the old and new image). Finally for the change type any-change, based on the number of changes detected we use a heuristic cost model for choosing the presentation mechanism between the Dual Frame Approach, Only Change and single Frame Approach for displaying changes. An example of WebVigiL's Dual Frame output is shown in Fig. 9 for the given keywords {CSE2315,

CSE2320, ALGOR&DATASTRUC, CSE3310}. Markups are used to highlight deleted and inserted objects. Deleted text is displayed in "struck-out" font using <STRIKE><B> which, as experimentally determined in [8], is rarely used in HTML and XML documents. And for displaying inserted text, we are currently using colors and <I><B> to highlight. Modified "content-defining" markups are highlighted as, change to the URL or IMG (image) in the anchor is highlighted using an arrow which points to the text between <A>.</A> in case of a URL and points to the image, in case of change in the source for the image. These techniques have been implemented for HTML documents. We are currently investigating, mapping of the above approaches to change presentation to XML pages.

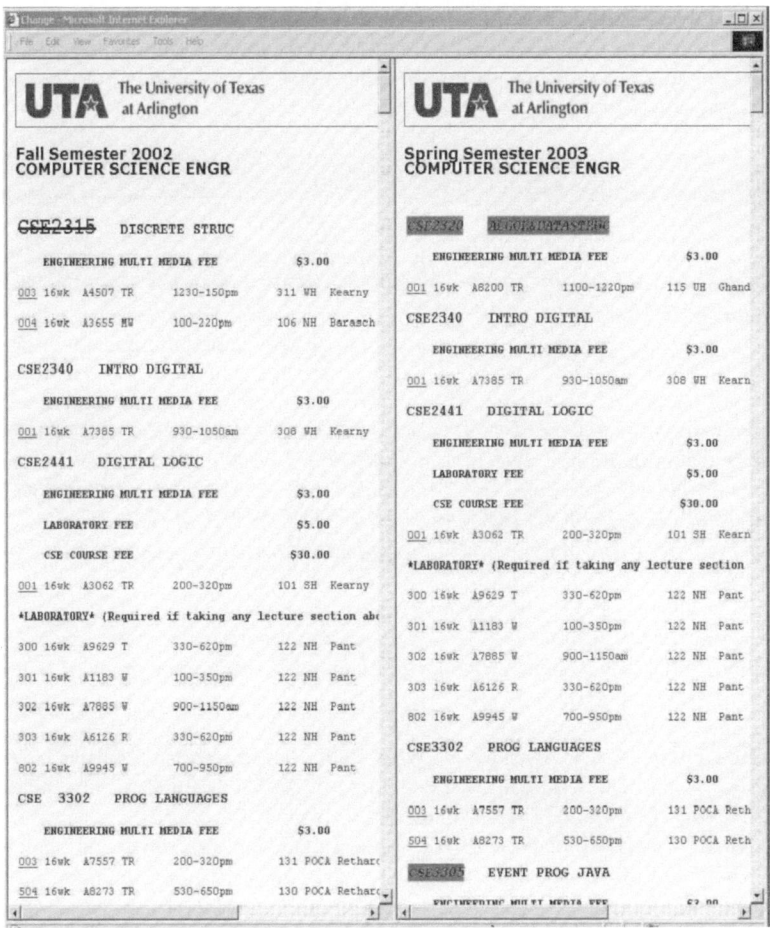

Fig. 9. A dual-frame presentation scheme for presenting changes to keywords.

7   Conclusion

WebVigiL is a change monitoring system for the web that supports specification, management of Sentinels and provides presentation of detected changes in multiple ways (batch, interactive, for multiple devices). The first prototype has been completed and includes the following features: web-based sentinel specification [1], ECA rule based fetch that includes learning [3] to reduces the number of times a page is fetched, population of the knowledge base, detection of changes to HTML and XML pages as discussed in this paper. A simple presentation module for the schemes briefly outlined in this paper has been implemented.

Currently, the individual modules are being integrated to instrument the first version of a complete WebVigiL system. The first release of WebVigiL with the above features is expected to be ready by March. The performance evaluation of change detection algorithms and their comparison with other approaches are currently underway.

References

[1]   Chakravarthy, S., et al. WebVigiL: An approach to Just-In-Time Information Propagation In Large Network-Centric Environments. in Second International Workshop on Web Dynamics. 2002. Hawaii.

[2]   Jacob, J., et al., WebVigiL: An approach to Just-In-Time Information Propagation In Large Network-Centric Environments(to be published), in Web Dynamics Book. 2003, Springer-Verlag.

[3]   Chakravarthy, S., et al., WebVigiL: Architecture and Functionality of a Web Monitoring System (submitted). http://itlab.uta.edu/sharma/Projects/WebVigil/files/WVFetch.pdf.

[4]   J.W.Hunt and M.D.McIlroy, An algorithm for efficient file comparison. 1975, Bell Laboratories: Murray Hill, N.J.

[5]   E.Myers, An O(ND) difference algorithm and its variations. Algorithmica, 1986. 1: p. 251–266.

[6]   S.Wu, U.Manber, and E.Myers, An O(NP) sequence comparision algorithm. Information Processing Letters, 1990. 35: p. 317–323.

[7]   Hirschberg, D., Algorithms for the longest common subsequence problem. Journal of the ACM, 1977: p. 664–675.

[8]   Douglis, F., et al., The AT&T Internet Difference Engine: Tracking and Viewing Changes on the Web, in World Wide Web. 1998, Baltzer Science Publishers. p. 27–44.

[9]   Saeyor, S. and M. Ishizuka. WebBeholder: A Revolution in Tracking and Viewing Changes on The Web by Agent Community. in WebNet98. 1998.

[10]   Baker, S.B. A theory of parametrized pattern matching:algorithms and applications. in Proceedings of the 25th Annual ACM Symposium on Theory of Computing. 1993.

[11]   Balazinska, M., et al. Advanced clone-analysis to support object-oriented system refactoring. in Seventh Working Conference on Reverse Engineering. 2000.

[12]   Lucca, G.D., et al. Clone Analysis in the Web Era: an Approach to Identify Cloned Web Pages. in Seventh IEEE Workshop on Empirical Studies of Software Maintenance. 2001. Florence, Italy.

[13] Ulam, S.M. Some Combinatorial Problems Studied Experimentally on Computing Machines. in Zaremba S.K., Applications of Number Theory to Numerical Analysis. 1972: Academic Press.

[14] K.Zhang and D.Shasha, Simple Fast Algorithms for the Editing Distance between Trees and Related Problems. SIAM Journal of Computing, 1989. 18(6): p. 1245–1262.

[15] K.Zhang, R.Statman, and D.Shasha, On the Editing Distance between Unordered Labeled Trees. Information Processing Letters, 1992. 42: p. 133–139.

[16] S.Chawathe, et al. Change detection in hierarchically structured information. in Proceedings of the ACM SIGMOD International Conference on Management of Data. 1996. Montréal, Québec.

[17] Y.Wang, D.DeWitt, and J.Cai, X-Diff: An Effective Change Detection Algorithm for XML Documents. 2001, Technical Report, University of Wisconsin.

[18] G.Cobena, S.Abiteboul, and A.Marian, Detecting Changes in XML Documents. Data Engineering, 2002.

[19] F.P.Curbera and D.A.Epstein, Fast Difference and Update of XML Documents. XTech'99, 1999.

[20] Chen, Y.-F. and E. Koutsofios. WebCiao: A Website Visualization and Tracking System. in WebNet97. 1997.

[21] Extensible Markup Language(XML)., World Wide Web Consortium,http://www.w3.org/XML/.

[22] S.Abiteboul, P.Buneman, and D.Suciu, Data on the Web: From Relations to Semistructured Data and XML. 1999: Morgan Kaufmann.

[23] HTML-Parser, http://www.quiotix.com/downloads/html-parser/.

[24] Liu, L., C. Pu, and W. Tang. WebCQ: Detecting and Delivering Information Changes on the Web. in Proceedings of International Conference on Information and Knowledge Management (CIKM). 2000. Washington D.C: ACM Press.

[25] Java1.3, http://java.sun.com/j2se/1.3/docs/api/.

[26] Document Object Model(DOM)., http://www.w3.org/DOM/.

[27] Xerces-J, http://xml.apache.org/xerces2-j/index.html.

8 Appendix

Input (Page P1, Page P2, User given Phrase)

/*Parsing the page and extraction of words from the page */

1. Parse and Extract the words from P1 into Old_Set
2. Parse and Extract the words from P2 into New_Set

/*Extraction of signature of each instance of phrase from the words sets */

3. Extract the signature(phrase) from Old_Set into set K1
4. Extract the signature(phrase) from New_Set into set K2

/*Sort the set based on the hashCode of its elements forming a range [lowerbound, upperbound] */

5. Sort K1 based on hash code
6. lowerbound = hashCode (the first element in K1)
7. upperbound = hashCode (the last element in K1)

/*Finding inserts and deletes*/

8. for every element I in k2
10.   if (hashCode(I) > outerbound || hashCode(I) < lowerbound) append {I} to insert_set
12.   if (hashCode(I) <= outerbound || hashCode(I) >= lowerbound)
16.   if (I exists in K1)no change
17.   else append {I} to insert_set.
18. for every I in K1 that didn't participate in the previous phase, append {I} to delete_set

/*Detecting Updates*/

19. for every I in delete_set
20.   get lower_context_box = lower_context_box(I)
21.   get upper_context_box = upper_context_box(I)
22.   updatecontent = ExtractContentBetween(lower_context_box, upper_context_box, Old_Set)
23.   Length = LCS(phrase, updatecontent)
24.   If (Length /phrase.length < updateFactor) flag update
25.   Else flag delete

Fig. 10. Outline of the CH-Diff Algorithm for Phrase Change Detection.

/* Outline of CX-Diff for change detection to keywords. For keywords, move is not detected. But for any change on the leaf nodes of given two trees, the move is detected as follows:

In the function changeOperations, move is detected by comparing nodes $\notin$ common order subsequence C of tree T1 and tree T2. If n1 $\in$T1 and n2 $\in$T2 and (n1,n2)$\notin$C and v(n1)=v(n2), then move is detected. */

Input (Tree T1, Tree T2, User given Keywords)

1. /* Parsing, Extraction and Signature computation */

      a. Parse and Extract T1 nodes

      b. Parse and Extract T2 nodes

      c. Extract Keywords from T1

      d. Extract Keywords from T2

      e. Compute Signatures for all extracted leaf nodes

2. /* Filtering Unique Inserts and Deletes */

      f. Algorithm *totalMatch* – Generate hash codes for all extracted leaf nodes and signatures of T1 and T2 and find matching nodes such that the value of the leaf nodes with its associated signature are matching. Include matching nodes in the set matchNodes M.

      g. Algorithm *signatureMatch* - input the unique inserts/deletes and extract all matching signatures and insert in the set matchNodes M from T1 and T2.

      h. Extract the associated keywords for matched nodes and matched signatures in T1 and T2 and flag them as "matched". Flag rest of keywords in T1 as 'insert' and keywords in T2 as 'delete'.

      i. If all keywords are marked 'insert' and 'delete' in T1 and T2, stop.

   Else go to step 3.

3. /* Finding the Common Order Subsequence */

      j. Insert 'matched' keywords of T1 and T2 into set M.

      k. Sort M containing matched leaf nodes, signatures and keywords on the position of occurrence in the tree T1 and T2.

      l. Algorithm findCommonSubsequence – input the set M and compute the longest common subsequence on all the matched nodes.

      m. Algorithm changeOperations – detects deleted keywords in T1, inserted keywords in T2

Fig. 11. Outline of the CX-Diff Algorithm for Keyword Change Detection.

Aggregate Table-Driven Querying via Navigation Ontologies in Distributed Statistical Databases

Yaxin Bi[1], David Bell[1], and Joanne Lamb[2]

[1]School of Computer Science, The Queen's University of Belfast, Belfast BT7 1NN, UK
{y.bi, da.bell}@qub.ac.uk
[2]CES, University of Edinburgh, Holyrood Road, Edinburgh, EH8 8AQ, UK
j.m.lamb@ed.ac.uk

Abstract. In this paper we describe a query paradigm based on ontologies, aggregate table-driven querying and expansion of QBE. It has two novel features: visually specifying aggregate table queries and table layout in a single process, and providing users with an ontology guide in composing complex analysis tasks as queries. We present the role of the fundamental concept of ontology in the context of the content representation of distributed databases with large numbers of multi-valued attributes, and in query formulation and processing. The methods and techniques developed for representing and manipulating ontologies for query formulation and processing make extensive use of XML and DOM. The core functionalities of content representation, query formulation without prior knowledge about databases, statistical summary and result presentation are integrated into a front-end client within the underpinning MVC architecture, which has been implemented in Java and JAXP.

1   Introduction

Our focus in the present study is on relational databases with large numbers of multi-valued attributes which have been common for several years in a variety of applications – especially for those including statistical databases and scientific databases – and often they are distributed on the Internet. The tasks of content representation, statistical summary and result presentation (publishing) place significant demands on front-end interfaces and integrated access to these databases. The large number of multi-valued attributes means that their meaningful representation is essential for understanding the content of databases and for query formulation. Furthermore, because of the requirements of statistical analysis and the need to publish results in various tabular forms, it must be possible for users to bring both query composition and table layout definition together in a single process of query formulation. Novel query paradigms and data integration mechanisms are thus needed.

Our intention here is to address query paradigms and data integration in the context of a particular application – that of official statistics. The work described includes three major aspects. The first is the support of statistical summary queries in terms of macro (aggregate or summary) data table queries for distributed statistical databases with large number of multi-valued attributes. The second is the enhancement of database content representation by means of domain ontologies. The third aspect is a

A. James, B. Lings, M. Younas (Eds.): BNCOD 2003, LNCS 2712, pp. 58–66, 2003.

knowledge-based query paradigm, which integrates ontologies, macro table-driven querying and expansion of Query By Example (QBE) [1], allowing users to visually specify macro table queries and table layout in a single process, and providing users with an ontology guide in composing complex analysis tasks as queries.

Much of the work presented here has been implemented in the European fifth framework MISSION project (Multi-Agent Integration of Shared Statistical Information Over the [inter]Net). MISSION grew out of ADDSIA [2], [3] and early research project MIMAD [4]. The MISSION system is built on a three-tier architecture composed of the client, library and dataserver. The client is a presentation layer – a front-end interface, which is developed using the advanced technologies of MVC (Model-View-Controller) paradigm [5] and DOM (Document Object Model). The library is a mediation layer holding the ontology repository and it acts as a workspace for software agents. It plays a mediation role between the client and the dataserver, that is, by using agents to receive queries from the client, decompose the queries, send the queries to the dataservers and get the query results back to the client. The dataserver is the local site which holds the physical data storage and management tools for data registering and data access.

In this paper, we present concepts, methods, and techniques developed for the system client and data integration in the MISSION system. These concepts and methods have been employed in the system client and the library in order to implement the fundamental functionality of *browsing*, *query construction*, and *publishing*.

2   Motivation

Relational schemas developed for conventional database systems may not suit the representation of the content of very high dimensional data well. In particular, they are inadequate when raw (micro) data is of value – encoding form with spreadsheet formats, which are accompanied with a considerable amount of metadata for interpretation. In a broad sense, schemas are developed for modelling structured data – they have less ability to define the meaning of attributes used in a given domain.

Query interfaces built on schemas may not contain any information about the application domain and how it operates, and in the limited space of a user interface, there is little chance of the characteristics of the entities being explicitly given. As a result, instead of giving users information about the content of data sources, these interfaces require users to fill out lengthy forms to express their information needs. A common assumption for such interfaces is that users are aware of a system implementation model, for example, a relational schema, in terms of structures and data values [6].

Strong interest in enhancing the content representation and presentation of distributed databases to facilitate statistical analysis and query composition emerges in the HCI, database, and knowledge management research communities. Research in these areas has been documented in a number of publications [6], [7], [8]. In [4], the MIMAD (Micro-Macro Data) model was developed. It provides a means of aggregating high dimensional micro data to macro data for statistical summary, as illustrated in Table 1 (a). This work was extended in ADDSIA to take account of domain knowledge – metadata – in order to achieve interoperation and integration between diverse data sources [2], [3]. In MISSION, these ideas are further developed. We make use of domain onologies built up from metadata to represent the content of distributed databases and incorporate them into macro table query formulation and processing.

The concept of "ontology" is well-known in knowledge engineering and has been applied to data integration [8]. Basically, in this case, the ontology is used to define the meanings of terms used in data sources, and to ensure the consistent use of terminology in order to cope with semantic heterogeneity reflected in the integration of heterogeneous data sources. It can be argued that the ontology is also a good means of representing the content of data sources, because the ontology hierarchy can correspond to the relational schemas and the meanings of terms defined in the ontology can be used to represent and interpret attributes, as we will see in the following sections.

Table 1. An example of macro object (a: left, b: right)

Gender	Employment	Income_SUM
Male	Full-time (F)	2,122,000
Male	Part-time (P)	1,422,000
Female	Full-time	1,922,000
Female	Part-time	1,122,000

		Gender	
		Male	Female
Employment	F	2,122,000	1,922,000
	P	1,422,000	1,122,000

To achieve the best performance in the exploitation of the ontology for query formulation and processing, by expanding on QBE we develop a simple yet powerful query paradigm. It displays meaningful attributes along with ontologies and provides visual selection among them, and it allows users to specify complicated information needs visually in the form of macro object tables, as shown in Table 3 (b). Our approach is based on the conceptual hierarchy of attributes and relationships, which serves a wide range of user expertise and working styles. We adapt implicit Boolean connectives within such a hierarchy based on two operations: *aggregation* and *generalization*.

3   Data Model for Ontologies

An ontology is defined as a *shared formal conceptualization of a particular domain* [9], which can be used to specify what concepts represent and how they are related. In practice, an ontology can be regarded as a controlled vocabulary providing a concrete specification of term names and term meanings. An ontology can be represented in various ways, such as description logic, Datalog, and frames. To address issues in the context of content representation of databases, query formulation and processing, we employ XML to represent ontologies, which is an effective approach for the hierarchy generation of the ontologies on the fly, required by the system client.

In the MISSION project, we have developed a DTD for representing domain ontologies. It is a further development of our previous work [2]. The DTD offers a uniform framework for representing concepts over heterogeneous distributed databases. Fig. 1 illustrates a fragment of the DTD definition.

In this definition, the FRAME is the root element, and there are four high level elements under it, i.e. TITLE, SUBJECT, DESCRIPTION, and ONTOLOGY. The first three of these represent the conceptual frame, indicating application domains to which ontologies are related. The last element, ONTOLOGY, is broken down into smaller elements: DESCRIPTION, CLASSIFICATION, and VARIABLE, to cover essential information required in the system. In particular, the element VARIABLE is used to define the meanings of concepts which are associated with the attributes within data sets, and constraints indicating the properties of the concepts. The hierarchy reflected in the elements is an important structure because it depicts the explicit hierarchical relationship between the elements.

```
<!ELEMENT    FRAME    (TITLE?,    SUBJECT,    DESCRIPTION?,
ONTOLOGY+)>
<!ELEMENT    ONTOLOGY    (DESCRIPTION,    CLASSIFICATION,
VARIABLE+)>
<!ELEMENT VARIABLE (SET+)>
...
```

Fig. 1. A fragment of the DTD definition for modeling the ontologies ('+': one or more elements, '?': optional)

Note that, although the depth of the hierarchy embedded in the DTD is at only 4 levels, i.e. FRAME → ONTOLOGY → VARIABLE → SET, this is sufficient to represent the ontologies in our case.

Fig. 2 gives a fragment of the ontology of "Catewe" (Comparative Analysis of Transitions from Education to Work in Europe) encoded in XML. In order to access and manipulate ontology information in the system client, we make extensive use of the DOM model, which is increasingly becoming popular for accessing and manipulating XML documents.

```
<FRAME name = "Catewe">
  <TITLE name = "A Comparative Analysis of Transitions from Education to Work in Europe"/>
  <SUBJECT name = "Education"/>
  <ONTOLOGY name = "Catewe">
    <VARIABLE name = "Country" mnemonic="Land" vartype = "geographical">
      <SET value="Scotland"/>
      ...
    </VARIABLE>
    ...
  </ONTOLOGY>
</FRAME>
```

Fig. 2. A fragment of XML data

4   Modelling Client Functions

The MISSION client is an MVC application [5]. Fig. 3 presents a high-level block diagram of the client in terms of the MVC architecture. The client consists of three basic components which correspond to the functions of *browsing*, *query construction*, and *publishing*. These accommodate the functionality for the browsing, query construction, and publication of large volumes of statistical information required in the applications of the MISSION system. Each component is modelled to three distinct forms of functionality called *model*, *view* and *controller*, which inherit from the common MVC class and incorporate customizations for individual tasks. For example, the *browsing* component is broken down into three subcomponents: *BrowserView*, *BrowserModel*, and *BrowserController*. This architecture effectively takes advantage of the MVC design paradigm, ensuring the explicit isolation of the various functions, abstract representation for each function, and interactions of functions with one another.

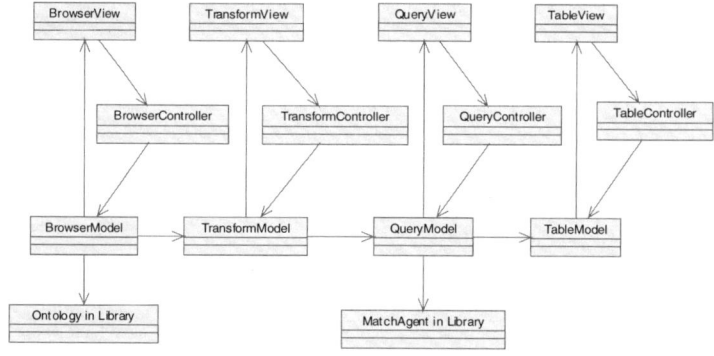

Fig. 3. The MVC and tier partitioning of the MISSION client

5   Visual Query Formulation

In this section, we investigate how concept ontologies are involved in query formulation and processing. Before looking at the process with respect to visual specification of queries, we begin with a brief description of macro table objects.

5.1   Macro Table Object and Table-Driven Queries

A macro object is defined as follows [4]:

$$MacroObject: \{C_1, C_2, ..., C_n; N_1, N_2, ..., N_m\}, count, sum, sum\text{-}of\text{-}squares$$

This representation abstractly defines macro table objects, where C_1 to C_n are categorical attributes, N_1 to N_m are numeric attributes, and *count*, *sum*, *sum-of-squares* are common primitive operations to be performed on the numeric attributes. In addition, the operations of *max* and *min* might also be included if applications demand these. In this expression, if the numeric attribute is empty, the *count* as a default operation which will be then applied to categorical attributes.

For queries which produce macro objects as illustrated in Table 1 (a), we need a mechanism to formulate queries in a tabular QBE style. A query table here is defined as an instance of a QueryView class that is managed by the Query Constructor component. A complete table configuration consists of three separate expressions in terms of *horizontal header, vertical stub* and *data cells*. The first two of the expressions define the configuration of the *x* and *y* axes of the table, partitioning the table into rows and columns. The third expression defines the data cells that hold aggregated values, corresponding to the Cartesian product of the value sets of categorical attributes. The table configuration provides the layout definition, and implicitly restricts attributes to be placed in either the *header* or *stub* only. For example, in formulating the macro object query (see Table 1(a)), the attribute *Gender* is placed on the header and *Employment* is put on the stub, and the cells hold aggregated values produced using the *sum* operation, as illustrated in Table 1 (b).

5.2 The Client Interface

Fig. 4 presents a screenshot of the user interface, including the three constituents: *browsing, query constructor* and *publishing* functions. Notice that the *publishing* function is implicitly specified with the configuration of the query table. These constituents are clearly important for supporting the broader user activities in flexible ways. As seen from the screenshot, the two functions of *browsing* and *query construction* are displayed on two parallel sub-windows. Users can interleave the functions through their views and track their progress. On the top of the query constructor, there exist two combo-boxes, one is to store numerical attributes (users can choose from them to compose queries), and the other presents a choice from the aggregation functions *count, sum, sum-of-squares*, which will be integrated into macro table queries.

The browsing component is the starting point for system access. It provides users with interactive and incremental functions, allowing users to discover a domain of interest and to interrogate the ontologies to find the fundamental concepts in which they are interested. This function offers a very important means for novices to learn about the data sources through the frames and ontologies. It fulfils the significant demand for the support in the formulation of valid queries without pre-knowledge about the databases. For example, the user can first find the *frames* that are available in the connected library. Generally knowledge of each frame can be gained through the descriptive information: *title, subject* and *description* as described in Fig 2. Once the frame has been chosen, the user can go straight to the concepts held in the ontologies to select the concepts in which he/she is interested. This process does not require the user to have pre-knowledge about the data sources – it can be learned during the browsing session.

The BrowserView presents ontologies as trees. The user can choose one of the ontology trees. For example, the user can choose the local ontologies of Catewe Scotland or the master ontology of Catewe as shown in Fig. 4. The ontology tree is

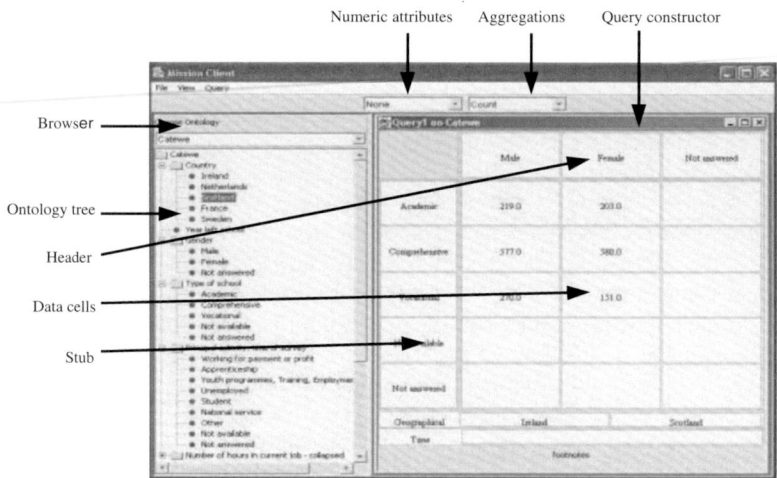

Fig. 4. A screenshot of the system client

composed of the nodes that are iteratively constructed with the ontology objects, but only the properties of the names and set values are visible. The remaining details within the objects are less useful for the user in understanding the content of databases, and so they only are used in the query process. On the other hand, the view can be switched from one to another, individual nodes and group nodes can be zoomed in to and out from independently without restrictions, according to users' preferences. This makes it possible to allow users to access multiple ontologies of data sources with the same style and avoid the screen being crowded by too many objects. This significantly enhances content representation for distributed data sources.

The idea of the macro table-driven query is to bring query composition and table layout definition together in a single process of query formulation. Defining a layout and style on the one hand and a query on the other hand are usually seen as two different tasks which should be done in two different ways. However, the two tasks are indeed related. It is difficult to define a layout without also defining the related queries. In the system client, the *query construction* component expands the QBE style as a way of query formulation, and incorporates the layout definition into the query formulation process, which acts as the client publishing function. The operator selection on the top field, such as *count*, determines which type of aggregation will be performed for the formulated query, and the configuration of the concepts placed on the QueryView implicitly determines the layout definition of query results. So, query formulation and layout definition are integrated in a single process.

5.3   An Example

Given an information need is to count "different types of school by gender within the countries of Scotland and Ireland", the user begins with the client interface as shown in Fig. 4. He/she first opens the Browser to connect to a library and obtain a list of ontologies such as *Catewe*, *Catewe Scotland*, etc. which are stored in the combo-box on the BrowserView. For the above request, the user chooses the master ontology of *Catewe*. Then, as illustrated in Fig. 4, he/she starts to navigate the ontology information to locate the three concepts "country, type of school and gender", respectively. Once these concepts are obtained, the user starts to drag an individual node of *Scotland* and *Ireland* from the ontology tree and drop them on the *Geographical Filed*, to drag *gender* and drop it on the header and place *type of school* on the stub, and then select the *count* operator. When complete, the query can be sent for execution. Simultaneously the visual expression formulated in the query constructor is internally converted into the expression of the table query language.

Looking at the query expression in Fig. 5, this expression explicitly demonstrates how the concepts drawn from the ontology hierarchy are incorporated into query formulation. For example, the concept of Gender, its type, its alias of Sex and a set of values have been included in the expression. Internally the query expression is passed as an object to a host library for query processing. More details for this can be found in [10].

```
<TQUERY>
<COMPUTE operand="table"/>
<WITH operand="generalization">
   <VARIABLE      name="Type      of      school"      mnemonic="SCHTYPE"
vartype="geographical">
      <VARIABLE name="Gender" mnemonic="Sex" vartype="categorical">
         <SET label="male" value=""/>
      ...
   <BROKENDOWNBY operand="aggregation">
   <VARIABLE name="Gender"/>
   <VARIABLE name="Type of school"/>
   ...
```

Fig. 5. The internal expression of the query corresponding to Fig. 4

6 Conclusion

This paper describes major concepts, methods and techniques developed for the system client and data integration in the MISSION project. We describe the use of the fundamental concept of ontology in the content representation of distributed databases, query formulation and processing, and underpinning methods and techniques for the macro objects, and the underlying client architecture of MVC. Although these have been developed specifically for statistical databases in the MISSION project, they can be readily tailored to general applications.

From the technology point of view we seek to use a novel query paradigm to reduce the burden on novices in understanding contents of databases and identifying pertinent attributes. We also present a user-friendly graphical interface to facilitate query formulation by the expansion of QBE style querying and table definition in a single process. For more advanced users, this front-end interface offers a powerful means of composing complex queries and publishing their analysis results, thereby supporting decision making and sharing expertise.

In the current state of the project, an ontology is automatically generated when a dataset and associated metadata are registered to the system. An exception in the frame description which data providers have to type in. With respect to ontology construction, there are three major classes in the metadata – identical, overlapping, and exclusive. The current approaches to coping with these issues are a) if two datasets have identical metadata, then the datasets will share the same ontology, b) if two datasets have different metadata, each dataset will have an individual ontology, and c) if two datasets have metadata with some overlap, then a master ontology has to be created using the two sets of metadata. The last approach involves complicated processing, but the possibility of handling such cases do exist. Some solutions have been proposed, in particular, the idea of mapping the local ontologies to a reference ontology which will be imported from public classification repositories. These solutions will be discussed in the other paper in future.

Acknowledgement. The work is partially supported by the MISSION project (IST 1999-10655) and partially supported by the ICONS project (IST-2001-32429). These are funded by the European Framework V. The authors would like to acknowledge the contributions made by the MISSION client development team.

References

1. Zloof, M.: Query by Example. AFIPS, 44, (1975).
2. Bi, Y., Murtagh, F. and McClean, S.I.: Metadata and XML for Organising and Accessing Multiple Statistical Data Sources, Proceedings of ASC International Conference, Edinburgh, (1999) 393–404.
3. Scotney, B.W., McClean, S.I., Rodgers, M. C.: Optimal and Efficient Integration of Heterogeneous Summary Tables in a Distributed Database. The Journal of Data and Knowledge Engineering, Vol. 29. (1999) 337–350.
4. Sadreddini, M. N. Bell, D. A. and McClean, S. I.: A Model for Integration of Raw Data and Aggregate Views in Heterogeneous Statistical databases. Database Technology, Vol. 4 (2), (1992) 115–127.
5. Gamma, E., Helm, R., Johnson, R., and Vlissides, J.: Design Patterns: Elements of Reusable Object-Oriented Software. Addison-Wesley (1994).
6. Tanin, E., Plaisant, C., Shneiderman, B.: Broadening Access to Large Online Databases by Generalizing Query Previews, Proceedings of the Symposium on New Paradigms in Information Visualization and Manipulation, (2000) 80–85.
7. Levy, A. Y., Rajaraman, A., Ordille, J. J.: Querying Heterogeneous Information Sources Using Source Descriptions. Proceedings of the 22nd VLDB Conference, Bombay, India. (1996).
8. Wache, H. V ogele, T. Visser, U. Stuckenschmidt, H. Schuster, G. Neumann, H., H ubner, S.: Ontology-based integration of information – a survey of existing approaches. In Stuckenschmidt, H. (ed.): IJCAI-01 Workshop: Ontologies and Information Sharing, (2001) 108–117.
9. Gruber,T.: A translation Approach to Portable Ontology Specifications. Knowledge Acquisition. Vol. **5**(2), (1993)199–220.
10. McClean, S., Páircéir, R., Scotney, B., Greer, K.: A Negotiation Agent for Distributed Heterogeneous Statistical Databases in SSDBM (2002) 207–217.

External Ontologies in the Semantic Web

Raphael Volz

Institute AIFB, University of Karlsruhe (TH), D-76128 Karlsruhe, Germany
volz@aifb.uni-karlsruhe.de

Abstract. The Semantic Web aims at easy integration and usage of content by building on a semi-structured data model where data semantics are explicitly specified through ontologies. The use of ontologies in real-world applications such as community portals has shown that a new level of data independence is required for ontology-based applications for example to allow the customization of information towards the needs of other agents. This requires control over the republishing of data and requires transformation of data across source databases. We address this issue and introduce external ontologies which are constituted of source data from several databases and views spanning across databases.

1 Introduction

The vision of the Semantic Web [2] incorporates distributed content that is machine understandable by relying on an explicit conceptual level. It builds on RDF [5], which is a semi-structured data model that allows the definition of directed labelled graphs. The required conceptual level is not given by a fixed schema, but rather by an ontology that specifies the formal semantics of content.

The use of ontologies in real-world applications such as community portals has shown that they can enhance interoperability between heterogeneous information resources and systems on a semantic level. However, what has also become clear is that ontologies and thereby ontology-based applications themselves suffer from heterogeneity.

To overcome this problem [11] propose a view language for RDFS-based lightweight web ontologies which allows easy selection, customization and integration of Semantic Web content. We extend this work by so-called external ontologies which group views and base entities into new data sets. External ontologies allow to customize and integrate distributed source databases towards application demands or other user communities.

One concrete application of external ontologies may be ontology mapping where data must be translated between different ontologies. Hence, the mechanisms described here may be used in the implementation of a mapping language such as proposed in [6].

The paper is structured as follows. Section 2 briefly recapitulates the fundamental technologies involved in our approach: RDFS as the target data model and an associated query language (RQL). Section 3 briefly sketches the view language based for RDFS introduced in [11]. Section 4 introduces the notion of external ontologies. Section 5 discusses implementation issues before we conclude in section 6.

A. James, B. Lings, M. Younas (Eds.): BNCOD 2003, LNCS 2712, pp. 67–74, 2003.

2   Fundamentals

RDF - A Semi-structured Data Model

The underlying data model of the Semantic Web is a semi-structured data model called Resource Description Framework (RDF) [5]. Data is organized around sets of statements or triples, which relate resources. Resources are identified via globally unique URIs. A set of statements constitutes a partially labelled directed pseudograph[1] and is commonly called an RDF model.

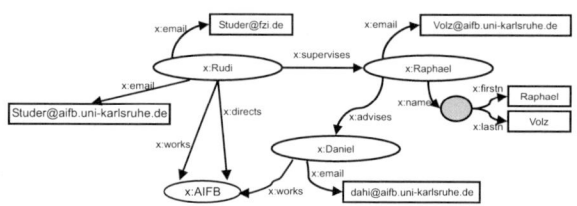

Fig. 1. A simple, exemplary RDF model

RDFS – Light-Weight Ontologies

Ontologies are usually constructed from classes and properties. Both are embedded in a class and a property inheritance hierarchy. One proposed standard for the Semantic Web is RDF Schema (RDFS)[4].

RDFS incorporates an unique notion of object orientation, which has to be considered in the design of both query and view languages. For example, subsumption hierarchies exist on both properties and classes and are partial orders (cf. Figure 2). RDFS permits both multiple inheritance and multiple instantiation.

Attributes and associations are not defined with the class specification itself. Instead, such class properties are defined as first-class primitives, so-called properties, which exist on their own. Thereby classes do not specify types. The definition of a property may include the specification of (multiple) domains and ranges.

RQL - A Query Language

Our approach is based on a version of RQL [1] which is augmented with view primitives. RQL is currently the only RDF query language that takes the semantics of RDFS ontologies into account. The need to be aware of these semantics is the main reason why query languages operating on the syntactic XML-serialization (e.g. XQuery [3]) are not suitable for our goal, however the notion of external ontologies presented later is not limited to a particular query language.

RQL is a typed language following a functional approach (in style of OQL) and aims at querying RDF at the semantic level. It's basic building blocks are generalized path expressions which offer navigation in a (single) RDF model. For example the following query would return the collection of all pairs of nodes which are related via the property email: `SELECT X,Y FROM {X}x:email{Y}`

---

[1] We can speak of pseudographs since multiple edges between (possibly identical) nodes are allowed.

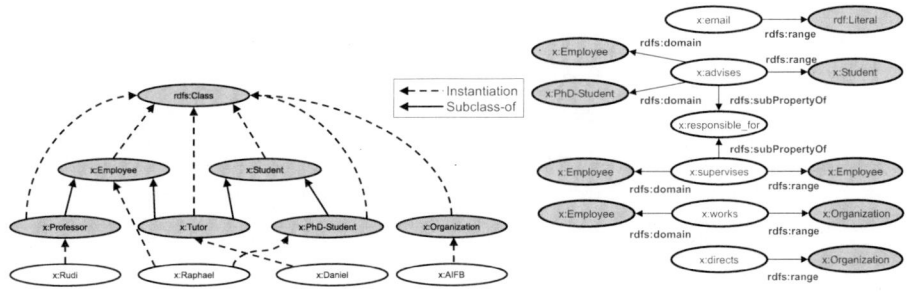

Fig. 2. Class and property hierarchies in RDFS

RQL interprets the superimposed semantic descriptions offered by an ontologies. For example, inheritance is considered when accessing class extents. Path expressions can be concatenated by a ".", which is just a syntactic shortcut for an implicit join condition: SELECT Y FROM Student{X}.x:advises{Y}

This query returns the identifiers of all students that are advised by other students. Since the class PhD-Student is a subclass of Student the above query would return "x:Daniel" for the RDF model depicted in Figure 1.

Furthermore, RQL supports set operators, such as union, intersection and difference. Boolean operations like $=, <, >$ can be used for selection in where-clauses.

3   View Language

[11] introduces a view language that follows the RDF(S) model and offers constructs for creating class and property views. Users are not able to make a distinction between views and base data and are able to state other queries or views on top of them. This mandates that the structure of views corresponds to the structure of base data. Hence, the view language allows both the definition of class views and property views.

Class Views
Class views can only be based on unary RQL queries. The result of the query constitutes the extension of the view. For example, Figure 3 defines the class view "StudentAssistant", which consists of PhD-Students that are employed and advise students.

Property Views
Similarly property views are based on binary RQL queries. For example, in Figure 3 also a property view that relates all PhD-Students with the email addresses of advised students is defined. View definitions may comprise assignment of super classes and properties. In case of property views the declaration may include the definition of (possibly multiple) domain and range constraints.

Semantic Characterization
The latter information is essential in RDFS. Unlike database schemas an RDFS ontology additionally gives a semantic characterization of data by means of class and property taxonomies. Therefore semantics of views have to be specified as well. The

Class view	Property view
CREATE CLASS VIEW x:StudentAssistant	CREATE PROPERTY VIEW x:mailsOfAdvised
SUBCLASSOF x:Employee	SET DOMAIN x:PhD-Student
SUBCLASSOF x:PhD-Student	SET RANGE rdf:Literal
USE	SUBPROPERTYOF x:email
(SELECT X FROM x:Employee{X})	USE
INTERSECT	SELECT DOMAIN, RANGE
(SELECT X FROM x:PhD-Student{X},	FROM x:PhD-Student{DOMAIN}.
{Y} x:advises {Z} WHERE X = Y)	x:advises{Y}. x:email{RANGE}

Fig. 3. Class and Property views

laborious manual classification is avoided in [11] by introducing convenience syntaxes for important types of queries. The system then classifies views defined via such syntaxes into the semantically appropriate location.

4   External Ontologies

Motivation
Many typical Semantic Web applications such as community portals are characterized by the fact that they rely on more than one information source and collect information from many distributed sources in the web. Distributed information can be aggregated and combined easily due to the characteristics of the RDF model. The integrated information can be understood if all information providers have used the same ontology to mark up their data. Hence, information that is not presented according to the ontology of the consumer cannot be understood. This mandates a means to transform data such as provided by database views.

Accordingly, views should not only be applied on one data source only, but on the integrated data of several data sources instead. This requires the ability to integrate information from several sources. A set of view definitions can then transform data outside of a particular data source.

The aggregated and transformed data is often intended to be republished as a new information artefact. Therefore it is necessary to exert control over which elements should be republished. This requires the adaption of the ontology. For example, the ontology should only talk about the aspects of the data that are visible, e.g. for security reasons.

Primitives
Figure 4 depicts the features offered by external ontologies. First, users can import classes and properties from multiple RDF databases and other external ontologies.

Second, users may state new views on top of the integrated data sources. View queries have access to all data not only the imported classes and properties. This allows to transform data without making the (raw) data itself visible to users.

One the one hand, this provides *external schemata* in the sense of the ANSI SPARC three-level architecture for databases, where applications or users can access a database

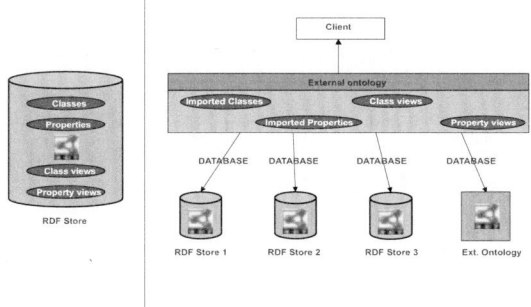

Fig. 4. Classical and external ontologies approach

through a specified subschema, e.g. to issue queries. On the other hand, this differs from the ANSI SPARC approach since external ontologies are hosted and specified completely outside of the data sources.

Example

The following example provides an external ontology that captures an administration perspective for a scientific department. This includes all information about people who actually receive payments. The view x:WorkingStudents captures that students might be employed by a faculty other than the one they are enrolled in. The latter information would not be possible within an isolated faculty database.

```
CREATE EXTERNAL ONTOLOGY x:HumanResources
DATABASE x:Faculty_1
DATABASE x:Faculty_2
IMPORT CLASS x:Scientist
IMPORT PROPERTY x:email
IMPORT PROPERTY x:supervises

CREATE CLASS VIEW x:WorkingStudents
 ON x:Student INTERSECT x:Employee
```

Data Input

External ontologies constitute virtual data sources that depend on other data sources. Such data sources may either be RDF databases (or external ontologies) within the same RDF DBMS or be located somewhere on the web outside the database. In the latter case we assume that the data is copied from their original source into a new auxiliary database. The DBMS may employ a dedicated component that (re)visits the url and updates the cached data source if updates occur (in style of [9]). The "DATABASE" statement from the above example may be augmented with update intervals for external data sources.

The IMPORT statement guarantees that only the mentioned extends are visible to clients. Users can restrict the IMPORT to a particular data source (via FROM) and may also import all resources whose URI matches a given regular expression.

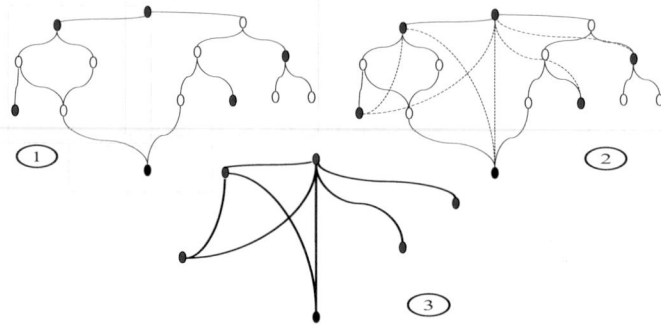

Fig. 5. Steps in the computation of the class hierarchy.

5   Implementation

5.1   Query Answering

Remote data sources are cached into an auxiliary database. This avoids network latency and increases the robustness of the system. Additionally, we are now able to process all queries towards the external ontology in an uniform manner. Queries are processed in three steps. First, the query graph is decomposed into appropriate sub-queries. In the second step sub-queries are matched with individual source data catalogues and passed to those sources which are able to handle the query, viz. queries for data residing in the source. Eventually partial results are gathered and composed to form the integrated answer.

The decomposition phase cuts the query graph into two parts. First, selections are pushed down as far as possible. Leaf nodes and selections acting on single leaf-nodes are passed to each source where appropriate[2]. Hence, an appropriate selection query is answered by each source individually. Answers of multiple sources are then merged (union) in memory and the upper levels of the query graph are processed in memory. Further optimizations of this strategy are taken in the implementation, but are beyond the scope of this paper. Queries underlying views are processed in a similar manner. The system detects, if a leaf node matches a view and computes the view on demand. Control on the visibility of classes and properties from the sources stated via imports are enforced at query processing time and implemented by (transitively) deleting all nodes that are not explicitly declared to be visible.

5.2   Materialization

Requests for serializing the external ontology to a RDF file lead to a materializiation of all views and export of all imported classes and properties. The inheritance hierarchies of the external ontology have to be adopted to those classes and properties and views

---

[2] if the property or class uri that constitutes the leaf appears in the source class/property catalogue

---

Algorithm 1 Computation of the class hierarchy

Require: IC set of imported classes, CV set of class views, S set of RDF sources
  $subclassof = \{\}$
  for all $s \in S$ **do**
    $subclassof = subclassof \cup s.subclassof$
  end for
  for all $v \in CV$ **do**
    $subclassof = subclassof \cup v.subclassof$
  end for
  $subclassof = subclassof^*$
  $newsubclassof = \{\}$
  for all $c_1 \in (IC \cup CV)$ **do**
    for all $c_2 \in (IC \cup CV)$ **do**
      if $(c_1, c_2) \in subclassof$ **then**
        $newsubclassof = newsubclassof \cup (c_1, c_2)$
      end if
    end for
  end for
Ensure: new class hierarchy ($newsubclassof$)

---

that are visible to the users. This is done by Algorithm 1 for the class hierarchy[3]. Following Figure 5, all inheritance information and is gathered from all sources and and augmented with the information about the classification of views in the first step. Then, the full transitive closure of this merged inheritance hierarchy is computed. In the final, third step only those links that connect visible nodes remain. The property hierarchy is computed in a similar fashion. Furthermore, the domain and range constraints for properties must be adopted to the visible classes, cf. [10] for the proposed solution.

6 Discussion

We have presented an extension of a view mechanism that picks up the unique situation of data in the Semantic Web. From our perspective, external ontologies are an important step in putting the idea of the Semantic Web into practice. Based on our own experiences with building Semantic Web based community portals [7] and ontology mapping frameworks [6] we devise that external ontologies will be a crucial cornerstone to achieve many different, exciting objectives.

If the vocabulary of another ontology is used, external ontologies allow to integrate otherwise disparate ontologies both by data transformation through views and by semantic integration through establishing integrated subsumption hierarchies between the classes and properties of both vocabularies leading to a proper articulation of both ontologies [8].

---

[3] This algorithm is simplified, since the implementation can avoid unnecessary computation of the transitive close and has only to consider all upwards links from visible nodes, hence the algorithm can bring visible nodes into a topological order and do an incremental computation instead of the presented algorithm)

We are currently investigating how updates can be consistently integrated. Additionally the materialization of views is of great importance in Web scenarios, we are therefore also investigating how such materialized views can be incrementally maintained in presence of updates. We also plan to adapt the implicit classification approach to allow full description-logic style subsumption which might have benefits for using views in query rewriting.

Acknowledgements. This work was done while staying at the University of Manchester and is funded by the EU in the WonderWeb project (IST-2001-33052) and a scholarship from the German Academic Exchange Programme (DAAD).

References

1. S. Alexaki, V. Christophides, G. Karvounarakis, D. Plexousakis, K. Tolle, Bernd Amann, Irini Fundulaki, Michel Scholl, and Anne-Marie Vercoustre. Managing RDF metadata for community webs. In *(WCM'00), Salt Lake City, Utah*, pages 140–151, October 2000.
2. Tim Berners-Lee. XML 2000 - Semantic Web Talk. Internet: http://www.w3.org/2000/Talks/1206-xml2k-tbö/slide10-0.html, december 2000.
3. S. Boag, D. Chamberlin, and al. XQuery 1.0: An XML Query Language. Technical report, W3C, April 2002.
4. Dan Brickley and R. V. Guha. Resource description framework (RDF) schema specification 1.0. Internet: http://www.w3.org/TR/2000/CR-rdf-schema-20000372/, 2000.
5. O. Lassila and R. Swick. Resource description framework (RDF) model and syntax specification. Internet: http://www.w3.org/TR/REC-rdf-syntax/, 1999.
6. Alexander Maedche, Boris Motik, Nuno Silva, and Raphael Volz. MAFRA - a mapping framework for distributed ontologies. In *Proc. of EKAW02, Siguenza, Spain*, October 2002.
7. Alexander Maedche, Steffen Staab, Rudi Studer, York Sure, and Raphael Volz. Seal tying up information integration and web site management by ontologies. In *IEEE Data Engineering Bulletin*, volume 25, March 2002.
8. Prasenjit Mitra, Gio Wiederhold, and Martin L. Kersten. A graph-oriented model for articulation of ontology interdependencies. In *Proc. of Extending Database Technology (EDBT) 2000*, pages 86–100, 2000.
9. B. Nguyen, S. Abiteboul, G. Cobena, and A. Marian. Monitoring xml data on the web. In *SIGMOD*, 2001.
10. Daniel Oberle and Raphael Volz. Implementation of a view mechanism for ontology-based metadata. Technical report, University of Karlsruhe (TH), 2002. http://www.aifb.uni-karlsruhe.de/WBS/dob/pubs/KAON-Views.pdf.
11. Raphael Volz, Daniel Oberle, and Rudi Studer. Views for light-weight web ontologies. In *ACM Symposium on Applied Computing (SAC), Orlando, Florida*, pages 1168–1173, March 2003.

Quantization Techniques for Similarity Search in High-Dimensional Data Spaces

Christian Garcia-Arellano[12] and Ken Sevcik

[1] Department of Computer Science, University of Toronto, Canada
cgarciaa,kcs@cs.utoronto.ca
[2] IBM Toronto Lab, Toronto, Canada cmgarcia@ca.ibm.com

Abstract. In the recent years, several techniques have been developed for efficient similarity search in high-dimensional data spaces. Some of the techniques, based on the idea of vector approximation via quantization, have been shown to be the most effective. The VA-file was as the first technique to use vector approximation. The IQ-tree and the A-tree are subsequent techniques that impose a directory structure over the quantized VA-file representation. The performance gains of the IQ-tree result mainly from an optimized I/O strategy permitted by the directory structure. Those of the A-tree result mainly from exploiting the clustering of the data itself. In our work, first we evaluate the relative performance of these two enhanced approaches over high-dimensional data sets with different clustering characteristics. Second, we present the Clustered IQ-Tree, which is an indexing strategy that combines the best features of the IQ-tree and the A-tree, leading to better query performance than the former and more stable performance than the latter across different types of data sets.

1 Introduction

In this paper, we investigate the problem of efficient *similarity search* Similarity search his distinguished from other database access problems in three ways:(i) each record in the data set is a vector of D elements (called a *feature vector*), where D is the *dimensionality* of the data set, (ii) the difference between feature vector pairs is expressed in terms of a distance measure, and (iii) queries focus on similarity of feature vectors rather than exact or partial matches.

The simplest kind of similarity query of this type is a range query, which returns all vectors in the data set for which the distance to a specified query vector is less than or equal to a given threshold. However, the cardinality of the set of vectors returned by a range query is difficult to estimate in advance, which is a disadvantage in some situations. Another type of query the K-nearest neighbor query(Knn), overcomes this problem in that, by definition, the answer set contains the K closest vectors, ordered by their distance from the query vector.

When the vectors have high-dimensionality (i.e., a large number of elements), several studies [20, 3] have shown that a simple sequential scan outperforms traditional indexing methods for multi-dimensional databases (e.g. the R-tree and

A. James, B. Lings, M. Younas (Eds.): BNCOD 2003, LNCS 2712, pp. 75–94, 2003.

its derivatives) New techniques, developed specifically for similarity search in high-dimensional data spaces, have been designed to overcome these difficulties. In particular, we focus on those techniques that use vector approximations, i.e., quantized versions of the vectors, as the key to improving query performance.

The VA-file was the first method that used vector approximations to improve the performance of nearest neighbor queries for high-dimensional data [20]. The IQ-tree [2] and the A-tree [18] were developed subsequently, each with the goal of improving query performance relative to the VA-file. We compare the performance of these similarity search techniques under a variety of scenarios. In our study, we have used both real and synthetic data sets with dimensionalities as high as 139, and searched for various numbers of neighbors, using both Euclidean and maximum distance metrics.

Finally, we have developed the CIQ-tree, a variation of the IQ-tree, which uses a spatial clustering algorithm to cluster the vectors on disk. The CIQ-tree integrates the best features of the IQ-tree and the A-tree, and obtains better query performance than the former and more stable performance than the latter across different types of data sets.

1.1   Problem Statement

The feature vectors of a data set consist of D numeric elements, and thus correspond to points in a D-dimensional space. We call D the *dimensionality* of the data set. Because both integers and real numbers are commonly represented in 32 bits in most computer architectures, we assume that each element is a 32-bit number, so that each feature vector requires $32D$ bits to represent.

The similarity search problem we address is defined as follows: In a data set consisting of N feature vectors of D elements, given a query vector and an integer K, return the K feature vectors from the data set that are closest to the query vector, while keeping the average query execution time as low as possible. We assume that D is relatively large, that K is much smaller than N, and that N is sufficiently large that the vectors and auxiliary information must reside on disk rather than in main memory.

For most of the experiments reported in this paper, we use the Euclidean distance measure to quantify the (dis-)similarity between two vectors:

$$distance(\vec{v_x}, \vec{v_y}) = \sqrt{\sum_{i=1}^{D} (\vec{v}_{xi} - \vec{v}_{yi})^2} \, .$$

We focus on dimensionalities of twenty or greater ($D >= 20$), with real and synthetic data sets of dimensionalities up to about 140.

The query execution times are composed of three components: i) CPU time; ii) disk positioning time (seek and rotation); and iii) page transfer time. The specific activities that contribute to each of these components differ from one technique to another.

Two of the similarity search implementations with which we experiment (IQ-tree and A-tree) use simulated rather than actual I/O operations. To achieve a fair comparison over all approaches, we measure the CPU time (c) directly, and count the number of disk head positionings (p), and page transfers (t). The average query execution time is then calculated as:

$$R = c + p \cdot T_p + t \cdot T_t \ .$$

where T_p and T_t are the average positioning time and the average page transfer time as measured on a chosen disk drive.

The extended version of this paper [15] explores some variations of the problem involving (1) use of a *maximum* (L_∞ norm) rather than a Euclidean (L_2 norm) distance measure, (2) partial overlap of I/O operations with CPU processing, and (3) use of main memory to cache index structure pages.

We assume the data sets to be *static* (i.e., insertions or deletions are not allowed). Thus, any cost of pre-processing the data set before it is subjected to queries is amortized over all subsequent queries. (Some of the approaches we compare can also handle *dynamic* data sets by efficient support of insertion and deletion operations.)

1.2 Plan and Contributions

Our goals in this paper are:

- to review three approaches to supporting K-nearest neighbor similarity queries based on quantized vector approximations (Section 2);
- to perform a detailed performance comparison of these three approaches on some real data sets with dimensionalities higher than have been previously investigated (Section 3);
- to propose a new approach, called the CIQ-tree, which is derived from the IQ-tree (Section 4);
- to compare the performance of the CIQ-tree to that of the other approaches based on both real and synthetic data sets (Section 5).

In Section 6, we present our conclusions.

2   Related Work

Previous work related to our study comes from the areas of indexing, clustering, and quantized vector approximations. Each of these areas is treated in a subsection below.

2.1 Indexing Techniques

The problem of querying a database containing multi-dimensional vectors has been studied extensively. A comprehensive survey of multi-dimensional data indexing structures is provided by Gaede and Günter. It includes descriptions of many structures for efficiently indexing data sets with low dimensionality (i.e., 2 to 3 dimensions) [13]. A survey by Böhm, Berchtold and Keim [7] describes recent approaches to dealing with higher dimensionalities.

2.2   Clustering

The use of clustering algorithms for similarity search has been proposed recently by several authors. Chakrabarti and Mehrotra present a clustering technique that, assuming the existence of subsets of data that are locally correlated, tries to find these subsets [8]. The technique is called Local Dimensionality Reduction (LDR) because the dimensionality reduction is applied independently to each of the detected clusters. Chakrabarti and Mehrotra also propose a two-level indexing structure on the clusters that can be used for similarity search. Barbara and Chen also propose a clustering algorithm, called Fractal Clustering (FC), that strives to minimize the fractal dimensionality of each of the independent clusters [1]. Also, in the context of similarity search, the k-Means algorithm was applied previously by Ferhatosmanoglu, Tuncel, Agrawal, and El Abbadi [11]. They use the resulting clustering of the vectors to answer approximate nearest neighbor queries.

2.3   Quantization Techniques

Recently, several approaches to searching in vector spaces have been developed around the concept of a *quantized* representation of the vectors. A vector of D 32-bit elements is quantized by the independent compression of each vector component into b bits ($b < 32$). The quantization of a vector component is obtained by partitioning the dimension range into 2^b non-overlapping subranges, and assigning a different code of length b bits to each subrange. The quantized version of a vector, also called a *vector approximation* (VA), is the concatenation of the b-bit quantized values for each vector component. The quantized version of a vector determines a set of D orthogonal subranges, which together specify a small D-dimensional hyper-rectangular cell in which the actual vector is enclosed. In general, the value of b may differ from one component of a vector to another, but, for our purposes, we assume that a single value of b is used for all the vector elements. Our experiments have shown that this simple approach yields the best results [14].

VA-file. Weber, Schek and Blott were the first to propose the use of vector approximations in the context of similarity search. They employed this idea in the Vector Approximation File (VA-file) [20]. This method does not partition and cluster the vectors of a data set as traditional indexing techniques do. Instead, it quantizes each dimension, generates a vector approximation for each vector in the data set, and stores these VAs in the VA-file, following the same order as the vector file, as is indicated in Figure 1(a). For each VA page containing VAs, there are multiple vector pages in the next level containing the corresponding vectors. (In the figure, each group of vector pages is represented as a unit by a circle.)

Given a query vector, the search in this data structure is performed in two phases. In the first phase, the VA-file is scanned, and, for each VA, the *minimum distance* and the *maximum distance* from the query vector to any point in the hyper-rectangular cell corresponding to the VA are computed, creating two priority lists using these distances. In the second phase, the VAs are examined

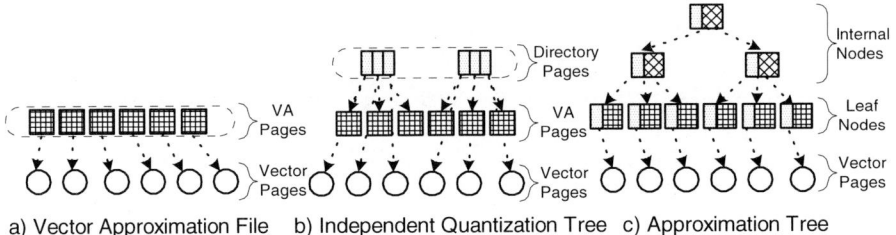

a) Vector Approximation File   b) Independent Quantization Tree   c) Approximation Tree

Fig. 1. Data Structures

in the order indicated by the minimum distance priority list, and the actual corresponding vectors are accessed. A third priority list is generated containing the K-nearest neighbor vectors themselves, ordered by increasing distance from the query point. The minimum distance list is processed until the minimum distance from the query vector to the next VA in the list is greater than the distance from the query point to the Kth nearest vector found already.

IQ-tree. Berchtold, Böhm, Jagadish, Kriegel and Sander also used the idea of vector quantization, and proposed the Independent Quantization Tree (IQ-tree), a multilevel indexing structure specially designed to perform fast nearest neighbor searches over high-dimensional data sets [2]. The IQ-tree is derived from the X-tree [4], and uses the partitioning strategy proposed with the X-tree bulk-loading algorithm. The structure has three levels: Directory Pages, Vector Approximation Pages and Vector Pages. As indicated in Figure 1(b), for each entry of the directory, there is a page containing VAs in the second level, and multiple pages containing vectors in the third level (represented all together by a circle). The number of vector pages associated with a directory entry is variable, and depends on the capacity of the associated VA page. The *capacity* of a VA page is the number of VAs that fit in a disk page, which depends on the number of bits per dimension used for the quantization of the vectors. Each directory entry contains the coordinates of the minimum bounding rectangle that encloses all the vectors corresponding to that entry. The VAs contained in a page of the second level are computed with respect to the MBR of the corresponding directory entry, and each page can use a different number of bits per dimension for the approximations.

The IQ-tree uses a recursive binary partitioning of the data space, choosing at each step to split the dimension of the MBR that has the maximum extension. The split point is chosen to cause an equal number of vectors to be in each of the two resulting nodes. This partitioning process is repeated until the number of vectors in each node fits within the capacity of the VA page. In the simplest version, a single number specifies the number of bits per dimension, which determines the capacity of all the vector approximation pages. Due to the recursive binary partitioning, the number of bits per dimension must be a power of 2 in the range [1,32].

Berchtold et al. also propose an auto-tuning algorithm based on the cost model published by Böhm [6] that can be used for data sets with self-similar or fractal structure. The auto-tuning algorithm determines the optimal capacity of each VA page, i.e., it determines the number of bits per dimension that leads to the lowest total I/O time. For our experimental evaluation, we will use the same number of bits for compressing each page, since the performance of the auto-tuned version depends on the fractal dimension parameter, the calculation of which is not reliable for high-dimensional data sets [14].

For the IQ-tree, Berchtold et al. also presented a nearest neighbor search algorithm that uses a smart page access strategy based on an I/O optimization developed by Seeger, Larson and McFayden [19]. Given a list of pages to be read, the strategy involves (i) ordering the list of pages by their position in the file, and then (ii) performing a single read request for any contiguous (or even nearly contiguous) sequence of pages in the list. This optimization reduces the number of (expensive) positionings at the cost of a few extra (cheap) page transfers.

In the IQ-tree context, it is not known initially exactly which pages hold the K nearest neighbors, but Berchtold et al. propose a probabilistic model for estimating the probability that each page will eventually have to be read in order to satisfy the query. The model specifies the set of pages that should be read in order to minimize the expected overall I/O cost. This strategy, called *sequential scan optimization* (SSO), was implemented to read the VA pages of the IQ-tree to support 1st-nearest neighbor queries [2]. The implementation was generalized to support K-nearest neighbor queries in our work[14]. In our study, we found that the use of the SSO is a critical factor in the good performance of the IQ-tree.

A-tree. Sakurai, Yoshikawa, Uemura and Kojima also make use of the idea of quantization in proposing the Approximation Tree(A-tree) [18]. The A-tree structure and construction algorithm are derived primarily from the SR-tree [16]. The A-tree design introduces the concept of virtual bounding rectangle (VBR), which is a compressed approximation using only a few bits per dimension of a minimum bounding rectangle (MBR). In a more general form of quantization, VBRs approximate MBRs in a manner analogous to how VAs approximate vectors. That is, the VBR defines a hyper-rectangle guaranteed to fully enclose the corresponding MBR. The use of VBRs, which are smaller than MBRs, increases the fanout of the nodes, which in turn reduces the height of the index tree and speeds up the search.

As indicated in Figure 1(c), an A-tree is a hierarchical index, with three levels: Internal Nodes, Leaf Nodes, and Vector Pages. Each of these levels has its own type of node. Internal nodes and leaf nodes together form a hierarchical index. Vector nodes each contain a cluster of neighboring vectors. Both internal and leaf nodes contain a header and multiple entries. The headers include an MBR that encloses all the vectors of the subtree rooted at the node. The entries of an internal node each contain a VBR that bounds the MBR of the corresponding child node. The entries of a leaf node are VAs of the vectors in the associated vector pages. Each node entry includes the centroid of the vectors within the associated MBR. The centroid is used only by the insertion algorithm and not by the search algorithm.

As this data structure can be created incrementally (i.e., is dynamic), the partitioning strategy is closely related to the insertion algorithm, which is based on that of the SR-tree [16].

The same sequential scan optimization dev elop ed for the IQ-tree could be applied in reading the leaf no des of the A-tree. This w ould require an extension of the data structure similar in spirit to the prefetc hing strategy proposed b y Chen, Gibbons, Mowry and V alen tin for range queries o v er B⁺-trees [9]. In our study ,w e found that a critical factor in the p erformance of the A-tree is the extent to w hich ts index no des correspond to tigh t clusters of v ectors.

2.4 Clustering and V ector Quantization

More recen tly,and concurrent to our w ork, Li, Chang, Garcia-Molina, and Wiederhold dev elop ed CLINDEX, an index structure for approximate similarity searc h that uses b oth a clustering tec hnique and v ector quantization [17]. The data structure is similar to the IQ-tree (and also to our CIQ-tree), b ecause it also has three lev els: v ector approximations, directory and data p oin ts. Ho w ev er, the query algorithm pro cesses these lev els in a different order: it first scans the v ector approximation lev el, then scans the directory, and finally it accesses the data pages. This tec hnique has not b een included in our exp erimental study b ecause it was dev elop ed to only handle approximate nearest neighb or queries.

3   Comparison of Three Techniques

Previously, the p erformance of the IQ-tree w as compared to that of the V A-file, the X-tree and sequential scan for dimensionalities from 4 to 16 [2], and the p erformance of the A-tree w as compared to that of the V A-file and the SR-tree [18] for dimensionalities up to 64. T o our kno wledge, the exp erimental study rep orted in this section is the first one to compare all three of V A-file, IQ-tree, and A-tree on a v ariety o f typ es of data sets. The range of dimensionalities w e address is 50 to 140.

3.1 Data Sets

F or our exp erimen ts, w e start with the v ectors of the data set stored in a binary file, where each vector element is stored as a 32-bit n um b er. Only the V A-file uses this initial v ector file without modification. The A-tree and the IQ-tree modify the order of the v ectors in the v ector file, eac h using their o wn space partitioning strategy for page clustering. Query v ectors for the exp erimen ts w ere selected b y cho osing 100 v ectors at random from eac h data set. Thus, the distribution of query v ectors reflects the distribution of the en tire data set. These v ectors selected to b e query v ectors w ere then remov ed from the data set. The av erage query execution times that w e presen t are the av erage K nn query times o v er the 100 selected query v ectors.

We used three real data sets with dimensionalities ranging from 54 to 139. In the COREL64 data set, each vector describes the color histogram of an im-age, computed using the Hue, Saturation, and V alue (HSV) color system. In the

T able1. Characteristics of the Real Data Sets

Name	Size (N)	Dim (D)	Source
F OREST54	500,000	54	UCI[3]
COREL64	68,040	64	US F orest Serv.[4]
CENSUS139	20,000	139	DELVE[5]

F OREST54 data set, each vector describes the forest co v ertyp e of a 30 meter
b y 30 meter cell of forest land. The dimensions represent wilderness and soil
typ es present in the area as 10 real v alues and 44 binary v alues. Finally, the
v ectors of the CENSUS139 data set eac h represent a region of the U.S.A., and
con tain dimensions lik e state and area co de, total n umb er of p ersons and fam-
ilies, p ercen tage of males and females, p ercen tage living inside urbanized area,
rural area, etc. The sizes, dimensionalities and sources of the three data sets are
summarized in T able1.

In each d ata set, w e performed a standardization and normalization pro cess
as a preprocessing step [14] causing each vector component to b e a 3 2 b it b in ary
fraction in the range $[0, 1)$. In data sets, it is frequently the case that features
are encoded in such a w ay that just a few attributes ha v ea dominant effect in
determining K nearest neighb or groups. One goal of our adjustments of the data
v alues w as to allow e ach dimension to ha v e comparable influence. This allo w ed
our exp erimen ts to address the full dimensionalities of the chosen data sets,
rather than artificially lo w erdimensionalities caused b y the (often arbitrarily)
selected ranges for feature v alues.

The distribution of pairwise distances be tween v ectors is a useful characterization of a data set in the con text of similarity s earch. Figure 2 sho ws the
distributions of pairwise distances for the three real data sets. We h av e adjusted
the distances b y dividing b y the length of the longest diagonal in the data space
($\sqrt{D}$) to present comparable v alues. These distributions w erecomputed using
randomly selected samples of 10,000 records of eac h data set (i.e., 10^8 pairwise
distances). Observe that the distributions of distances of the COREL64 and
F OREST54 data sets are more concentrated than is the one of CENSUS139. In

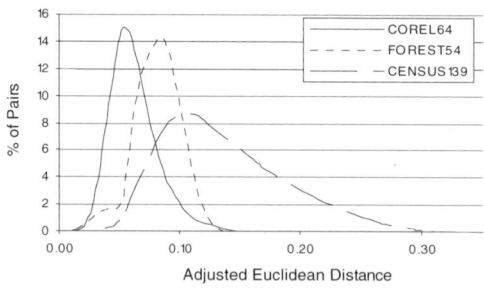

Fig. 2. Real Data Sets; Distrib. of P airwiseDistances

---

[3] h ttp://kdd.ics.uci.edu/databases/

[4] h ttp://nationalatlas.gov/fort yp em.html

[5] h ttp://www.cs.toronto.edu/~delv e/data/census-house

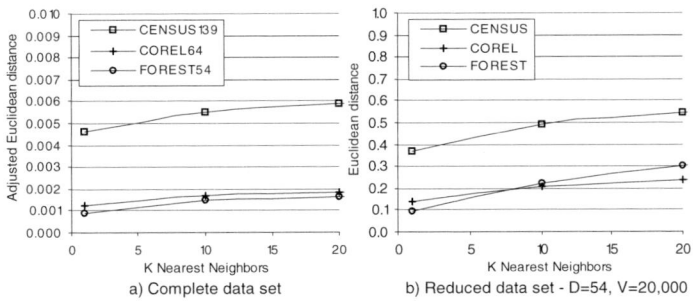

Fig. 3. Real Data Sets; Av erage$K$nn Distance

the case of F OREST54, w ecan distinguish the lo cal neighbo rh oodof a vector
(indicated b y the initial bulge b etw een0.02 and 0.04).

To in vestigate the lo cal neighbo rh oodof a vector further, we h av e measured
the av erage distances from eac h v ector to its 20 nearest neighbo rs using the
complete data sets. Figure 3(a) sho wsthe adjusted (divided b y $\sqrt{D}$) distances
for the real data sets. The av erage distances to the K nearest neighbo rs are
smaller in the case of F OREST54for all K from 1 to 20. Relating this fact to
the curv esof Figure 2, w esee that, ev en though at a lo cal lev el the distances
in F OREST54are smaller than in the case of COREL64, at a global lev el, the
majority o f the v ectors in F OREST54are more distant from a v ector than in
COREL64.

T oobtain more comparable data sets, we h av egenerated reduced v ersions of
eac h real data set with the same dimensionality ($D = 54$) and the same n umbe r
of v ectors ($N = 2$ 0000). The dimensions and v ectors retained in these reduced
data sets w ererandomly selected. Using the reduced data sets, the selectivit y
of a Knn query is the same in all three cases (e.g., the selectivit y of a 20-
nearest neighb or query is 0.001% of the reduced data set). Here the distances
are comparable without adjustment since the dimensionality of eac h reduced
data set is the same. Figure 3(b) sho wsthe av erage distances to eac h of the K
nearest neighb ors in the reduced data sets. As with the full data sets, at a lo cal
lev el ($K < 8$), the nearest neighb ors are closer in the reduced F OREST54than
in COREL64, and more distant at a global lev el ($K > 8$).

F romthis evidence, w e concludethat the F OREST54data set is highly clustered, formed b y a largen umbe r of very tigh t clusters.COREL64 is less clustered,
and the CENSUS139 data set has a distribution that is closer to uniform.

3.2   Environment

F or our exp erimens, w eused our own V A-fileco de [14], the IQ-tree co de de-
v elop edb y Berch told et al., and the A-tree co de dev elop edb y Sakurai et al.
Both the IQ-tree and the A-tree w eregeneralized to p erform K-nearest neigh-
b or searc hfor arbitrary v alues of K, and to allo w the choice of either Euclidean
or maximum distance.

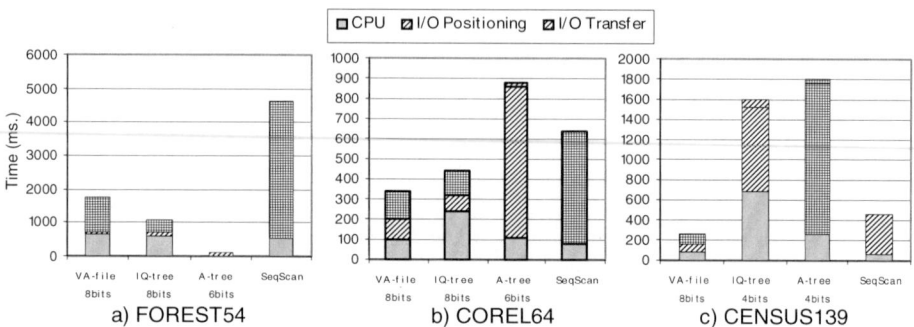

Fig. 4. Query Componen ts;$K = 1\ 0$

Our exp erimen ts w ere p erformed on a Dell Optiplex 200 with a 933-Mhz P en tiumIII pro cessor, 256 MB of main memory and a 10GB Maxtor 5T010H1 hard disk. The w orkstation runs Lin ux.

F or all the query p erformance results, the I/O time is computed b y counting the n umb er of randomp ositionings and pages read, and using the reference v alues of 5.5 ms p er page for p ositioning time and 30 MB/s for transfer rate (0.13 ms pe r 4KB page), obtained exp erimen tally based on our Maxtor 5T010H1 disk. These reference v alues giv e a ratio of approximately 40:1 be tween p ositioning time and transfer time for one 4KB page. (This motivates the use of the SSO to a v oid p ositionings where p ossible.)

The CPU time w as measured using standard system calls to determine the user time consumed in the execution of a p ortion of the co de. In most exp eri-ments, w e assume that initially the index structure and the v ector file are com-pletely in secondary storage, and read op erations must be performed for an y p ortion that is used for answering the query. In all cases, if a page is used more than once in the same query, only one read is counted, assuming that the page remains in main memory for subsequent op erations.

In the extended v ersion of the paper [15], we p resen t the p erformance results under the assumption that the reused components of the data structure are stored in main memory from the start of the exp erimen t.

3.3   Evaluation Results

F or eac h of the data structures and data sets, w e p erformed exp erimen ts with $K = 10$ to determine the b est configuration of n umb er of bits p er dimension to use. F or the V A-File and the IQ-tree the page size is 4KB, and for the A-tree it is 8KB. These v alues w ere chosen b ecause they led to the b est p erformance of the resp ectiv e techniques.

Figure 4 sho ws the components of the a v erage query time on each d ata s et for eac h of the techniques, including sequential scan. In the case of F OREST54 (Figure 4(a)), the A-tree sho ws outstanding query p erformance, follo w ed by t h e IQ-tree and by th e VA-file. The A-tree p erforms w ell due to the combination of a highly-clustered data set with the cen troid-based partitioning strategy, w h ich generates a go o d disk clustering of the v ectors. Also, the tigh t clusters separated

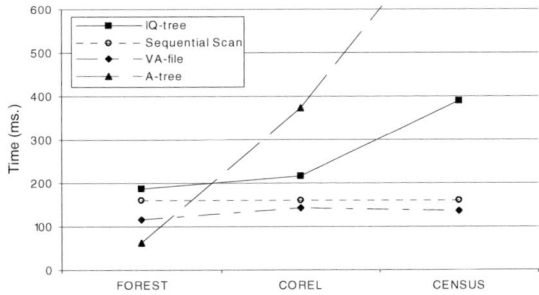

Fig. 5. Real Data Sets (Reduced) with K=10; D=54; N=20,000

by areas of low vector densit y fully exploit the hierarc hical structure. The a verage execution time of sequential scan is larger due to the large n umbe r of vectors in this data set (580,000).

F or the COREL64 data set (Figure 4(b)), the V A-file yields the b est query p erformance. The CPU component for the IQ-tree is quite large, and approaches the averagequery time of the V A-file. The A-tree do es p o orly due to the large n umb er of random reads required, mostly at the leaf lev el of the data structure. Of the total n umb er of randomreads p erformed, more than 80% are p erformedat the leaf lev el, and the remaining 20% correspond to random accesses to in ternal no des and v ector pages, in almost equal proportion. The clusters in the case of COREL64 are muc h larger than in the case of F OREST54, which means that more v ectors ha v e to be examined to determine which are the closest. Thus, the hierarc hical structure of the A-tree is not exploited, and the sequential scan optimization of the IQ-tree pro v es its usefulness.

F or the CENSUS139 data set (Figure 4(c)), due to the smaller n umbe r of v ectors, only the V A-file sho ws an improv ement o ver the sequential scan, and the A-tree and IQ-tree b oth do much worse due to the v ery lo w degree of clustering of this data set. F or the IQ-tree, its CPU time alone is greater than the a verage total execution time for sequential scan.

In Figure 5, w e sho wthe query p erformanceresults using the reduced v ersions of the real data sets. The relative b eh avior of the techniques using the reduced data sets is consistent with that obtained with the complete data sets. This means that there is an in trinsic characteristic in eac h of them that depends neither on the n umbe r of vectors nor on the dimensionality. W e believ e thatthis characteristic is the degree of clustering of the data set, which is high in the case of F OREST54,and lo w in the case of CENSUS139. Sequential scan remains v ery competitiv e b ecause the reduced data sets con tainonly 20,000 records eac h.

4   Clustered IQ-Tree

We propose a new indexing strategy, th e *Clustered IQ-Tree* or *CIQ-tree*, w hich is deriv edprimarily from the IQ-tree. The CIQ-tree ac hiev esgo o dv ector clustering (which w as critical in the A-tree) while employing the sequential scan optimization (which was critical in the IQ-tree). We chose to do this b y adding

a cen troid-basedpartitioning step to the IQ-tree approach, although an alternative would ha v eb een to add the sequential scan optimization to the reading of
leaf no desin the A-tree.

We characterize the *precision*(or qualit y) of a A'b y the in v erse of the volume
of hyp er-rectangle it defines. The A-tree, due to its cen troid-based partitioning
strategy and multiple index tree lev els, generatespage regions with small v olume.
This leads in turn to high precision V As.How ev erin cases where the data set
do es not con tain tigh t clusters, the A-tree requires a large n umbe r of random
reads to access the no depages on disk. Although the precision of the V Asfor the
IQ-tree is lo w er than that of the A-tree, due to the sequential scan optimization,
the IQ-tree p erforms b etter than the A-tree when the data structures reside on
disk.

4.1   Data Space P artitioning

The CIQ-tree partitioning strategy uses a varian t of th e k-Means spatial clustering algorithm [12] to cluster the v ectors and obtain V Aswith comparable
precision to those obtained with the A-tree. Because w e wishto place eac hclus-
ter of V Ason a disk page, w erequire that clusters b e of a b ounded maximum
size. We adapt the k-Means algorithm to enforce this constraint.

F or example, consider the 64-dimensional COREL64 data set and assume
a page size of 4KB. The exact 32D-bit representation of a v ector o ccupies 256
b ytes, which p ermits a maximum of 16 v ectorsp er 4KB disk page. If the n umbe r
of vectors in a cluster is b etw een1 and 16, the v ectors will b e stored in a V A
page using the full 32-bit representation. If w ereduce the n umbe r of bits pe r
dimension to 16, w e doublethe n umbe r of VAs that can fit on a disk page to as
many as 32, etc.

4.2   Clustering b y a Modified k-Means Algorithm

F orclustering, w euse a modification of the k-Means clustering algorithm [12].
The modification makes it p ossibleto assure that cluster sizes will b e constrained
b y upper and lo w er b ounds so that they map efficiently to disk pages. Pseudo-
co de of the algorithm is giv en in Figure 6. The inputs to the algorithm are (i)
the set of v ectors $V = \{\overrightarrow{v_1}, \ldots, \overrightarrow{v_N}\}$, (ii) the initial proposed v alue, k_{init}, for th e
numbe r of clusters, (iii) $size_{min}$ and $size_{max}$, the upper and lo w erb ounds on
the sizes of clusters, and (iv) Δ_{min}, the minimum improv ement in eac hiteration
to justify additional iterations. The outputs are (i) the final n umb er ofclusters,
k, (ii) the list of k cen troids, $\Omega = (\omega_1, \ldots, \omega_k)$, and (iii) the sets of v ectors,
$S = \{S_1, \ldots, S_k\}$, assigned to each o f th e k clusters.

We define the functions $closest(\overrightarrow{v_i})$ and $disor\,der(\Omega, S)$ for u se in th ealgo-
rithm:

$$closest(\overrightarrow{v_i}) = \{\; cluster\; C_j \mid distance(\omega_j, \overrightarrow{v_i}) = \min_{1 \leq h \leq k} distance(\omega_h, \overrightarrow{v_i})\; \}.$$

$$disor\,der(\Omega, S) = \sum_{j=1}^{k} \sum_{\overrightarrow{v_i} \in S_j} distance(\omega_j, \overrightarrow{v_i}).$$

kMeans_Restricted_Size_Clustering

Inputs: V, k_{init}, $size_{min}$, $size_{max}$, Δ_{min}

Outputs: k, S, Ω

1. Setting $k = k_{init}$, create set $S = \{S_j\}$ with k empty sets of vectors, S_j, one for each cluster, C_j
2. For each cluster, C_j, select randomly from V a vector $\vec{v_i}$ as the centroid, ω_j, of C_j
   Loop
3.   For each vector $\vec{v_i} \in V$, add it to cluster $closest(\vec{v_i})$
4.   For each cluster C_j, recompute ω_j as the centroid of the vectors in S_j
5.   For each cluster with size less than $size_{min}$, remove the cluster and re-assign each orphan vector $\vec{v_i}$ to set $closest(\vec{v_i})$, and decrement k
6.   For each cluster with size greater than $size_{max}$, split the cluster using recursive binary partitioning, and increase k accordingly
7.   Again, for each cluster C_j, recompute ω_j as the centroid of the vectors in S_j
8.   Compute the disorder of the clustering, $disorder(k, S, \Omega)$
9.   Exit loop if the disorder has not decreased by at least Δ_{min} from the previous iteration
10.   Re-initialize each cluster C_j, by setting $S_j = \emptyset$
   End Loop

Fig. 6. k-Means Clustering with Restricted Cluster Size

The algorithm works as follows. A collection S of k (initially, k_{init}) sets of vectors, are initialized empty (step 1), and the initial center of each cluster is (uniform) randomly selected from the set of vectors V (step 2). Within the main loop (step 3), each vector of the data set is assigned to the cluster having the center to which the vector is closest. After this assignment, the center of each cluster is re-computed to be the centroid of the vectors assigned to the cluster (step 4).

Next (step 5), all clusters of size less than $size_{min}$ are removed, and k is adjusted downward accordingly. Each vector orphaned by the removal of the cluster to which it had been assigned is re-assigned to the remaining cluster having the center to which the vector is closest. Then (step 6), each cluster with size greater than $size_{max}$ is split in two (recursively, if necessary) to make the size of each cluster no more than $size_{max}$, and the value of k is adjusted upward accordingly. The split algorithm splits the dimension for which the vectors in the cluster have the highest variance at a value such that the sum of the variances in the attribute in the two resulting clusters is minimized. (This split policy is similar to the one used in the A-tree for handling node overflow.) Then (step 7), the center of each cluster is recomputed.

At the end of the main loop, the measure of clustering quality ($disorder$) is calculated (step 8), and (step 9) if the improvement in the quality measure value from the previous iteration is not significant (i.e., is less than Δ_{min}), then the algorithm terminates; otherwise (step 10), remove all vector assignments to clusters and return to the top of the loop with the current set of centroids. The fact that the quality measure value is monotonically non-increasing from one iteration to the next guarantees termination of the algorithm for any positive

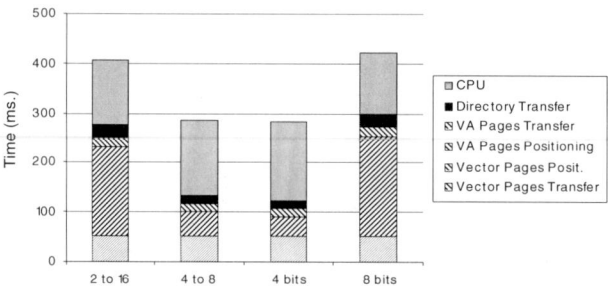

Fig. 7. CIQ-tree; Cluster Compression Sizes; $K = 10$; COREL64

value of Δ_{min}. Empirically, w e observed that the algorithm typically con verged in fiv e toten iterations.

4.3   CIQ-Tree Performance

We present four different exp eriments with the COREL64 and F OREST54 data sets, varying the compression range allo w ed. In our exp eriments, w e consider cases where the n umb er of bits p er dimension (i) is an ywhere from 2 to 16, (ii) is either 4 or 8, (iii) is fixed at 4, and (iv) is fixed at 8 for all clusters of V As Having chosen the p ermitted range of n umb er of bits p er dimension, the parameters $siz e_{min}$ and $siz e_{max}$ can b e set to constrain cluster sizes accordingly. Table 2 sho ws the configurations that result from applying the clustering algorithm to the COREL64 data set. Each row of the table sho ws the n umb er of clusters (and also V A pages) with eac h compression ratio. F or example, if w e set the minimum cluster size to 17 (requiring 16 bits p er dimension) and the maximum cluster size to 256 (using 2 bits p er dimension), then the resulting tree con tains 200 V A pages with 4 bits, 964 with 8 bits and 301 with 16 bits.

Figure 7 sho ws the query p erformance results for the COREL64 data set for $K = 10$. The b est p erformance is obtained with 4 bits for eac h dimension. Among these cases, the p ositioning time for the v ector approximation pages is the query component that v aries most significantly for the different compression ranges. (Note that the transfer time for the v ector pages is too small to b e visible in the figure.) F or F OREST54, on the other hand, the transfer time of the directory is the most significant query component, and its v ariation is what makes the difference in p erformance b etw een the different compression ranges.

Figures 8(a) and 8(b) sho w the a verage total query execution times for COREL64 and F OREST54 v arying the v alue of K from 1 to 20. As observed for COREL64 with $K = 10$, compression to 4 bits is b est for b oth data sets for an y v alue of K.

T able 2. Numb er of clusters with each numb er of bits p er dim. for COREL64

Compression Range	$siz e_{min}$	$siz e_{max}$	2 bits	4 bits	8 bits	16 bits
2 to 16 bits	17	256	0	200	964	301
4 to 8 bits	33	128	–	625	242	–
4 b its	65	128	–	739	–	–
8 b its	33	64	–	–	1454	–

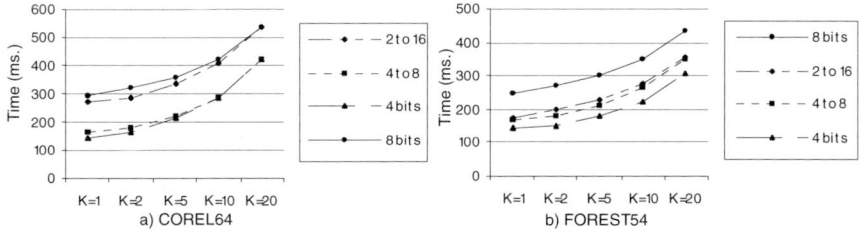

Fig. 8. CIQ-tree; V aryingCompression Range and K

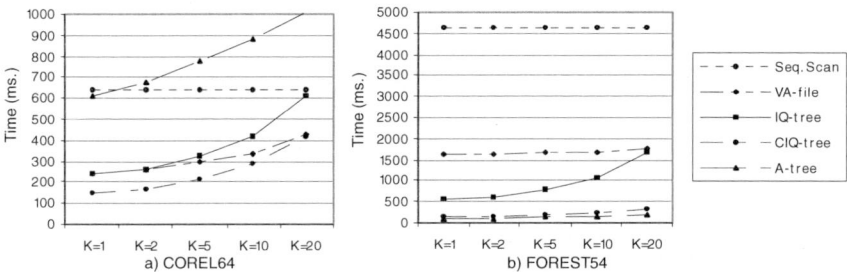

Fig. 9. Knn Queries

5   Comparison of CIQ-Tree with the Other Techniques

5.1   Experiments Based on Real Data Sets

In this section, w ecompare the query p erformance of the CIQ-tree with that of the alternative quantization techniques. F or eac h technique, on eac h data set, w eha veused the n umbe r of bits pe r dimension that giv es the b est query p erformance, and these are sho wn in T able3.

Varying the Number of Neighbors. Figure 9(a) sho ws the a verage query execution times for the COREL64 data set for different values of K. The CIQ-tree p erforms b etter than the IQ-tree for all tested v alues of K and b etter than the alternative techniques for values of K b elow 2 0.

F or values of K ab o ve 20 the V A-file is the b est alternativ e to obtain b etter p erformance than the sequential scan. This is due to the fact that, as K gro ws, the exp ecteddistances to the Kth nearest neighb or and the $2K^{th}$ b ecomes v ery small [5], so that no lo cal clustering strategy can b e successful.

In the case of the F OREST54 data set (Figure 9(b)), the CIQ-tree giv es a lo w era verage query time than the IQ-tree. Figure 10 compares the query time components for the CIQ-tree and the A-tree with $K = 10$. The CIQ-tree CPU time component is larger than that of the A-tree due to the CPU time

T able3. Number of B its Pr Dim. that Gives the Best Query P erf. for Eac HIndex

	V A-file	IQ-tree	A-tree	CIQ-tree
COREL64	8	8	6	4
F OREST54	8	8	6	4

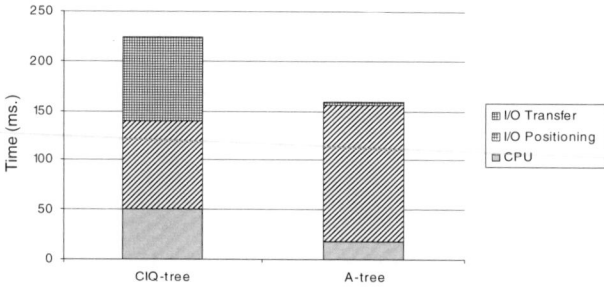

Fig. 10. Query Time Componen ts; F OREST54;$K = 1 0$

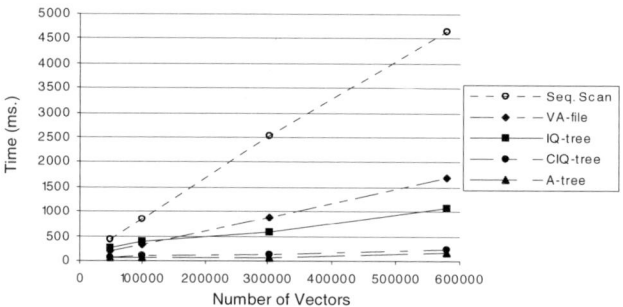

Fig. 11. V aryingthe data set size; F OREST54; $K = 1 0$

required for the sequential scan optimization. The adv an tages that the CIQ-tree requires few er random p ositionings. How ev er, theCIQ-tree tak es moretime in the transfer of the directory pages, which is the major difference in the query p erformance. Due to the many tigh t clusters in F OREST54,the A-tree makes full use of the no de hierarc h y gaining an adv an tage v er the CIQ-tree, which requires a full scan of the directory.

In the case of CENSUS139,the data set with the smallest degree of clustering, the CIQ-tree sho wslittle improv ement o ver the IQ-tree and the A-tree, and the V A-filestill ac hiev es the b est p erformance on this data set.

Data Set Size. Figure 11 sho wsthe average query times of the different techniques for subsets of different sizes of the F OREST54 data set with $K = 10$. The query p erformance of the CIQ-tree is v ery close to that of the A-tree, and the p erformance improv ement relativ e to the IQ-tree increases for larger data set sizes.

5.2   Experiments Based on Synthetic Data Sets

We ha v e also generated syn thetic clustered data sets to allo w more flexibility in our ev aluation. We h a v e performed three sets of exp erimets with syn thetic data sets to sho w the b eha vior of the alternative quantization techniques under different scenarios. In eac h case, the dimensionality o f the sy thetic data set is 50, and the size of the data set is 50,000 v ectors.

Synthetic Data Set Generation. The cen ters of the clusters in each syn thetic data set w ere generated follo wing a uniform distribution in a C-dimensional

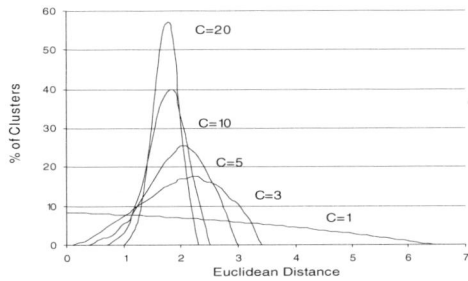

Fig. 12. Syn theticData Sets - Distrib. of In ter-Cluster Distances

space, and they w ereemb edded in to a D-dimensional space (for $D > C$) u sin g a random orthonormal rotation matrix generated using the Gram-Schmidt method in MATLAB. We refer to dimensionality C as the *intrinsic dimensionality* of the cen ters, and to dimensionality D as the *embedding dimensionality*. T h e vectors of eac h cluster w ere generated uniformly within a sphere around the cluster cen ter in the D-dimensional space based on the parameters m, M, μ_r, and σ_r. The n umbe r of v ectors in eac h cluster w asgenerated follo wing a uniform distribution be tween minimum and maximum v alues ($U(m, M)$). The radii of the spheres w ere generated follo wing a Gaussian distribution with sp ecified mean and standard deviation ($G(\mu_r, \sigma_r)$). The v ectors of eac h cluster w eregenerated uniformly within the sphere of the chosen radius using the method of the Normal deviation.

Varying the Global Clustering Structure. In this exp eriment w e vary the global structure of the clustering, maintaining a constant lo cal densit y within the clusters. The in trinsic dimensionality of the cen ters, C, ranged from 1 to 20. The cluster size distribution w as $U(100, 200)$, and the cluster sphere radius distribution w as $G(0.3, 0.1)$. Figure 12 sho ws the distribution of distances be - tween the cen tersof the clusters for v arious v alues of C. Note that, with larger in trinsic dimensionality of the clusters, the distances be tween pairs of cen ters are less v ariable, and also the clusters are more disp ersein the space.

The query p erformance results for this set of data sets are sho wnin Figure 13(a). As w e cansee, the more disp ersedthe clusters are in the space, the b etter the p erformanceof the A-tree. This is b ecausethe combination of a hierarc hical structure with the cen troid-basedpartitioning is more useful in the cases where there are clusters with high densit ysurrounded b y areas with lo w densit y.A t the other extreme, when the cluster cen tersw eregenerated in a 1-dimensional space ($C = 1$) and emb edded in to a 50-dimensional space, the IQ-tree sho wsa significant adv an tageover the A-tree, due to the recursiv ebinary partitioning of the data space. The CIQ-tree ac hiev esb etter query p erformance than an y alternative technique for all v alues of C. This is p ossible b ecause the CIQ-tree combines the b est features of the A-tree and the IQ-tree.

Varying the Local Density o f the Clusters. The second group of syn thetic data sets w asgenerated v arying the lo cal densit yof the clusters. In this case, w e used the cluster sphere radii distributions $G(0.05, 0.01)$, $G(0.2, 0.05)$, $G(0.3, 0.1)$

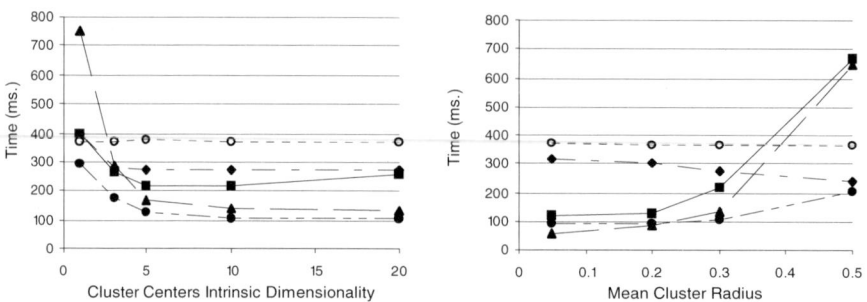

a) Varying the Cluster Centers Intrinsic Dimensionallity b) Varying the Cluster Sphere Radii Distrib; C=10

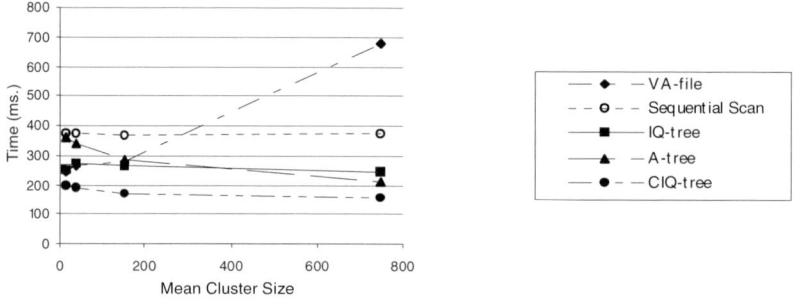

c) Varying the Cluster Sizes Distribution; C=3

Fig. 13. Syn theticdata sets; $K = 10$; $D = 5 0$

and $G(0.5, 0.1)$. The in trinsic dimensionality of the distribution of the cluster centers w as $C = 10$ in all cases, and the distribution of cluster sizes w as $U(100, 200)$.

Figure 13(b) sho wsthe a verage query time as a function of the mean of the Gaussian distribution of the cluster sphere radii. F or a fixed global sparseness of the clusters, the tigh ter the clusters are, the b etter the query p erformance of the A-tree is. Also, the lo w er th do cal density of the clusters, the closer the data set is to a uniformly distributed data set, and the b etter the p erformance of the V A-file.The CIQ-tree query p erformance is not to o sensitiv e to the lo cal density of the clusters, resulting in more stable results than those of the alternative techniques. Overall, the CIQ-tree yields the b est p erformance, although the A-tree is somewhat b etter when the clusters are v ery tigh t.

Varying the Number of V ectors per Cluster. The last group of syn thetic data sets w as generated v arying the distribution of cluster sizes. Since the total n umbe r of vectors in eac h data set is fixed (at 50,000), the n umb er of clusters in the data set is approximately N divided b y the mean cluster size, $(m + M)/2$. We generated four data sets, with cluster sizes distributions $U(5, 20)$, $U(25, 50)$, $U(100, 200)$ and $U(500, 1000)$. The in trinsic dimensionality of the distribution of cluster cen ters w as $C = 3$ in all cases, and the distribution of cluster sphere radii w as $G(0.3, 0.1)$.

Figure 13(c) sho wsthat the CIQ-tree obtains the b est a verage query p erfor-mance in all cases. The p erformance of the V A-file degrades rapidly as the mean cluster size increases (leading to greater lo cal density of the clusters).

6   Conclusions

Sev eraltec hniques for similarity searc h h av ebe en dev elop edusing the idea of v ector approximation through quantization. The first con tributionof our w ork is the comparative e valuation of the p erformanceof these tec hniques using b oth real and syn theticdata sets with v arious degrees of clustering. We considered dimensionalities from 50 to 140, whereas previous studies of these methods ha v e addressed dimensionalities only as high as 64. We h av e sen that, for data sets with a high degree of clustering, the hierarc hicalstructure of the A-tree leads to the b est p erformanceresults. But the p erformanceof this tec hnique degrades rapidly for data sets that are not highly clustered, due to the large n umbe r of random p ositioningsrequired to read the no desof the tree. A t theother extreme, when the data sets ha v e amore uniform distribution, we h av eseen that the V A-file is the b est alternative.

The second con tributionof our w orkis the in tro ductionof the CIQ-tree, a v ariation of the IQ-tree. We ha v esho wn that it p erforms b etter than the IQ-tree in all the cases examined. The cen troid-basedpartitioning strategy , adopted from the A-tree, generates a b etter page clustering of the v ectors, which l ead s to b etter v ector approximation precision and also to b etter query p erformance. Relative to the A-tree, the p erformanceof the CIQ-tree w assho wnto b e more consistently go o dov er datasets with different degrees of clustering. F or a data set that is kno wnto b e highlyclustered, the A-tree will probably lead to the b est p erformance.How ev er, theCIQ-tree p erformsconsistently w ell ov er a widerange of degrees of clustering, and is the b est alternative for datasets with an in terme-diate degree of clustering (suc h as COREL64). F orthis consistent p erformance, w eb eliev ethat the CIQ-tree is the b est alternative o verall in situations where the main limitation noted in Section 1.1, lac k of support for efficient insertions and deletions, is not an issue.

There are sev eral p ossibldirections for future w ork.First, to complemen t ou r modification of the IQ-tree to obtain the CIQ-tree, w e couldinstead modify the A-tree implementation to incorporate the sequential scan optimization (SSO) from the IQ-tree, and assess the p erformance of this approach relativ eto the CIQ-tree. Second, the same set of quantization techniques could be compared with resp ect to p erformance for range queries or *constr aine dne ar estneighbor* queries [10], instead of on Knn queries. Third, the quantization-based methods we h av eaddressed in this paper could b e ev aluated relativ e toclustering-based methods (suc h as LDR [8] and fractal clustering [1]).

As w asargued b y Web er et al. [20], for an y indexing tec hnique, there is a dimensionality sufficiently large that the V A-filewill p erform b etter. How ev er, through the dev elopmen t of improv ed indexing tec hniques lik e the CIQ-tree, it is p ossibleto push that dimensionality threshold to higher lev els.

References

1. D. Barbara and P . Chen. Using the fractal dimension to cluster data sets. In *Pr oc. of the 6th KDDM*, pages 260–264, 2000.

2. S. Berc htold,C. B¨ohm,H. V. Jagadish, H.-P. Kriegel, and J. Sander. Independen t quan tization:An index compression technique for high-dimensional data spaces. In *Pr oc. ofthe 16th ICDE*, pages 577–588, 2000.

3. S. Berc htold,C. B¨ohm,and H.-P. Kriegel. The p yramid-technique: tow ardsbreaking the curse of dimensionality. In *Pr oc. of A CM SIGMOD Int. Conf.*, pages 142–153, 1998.

4. S. Berc htold,D. Keim, and H.-P. Kriegel. The X-tree: An index structure for high-dimensional data. In *Pr oc. ofthe 22nd VLDB*, pages 28–39, 1996.

5. K. Bey er, J.Goldstein, R. Ramakrishnan, and U. Shaft. When is "nearest neighb or" meaningful? In *In* Pro c. ofthe 7th ICDT, pages 217–235, 1999.

6. C. B¨ohm. A cost model for query pro cessing in high-dimensional data spaces. *A CM T ransactions on Database Systems*, 25:129–178, 2000.

7. C. B¨ohm,S. Berc htold,and D. Keim. Searc hing in high-dimensional spaces: Index structures for improving the p erformance of m ultimediadatabases. *A CM Comp. Surveys*, 33(3):322–373, 2001.

8. K. Chakrabarti and S. Mehrotra. Lo cal dimensionaliy reduction: A new approach to indexing high dimensional spaces. In *The VLDB Journal*, pages 89–100, 2000.

9. S. Chen, P . Gibbons, T. Mowry ,and G. V alen tin. F ractal prefetc hing b+-trees: Optimizing b oth cache and disk p erformance. *Pr oc. of A CM SIGMOD Int. Conf.*, pages 157–168, 2002.

10. H. F erhatosmanoglu,I. Stanoi, D. Agraw al, andA. E. Abbadi. Constrained nearest neigh bo r queries. In *In* Pro c. of the 7th In t. Symp. on Spatial and T emporal Databases SSTD, pages 257–278, 2001.

11. H. F erhatosmanoglu, E. T uncel, D. Agraw al, and A. E. Abbadi. Approximate nearest neigh b orsearc hing in m ultimediadatabases. In *Pr oc. of the 17th ICDE*, pages 503–511, 2001.

12. E. F orgy . Cluster analysis for m ultiv ariatedata: Efficiency vs. in terpretability o f classifications. *Biometrics*, 21, 1965.

13. V. Gaede and O. Gu¨n ther.Multidimensional access methods. *A CMComp. Surveys*, 30(2):170–231, 1998.

14. C. Garcia-Arellano. Quantization techniques for similarity search in high-dimensional data spaces, 2002. Master's Thesis. Computer Science Deptartment, University o f Toron to, Canada.

15. C. Garcia-Arellano and K. Sev cik. Quantization techniques for similarity search in high-dimensional data spaces, 2003. T echnicalReport CSRG-471. Computer Science Deptartment, University o f Toron to, Canada.

16. N. Katayama and S. Satoh. The SR-tree: an index structure for high-dimensional nearest neigh b orqueries. In *Pr oc. of A CM SIGMOD Int. Conf.*, pages 369–380, 1997.

17. C. Li, E. Chang, H. Garcia-Molina, and G. Wiederhold. Clustering for appro ximate similarity searc h in igh-dimensional spaces. *IEEE T rans. on Knowledge and Data Engineering*, 14(4):792–808, 2002.

18. Y. Sakurai, M. Y oshik aw a,S. Uemura, and H. Kojima. The A-tree: An index structure for high-dimensional spaces using relativ e appro ximationIn *Pr oc. of the 26th VLDB*, pages 516–526, 2000.

19. B. Seeger, P . A.Larson, and R. McFayden. Reading a set of disk pages. In *Pr oc. of the 19th VLDB*, pages 592–603, 1998.

20. R. Web er, H.-J. Sc hek, and S. Blott. A quan titativ eanalysis and p erformance study for similarity-searc h methods in high-dimensional spaces. In *Pr oc. of the 24th VLDB*, pages 194–205, 24–27 1998.

Performance Evaluation and Analysis of K-Way Join Variants for Association Rule Mining[1]

P. Mishra and S. Chakravarthy

Information and Technology Laboratory and
The University of Texas at Arlington, Arlington, TX 76019
{pmishra,sharma}@cse.uta.edu

Abstract. Data mining aims at discovering important and previously unknown patterns from the dataset in the underlying database. Database mining performs mining directly on data stored in (relational) database management systems (RDBMSs). The type of underlying database can vary and should not be a constraint on the mining process. Irrespective of the database in which data is stored, we should be able to mine the data. Several SQL92 approaches (such as K-way join, Query/Subquery, and Two-group by) have been studied in the literature.

In this paper, we focus on the K-way join approach. We study several additional optimizations for the K-way join approach and evaluate them using DB2 and Oracle RDBMSs. We evaluate the approaches analytically and compare their performance on large data sets. Finally, we summarize the results and indicate the conditions for which the individual optimizations are useful. The larger goal of this work is to feed these results into a layered optimizer that chooses specific strategies based on the input dataset characteristics.

1   Introduction

The rapid improvement in the storage technology with steep drop in the storage cost and increase in the computing power has made it feasible for organizations to store huge amounts of data and process it. To compete effectively in today's market, decision makers need to identify and utilize the information hidden in the collected data and take advantage of the high return opportunities in a timely fashion. Data Mining is the process of inferring knowledge from such data repositories, and database mining incorporates the ability to directly access data stored in a database.

Association rule mining is a process of identifying the co-occurrences of one or more items that satisfy user-defined frequency (specified as support and confidence). These models are often referred to as Market Basket analysis when they are applied to retail industries to study the buying patterns of their customers. Here an attempt is made to identify whether a costumer buys item "B" also, whenever he/she buys item "A". If so, then how many customers buy item "B" along with item "A" is of interest. This is stated as an association rule of the form A $\Rightarrow$ B. Where A is called the

---

[1] This work was supported, in part, by the Office of Naval Research, the SPAWAR System Center-San Diego & by the Rome Laboratory grant F30602-02-2-0134, and by NSF grants IIS-0097517 and ITR -0121297.

A. James, B. Lings, M. Younas (Eds.): BNCOD 2003, LNCS 2712, pp. 95–114, 2003.
© Springer-Verlag Berlin Heidelberg 2003

antecedent of the rule and B the consequence. In a more generalized form of the rule, antecedent and consequence can have more than one item (are sets).

The work on association rule mining started with the development of the AIS algorithm [1] and then some of its modifications as discussed in [2]. Since then, there have been continuous attempts in improving the performance of these algorithms. The partition algorithm [3] improves the overall performance by reducing the number of passes needed over the complete database to two. The turbo-charging algorithm [4] incorporates the concept of data compression to boost the performance of the mining algorithm. [5] builds a special tree structure in main memory to avoid multiple passes over database. However, most of these algorithms are applicable to data present in flat files. The basic characteristics of these algorithms are that they are main memory algorithms, where the data is either read directly from the flat files or is first extracted from the DBMS and then processed in the main memory. These algorithms implement their own buffer management strategies. The performance of these algorithms is due to their capability of building specialized data-structures, which is more suited to the specific algorithm. There have been very few attempts until now to build database based mining models. Here we assume that the data is already present in the form of tables in the underlying DBMS and we use the SQL capabilities provided by the RDBMS to churn it and to produce so far unseen and interesting rules. SETM [6], showed how the data stored in RDBMS can be mined using SQL and the corresponding performance gain achieved by optimizing these queries.

Recent research in the field of database-based mining has been in integrating the mining functions with the database. Various extensions to the SQL have been proposed. These proposals are to load the SQL with certain mining operators. The Data Mining Query Language DMQL [7] proposed a collection of such operators for classification rules, characteristics rule, association rules, discriminant rules, etc. [8] proposed the *MineRule* operator for generating general/clustered/ordered association rules. [9] presents a methodology for tightly-coupled integration of data mining applications with a relational database system. In [10] the authors have tried to highlight the implications of various architectural alternatives for coupling data mining with relational database systems. They have also compared the performance of the SQL-92 based architecture with SQL-OR based architecture and when mining is done outside the database address space.

Some of the research has focused on the development of SQL-based formulations for association rule mining. Most of these algorithms use the a priori algorithm directly or indirectly with some modifications to it. [10] and [11] deal with the SQL implementation of the apriori algorithm and have compared some of the optimizations to the basic k-way join algorithm for association rule mining but the relative performances and all possible combinations for optimizations were not explored. In this paper, we will analyze the characteristics of these optimizations in detail both analytically and experimentally. We conclude why certain optimizations are always useful and why some perceived optimizations do not seem to work as intended.

There are many commercial mining tools available today in the market, viz., the IBM's Intelligent Miner, DBMiner, etc., which use the capabilities provided by the underlying database management system for mining. Though these mining tools are quite efficient, they are developed for a particular RDBMS. Hence, they cannot be used if the relevant database is not used. To overcome this limitation, our approach uses a database independent architecture introduced in [12]. To make the implementation operating system independent, we have used java and along with it, we use JDBC API's to make our implementation independent of the underlying database. For the purpose of our evaluation, we have run the experiments on both Oracle 8i and IBM DB2/UDB 6.1.

1.1   Focus of This Paper

With more and more use of RDBMS to store and manipulate data, mining directly on RDBMSs gives us the advantage of using the fruits of decades of research done in this field. As the main memory always imposes a limitation on the size of data that can be processed, using RDBMSs provides us the benefits of using a sophisticated buffer management systems implemented in them. Building mining algorithms to work on RDBMSs directly also gives us the advantage of mining over very large datasets as RDBMSs have been built to manage such large volumes of data. File based mining algorithms or those that work on data outside the database, generally have an upper limit to the number of transaction that can be mined. For example, the DBMiner has an upper limit of 64K on the number of unique transactions that it can process for mining. With the user having a choice of RDBMS to use for his application, the mining algorithms should be developed using such accepted standards so that the underlying system is not a limitation and should be portable on other RDBMSs. Keeping this in mind, our focus in this paper is on the use of SQL-92 features for association rule mining over RDBMSs.

The goal of this paper is to study all aspects of the basic k-way join approach for association rule mining and then explore additional performance optimizations to the k-way join. The other goal of our work is to be able to use the results obtained from mining various relations to make the mining optimizer mining-aware. Most of the relational query optimizers were not designed to optimize queries that are typically used in mining. Furthermore, current optimizers cannot be given any external input in guiding them towards generating a specific query plan. Hence, the results collected from the performance evaluations of these algorithms are critical for developing a knowledge base that can be used for selecting appropriate approaches as well as optimizations with in a given approach. Due to lack of availability of real datasets, we use synthetic datasets (generated by the program developed at IBM Almaden) for performance evaluation. Nevertheless, the results are useful in understanding the approaches and can certainly be converted into meta-data for use by mining application.

The rest of the paper is organized as follows. Section 2 introduces the association rules and the apriori algorithm. Section 3 covers in detail the k-way join method for support counting and its basic optimizations along with their performance analysis. Section 4 considers the combinations of the optimizations discussed in section 3 and reports some of the results due to space limitations. The details can be found in [13] available on the web. In section 5 we have compiled the summary of results obtained from mining various datasets. We conclude and present the future work in section 6.

2   Association Rules

The problem of association rule mining was formally defined in [2]. In short, it can be stated as: Let I be the collection of all the items and D be the set of transactions. Let T be a single transaction involving some of the items from the set I. The association rule is of the form A $\Rightarrow$ B (where A and B are sets). If the support of itemset AB is 30%, it means "30% of all the transactions contain both the itemsets – itemset A and itemset B". And if the confidence of the rule A $\Rightarrow$ B is 70%, it means "70% of all the transactions that contain itemset A also contains itemset B". In this section, we discuss SQL92 formulation for the generic apriori algorithm that serves as the basis for our analysis. An association rule mining problem is broken down into two sub-problems: 1) select all the item combinations (itemsets) whose support is greater than the user specified minimum support. Such itemsets are called the frequent itemsets and 2) use the identified frequent itemsets to generate all rules that satisfy user specified confidence.

2.1   Apriori Algorithm

The apriori algorithm is based on the above-mentioned two steps: generate frequent itemsets and generate corresponding rules. Frequent itemsets of length k are generated in two steps. In the first step all the possible combinations of items, called the candidate itemsets (C_k) are generated. In the second step, support of each candidate itemset is counted and all those candidate itemsets, which have support values greater than the user specified minimum support value, form the set of frequent itemsets (F_k). The algorithm is depicted below.

```
F₁ = {frequent itemsets of length 1}
for (k = 2; Fₖ₋₁ ≠ 0; k++) do
      Cₖ = generate(Fₖ₋₁)
      for all transactions t ∈ D do
            Cₜ = subset(Cₖ, t)
            for all candidates, c ∈ Cₜ do
                  c.count++
            end for
      end for
      Fₖ = { c ∈ Cₖ | c.count ≥ minsup}
end for
Answer = ∪ₖ{Fₖ}
```

The generate function uses frequent itemsets of length k-1 to generate candidate itemsets of length k, while the subset function, produces only that subset of candidate itemsets from C_k which can be generated from the items bought in any transaction t.

2.2   Candidate Generation

In the kth pass, the set of candidate itemsets C_k is generated from the frequent itemset F_{k-1} as shown below. F_{k-1} is generated in the $(k-1)^{th}$ pass. Relations C_k and F_k have following attributes (item1, item2,..., itemk)

```
Insert        into Cₖ
Select        I₁.item₁, … ,I₁.itemₖ₋₁, I₂.itemₖ₋₁
From          Fₖ₋₁ I₁, Fₖ₋₁ I₂
Where         I₁.item₁ = I₂.item₁ and
                            :
              I₁.item ₖ₋₂ = I₂.itemₖ₋₂ and
              I₁.item ₖ₋₁ < I₂.itemₖ₋₁
```

The number of candidate itemsets generated by the above step can be reduced by deleting all itemsets $c \in C_k$, where some subset of c of length k-1 is not in F_{k-1}. This has been introduced in [2].

2.3   Support Counting

This is an important and most time-consuming part of the mining process. This step is needed to identify those candidate itemsets that are frequent.. The basic approach for support counting is that in any pass k, k copies of the input table are joined with the candidate itemsets C_k followed by a *group by* on the itemsets. The k copies of the input table are needed to compare the k items in the candidate itemset C_k with one item from each of the k-copies of the input table. The *group by* clause on the k items is done to identify all itemsets whose count is $\geq$ support value, as frequent itemsets. These frequent itemsets are then used in the rule generation phase. The tree diagram for support counting using k-way join approach is shown below [10], [11], [12].

3   Analysis of Basic K-Way Join Method and Its Optimizations

In this section we analyze the k-way join approach more closely. This section, also discusses a number of basic optimization and their combinations. The purpose of these optimizations and their analysis (along with performance evaluation) is to understand the impact of various optimizations on datasets having different characteristics (size, average transaction length, support, confidence, number of passes needed etc.) and to obtain heuristics that relate various optimization techniques and their effect on the characteristics of the input dataset. Though, not all optimizations always produce better timings, our belief is that the study of these optimizations can give us a better insight in formulating the metadata that can be used for making a mining-aware mining optimizer. We will here present the performance evaluation and the results obtained when datasets with different characteristics were mined using them.

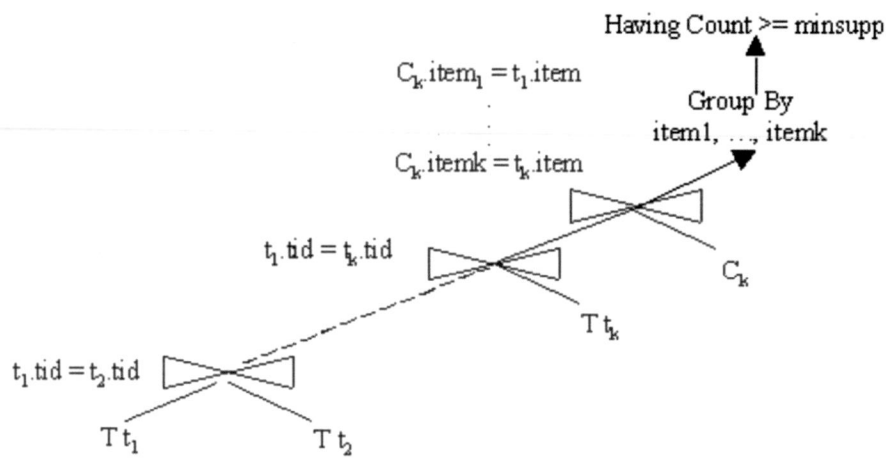

Fig. 1. Support counting by K-way join approach

3.1   Methodology for Experimental Evaluation

The results shown here are on datasets generated synthetically using the IBM's data-generator. The nomenclature of these datasets is of the form TxxIyyDzzzK. Where xx denotes the average number of items present per transaction. yy denotes the average support of each item in the dataset and zzzK denotes the total number of transactions in K (1000's). The experiments have been performed on Oracle 8i (installed on a Solaris machine with 384MB of RAM) and IBM DB2/UDB (over Windows NT with 256MB of RAM). Each experiment has been performed 4 times. The values from the first results are ignored so as to avoid the effect of the previous experiments and other database setups. The average of the next 3 results is taken and used for analysis. This is done so as to avoid any false reporting of time due to system overload or any other factors. For most of the experiments, we have found that the percentage difference of each run with respect to the average is less than one percent. Before feeding the input to the mining algorithm, if it is not in the (tid, item) format, it is converted to that format (by using the algorithm and the approach presented in [12]). On completion of the mining, the results are remapped to their original values. Since the time taken for mapping, rule generation and re-mapping the results to their original descriptions is not very significant, they are not reported.

For the purpose of reporting the experimental results in this paper, for most of the optimizations we have shown the results only for three datasets – T5I2D500K, T5I2D1000K and T10I4D100K. Wherever there is a marked difference between the results for Oracle and IBM DB2/UDB they are also shown; otherwise the result from anyone of the RDBMSs have been included.

3.2   Cost Analysis of the Basic K-Way Join (Kwj) Approach

Fig. 2 compares the time required for mining the relation T5I2D1000K on DB2, with break-up for each pass for support values of 0.20%, 0.15% and 0.10%, while Fig. 3 shows the same on Oracle. (On DB2, for support value of 0.10%, the experiment didn't complete even after running it for over 9 hrs). The analysis for time required for each pass shows that, of all the passes, second pass is most time consuming. This is true as in second pass $^{n}C_{2}$ (all combinations of two elements from frequent 1-itemsets) candidate itemsets are generated, where n is the cardinality of frequent-1 itemset.

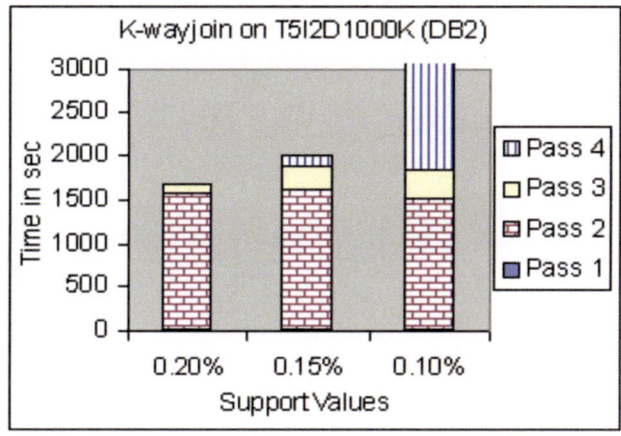

Fig. 2. K-way Join on T5I2D1000K (DB2)

Fig. 4 shows the time required for mining relation T10I4D100K for different support values on Oracle and Table 1 shows the number of candidate itemsets generated in respective passes, when different tables were mined with different support values. The analysis of the theses figures shows that for mining configuration, where the length of the largest frequent itemsets is small, the time required for support counting at higher passes is not very significant. This is because there is a great reduction in the size of the candidate itemset (C_k). However, for relations with long frequent itemsets, even though the cardinality of the C_k decreases with the increase in the number of passes, even then joining k-copies of input table for support counting at higher passes is quite significant.

In Kwj, for support counting of any pass k, the input table is joined k-times. Hence an obvious way to optimize this would be by reducing the cardinality of the input table. Section 3.3 discusses about this in more detail. Once again, if we analyze the first and the second pass, frequent itemsets of length 1 (F_1) are generated in pass 1. F_1 is then used to generate C_2, which is followed by support counting of C_2. An efficient way to get around with this time consuming process would be generating the frequent itemsets of length 2 (F_2) directly, by joining the input table with itself with the group-by on the items of the input table that have the same tid. This way Pass 1 can be

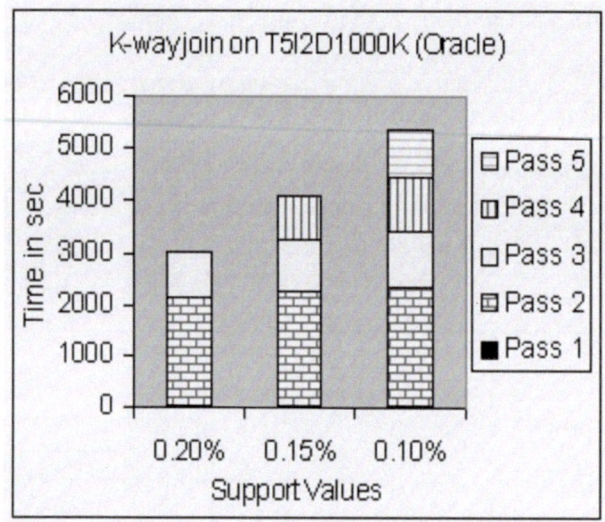

Fig. 3. K-way Join on T5I2D1000K (Oracle)

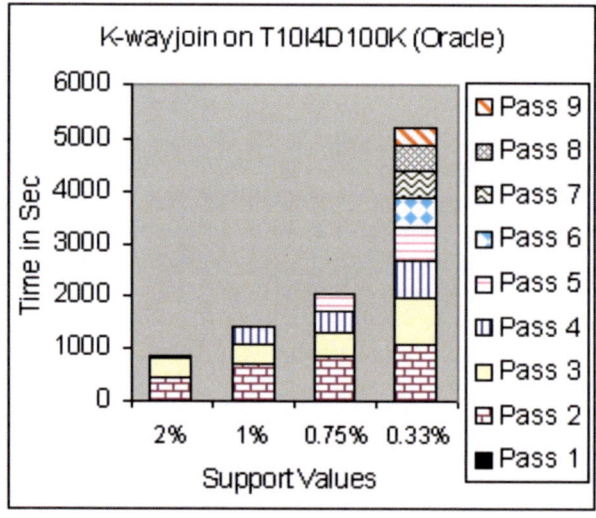

Fig. 4. K-Way Join on T10I4D100K (Oracle)

skipped all together (as there are no rules on F_1) and also there is no need for candidate generation for pass 2 as F_2 is generated directly by the above step. Section 3.4 discusses this second pass optimization in more detail.

Table 1. Number of Candidate Itemsets in different passes

	C_2	C_3	C_4	C_5	C_6	C_7	C_8	C_9
T5I2D500K. Support = 0.10%	307720	126	7	0	--	--	--	--
T5I2D1000K. Support = 0.10%	309291	127	61	0	--	--	--	--
T10I4D100K. Support = 0.75%	12470	65	3	0	--	--	--	--
T10I4D100K. Support = 0.33%	216153	2453	905	354	109	20	2	0

Let us compare the SQL tree for support counting (Fig. 1. Support counting by K-way join approach) for two successive passes, say pass 4 and pass 5. In the 4th pass C_4 is joined with 4 copies of input table, to identify all frequent itemsets of length 4. In the 5th pass, again input table is joined 4 times for determining the frequent itemsets of length 4 and then the support of 1-extensions of these frequent items, present as the fifth item in C_5, are counted by joining one more copy of the input table with C_5. Thus if all the frequent itemsets contained in any transaction is saved at the end of the pass 4, they can be used for support counting in pass 5, as frequent itemsets of length 5 are 1-extensions of these frequent itemsets of length 4. Section 3.5 discusses about this optimization and its effects.

3.3   Pruning the Input Table (Pi)

Smaller the size of the input table, the faster should be the join computation. Eliminating the records of those single itemsets from the input table, whose support is lower than the user specified minimum value, can reduce the size of the input table. Instead of deleting these tuples, a new relation, say, pruned input (T_f) is created to contain the tuples (transactions) of only frequent itemsets of length 1. This is done by generating F_1, as before. Then F_1 is joined with T on the "item" column, and tuples of only those items whose support $\geq$ user defined support value are inserted in T_f. The SQL for creating the pruned input table is given below:

```
Insert into Tf select t.tid, t.item
From            T t, F1 f
Where           t.item = f.item
```

Thus the overall cost of this optimization includes the cost of producing the pruned input table T_f + cost of support counting in every pass. The difference between basic Kwj and Pi is that, in Pi, an additional cost for materializing the pruned input table is involved. And then this pruned input table is used instead of the original input table in the joins for the support counting of every pass. The pruning of non-frequent 1-itemset is more effective with higher support values or for relations with a very large number of distinct items, which results in pruning out a large number of non-frequent 1-itemsets. Fig.5 shows the reduction in size of input table T5I2D1000K for different support values.

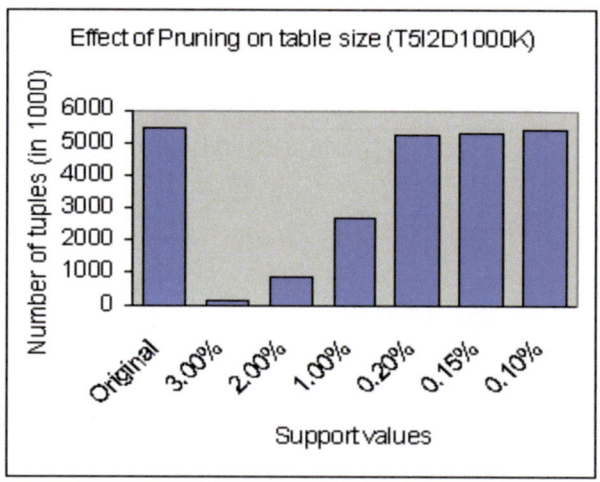

Fig. 5. Reduction in Table size due to Pruning

The reduction in the size of the input table is very marked for higher support values. But, pruning might not always end up in giving better performance. Fig.6 compares the total cost of mining the relation T5I2D1000K on oracle, using the pruned input (time for pruning also considered and is shown as "Ohead" in the figure) with the basic Kwj approach, for different support values. For higher support values, (3.0%, 2.0% and 1.0%), the total time taken is less when pruned input was used, but the reverse is true for lower support values. This is because for low support values, the reduction in the size of the input table is almost negligible; hence use of pruned input hardly has any effect on the running time of any pass, rather, there is an additional cost involved in generation of the pruned input. Because of this overhead, the overall time of using pruned input comes out more than the basic Kwj.

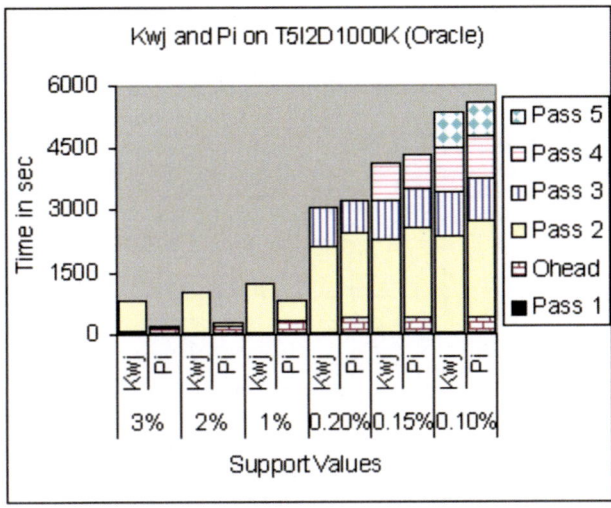

Fig. 6. K-way join and Pruned Input

3.4   Second Pass Optimization (Spo)

As indicated earlier and is apparent as well from the figures shown above that of all the passes, second pass is the most time consuming. In most of the cases, because of the immense size of C_2, the cost of support counting for C_2 is very high. In addition, for candidate sets of length 2, as all the subsets of length 1 are known to be frequent, there is no gain from pruning during the candidate generation. The process of generating F_1 then C_2 followed by its support counting phase can be replaced by directly generating F_2 by joining two copies of the input table. The SQL for this is as follows:

```
Insert into F₂     select t₁.item, t₂.item, count(*)
From               T t1, T t2
Where              t1.tid = t2.tid and t1.item < t2.item
Group by           t1.item, t2.item.
Having             count(*) > support
```

Fig. 7 compares the over all time required for mining table T5I2D500K using Kwj and Spo. For table T5I2D500K, the overall time required for mining is reduced by 3 to 4 times with this optimization alone.

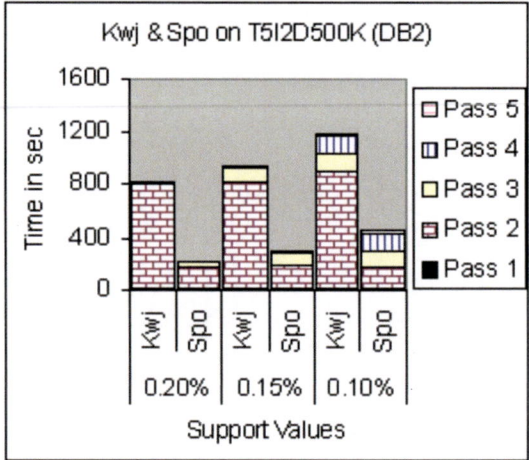

Fig. 7. K-way join and Second Pass Optimization

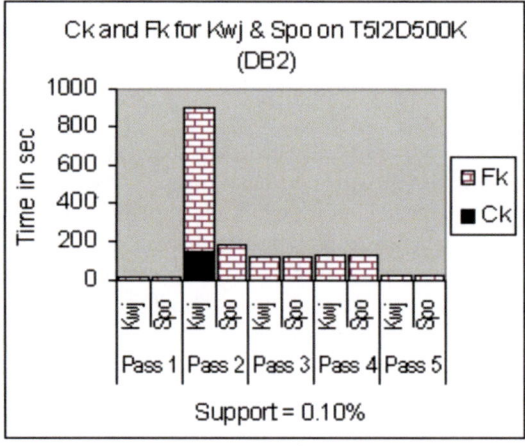

Fig. 8. Ck and Fk for Kwj and Spo

Fig. 8 compares the time taken for the candidate generation phase (C_k) and support counting phase (F_k) in each pass for the Kwj and the Spo. The values in Pass-2 of this figure show that the improvement in performance for Spo is due to savings on the join cost at two stages – during generation of C_2 and during generation of F_2. The saving in the former case is due to totally bypassing the generation of candidate itemsets C_2. For the latter case, in Spo, input table (T) is directly joined with itself, instead of joining three tables – C_2 and 2 copies of input table (as is done in second pass of Kwj), which results in decrease in the computation time for F_2.

3.5   Reuse of Item Combinations (Ric)

This optimization aims to reduce the cost of support counting by avoiding the join of k copies of input table with C_k. This is done by materializing the frequent itemsets obtained from a particular transaction in pass k-1 (F_{k-1}), and using it for support counting in the kth pass. This saves from redoing the same series of joins that were done in the previous pass, which proves to be very effective for cases where the length of the frequent itemset is large by avoiding large number of joins. So in k^{th} pass for support counting, a relation $Comb_k$, having the following attributes: tid, $item_1$, $item_2$, ..., $item_k$, is created. The tuples in $Comb_k$ is the result of the join between $Comb_{k-1}$, T and C_k to select all those transactions in T which contains 1-extensions to the frequent itemsets of length k-1 (F_{k-1}). Then F_k is generated from $Comb_k$ by grouping on k items ($item_1$, $item_2$, ..., $item_k$) and filtering those that don't satisfy the minimum support criteria. Due to space constraints the SQL formulation is not given here. Please refer to [13] for details.

The analysis of this optimization shows that instead of joining the input table k times, in any pass k, only 3 relations – C_k, T, and $Comb_{k-1}$ are joined. However, the downside of this approach is that, $Comb_{k-1}$ has to be materialized so that it can be used in the next pass.

Fig. 9 compares the total time taken to mine table T10I4D100K using Kwj and Ric for different support values on Oracle. Fig. 10 shows the same for DB2. For higher support values, the experiments run for less number of passes and hence the cost of support counting using the Kwj, does better than when $Comb_k$ is materialized for using it in the next pass. But for low support values, at higher passes, the cost of joining input table k-times with C_k turns out to be more costly than materializing $Comb_{k-1}$ and using it for support counting. In Fig. 10. , for support value of 0.75%, Kwj didn't complete (even after running for 9 hrs.), while the reuse of item combinations did. In Kwj, for support counting of the 3rd pass, 4 relations are joined - 3 copies of the input table and C_3, while in Ric just 3 relations are joined - $Comb_2$, T and C_2 to get $Comb_3$ and then group by on $Comb_3$ is done for F_3. As the size of these tables is huge and also there are more number of joins, the experiments (on DB2) in the former case, didn't complete.

4   Combinations of Basic Optimizations

Sections 3.3, 3.4 and 3.5 discussed, respectively, the use of pruned input, optimization of the second pass and reusing the item combinations generated in the previous pass. In this section we will discuss the optimization obtained by combining these optimizations.

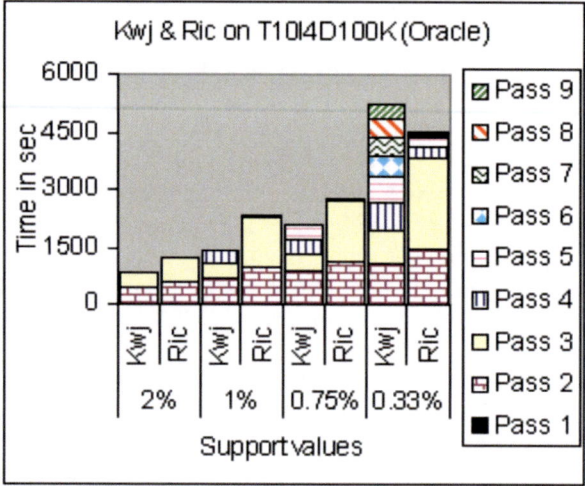

Fig. 9. Reuse of Item Combination (Oracle)

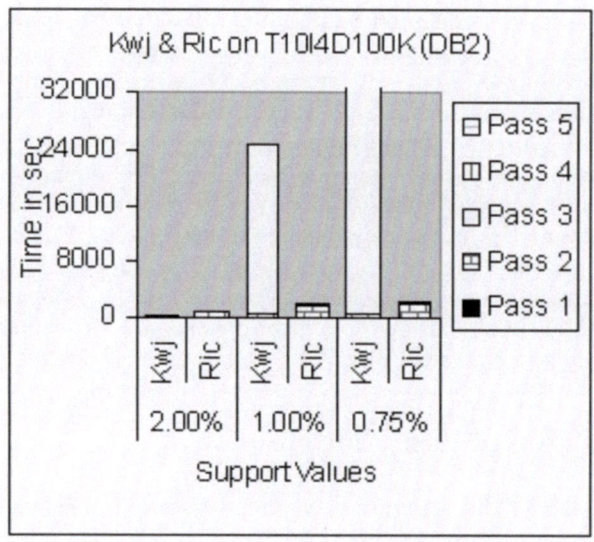

Fig. 10. Reuse of Item Combination (DB2)

4.1   Second Pass Optimization on Pruned Input (SpoPi)

As the Spo does results in some performance gain under all situations, but the same is not true with Pi, hence the overall performance obtained from this combination is limited by the overhead of pruning. For low support values, the overhead of building pruned input outweighs any performance gained due to optimization of the second pass. Hence at a low support value, SpoPi does better than when only pruned input is used, but its performance is worse than when only Spo is used. In all the experiments performed, the performance of this combination has not been very impressive, hence the details of this combination are not reported here, they can be seen in [13].

4.2   Reuse of Item Combinations on Pruned Input (RicPi)

This optimization is similar to the one discussed in the section 3.5, except that instead of using the input table as it is, non-frequent itemsets of length-1 are pruned out and then this pruned input table is used in all passes for joining with $Comb_{k-1}$ to produce $Comb_k$. The analysis of this combination also shows that almost nowhere it produced the added performance of both - (1) reusing the frequent itemsets generated in the previous pass and (2) use of pruned input for support counting. The overall performance for this combination is dominated either by the cost of building the pruned input at low support values or by the cost of materializing the $Comb_2$ (for using it in the next pass for support count) at high support values. This seems to be quite logical because, as seen earlier the effect of pruning dominates only for high support values and reuse of item combinations is effective for cases where the maximum length of the frequent itemset is large. But since for large support values, the maximum length of the frequent itemset is quite small, we never obtain the benefits of materializing the transactions with frequent itemsets of the previous pass. Similarly for low support values, where there is hardly any effect of pruning on the input table size, the overhead of pruning eclipses any time saved by reusing the item combinations. As the results of this combination too are not very impressive, we don't report them here. They can be found in [13].

4.3   Reuse of Item Combinations and Spo (RicSpo)

This section describes the effect of combining Spo with the optimization where frequent itemsets generated in the previous pass are materialized and used for support counting. As described in section 3.4 for Spo, first pass and candidate generation in second pass is skipped. Since in Spo, C_2 is not generated hence in RicSpo, instead of generating $Comb_2$, input table is joined thrice with C_3 to produce $Comb_3$ directly (C_3 is produced in the same way as is done in the Spo). And then for subsequent passes, the query is similar to one discussed in section 3.5. The SQL for generating $Comb_3$ directly is shown below:

```
Insert into Comb₃ select t₁.tid, t₁.item, t₂.item, t₃.item
From                  T t₁, T t₂, T t₃, C₃
Where                 t₁.item = C₃.item₁ and
                      t₂.item = C₃.item₂ and
                      t₃.item = C₃.item₃ and
                      t₁.tid = t₂.tid and
                            t₂.tid = t₃.tid
```

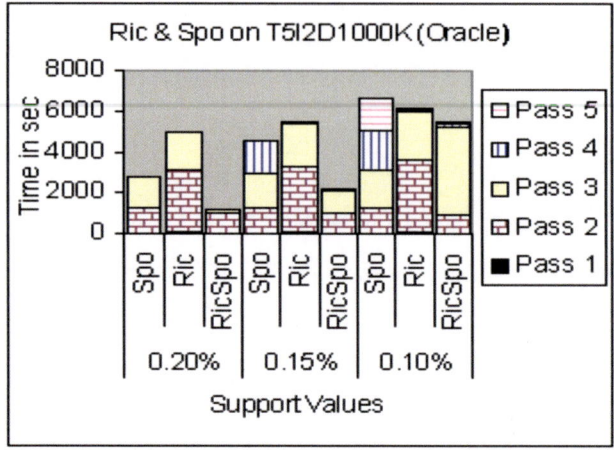

Fig. 11. Ric and Spo (Oracle)

Fig. 11 compares second pass optimization and reuse of frequent itemsets of the previous pass with their combination for table T5I2D1000K on Oracle. Fig.12 shows the same on DB2. As seen from these figures, in reuse of item combination, second pass takes most of the time. This is to materialize $Comb_2$, which is very expensive (Table 2 shows the number of tuples in $Comb_k$ for any pass-k for different support values).

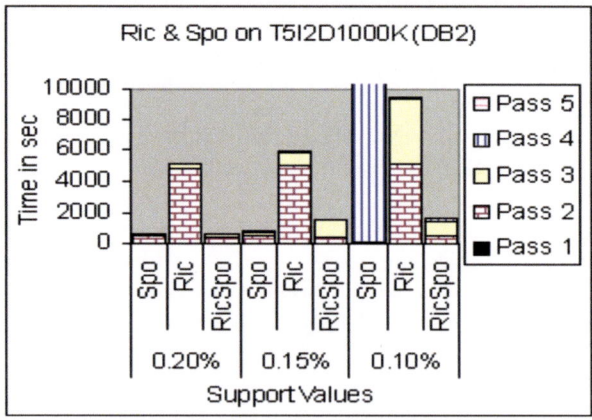

Fig. 12. Ric and Spo (DB2)

Hence the combined optimization does better than just the reuse of item combination as it skips the generation of C_2 and $Comb_2$. Thus for most of the experiments, this combination of optimization has resulted as one of the best optimization.

Table 2. Number of records in Comb$_k$ (in 1000's)

Table Characteristics	Number of tuples in 1000's		
	Comb$_2$	Comb$_3$	Comb$_4$
T5I2D1000K. Support = 0.20%	13267	0	0
T5I2D1000K. Support = 0.15%	13756	22	0
T5I2D1000K. Support = 0.10%	14165	111	6

4.4   Reuse of Item Combinations on Pruned Input with Spo (All)

This is the last optimization, which is basically the combination of all the three individual optimizations discussed in sections 3.3, 3.4 and 3.5. The SQL for this plan is similar to the one discussed in section 4.3, except that instead of using the input table as such, we first prune out all the non-frequent itemsets and then in place of input table use this pruned table for support counting. As seen above, optimizing the second pass does save some time in almost all cases and also the combination of second pass optimization with reuse of item combination has shown to be one of the most effective combination of optimizations, but at the same time use of pruned input with reuse of item combination has never given added performance. Out of the two sets of extreme sub-combinations - (1) reuse of item combination with pruned input and (2) reuse of item combination with second pass optimization, for lower support values, this combination of all individual optimizations is dominated by the former sub-combination, which eclipses any performance gained by the second sub-combination. Hence for most of the experiments, this combination, of all the optimizations has shown better performance than others, but worse than just the RicSpo. The details of this combination can be seen in [13].

5   Summary of Experimental Results

We have compiled the results obtained from mining different relations into a tabular form. This can also be made available to the mining optimizer that can use these values as a cue for choosing a particular optimization for mining a given input relation. Here it is assumed that we can easily figure out the characteristics of the input table.

Table 3 and Table 4 below, summarizes the ranking of various optimizations based on their performance and also the trend seen in the performance of these optimizations in mining three relations (T5I2D1000K, T5I2D500K and T10I4D100K) with different support values on Oracle and IBM DB2/UDB respectively.

Table 3. Trends in Oracle

RDBMS: ORACLE					
Table Name	Ranking	Support			
		0.20%	0.15%	0.10%	
T5I2D1000K	First	**RICSPO**	**RICSPO**	*KWJ*	
	Second	*ALL*	*ALL*	**RICSPO**	
	Last	RICPI	RICPI	RICPI	
T5I2D500K	First	**RICSPO**	**RICSPO**	SPO	
	Second	SPO	SPO	**RICSPO**	
	Last	RICPI	RICPI	RICPI	
		2.00%	1.00%	0.75%	0.33%
T10I4D100K	First	*ALL*	**RICSPO**	**RICSPO**	RIC
	Second	**PI**	*ALL*	*ALL*	SPO
	Last	RIC	RICPI	RICPI	**RICSPO**

For each of these relations, and for different support values, the summary table contains 3 columns. The first two columns specify the two best optimizations and the last column lists the worst optimization for that relation. The format is same for both – Oracle and IBM DB2/UDB. For the purpose of understanding how the meta-data might look, in Table 5 below, we provide a summary of results obtained from mining various other tables on both IBM DB2/UDB and Oracle. Because of the space constraint, their details are skipped. The focus of this summary table is to aid the optimizer in picking up the proper optimization based on a couple of easily determinable constraints. These constraints are: RDBMS to use (if there is a choice), the cardinality of the input table and if there is enough additional space to materialize the intermediate results.

Table 4. Trends in IBM DB2/UDB

RDBMS: DB2				
Table Name	Ranking	Supp = 0.20%	Supp = 0.15%	Supp = 0.10%
T5I2D1000K	First	**RICSPO**	SPO	**RICSPO**
	Second	SPO	**RICSPO**	*ALL*
	Last	RICPI	SPOPI	SPOPI
T5I2D500K	First	SPO	SPO	SPO
	Second	**RICSPO**	**RICSPO**	**RICSPO**
	Last	SPOPI	SPOPI	SPOPI
	Ranking	Supp = 2.00%	Supp = 1.00%	Supp = 0.75%
T10I4D100K	First	SPO	**RICSPO**	**RICSPO**
	Second	**RICSPO**	*ALL*	*ALL*
	Last	RIC	*KWJ*	*KWJ*

Table 5. Meta-data Table

Table Size T5I2Dzzz K	DB2		Oracle		Support Value
	Extra Space	No Extra Space	Extra Space	No Extra Space	
10K	RicSpo	Spo	RicSpo	Spo	S = 0.20%
	RicSpo	Spo	RicSpo	Spo	S = 0.15%
	RicSpo	Spo	Spo	Spo	S = 0.10%
50K	RicSpo	Spo	RicSpo	Spo	S = 0.20%
	Spo	Spo	RicSpo	Spo	S = 0.15%
	Spo	Spo	Spo	Spo	S = 0.10%
100K	RicSpo	Spo	RicSpo	Spo	S = 0.20%
	Spo	Spo	RicSpo	Spo	S = 0.15%
	Spo	Spo	Spo	Spo	S = 0.10%
500K	Spo	Spo	RicSpo	Spo	S = 0.20%
	Spo	Spo	RicSpo	Spo	S = 0.15%
	Spo	Spo	Spo	Spo	S = 0.10%
1000K	RicSpo	Spo	RicSpo	Spo	S = 0.20%
	Spo	Spo	RicSpo	Spo	S = 0.15%
	Spo	Spo	Kwj	Kwj	S = 0.10%

6   Conclusions and Future Work

In this paper, we have explored the various optimizations and their combinations for the SQL–92 implementation of the basic K-way join (Kwj) for support counting phase of the association rule mining. We have experimentally compared these optimizations in an attempt to provide better insight to the effect of these optimizations on the total mining time for relations with varying characteristics and changing support values. Although combination of individual optimizations makes sense intuitively, our analysis and performance evaluation clearly indicates that it is not a given. Also, depending upon the storage available different choices of optimization may have to be used by the mining optimizer.

From most of these experimental results it seems that the best optimization is the reuse of item combinations or reuse of item combinations combined with second pass optimization when we have enough space for materializing the intermediate relations (Comb$_k$). But when additional space is an issue, then second pass optimization comes out as the best approach. On the other hand for low support values, use of pruned input along with reuse of item combinations was found to be the worst combination for most of the input tables.

The work presented here tries to build this metadata by considering the different optimizations to the basic k-way join approach to association rule mining. A natural extension to this work would be trying to mix these optimizations at different passes. The other possibility would be to use the SQL-OR features provided by these commercial RDBMS's and develop association rule mining algorithms to use them efficiently. We can then try evaluating these mixed approaches and the SQL-OR based optimizations with the current SQL92 based implementations and if they are comparable, we can include them in the meta-data.

References

1. Agrawal, R., T. Imielinski, and A. Swami. Mining Association Rules between sets of items in large databases. in ACM SIGMOD 1993.
2. Agrawal, R. and R. Srikant. Fast Algorithms for mining association rules. in 20th Int'l Conference on Very Large Databases (VLDB). 1994.
3. Savasere, A., E. Omiecinsky, and S. Navathe. An efficient algorithm for mining association rules in large databases. in 21st Int'l Cong. on Very Large Databases (VLDB). 1995. Zürich, Switzerland.
4. Shenoy, P., et al. Turbo-charging Vertical Mining of Large Databases. in ACM SIGMOD Int'l Conference on Management of Data. 2000. Dallas.
5. Han, J., J. Pei, and Y. Yin. Mining Frequent Patterns wihtout Candidate Generation. in ACM SIGMOD 2000. Dallas.
6. Houtsma, M. and A. Swami. Set-Oriented Mining for Association Rules in Relational Databases. in 11th ICDE, 1995.
7. Han, J., et al. DMQL: A data mining query language for relational database. in ACM SIGMOD workshop on research issues on data mining and knowledge discovery. 1996. Montreal.
8. Meo, R., G. Psaila, and S. Ceri. A New SQL-like Operator for Mining Association Rules. in Pro. of the 22nd VLDB Conference. 1996 India.
9. Agrawal, R. and K. Shim, *Developing tightly-coupled Data Mining Applications on a Relational Database System*. 1995, IBM Almaden Research Center: San Jose, California.
10. Sarawagi, S., S. Thomas, and R. Agrawal. Integrating Association Rule Mining with Rekational Database System: Alternatives and Implications. in ACM SIGMOD 1998. Seattle, Washington.
11. Thomas, S., Architectures and optimizations for integrating Data Mining algorithms with Database Systems, in CSE. 1998, University of Florida.
12. Dudgikar, M., A Layered Optimizer or Mining Association Rules over RDBMS, in CSE Department. 2000, University of Florida: Gainesville.
13. Mishra, P. *Evaluation of K-way Join and its variants for Association Rule Mining*. MS Thesis 2002, Information and Technology Lab and CSE Department at UT Arlington, TX.

External Sorting with On-the-Fly Compression

John Yiannis and Justin Zobel

School of Computer Science and Information Technology
RMIT University, Melbourne, Australia, 3000
{jyiannis,jz}@cs.rmit.edu.au

Abstract. Evaluating a query can involve manipulation of large volumes of temporary data. When the volume of data becomes too great, activities such as joins and sorting must use disk, and cost minimisation involves complex trade-offs. In this paper, we explore the effect of compression on the cost of external sorting. Reduction in the volume of data potentially allows costs to be reduced – through reductions in disk traffic and numbers of temporary files – but on-the-fly compression can be slow and many compression methods do not allow random access to individual records. We investigate a range of compression techniques for this problem, and develop successful methods based on common letter sequences. Our experiments show that, for a given memory limit, the overheads of compression outweigh the benefits for smaller data volumes, but for large files compression can yield substantial gains, of one-third of costs in the best case tested. Even when the data is stored uncompressed, our results show that incorporation of compression can significantly accelerate query processing.

1   Introduction

Relational database systems, and more recent developments such as document management systems and object-oriented database systems, are used to manage the data held by virtually every organisation. Typical relational database systems contain vast quantities of data, and each table in a database may be queried by thousands of users simultaneously. However, the increasing capacity of disks means that more data can be stored, escalating query evaluation costs. With the amount of data being so large, each stage of the entire storage hierarchy of disk, controller caches, main-memory, and processor caches becomes a bottleneck. Processors are not keeping pace with growth in data volumes [1], particularly for tasks such as joins and sorts where the costs are superlinear in the volume of data to be processed.

In this paper we focus on reducing the costs of external sorting through making better use of the storage hierarchy. A current problem is that tens to hundreds of processor cycles are required for a memory access, and tens of millions for a disk access, a trend that is continuing: processor speeds are increasing at a much faster rate than that of memory and disk technology [2]. Thus, during an external sort, total processing time is only a tiny fraction of elapsed time.

A. James, B. Lings, M. Younas (Eds.): BNCOD 2003, LNCS 2712, pp. 115–130, 2003.

Most of the time is spent writing temporary files containing sorted runs to disk, then reading and merging the runs to produce the final sort; each run is the result of sorting one buffer of data. This imbalance, where disk activity dominates, can be partly redressed through use of compression.

For external sorting, it should in principle be possible to use spare cycles to compress the data on the fly, thus reducing the number of runs. However, a compression technique for this application must meet strong constraints. First, in contrast to adaptive compression techniques, which treat the data as a continuous stream and change the codes as the data is processed, it must allow the records to be accessed individually and reordered. Second, in contrast to standard semi-static techniques, the data cannot be fully pre-inspected to determine a model. Third, the coding and decoding stages must be of similar speed to the transfer rate for uncompressed data. Last, the compression model must be small, so that it does not consume too much of the buffer space needed for sorting. No standard technique meets these constraints.

We propose that compression proceed by allowing pre-inspection of the first buffer-load of data, and building a model based on this data alone. This partial (and probably non-optimal) model can then be used to guide compression and decompression of each subsequent run. In this framework we test several compression techniques: canonical Huffman coding and two new methods that we have developed, both of which are based on identifying the commonest letter sequences and representing them in computationally efficient bytewise codes. Our experiments show that these methods reduce sorting costs for large files. Data compression is therefore an effective means of increasing bandwidth – not by increasing physical transfer rates, but by increasing the information density of transferred data – and can relieve the I/O bottlenecks found in many high performance database management systems [3].

Previous research [4,5,6,7,8,9] has shown the benefits of decompressing data on the fly where the data is stored compressed. However, it was found [9] that compression on the fly had significantly higher processor costs, indicating that compression is only beneficial to read-only queries. Our results show, in contrast to previous work, that compression is useful even when the data is stored uncompressed.

2   Compression in Retrieval Systems

The value of compression in communications is well-known: it reduces the cost of transmitting a stream of data through limited-bandwidth channels. Much of the research into compression has focused on this environment, in which the order of the data does not change and pre-inspection of the data is not necessarily available, leading to the development of high-performance *adaptive* techniques. Compression depends on the presence of a *model* that describes the data and guides the coding process. A model is in principle a set of symbols and probabilities; in adaptive compression, the model is changed with each symbol encountered.

Compression is achieved by using short codes for highly probable symbols, and longer codes for rarer symbols.

Adaptive techniques are largely inapplicable to the database environment, in which the stored data is typically a bag of independent records that can be retrieved or manipulated in any order. In such applications, the only option is to use *semi-static* compression, in which the model is fixed after some training on the data to be compressed, so that the code allocated to a symbol does not change during the compression process. (Adaptation can be used while a record is being compressed [10], but at the start of the next record it is necessary to revert to the original model.) Further difficulties are that the data changes as records are added, modified, or deleted; that the volume of memory available to store a compression model is very much smaller than the volume of data to be compressed, a situation that is likely to lead to poor compression; that the presence of a compression model reduces the buffer space available to evaluate the query; and that coding and decoding must have low processor overhead so as not to eliminate the benefits of reduced data transfer times.

The best-known semi-static compression technique is zero-order frequency modeling coupled with canonical Huffman coding, in which the frequency of each symbol (which might be a byte, Unicode character, character-pair, English word, and so on) is counted, then a Huffman code is allocated based on the frequency. In canonical Huffman coding, the tree is not stored and decompression is much faster than traditional implementations [11,12].

Semi-static compression has been successfully integrated into text information retrieval systems, resulting in savings in both space requirements and query evaluation costs [12,13,14,15,16]. The compression techniques used are relatively simple – Huffman coding for text, and integer coding techniques [15] for indexes – but the savings are dramatic. Index compression in particular is widely used in commercial systems, from search engines such as Google to content managers such as TeraText. Moreover, integer coding is extremely fast. We have shown [14] that even the cost of transferring data from main-memory to the on-processor cache can be reduced through appropriate use of compression based on elementary byte-wise codes.

However, compression has not traditionally been used in commercial database systems [4,7], and has been undervalued in query processing research [3]. Earlier papers investigated the benefits of compression in database query evaluation theoretically [6,7,8], and only in the last few years have researchers reported compression being incorporated into database systems [4,5,9].

Most of the research in this area has focused on reducing storage and query processing costs when data is held compressed. Graefe et al. [6] recommend compressing attributes individually, employing the same compression scheme for all attributes of a domain. Ng et al. [7] describe a page-level compression scheme based on a lossless vector quantisation technique. However, this scheme is only applicable to discrete finite domains where the attribute values are known in advance. Ray et al. [8] compared several coding techniques (Huffman, arithmetic, LZW, and run-length) at varying granularity (file, page, record, and attribute).

They confirm the intuition that attribute-level compression gives poorer compression, but allows random access.

Goldstein et al. [5] described a page-level compression algorithm that allows decompression at the field level. However, like the scheme described by Ng et al. [7], this technique is only useful for records with low cardinality fields. Westmann et al. [9] used compression at the attribute level. For numeric fields they used null suppression and encoding of the resulting length of the compressed integer [17]. For strings they used a simple variant of dictionary-based compression. This is particularly effective if a field can only take a limited number of values. For example, a field that can only take the values "male" and "female" could be represented by a single bit which could then be used to look up the decompressed value of the field in the dictionary. They saw a reduction in query times for read-only queries, but significant performance penalties for insert and modify operations. Chen et al. [4] used the same scheme as Westmann et al. for numerical attributes, and developed a new hierarchical semi-static dictionary-based encoding scheme for strings. They also developed a number of compression-aware query optimization algorithms. Their results for read-only queries showed a substantial improvement in query performance over existing techniques. A consensus from this work is that, for efficient query processing, the compression granularity should be small, allowing random access to the required data and thereby minimising unnecessary decompression of data; and the compression scheme should be lightweight, that is, have low processor costs, so as not to eliminate the benefits of reduced data transfer times

When examining the benefits of compression, Westmann et al. [9] saw that compression of a tuple had significantly higher processor costs than decompression, and so did not believe that compression could improve the performance of online transaction processing (OLTP) applications. All the other papers presupposed a compressed database, so the only compression-related cost involved in query resolution was the decompression of data.

For query processing, compression has value in addition to improved I/O performance, because decompression can often be delayed until a relatively small data set is determined. Exact-match comparisons can be on compressed data. During sorting, the number of records in memory and thus per run is larger, leading to fewer runs and possibly fewer merge levels [3].

3   External Sorting

External sorting is used when the data does not fit into available memory. It is of general value for sorting large files, but is of particular value in the context of databases, where a machine may be shared amongst a large number of users and queries, and per-query buffer space is limited. External sorting has two phases [18,19], as below. The process assumes that a fixed-size buffer is available, which is used for sorting in the first phase and for merging in the second. The process is illustrated in Figure 1, and is described in detail by Knuth [20].

Phase 1: Process buffer-sized amounts of data in turn. The following is repeated as many times as necessary:

1. Fill the buffer with records from the relation to be sorted.
2. Sort the records in memory.
3. Write records in sorted order into new blocks, forming one sorted run.

Phase 2: Merge all the sorted runs into a single sorted list, repeating until all runs have been processed:

1. Divide input buffer space amongst the runs, giving per-run buffers, and fill these with blocks from runs.
2. Using a heap, find the smallest key among the first remaining record in each buffer, then move the corresponding record to the first available position of the output buffer.
3. If the output buffer is full, write it to disk and empty the output buffer.
4. If the input buffer from which the smallest key was just taken is now exhausted, fill the input buffer from the same run. If no blocks remain in the run, then leave the buffer empty and do not consider keys from that run in any further sorting

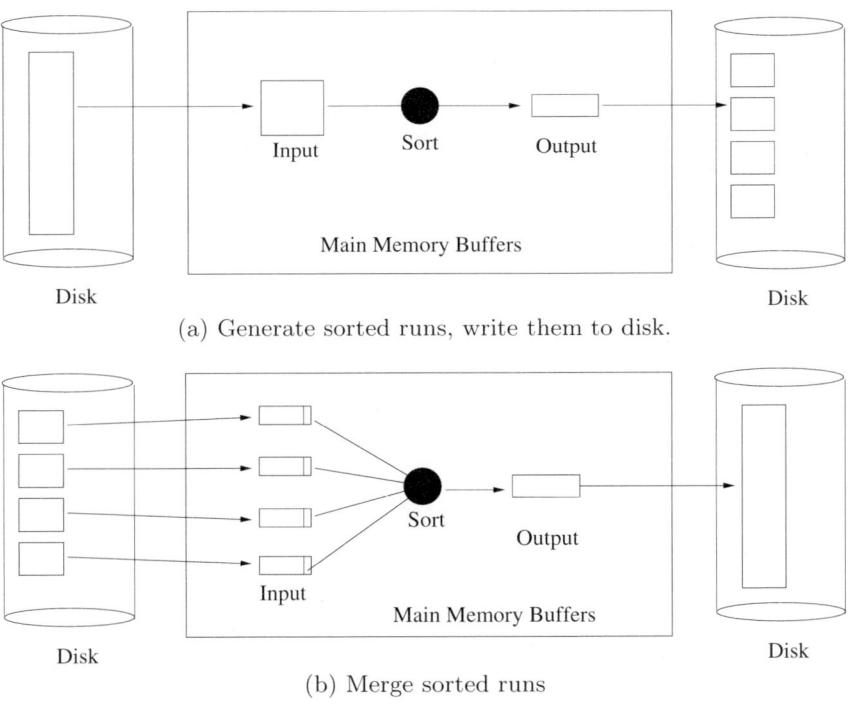

(a) Generate sorted runs, write them to disk.

(b) Merge sorted runs

Fig. 1. A simple external sort, with sorted blocks of records written to intermediate runs that are then merged to give the final result.

There are many variants on these algorithms. One is that, with a large number of runs, there can be housekeeping problems for the operating system, and the per-run buffers may become too small. A solution is then to merge the runs hierarchically, which however incurs significant penalties in data transfer, and should be avoided if at all possible. The Unix command-line sort utility takes this approach. (We do not test hierarchical merging in our experiments.) Another variant is that, if the merged results are to be written to disk, they can be written in-place; in the context of database query processing, however, it is often the case that the results are immediately used and discarded.

4   External Sorting with Compression

By incorporating compression into the sort algorithm, we aim to reduce the time taken to sort due to better use of memory, reduced transfer costs, and generation of fewer runs. The two key questions to answer when integrating compression into external sorting are, first, at what stage should the data be compressed, and, second, what compression technique to use.

Considering the first of the key questions, compression could be used simply to speed memory-to-disk transfers, by compressing runs after they have been sorted and decompressing them as they are retrieved. This approach has the advantage that high-performance adaptive compression techniques could be used, but also has disadvantages. In particular, it does not allow reduction in the number of runs generated, and at merge time a separate compression model must be used for each run.

The alternative is to compress the data as it is loaded into the buffer, prior to sorting. This allows better use to be made of the buffer; reduces the number of runs; and, since semi-static compression must be used, the same model applies to all runs. However, the compression is unlikely to be as effective. Nonetheless, given the cost of adaptive compression and the advantages of reducing the number of runs – such as increasing the buffer space available per run and reducing disk thrashing – it is this alternative that we have explored in our experiments.

In this approach, external sorting with compression proceeds as follows. Referring to Figure 2, assume that we have an input buffer of size A and an output buffer of size B, and that compression model size is M.

Phase 1: Build the compression model.
>The arrangement of buffers in shown in Figure 2(a). The input buffer has capacity $A - M$ for records.
> 1. Fill input buffer with records.
> 2. Build a model based on the symbol frequencies in these records.

Phase 2A: Generate the first compressed run.
> 1. Sort the keys of the records in the input buffer.
> 2. In sorted order, compress the records then write them to disk as a sorted run.

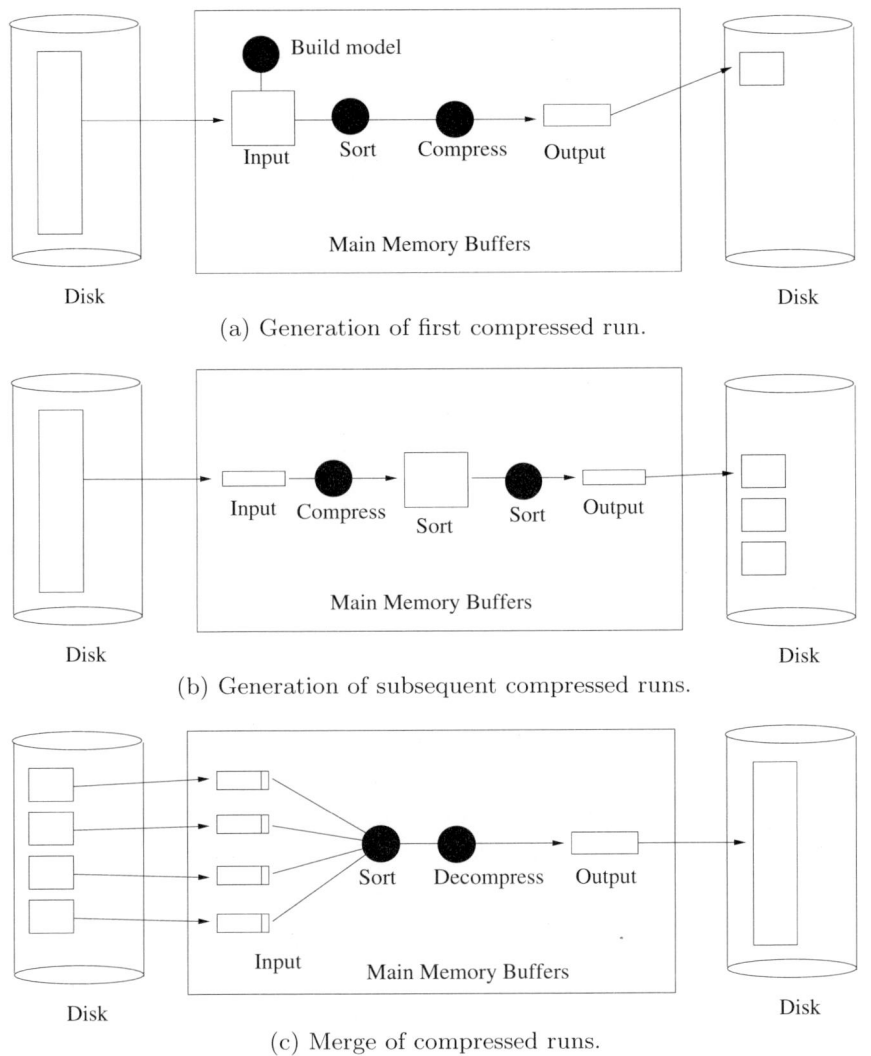

(a) Generation of first compressed run.

(b) Generation of subsequent compressed runs.

(c) Merge of compressed runs.

Fig. 2. External sorting with compression. The first stage is using the initial data to determine a model. Then runs are generated and merged as before, but compression is used to increase the number of records per run.

Phase 2B: Generate the remaining compressed runs.

The arrangement of buffers is shown in Figure 2(b); note that the data can no longer be read directly into a buffer for sorting, as it must first be compressed. The input and output buffers are of size $B/2$ each, and the sort buffer is of size $A - M$.

Repeat the following until all data has been processed:

1. Fill the input buffer with data.

2. Compress each record in the input buffer, then write it to the sort buffer. Continue until the sort buffer is full, reloading the input buffer as necessary.

3. Sort the records in the sort buffer.

4. In sorted order, write the compressed records to disk, forming one run.

Phase 3: Merge all the runs into a single sorted list.

The arrangement of buffers in shown in Figure 2(c). The input buffer is of size $A - M$, the output buffer is of size B. Note that the model required for decoding may be smaller than that required for encoding.

1. Divide the input buffer space amongst the runs and fill with data from the compressed runs.

2. Find the smallest key among the first remaining record in each buffer, and move the corresponding record to the first available position of the output block and decompress.

3. If the output buffer is full, write it to disk and reinitialise.

4. If the input buffer from which the smallest key was taken is exhausted, read from the same run and fill the same input buffer. If no blocks remain in the run, then leave the buffer empty and do not consider keys from that run in any further sorting.

In this algorithm, the sort key must be left uncompressed, and to simplify data management each compressed record should be prefixed with a bytelength. In comparing sorting techniques, each should use the same fixed amount of buffer space. If compression is not used, all the buffer space is available for sorting. For the compression-based sort algorithms, the buffer space available for sorting will be reduced by the memory required by the compression model.

5   Compression Techniques for External Sorting

The second key question of this research program is choice of compression technique. As outlined earlier, "off the shelf" compression systems (with one exception, XRAY, discussed below) do not satisfy the specific constraints of this application.

Several observations can be made. We need to investigate semi-static coding techniques that can be used in conjunction with a model based on inspection of only part of the data; if some symbol does not occur in this part of the data, it is nonetheless necessary that it have a code. Bitwise or bytewise codes are much faster than arithmetic coding [12], which is too slow for this application. Bytewise codes are much faster than bitwise codes [14], but may lead to poor compression efficiency. Both coding and decoding must be highly efficient: for example, given a symbol it is necessary to find its code extremely fast. Zero-order models are an obvious choice, because higher-order models lead to high symbol probabilities – and thus poor compression efficiency – with bitwise or bytewise codes (for a given model size). And model size must be kept small.

In view of these observations, Huffman coding is one choice of coding technique, based on a model built on symbol frequencies observed in the first bufferload of data. Bytewise codes are another option. These are discussed below. Another choice would be to use XRAY [21], in which an initial block of data is used to train up a model. Each symbol, including all unique characters, is then allocated a bitwise code. XRAY provides high compression efficiency and fast decompression; in both respects it is superior to gzip on text data, for example, even though the whole file is compressed with regard to one model. (In gzip, a new model is built for each successive block of data. Compression efficiency depends on block size, which is around 100 Kb in standard configurations; with small blocks no size reduction is achieved.) However, the training process is much too slow. Development of new XRAY-based compression techniques for this application is a topic for further research.

Likely buffer sizes are a crucial factor in design of algorithms for this application. We have assumed that tens of megabytes are a reasonable minimum volume for sorting of data of up to gigabytes; in our experiments we report on performance with 18.5 Mb and 37 Mb buffers. In this context, model sizes need to be restricted to at most a couple of megabytes.

Huffman Coding of Bigrams

In compression, it is necessary to choose a definition of symbol. Using individual characters as symbols gives poor compression; using all trigrams (sequences of three distinct characters) consumes too much buffer space. Using variable-length symbols requires an XRAY-like training process. We therefore chose to use *bigrams*, or all character pairs, as our symbols, giving an alphabet size of 2^{16}. The amount of memory required for the model is approximately 800 Kb (528 Kb for the decode part and 264 Kb for the additional encode part).

Huffman coding yields an optimal bitwise code for such a model. Standard implementations of Huffman coding are slow; we used canonical Huffman coding, with the implementation of Moffat and Turpin [22].

Bytewise Bigram Coding

Bitwise Huffman codes provide a reasonable approximation to symbol probabilities; a symbol with a 5-bit code, for example, has a probability of approximately 1 in 32. Bytewise codes can be emitted and decoded much more rapidly, but do not approximate the probabilities as closely, and thus have poorer compression efficiency. However, their speed makes them an attractive option.

One possibility is to use radix-256 Huffman coding. However, given that the model is based on partial information, it is attractive to use simple, fast approximations to this approach – in particular, the bytewise codes that we have found to be highly efficient in other work [14]. In these codes, a non-negative integer is represented by a series of bytes. One flag bit in each byte is reserved for indicating whether the byte is final or has a successor; the remaining bits are used for the integer. Thus the values 0 to $2^7 - 1$ can be represented in a single byte, 2^7 to $2^{14} - 1$ in two bytes, and so on.

Using these bytewise codes, the calculation of codes for bigrams can be dispensed with. The bigrams are simply sorted from most to least frequent and held in an array, and each bigrams's array index is its code. The first 2^7 or 128 most frequent bigrams are encoded in one byte, the next 2^{14} are be encoded in two bytes, and so on.

This scheme is simple and fast, but does have the disadvantage that compression can no more than halve the data size, regardless of the bigram probabilities, whereas Huffman coding could in principle provide reduction by around a factor of 16 (ignoring the uncompressed sort key and record length). The model sizes are identical to those for Huffman coding of bigrams above.

Bytewise Common-Quadgram Coding

To achieve better compression than is available with bigrams, we need to include more information in each symbol. Longer character sequences can yield better compression, but models based on complete sets of trigrams and quadgrams are too large. Another approach is to model common grams and use individual characters to represent other letter sequences. In a 32-bit architecture, it is efficient to process 4-byte sequences, and thus we explored a compression regime based on quadgrams and individual characters.

Because buffer space is limited, we cannot examine all quad-grams and choose only the commonest. As a heuristic, our alphabet is the first L quadgrams observed, together with all possible 256 single characters. We use a hash table with a fast hash function [23] to accumulate and count the first L overlapping quadgrams, and simultaneously count all character frequencies. The symbols – quadgrams and characters together – are then sorted by decreasing frequency, and indexed by bytewise codes as for bytewise bigram coding. This scheme is not perfect; for example, "ther" and "here" may both be common, but they often overlap, and if one is coded the other isn't. Determining an ideal set of quad grams is almost certainly NP-hard. However, the frequencies are in any case only an approximation, as only part of the data has been inspected. Also, in the presence of overlap, choosing which quadgram to code (rather than greedily coding the leftmost) can improve compression, but is slower. We use the simple greedy approach.

We varied L for the two buffer sizes tested, using $L = 2^{16}$ for the 18.5 Mb buffer and $L = 2^{17}$ for the 37 Mb buffer. The amount of memory required for the model is approximately 1.8 Mb (528 Kb for the decode part and 1.3 Mb for the encode part) or 3.0 Mb (528 Kb for the decode part and 2.5 Mb for the encode part). As for bigram coding, the commonest 2^7 symbols are represented in a single byte.

Coding then proceeds as follows. If the current four characters from the input form a valid quadgram, its code is emitted, and the next four characters are fetched. Otherwise, the code for the first character is emitted, and the next character is fetched. Decoding proceeds by replacing successive codes by the corresponding symbols, which can be characters or quadgrams. We observed in our experiments that about two-thirds of the output codes represented quadgrams.

6   Results

To test the effect of compression on external sorting, we implemented a fast external sorting routine, and added as options the three compression schemes described above. Runs were sorted with the best implementation of sorting we able to locate; as part of a separate project we are investigating high-performance sorting algorithms [24,25].

We are confident that the implementation is of high quality. For example, on the same data and with similar parameters, the Unix sort utility takes almost twice as long (or four times as long to sort on strings, for experiments not reported here). Two buffer sizes were used. The larger was 37 Mb, chosen as 36 Mb for data plus 1 Mb for housekeeping; the smaller was half that, 18.5 Mb. These choices were arbitrary.

For data, we required a large number of records representing a realistic task. We used a log derived from a web cache, in which each line includes information such as file size, time and date, and HTML page request. Data volumes tested ranged from 100 Mb to 10 Gb of distinct records. The task was to sort these on one of the numerical fields.

All experiments were carried out on an Intel 1 GHz Pentium III with 512 Mb of memory running the Linux operating system. Other processes and disk activity were minimised during experiments, that is, the machine was under light load.

Tables 1 and 2 show the effect that incorporating compression into external sorting has on elapsed time and temporary disk requirements. The "build model" time is the time to determine the model. The "generate runs" time is the time to read in the data and write out all the runs. The "merge runs" time is the time to read in and merge the runs and write out the result. The total sort times are illustrated in Figure 3, including additional data points.

These results show that, as the volume of data being sorted grows – or as the amount of buffer space available decreases – compression becomes increasingly effective in reducing the overall sort time. The gains are due to reduced disk transfer, disk activity, and merging costs, which can clearly outweigh the increased processor cost incurred by compression and decompression of the data. In the best case observed, with an 18.5 Mb buffer on 10 Gb of data, total time is reduced by a third. The computationally more expensive methods, such as Huffman coding and common-quadgram coding, are slow for the smaller data sets, where the disk and merging costs are a relatively small component of the total. (For a given buffer size, the cost of building each run is more or less fixed, and thus run construction cost is linear in data size; merge costs are superlinear in data size, as there is a $\log K$ search cost amongst K runs for each record merged. Use of hierarchical merge and other similar strategies does not affect the asymptotic complexity of the merge phase.) However, because Huffman coding

Table 1. Results for sorting with 18.5 Mb of buffer space, using no compression and using three alternative compression techniques. Results shown include time to sort and temporary space required.

	No compression	Huffman	Bigram	Quadgram
Build model (sec)	—	0.34	0.26	2.84
Generate runs (sec)	10.62	14.37	11.29	15.69
Merge runs (sec)	12.85	19.31	14.99	13.27
Total time to sort (sec)	23.47	34.02	26.54	31.80
Comparative (%)	100.0	145.0	113.1	135.5
Number of runs	6	5	5	5
Size of runs (Gb)	0.101	0.066	0.078	0.057
Comparative (%)	100.0	64.6	76.5	56.5

(a) Results for sorting 100 Mb of data with 18.5 Mb of buffer space

	No compression	Huffman	Bigram	Quadgram
Build model (sec)	—	0.33	0.26	2.84
Generate runs (sec)	109.23	134.49	115.68	146.83
Merge runs (sec)	176.24	197.58	161.82	142.09
Total time to sort (sec)	285.47	332.41	277.76	291.76
Comparative (%)	100.0	116.4	97.3	102.2
Number of runs	56	39	46	36
Size of runs (Gb)	0.976	0.641	0.757	0.561
Comparative (%)	100.0	65.7	77.6	57.5

(b) Results for sorting 1 Gb of data with 18.5 Mb of buffer space

	No compression	Huffman	Bigram	Quadgram
Build model (sec)	—	0.34	0.26	2.83
Generate runs (sec)	1305.25	1562.52	1262.95	1699.38
Merge runs (sec)	6140.86	4736.35	4769.87	3237.10
Total time to sort (sec)	7446.11	6299.21	6033.08	4939.32
Comparative (%)	100.0	84.6	81.0	66.3
Number of runs	568	394	462	372
Size of runs (Gb)	9.921	6.584	7.742	5.848
Comparative (%)	100.0	66.4	78.0	58.9

(c) Results for sorting 10 Gb of data with 18.5 Mb of buffer space

and common-quadgram coding achieve greater compression than does bigram coding, the sort times decrease faster as database size grows. This is most noticeable in the upper graph in Figure 3, which shows that, for smaller volumes of data, compression and decompression speed is the dominating factor; and that at larger volumes, the amount of compression achieved becomes the dominating factor in determining the sort time.

Despite the greater compression achieved by Huffman coding in comparison to bigram coding, the latter is always faster. This confirms that bytewise codes are much more efficient, with the loss of compression efficiency more than com-

Table 2. Results for sorting with 37 Mb of buffer space, using no compression and using three alternative compression techniques. Results shown include time to sort and temporary space required.

	No compression	Huffman	Bigram	Quadgram
Build model (sec)	—	0.66	0.51	6.02
Generate runs (sec)	8.39	13.41	12.17	15.13
Merge runs (sec)	12.79	19.37	15.09	13.20
Total time to sort (sec)	21.18	33.44	27.77	34.36
Comparative (%)	100	157.9	131.1	162.2
Number of runs	3	3	3	3
Size of runs (Gb)	0.101	0.0652	0.0773	0.0561
Comparative (%)	100	64.3	76.3	55.3

(a) Results for sorting 100 Mb of data with 37 Mb of buffer space

	No compression	Huffman	Bigram	Quadgram
Build model (sec)	—	0.66	0.52	5.99
Generate runs (sec)	108.67	146.36	126.43	143.71
Merge runs (sec)	168.81	213.62	177.93	155.36
Total time to sort (sec)	277.49	360.65	304.88	305.06
Comparative (%)	100	130.0	109.9	110.0
Number of runs	28	19	23	18
Size of runs (Gb)	0.976	0.640	0.752	0.552
Comparative (%)	100	65.5	77.0	56.6

(b) Results for sorting 1 Gb of data with 37 Mb of buffer space

	No compression	Huffman	Bigram	Quadgram
Build model (sec)	—	0.66	0.51	5.98
Generate runs (sec)	1291.94	1675.52	1395.19	1593.98
Merge runs (sec)	2852.07	2442.40	2245.25	1796.71
Total time to sort (sec)	4144.02	4118.58	3640.95	3396.66
Comparative (%)	100	99.4	87.9	82.0
Number of runs	287	193	226	181
Size of runs (Gb)	9.918	6.569	7.694	5.751
Comparative (%)	100	66.2	77.6	58.0

(c) Results for sorting 10 Gb of data with 37 Mb of buffer space

pensated for by the gain in processing speed. The common-quadgram method had both better compression efficiency and high processing efficiency, and thus was for large files superior to the other methods.

The tables also include the size of the resulting runs, giving an indication of the amount of compression achieved. Because we are making a number of compromises (compression and decompression must be fast, and the model must not consume too much memory), only modest compression was achieved. Also, as discussed earlier the key is not compressed, and there is the extra overhead of storing the number of bytes encoded in the record, as this value is needed

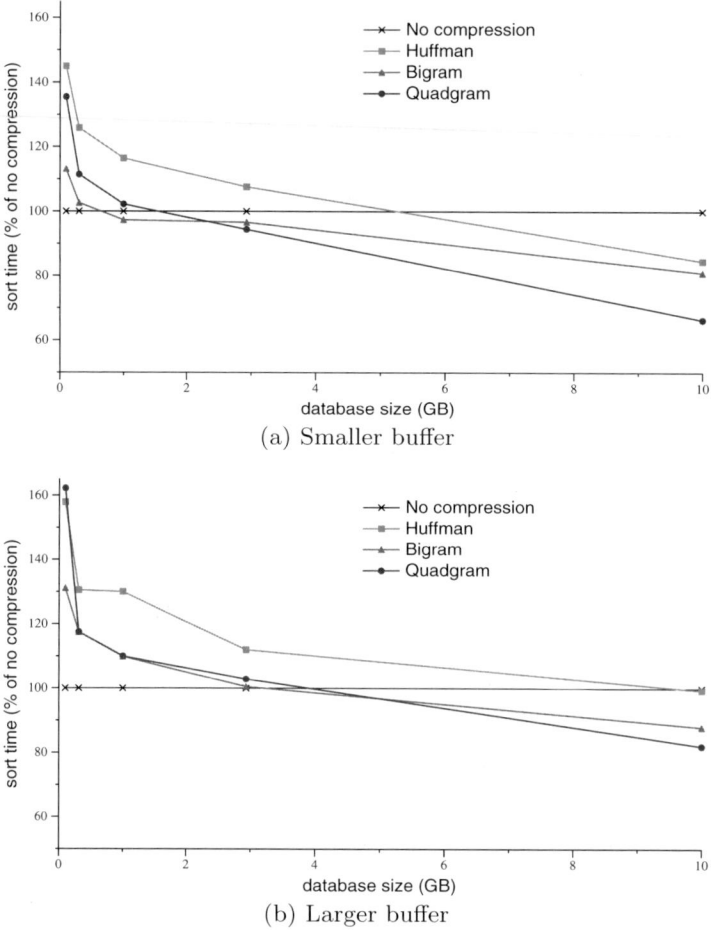

Fig. 3. Sort times as a percentage of the time to sort without compression. (a): with 18.5 Mb of buffer space. (b): with 37 Mb of buffer space.

by the decoder. The model is only built from symbols encountered in the first buffer, not the entire database, so the model may not be optimal. However it is worth noting that when compressing 10 Gb of data, comparing the values in Tables 1(c) and 2(c), using 36 Mb to build the model instead of 18 Mb only resulted in an extra 1 to 2 percent decrease in size.

Even though the degree of compression is relatively small, from Table 2(c) for bigram coding, we can see that a 22.4% saving in space due to the use of compression has resulted in a 12.1% saving in time. From Table 1(c) for bigram coding, a 22.0% saving in space has resulted in a 19.0% saving in time. For common-quadgram coding, a 41.1% reduction in the size of the runs has resulted in a 33.7% reduction in the sort time. It seems clear that more effective compression should lead to further reduction in costs in both space and time.

7 Conclusions

We have developed new compression methods that accelerate external sorting for large data files. The methods are simple; the most successful is based on the expedient of identifying common quadgrams and replacing characters and quadgrams by bytewise codes. The gain is greatest when memory is limited, showing that the reduction in merging costs is a key reason that time is saved. Even though the compression gains were only moderate, significant reductions in costs were achieved.

For the largest file considered, most of the savings in data volume translate directly to savings in sorting time. This strongly suggests that more effective compression techniques will yield faster sorting, so long as the other constraints – semi-static coding, rapid modelling, compression, and decompression, and low memory use – continue to be met. It is also likely that similar techniques could accelerate other database processing tasks, in particular large joins. That is, our results indicate that compression of this kind could be used to reduce costs for a range of applications involving manipulation of large volumes of data.

Acknowledgements. This research was supported by the Australian Research Council.

References

1. Zobel, J., Williams, H.E., Kimberley, S.: Trends in retrieval system performance. In Edwards, J., ed.: Proceedings of the Australasian Computer Science Conference, Canberra, Australia (2000) 241–248
2. Boncz, P.A., Manegold, S., Kersten, M.L.: Database architecture optimized for the new bottleneck: Memory access. In: The VLDB Journal. (1999) 54–65
3. Graefe, G.: Query evaluation techniques for large databases. ACM Computing Surveys **25** (1993) 152–153
4. Chen, Z., Gehrke, J., Korn, F.: Query optimization in compressed database systems. In: Proceedings of ACM SIGMOD international conference on Management of Data, Santa Barbara, California, USA (2001) 271–282
5. Goldstein, J., Ramakrishnan, R., Shaft, U.: Compressing relations and indexes. In: Proceedings of the Fourteenth International Conference on Data Engineering, Orlando, Florida, USA, IEEE Computer Society (1998) 370–379
6. Graefe, G., Shapiro, L.: Data compression and database performance. In ACM/IEEE-CS Symposium On Applied Computing (1991) 22–27
7. Ng, W.K., Ravishankar, C.V.: Relational database compression using augmented vector quantization. In: Proceedings of the Eleventh International Conference on Data Engineering, Taipei, Taiwan, IEEE Computer Society (1995) 540–549
8. Ray, G., Harista, J.R., Seshadri, S.: Database compression: A performance enhancement tool. In: Proceedings of the 7th International Conference on Management of Data (COMAD), Pune, India (1995)

9. Westman, T., Kossmann, D., Helmer, S., Moerkotte, G.: The implementation and performance of compressed databases. ACM SIGMOD Record **29** (2000)
10. Moffat, A., Zobel, J., Sharman, N.: Text compression for dynamic document databases. IEEE Transactions on Knowledge and Data Engineering **9** (1997) 302–313
11. Larmore, L.L., Hirschberg, D.S.: A fast algorithm for optimal length-limited Huffman codes. Journal of the ACM **37** (1990) 464–473
12. Witten, I.H., Moffat, A., Bell, T.C.: Managing Gigabytes: Compressing and Indexing Documents and Images. Second edn. Morgan Kaufmann, San Francisco, California (1999)
13. Bell, T.C., Moffat, A., Nevill-Manning, C.G., Witten, I.H., Zobel., J.: Data compression in full-text retrieval systems. Journal of the American Society for Information Science **44** (1993) 508–531
14. Scholer, F., Williams, H.E., Yiannis, J., Zobel, J.: Compression of inverted indexes for fast query evaluation. In: Proceedings of the 25th annual international ACM SIGIR conference on research and development in information retrieval. (2002) 222–229
15. Williams, H.E., Zobel, J.: Compressing integers for fast file access. Computer Journal **42** (1999) 193–201
16. Zobel, J., Moffat, A.: Adding compression to a full-text retrieval system. Software Practice and Experience **25** (1995) 891–903
17. Roth, M., Horn, S.V.: Database compression. ACM SIGMOD Record **22** (1993) 31–39
18. Garcia-Molina, H., Ullman, J.D., Widom, J.: Database Systems Implementation. First edn. Prentice Hall (2000)
19. Ramakrishnan, R., Gehrke, J.: Database Management Systems. Second edn. McGraw-Hill (2000)
20. Knuth, D.E.: The Art of Computer Programming, Volume 3: Sorting and Searching, Second Edition. Addison-Wesley, Massachusetts (1973)
21. Cannane, A., Williams, H.: A general-purpose compression scheme for large collections. ACM Transactions on Information Systems **20** (2002) 329–355
22. Moffat, A., Turpin, A.: Compression and Coding Algorithms. First edn. Kluwer (2002)
23. Ramakrishna, M.V., Zobel, J.: Performance in practice of string hashing functions. In: Proceedings of the Databases Systems for Advanced Applications Symposium, Melbourne, Australia (1997) 215–223
24. Sinha, R., Zobel, J.: Efficient trie-based sorting of large sets of strings. In Oudshoorn, M., ed.: Proceedings of the Australasian Computer Science Conference, Adelaide, Australia (2003) 11–18
25. Sinha, R., Zobel, J.: Cache-conscious sorting of large sets of strings with dynamic tries. In Ladner, R., ed.: Proceedings of the ALENEX Workshop on Algorithm Engineering and Experiments, Baltimore, Maryland (2003)

MaxDomino: Efficiently Mining Maximal Sets

Krishnamoorthy Srikumar, Bharat Bhasker, and Satish K. Tripathi

Indian Institute of Management, Lucknow. INDIA.
Phone: 091-0522-361 889 to 091-0522-361 897
Fax: 091-0522-361 843
{srikumar, bhasker}@iiml.ac.in, tripathi@cs.umd.edu

Abstract. We present MaxDomino, an algorithm for mining maximal frequent sets using a novel concept of dominancy factor of a transaction. We also propose a hashing scheme to collapse the database to a form that contains only unique transactions. Unlike traditional bottom up approach with look-aheads, MaxDomino employs a top down strategy with selective bottom up search for mining maximal sets. Using the connect dataset [Benchmark dataset created by University California, Irvine], our experimental results reveal that MaxDomino outperforms GenMax at higher support levels. Furthermore, our scalability tests show that MaxDomino yields an order of magnitude improvement in speed over GenMax. MaxDomino is especially efficient when the maximal frequent sets are longer.

1 Introduction

Frequent set mining is a fundamental and essential operation in the process of discovering the association rules. The concept of association rule mining introduced by [1] mines the frequent sets based on the Apriori principle. As Apriori based algorithms employ a pure bottom-up, breadth first search, mining a frequent set of length m require mining all its $2^m - 2$ subsets, which would be computationally expensive if m is very large (> 30). Hence, there has been recent interest in mining maximal frequent sets. Maximal frequent sets are frequent sets whose supersets are infrequent and all its subsets are frequent. Thus, they can be used for generating all possible association rules.

Recent approaches to maximal frequent set mining include, GenMax [5], Depth-Project [3] and MAFIA [4]. GenMax uses vertical data representation and tidset based intersections for mining the maximal frequent sets. DepthProject employs a transaction projection mechanism for counting the support of itemsets. Mafia uses parent equivalence and superset pruning (PEP, FHUT and HUTMFI) strategies to remove non-maximal sets.

Our primary motivation in this paper is to demonstrate that it is possible to mine quickly the entire set of maximal frequent sets quickly by employing a top-down strategy with selective bottom-up search in dense domains. Our algorithm employs a

A. James, B. Lings, M. Younas (Eds.): BNCOD 2003, LNCS 2712, pp. 131–139, 2003.
© Springer-Verlag Berlin Heidelberg 2003

novel concept of dominancy factor and is especially efficient when the maximal sets are longer.

The organization of the rest of paper is as follows: In the next section we introduce the notations, model and pruning properties used in MaxDomino. Section 3 gives the implementation aspects of MaxDomino in various phases. In Section 4, we present our experimental results. Finally, in section 5, we conclude with a discussion of future work.

2   The Model and Notations

The mining algorithm introduced in this paper presumes a data set consisting of transactions that contain multiple items in each transaction. A set of items present in a transaction is referred to as an itemset. We assume that the items in the transaction are ordered sequence of numbers as per IBM artificial data set generator format [2].

Let $I = \{i_1, i_2, ...i_m\}$ be a set of distinct items. A set $X \subseteq I$ is called an itemset. An itemset X with k items is succinctly referred as k-itemset.

A transaction, $T_i = \{x_\ell \mid \ell = 1, 2...N_i; x_\ell \in I\}$, where N_i is the number of items in transaction T_i. A transaction T_i is said to support an itemset $X \subseteq I$ iff $X \subseteq T_i$. The support of an itemset X, denoted by Sup (X), is the number of transactions in the dataset that supports X. The user defined minimum support is denoted as minsupport. An itemset $X \in \mathfrak{I}$ (Frequent itemsets) iff Sup (X) $\geq$ minsupport.

We define, the dominancy factor of a transaction T_i, denoted by DF_i, as the sum of supports of individual items that appear in the transaction. For $T_i = \{x_\ell \mid \ell = 1, 2....N_i; x_\ell \in I\}$, $DF_i = \sum_{\ell=1}^{N_i} Sup (x_\ell), \forall x_\ell \in T_i$. Similarly, the dominancy factor of an itemset X_k, denoted as DF (X_k), is the sum of supports of each item belonging to itemset X_k. For $X_k = \{x_m \mid m = 1, 2....k ; x_m \in I\}$, DF $(X_k) = \sum_{m=1}^{k} Sup (x_m), \forall x_m \in X_k$.

The algorithm proposed in this work utilizes the dominancy factor for pruning the search space. Thus, during the preparatory phase we sort the entire dataset based on descending order of DF as shown in Table 1.

In a dataset sorted based on descending order of DF, for an itemset X to be present in a transaction T_i it should satisfy the property DF (X) $\leq DF_i$. So, as we are walking down the transactions, we can determine a point beyond which a subset, X, would not exist. For example in Table 1, for the itemset X = (1,3,5,2) the dominancy factor, DF (1,3,5,2) computes to the value of 19. Hence, we need to traverse the transaction list up to the point at which the dominancy factor of transactions is at least equal to that of itemset X. In this case, we need to scan till T_4 only as DF_4 = 19. So, we define the point (transaction id) beyond which a subset X of size k would not exist as the Maximum Depth of Traversal (MDT_k). The point beyond which any itemset of size k will not exist is defined as $MaxMDT_k$. In Table 1, $MaxMDT_5$ = 1; $MaxMDT_4$ = 4; and $MaxMDT_3$ = 6.

In the initial phase of the algorithm the original dataset is transformed and prepared for the mining algorithm. The preprocessed dataset used by the algorithm consists of transactions sorted on descending order of the dominancy factor. Furthermore, the items within a transaction are sorted based on ascending order of its support. In other words, the dataset or transaction list, D, is an ordered set of quadruplet Q,

$D = \{ <Qi> \mid DF_i \geq DF_{i+1} \}$

    where $<Qi> = \{ (T_i, N_i, DF_i, Sup_i) \mid i = 1, 2, \ldots L;$

        T_i is the ith transaction containing itemset x_ℓ;

        N_i is the number of items in T_i;

        $DF_i = \sum_{\ell=1}^{Ni} Sup(x_\ell)$; $Sup_i = Sup(T_i)$;

$\}$ Where L is the total number of transactions in the dataset.

Table 1. Transactions sorted based on Dominancy Factor

TID	Itemsets	Dominancy Factor
T1	1 3 4 5 2	23 (4+4+4+5+6)
T2	1 4 5 2	19 (4+4+5+6)
T3	1 4 5 2	19 (4+4+5+6)
T4	1 3 5 2	19 (4+4+5+6)
T5	3 5 2	15 (4+5+6)
T6	3 4 2	14 (4+4+6)

Note: Sup (1) = 4; Sup (2) = 6; Sup (3) = 4; Sup (4) = 4; Sup (5) = 5

We define hash value for a transaction T_i as, $Hval_i = \sum_{\ell=1}^{Ni} \log (x_\ell^{th}$ prime number).

We know that the product of prime numbers is unique and log $(m*n)=\log(m)+\log(n)$. Hence, it can be easily verified that two transactions will have the same hash value if and only if all the items in both the transactions are identical. The hash values are used for collapsing the duplicate transactions in the dataset.

The preprocessed dataset with the sorted transaction list has several properties that can be used for pruning the search space. These properties are described in the lemmas that follow:

Lemma 1. A candidate k-itemset, $X_k \not\subset T_i$ $\forall T_i > MDT_k$. In other words, a candidate subset X_k is definitely not a subset of Transaction T_i beyond the Maximum Depth of Traversal, MDT_k of the candidate subset, X_k.

Proof. As the transactions in the dataset, D are sorted based on descending order of DF_i, we can identify a transaction point at which $DF_i < DF(X_k)$. Further, the dominancy factor is just the sum of supports of individual items in a transaction list (DF_i). So, for an itemset to be present in a transaction, its dominancy factor should be more than the sum of supports of the subset to be evaluated $DF(X_k)$.

In the process of mining, MaxDomino generates a hash table, denoted as HT_k, for all k-itemsets. We define a hash table, HT for all itemsets of size k as, $HT_k = \{ (X_k, Sup_k) \mid X_k = \{ x_\ell \mid \ell = 1, 2 \ldots k ; x_\ell \in I \}; Sup_k = Sup(X_k) \}$. Detailed explanations for hash table (HT) construction is deferred till Section 3.2.

Corollary of Lemma 1. For all subsets $X_k \in HT_k$, $\exists MaxMDT_k = Max(MDT_k) \mid X_k \not\subset T_i \forall T_i > MaxMDT_k$.

Proof. The proof of this corollary is obvious, as each and every k-itemset, X_k has MDT_k, the maximum depth of traversal for any itemset belonging to hash table will be decided by the maximum values of MDT_k. Hence, any k-itemset $X_k \in HT_k$ cannot exist beyond $MaxMDT_k$.

Lemma 2. For an itemset X_k to be frequent, the upper bound of the support should be at least equal to the user defined minimum support, minsupport. That is, if $X_k \in \Im$, then minsupport $\leq$ Upper Bound (X_k), otherwise $X_k \notin \Im$.

Proof. The duplicate transactions are combined together in the preprocessing stage and the support (sup_i) is incremented for the ith transaction appropriately. Thus, the support upper bound on support can be computed as Upper Bound $(X_k) = \sum_{m=fk}^{MDTk} (Sup_m)$. As each and every itemset in a transaction is distinct, any itemset can occur at-most as many times as the support of a particular transaction. Further, we have established in lemma 1 that any itemset X_k cannot exist beyond its MDT_k. So, once we know MDT_k and the itemset's first occurrence in transaction list D, we can ascertain the maximum support by summing up the support of all transactions between these two points. It assumes that the itemset is supported by every transaction between these two points and thus can be upper bound of the support. This property is used to prune infrequent itemsets even before adding the itemset to hash table.

Corollary of Lemma 2. If a k-itemset with smallest dominancy factor doesn't satisfy upper bound property, no other k-itemset can.

Proof. As the transactions in D are sorted based on descending order of dominancy factor, the smaller the dominancy factor of the itemset, X_k, the larger its MDT_k. So, if a k-itemset with smallest dominancy factor doesn't satisfy Lemma 2, no other k-itemset can. Hence the corollary follows. We use this corollary effectively in earlier passes of the algorithm to come down many levels even without accessing the dataset.

A maximal tree, that stores all the maximal itemsets, is defined as,

$$MT = \{X \mid X \in \Im \text{ and } (X \cup \{x_\ell\}) \notin \Im ; \ell \geq 1;\}$$

In addition to the support upper bound property, MaxDomino also uses Apriori [1] and Reverse Apriori (all subsets of a frequent set are frequent) properties for pruning the search space.

3   Implementation of MaxDomino

In this section, we describe the implementation details of MaxDomino in various phases.

3.1   Transaction List Generation

During this phase, the algorithm scans the dataset and computes the support for all 1-itemsets. The infrequent 1-itemsets are removed from further evaluation (Apriori principle). In the second scan of the dataset, as we walk down the transaction we compute the dominancy factor and hash value for all frequent 1-itemsets. Before, we add a transaction to the Transaction List D, we check for uniqueness of transactions using hash values. If unique hash values already exist we increment the support of corresponding transaction. Otherwise, we sort the items in the transaction in ascending order of its 1-item support and add it as a new transaction in D. At the end of the pass, the transaction list is sorted on the descending order of dominancy factor. A sample transaction list, D is given in Table 2 (taking minsupport=2).

In order to reduce the complexity of logarithmic computations for hash values, we store a large set of logarithm of prime numbers in a file and read only as many as required for a particular dataset. Further, to avoid the complexity of floating point comparisons for large set of transactions, we hashed each transaction by a multi-hashing scheme: first_item $\rightarrow$ sum_of_all_items $\rightarrow$ hash value.

Table 2. Transaction List D

TID	$T_i(x_\ell)$	N_i	DF_i	Sup_i
T1	2 0 4 3	4	12	1
T2	0 4 3	3	10	1
T3	1 4 3	3	9	1
T4	0 3	2	7	1
T5	1 2	2	4	1

Note: Sup (0) = 3; Sup (1) = 2;Sup (2) = 2;Sup (3) = 4;Sup (4) = 3

After the transaction list, D is generated; we make a pass over D to compute supports for all 2-itemsets.

3.2 Hash Table Construction, Support Counting, and Itemset Pruning

As our algorithm follows a top down approach, we start with generating all itemsets of size, k equal to the maximum length of transaction in dataset, Maxlen. However, we maintain a list of frequent 1-itemsets in ascending order as well as dominancy factor of transactions in descending order in an array and apply corollary of Lemma 2 repeatedly to come down many levels even without accessing the dataset.

Top-down Phase. As soon as we generate a k-itemset, after checking for frequency of all its 2-itemsets, we apply the support upper bound property to check whether the subset could be infrequent. If the generated itemset is infrequent, it is pruned. Otherwise, we add the itemset generated to a hash table HT.

In the constructed hash table, we store the hash value of itemsets rather than the itemset itself. Here again, we use a multi-hashing scheme similar to the one described in section 3.1 to reduce the complexity of floating point comparisons. The support values are incremented against corresponding hash entries if the same itemset occurs again as we walk down the transaction list.

Selective Bottom-up Phase. As we scan the first transaction, we take the first k-items in it and store the support value of kth item as bup_sup. From these k-items, we generate all itemsets of size b (initially b=3). We put all the b-itemsets generated into a hash tree which is constructed similar to the one proposed in [1].

We repeat the Top-down phase and Selective Bottom-up phase for each transaction till $MaxMDT_k$ and $MaxMDT_b$ respectively, as no k-itemset would exist beyond $MaxMDT_k$ and no b-itemset would exist beyond $MaxMDT_b$ (refer Lemma 2). As soon as a k-itemset is found frequent in the top-down phase, it is written to the maximal tree. While inserting a maximal frequent set into the tree, the items are recursively placed in the form of itemset tree to speed-up maximality checking.

For the selective bottom-up phase, from the 2nd transaction till $MaxMDT_b$, we take all items in a transaction whose supports are less than or equal to bup_sup and generate all itemsets of size b. This is done to ensure that no b-itemset gets missed out for support counting. We add all the b-itemsets into the hash tree. At the end of the pass, the leaf nodes of hash tree will have the support information for b-itemsets. This information is used in subsequent passes by the top-down phase for pruning infrequent (k-1)-itemsets (Apriori principle).

All of the above procedures are repeated by decrementing k by 1 till 2 and incrementing b by 1 till $b \leq k$. The pseudo-code for MaxDomino is given in Figure 1.

4   Experimental Results

All our experiments were performed on a 450MHz Pentium-III PC with 64MB of memory, running RedHat Linux 7.2. For performance comparisons, we used the original source codes for GenMax [5] provided to us by their authors. A detailed comparison of MaxDomino with GenMax (tidset based intersections) was conducted on connect dataset. The timings reported in this paper include all pre-processing costs (such as time for horizontal-to-vertical conversion in GenMax and transaction collapsing in MaxDomino) and doesn't include the output time for displaying maximal frequent sets for both GenMax and MaxDomino.

Figure 2 shows the performance comparison of MaxDomino against GenMax on connect dataset. It is clearly evident from Figure 2 that MaxDomino outperforms GenMax at very high supports (above 87%). We have also carried out scalability experiments by multiplying connect dataset by 3times (named as 3connect) and 5times (named as 5connect). The graphs in Figure 2, clearly reveals that MaxDomino shows order of magnitude improvements over GenMax on 3connect and 5connect datasets.

As the search strategy employed by MaxDomino is primarily top-down, the algorithm would perform poorly if the maximal frequent sets lie far below maxlen. In many of the benchmark real world datasets such as chess, connect, pumsb, we find even the longest maximal patterns are lying far below maxlen,(atleast 45 to 50 percent below maxlen) and the number of infrequent nodes along the path are very large. So, the real application domain of MaxDomino is on those datasets for which the maximal sets are much closer to maxlen and the numbers of infrequent itemsets along the path are smaller. However, MaxDomino can be utilized effectively for mining at very high supports as shown in this paper for connect dataset. In addition, MaxDomino can also

MaxDomino (Data-set DB):

1. $\mathfrak{I}_1$ = {Frequent 1-itemsets}
2. For each $T_i \in$ DB do begin
3. $DF_i = \sum_{\ell=1}^{Ni} Sup(x_\ell)$;
4. $Hval_i = \sum_{\ell=1}^{Ni} \log(x_\ell^{th}$ prime number);
5.   Scan D and check for unique $Hval_i$, if exist increment its support,
       Otherwise, sort items in ascending order of support and add T_i to D
6. End
7. Sort list D in descending order of DF and write D to a NewDB;
8. Scan NewDB and compute $\mathfrak{I}_2$ supports (frequent 2-item supports)
9. MT={};
10. Initialize k to Maxlen (for top-down phase) and b to 3 (selective bottom-up phase)
11. For k = Maxlen to 2 do begin
12.   Check whether all k-itemsets could be infrequent, if so decrement k
         and continue //refer corollary of lemma 2
13.   HT= {};
14.   for each $T_i \in$ NewDB do begin
15.   if $(T_i \le MaxMDT_k)$ do //Top-down phase
16.   Generate k-itemsets, check for support upper bound, maximality &
             infrequency of subsets and add to HT_k (Infrequency of subsets checked
             with $\mathfrak{I}_2$ supports as well as information gathered in bottom-up phase)
17.   If the support of k-itemset just added to HT_k crosses minsupport
             requirement add the k-itemset to MT
18.   endif
19.   if $(T_i \le MaxMDT_b$ and $b \le k)$ do begin //Selective Bottom-up phase
20.   if (the transaction read is equal to first one i.e. T_1) do
21.   Set bottom-up support threshold (bup_sup) as the
                support of kth item in the first transaction
22.   endif
23.   for all sets of items in T_i whose supports are less than or equal bup_sup
             generate all possible b-itemsets and add it to hash tree
24.   endif
25.   End
26.   decrement k by 1 and increment b by 1
27. End
28. Return Output

Fig. 1. Pseudo-code for MaxDomino

be used efficiently for finding the longest maximal patterns (say, LM patterns) alone very quickly. Table 3 shows the results for MaxDomino on connect dataset in mining LM patterns at different support levels.

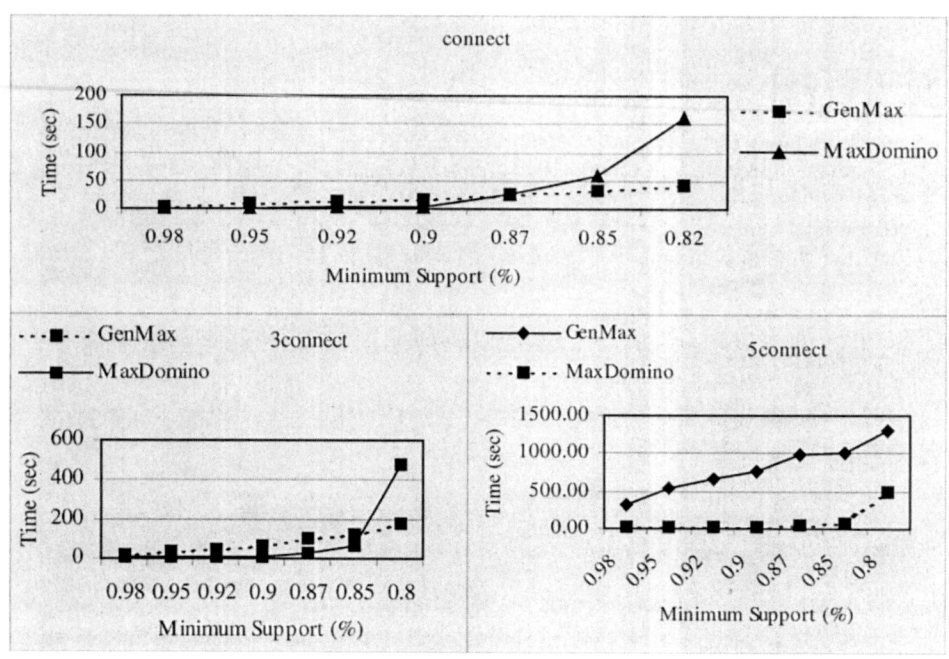

Fig. 2. Performance Comparison of MaxDomino Vs GenMax

Table 3. Mining Longest Maximal (LM) Patterns Using MaxDomino

Minimum Support (%)	Maxlen	LM Pattern Size	No. of Maximal sets	Time (sec)
0.95	17	9	1	0.78
0.92	19	11	1	0.83
0.90	21	12	1	0.90
0.87	24	13	4	1.41
0.85	25	13	55	2.25
0.82	26	14	59	3.63
0.80	28	15	24	4.11

5   Summary and Future Research Directions

In this paper, we presented and evaluated MaxDomino for mining maximal frequent sets using a novel concept of dominancy factor. We have demonstrated that MaxDomino yields better performance compared to GenMax, a state-of-the-art maximal set mining algorithm, at higher support levels. Furthermore, the utility of MaxDomino for mining Longest Maximal (LM) patterns is also evaluated.

As we noticed that our algorithm performs better at higher support levels compared to GenMax, we are planning to integrate the concepts of GenMax and MaxDomino in future and study the performance improvements.

References

1. Agrawal, R., Imielinski, T., Swami, A.: Mining association rules between sets of items in large databases. In proceedings of ACM SIGMOD Conference on Management of Data. (1993) 207-216. Washigton D.C.
2. Agrawal R. et al: The Quest Data Mining System, Technical report, IBM Almaden Research Center. (1996b) Retrieved October 10, 2002 from http://www.almaden.ibm.com/cs/quest/.
3. Agrawal, R., Aggarwal C., Prasad VVV.: Depth first generation of Long patterns. 7th International conference on Knowledge discovery and Data mining (2000)
4. Burdick, D., Calimlim, M., Gehrke, J.: MAFIA: A Maximal Frequent Itemset Algorithm for Transactional Databases. In Intl. Conf. On Data Engineering (2001)
5. Zaki, M.J., Gouda, K.: Fast vertical mining using diffsets. RPI Technical Report. 01-1. (2001)

Evaluating Maintenance Policies for Externally Materialised Multi-source Views

Henrik Engström[1] and Brian Lings[2]

[1] Department of Computer Science, University of Skövde, Sweden
henrik@ida.his.se
[2] Department of Computer Science, University of Exeter, UK
B.J.Lings@exeter.ac.uk

Abstract. In many applications data from distributed, autonomous, and heterogeneous sources need to be imported and materialised in a (client) system external to those sources. As changes are committed in the sources, the externally materialised view must be updated to reflect those changes. A maintenance policy determines when and how to conduct updates. As sources may not be cooperating maintenance of externally materialised views is different from traditional view maintenance. Previous studies on maintenance of externally materialised views have been heavily focused on algorithms that ensure view consistency. There are, however, other aspects of maintenance that, when considered, can affect choice of consistency algorithm. If, for example, auxiliary views are maintained in the view client it is possible to ensure strong consistency without complex algorithms.

In our previous work we have studied how to select a maintenance policy for a single source view. In this paper we extend the work to evaluating maintenance policies for externally materialised views based on several sources. We explore views that are defined as the join of two independent sources, identifying the solution space in terms of possible policies, their implications for consistency and their required source capabilities. We use a testbed system to evaluate policy performance. The work confirms that the earlier results on single source maintenance extend to the multi-source situation. In addition we show that the consistency preserving algorithms suggested in the literature are not always required. Actually, in all situations explored it has proved more efficient to use auxiliary views than policies which requires consistency preserving algorithms.

1 Introduction

Maintenance of materialised views is an area which has received substantial interest from the research community [5,16,15,14,22,17,20,1,4]. The original usage of views is as a mechanism in centralised and distributed database systems to increase data independence and query performance. A view is defined as a named query [20] over source data. A view can be referenced in user queries in the same way as the source data. If a view is materialised, the result of the defining query is physically stored. In such cases the view has to be maintained to reflect

A. James, B. Lings, M. Younas (Eds.): BNCOD 2003, LNCS 2712, pp. 140–156, 2003.

changes to the base data. There have been several studies on how to incrementally maintain views expressed using various data models and query languages [15,1,3].

An externally materialised view is different from traditional materialised views in that it is defined over autonomous and heterogeneous sources. Autonomy implies that sources may not be changed to participate in maintenance and may not be aware of the views defined over its data. Heterogeneity implies that sources may have a varying degree of support to participate in maintenance and that no common data model may be assumed. A common form of externally materialised views are those that constitute the contents in a data warehouse. For all such externally materialised views, it may not be possible to utilise all proposed view mechanisms as the underlying systems may not support them. It can, for example, be impossible to provide global transactions to ensure complete consistency between sources and views. This "inconsistency problem" has been studied extensively in the last 8 years [28,29,2,26,23]. This is, however, not the only issue that has to be considered when a maintenance policy is selected. We have shown in previous work that, for views based on a single source, the selection of a maintenance policy for externally materialised views depends on both quality of service requirements and the capabilities of underlying sources. When the view definition involves more than one source the maintenance of the view becomes more complex as it requires the synchronisation of several independent processes.

In this paper we analyse maintenance of a view expressed as the join of two sources. We present a set of possible policy combinations, consider implications for consistency preservation and analyse which source capabilities may affect their operation. We then evaluate the performance of these policies in TMID, a testbed for maintenance of externally materialised views. The results support the view that several multi-source policies are useful in that they can give optimal performance under certain conditions. In most situations it is advantageous to use incremental techniques and to keep auxiliary views. For this type of policy it is not necessary to use any of the many proposed consistency preserving algorithms - strong consistency can still be guaranteed.

2   Background

The concept of externally materialised views was first defined by Staudt and Jarke [22]. This work focuses on techniques for extending a data source to support the maintenance of external views stored in autonomous, heterogeneous clients. These views are based on data from a single source. In this paper we consider the reverse problem: how to devise a maintenance policy in a client for an externally materialised view that combines data from several autonomous, heterogeneous sources. We do not expect these sources to support any particular view maintenance mechanism and it may not be possible to change them to do so. Our problem is to maintain a view which is based on several data sources outside the control of the view client. This is a typical situation for Internet data sources. A client can request data from multiple Internet sources but these do not normally support view maintenance and cannot be extended to do so. It may be possible to wrap a source to provide some additional capabilities but this will have implications for performance [10].

In the data warehouse area there have been several studies on how to incrementally maintain views when they are based on multiple independent sources. Issues related to view consistency have been studied thoroughly by Zhuge [27], who defines four levels of consistency. Strong and complete consistency have received most attention. Complete consistency requires all state changes of sources to be visible in the warehouse. Strong consistency requires that consecutive view states are based on valid consecutive source states. Many algorithms have been proposed [28,29,2,25,26,23] that will ensure that a view is consistent with sources when join queries are sent to the sources. All this work assumes that the client is not maintaining sufficient auxiliary information to avoid sending join queries to sources. This implies that whenever changes are propagated from one source, the client has to send queries to the other sources to find matching objects. Another way to ensure consistency is addressed by Gupta et al. [13] who define the concept of self-maintainable views. By making an external view self-maintainable, inconsistency cannot arise and the load on the source systems may be reduced. Quass et al. [19] extend on this, suggesting algorithms for generating auxiliary views that make warehouse views self-maintainable.

This paper addresses the evaluation of maintenance policies. For centralised database environments it has been shown that the choice of policy is a complex trade-off affected by update and query patterns [16], quality of service requirements [21], and query complexity [4], and that there is a need to support multiple maintenance policies [6].

In our previous work we have studied the selection of maintenance policies in a data warehouse environment. We have established the framework for single source policy selection [8] and formulated the dependencies between policies, evaluation criteria, and source capabilities using a cost-based approach [11]. The analytical results have been validated empirically using a testbed system [10]. These results show that policy selection is highly dependant on quality of service requirements and system characteristics. An important quality of service evaluation criterion is the maximal view staleness that can be guaranteed. For a view with guaranteed maximum staleness Z, the result of any query over the view, returned at time t, will reflect all source changes prior to $t - Z$.

We have shown that although wrapping is a viable technique to extend the interface to a source, it has implications for performance (both quality of service and system overhead) and hence to policy choice. This means that it is important to consider source capabilities explicitly in policy selection. All these results apply to a single source external view. In this paper we extend the work to views based on multiple sources, and present performance evaluations in which a large number of join view maintenance policies have been compared.

Note that in this work we are considering externally *materialised* views. A view may also be virtual, in which case queries over the view are shipped to the underlying sources. Hybrid approaches are also possible, where some views are virtual and some are materialised. The latter is addressed by Hull and Zhou [17, 18] who study the trade-off between virtual and materialised views in a loosely coupled database system. Whilst relevant to this paper, our study differs mainly in that we do not make assumptions about sources providing any change detection capabilities.

3   Maintaining a Join View

In this paper we consider the maintenance of a view defined as a join of two data sources. We use the term *supporting view* to refer to the selected and projected part from each source used in the join. In other words, we adopt the standard optimisation that select-project should be pushed through a join. A supporting view is hence single source. We assume that each source provides a single set of objects which means all objects in a supporting view have a (value based) identifier. We do not consider the special case where a single source provides several supporting views.

As we are operating in a heterogeneous environment we adopt a generalised join definition. A *join view* contains a subset of the Cartesian product of two supporting views, where elements in the view are concatenations of parts of objects, one object from each supporting view. A join-predicate p(x,y) determines the relevant subset. This predicate is an arbitrary function which takes an object from each supporting view and returns true if the two objects should be combined and included in the join, false otherwise.

The possible maintenance policies for a join view are not well understood. As mentioned above, there has been much work on algorithms to preserve consistency. However, the relationship between supporting view policies and join policy is not considered. In this section we suggest a set of maintenance policies. We then analyse the level of consistency these policies may provide and the source capabilities that may be required or useful.

3.1   Alternatives for Join View Maintenance Policies

For a single source view we consider six different policies [11]. These are constructed by combining two different strategies (incremental and recompute) with three different timings (immediate, periodic and on-demand). This gives rise to six policies: Immediate Incremental (I_I), Immediate Recompute (I_R), Periodic Incremental (P_I), Periodic Recompute (P_R), On-demand Incremental (O_I), On-demand Recompute (O_R). Although more single source policies are possible, these represents the most commonly mentioned alternatives in the literature. For a join view each supporting view can, in principle, be maintained with any of these policies. In addition, the joining of the two supporting views can be done with the same set of policies, in principle independent of the choice of the supporting view policies. We will refer to this as the integrator policy (as it is assumed the join will be performed in an integrator component in the client). In addition to this, the supporting views can be materialised in the client or can be treated as virtual views. We will refer to a materialised supporting view as an *auxiliary view*.

When combined, the set of join policy combinations becomes: $6 \cdot 6 \cdot 6 \cdot 2 \cdot 2 = 864$ (left supporting view policy, right supporting view policy, integrator policy, left auxiliary view, right auxiliary view). Some of these combinations are not meaningful[1] but still the set of possible policies is large. In this paper we will study all principle types of policies: incremental and recompute for both supporting views and integrator views; all possible combinations of integrator and supporting view timings; policies with and without auxiliary views.

We will use the following naming conventions for join policies:

<Integrator policy>-<aux/noAux>-<left supporting view policy>-<right supporting view policy>

For example, I_R-aux-I_I-P_I denotes a policy which immediately recomputes the join view when changes are reported for the supporting views, and uses auxiliary views. For both supporting views incremental maintenance is used; the left sends changes immediately when the source reports them, while the right sends changes periodically.

3.2   Consistency Implications

An important quality of service characteristic for a view based on several autonomous sources is how consistent it is with its sources. In practice all previous research has addressed only strong and complete consistency. We claim that strong consistency is far more likely to be required in a heterogenous environment with autonomous sources. Complete consistency requires all sources to either actively notify that changes have occurred, or record all changes that are committed. A source that propagates *only net changes* (e.g. a tuple which is inserted and then immediately deleted corresponds to no change) will not be sufficient to ensure complete consistency. Only specialised applications are likely to require that *all* state changes of *all* sources should be reflected. Interestingly, Zhuge et al., who propose the consistency classification, state that [28, p.5] completeness "is too strong a requirement and unnecessary in most practical warehousing scenarios". For this reason, we have focused on strong consistency in our work.

When auxiliary views are used for a binary join, it is relatively easy to ensure strong consistency (that consecutive view states are based on valid consecutive source states). The state of each auxiliary view will always reflect a valid state of the source, and state changes will reflect the evolution of the source. As both maintenance of auxiliary views and joining are done in the integrator, it is

---

[1] For example, it is not possible to have an on-demand supporting view policy combined with a immediate integrator policy. The integrator will await changes from the wrapper which in turn is awaiting requests from the integrator. This means the view will never be maintained.

easy to ensure that updates of auxiliary views are not done concurrently with maintenance of the join view.

When auxiliary views are *not* maintained in the integrator, and the view is recomputed, strong consistency can be guaranteed. This is because each delivered supporting view will reflect states from each source. Moreover, when the view is recomputed, the supporting views will always reflect the same or a later state. When there are no auxiliary views, and the integrator policy is incremental, consistency cannot be guaranteed unless maintenance algorithms are modified appropriately (see for example [29]). We do not consider such algorithms in this paper.

3.3 Source Capabilities

Maintenance policy performance for externally materialised views depends on the capabilities provided by sources. Maintenance of auxiliary views is similar to maintenance of a single source view. This means that the same dependency on capabilities applies. We have shown that the most important capabilities in such cases are whether the source can actively notify changes and whether it can deliver the delta changes. We define a source as *change active* (CHAC) if it can actively notify to an external client that changes have been committed, and as *delta aware* (DAW) if it can deliver delta changes on request. Note that for a join view the sources can have different degrees of support which, for example, may mean that one source is DAW (which makes incremental maintenance preferable) and the other can be non-DAW (which may imply that recomputed policies are better). A goal with this paper is to analyse how to determine a join view maintenance policy and whether the results for a single source view may be useful for determining a supporting view policy.

For some join view policies additional interaction with sources is required. If an incremental join policy is used and no auxiliary views are maintained, changes from one source have to be joined with the other source. We will classify a source as *semi-join aware* (SAW) if, for a join with predicate p, and for any object O, it can return objects that match with O under predicate p. A relational database is trivially SAW for equi-joins (these join queries will be selections using the join attribute as condition). For other types of joins, e.g. matching using regular expressions, a relational database may not be SAW, which implies that the whole supporting view may have to be retrieved and matched against the other objects.

4 TMID – A Testbed for Maintenance of Integrated Data

In this section, we present a *Testbed for Maintenance of Integrated Data* (TMID), an implementation of view maintenance using sources such as a relational database and an XML web server. It enables measurement of policy performance, both in terms of quality of service and system overhead. This makes it possible to empirically compare the performance of any of the join policies discussed in the previous section. The system is publicly available[2], and can be downloaded and used for multi-source view maintenance.

The architecture of TMID corresponds to the one shown in Figure 1. Wrappers, integrators and other components can be located on any machine on the network. XML is used as the common data model used by the integrator. This means that data from various sources can be wrapped and sent to the client in XML format. The main components, from a maintenance perspective, are wrappers and the integrator. The wrappers can be tailored to handle different data sources.

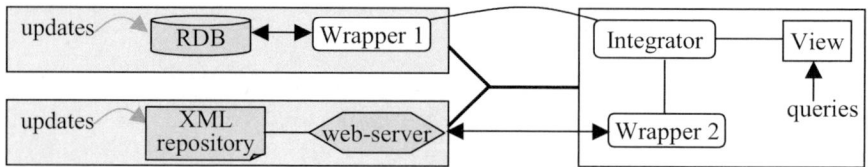

Fig. 1. The components of the TMID architecture, and an example of a possible configuration

Currently, a data source can be an InterBase database or an XML web server. Wrappers are responsible for providing the relevant data to the integrator according to the supporting view policies. The integrator is the most complex component, in that it is responsible for synchronizing wrapper activity, and computing and maintaining the join view. Currently, it is possible to use either hash-based or nested loop join in the integrator.

Although the system can be used for distributed data maintenance, the main purpose of TMID is for measuring performance. Experiments can be defined and executed, and performance can be measured and recorded. For this purpose, each data source will be updated by an updater component, and a querier will query the view. By specifying a number of policies and source characteristics to be varied, the system can be configured to automatically execute experiments and log results.

Any combination of integrator and wrapper policies can be used for experiments. This includes incremental or recomputed join, with periodic, immediate or on-demand timing and the possibility of using auxiliary views in the integrator. If auxiliary views are not maintained in the integrator, the incremental join algorithm will send join queries to the wrappers, which will either forward them to the source (if it is SAW) or retrieve the supporting view and perform the join. No consistency preserving algorithms have been implemented when auxiliary views are used which means the cost of such policies will currently be underestimated when strong consistency is required.

---

[2] at http://www.his.se/ida/~henrik/research/

5   Evaluating Maintenance Policies

The large number of possible join view policies and source configurations makes it difficult to evaluate and understand the trade-offs in policy selection. In this section we present the result of a performance evaluation where the staleness (Z), response time (RT) and system overhead[3] (SO) for a large number of policies have been measured under different system configurations. The experiments were designed to answer the following questions:

- Are all combinations of policy timings meaningful? Are there types of policies which give inferior performance irrespective of configuration?
- How is the choice between incremental and recomputed policies affected by join processing? Are high cost joins different from low cost joins?
- When is it beneficial to keep auxiliary views? How is this affected by the presence of SAW capability?

The same set of experiments has been conducted in two different system and data source configurations. The first configuration consists of three Sun Solaris machines with one relational database and one XML source. The second configuration consists of three Linux machines with two XML sources. In both configurations a 10Mbit hub is used to connect the machines. The relational data source consist of 10000 tuples each of size 1K. The XML sources contain 3000 XML objects of size 5K. Each experiment included 50 queries (which took approximately 25 minutes) and the same experiment was repeated three times with the median value being used. Unless explicitly stated, the join is performed using a hash-based algorithm and the result is for the Linux configuration [4].

5.1   Analysing Policy Timings

It is possible to use most combinations of timings in the integrator. To analyse the impact of supporting view and integrator timings we systematically selected 84 different policies representing all possible combinations of integrator and supporting view timings with both recomputed and incremental strategies (including those which have incremental maintenance of supporting views and recomputed join). The set of policies includes those that use auxiliary views and those that do not. The policies have been used in a number of source configurations where source capabilities have been varied. For each such configuration the costs of all policies have been compared under different evaluation criteria.

The result of one comparison of all policies is shown in an Appendix. It is clear from such a comparison that the different policies exhibit great variation in cost. When the combined cost is considered (all), the worst policy has a cost 42 times higher than the best policy.

---

[3] including the total delay caused by maintenance activity in both wrappers and integrator.

[4] All observations presented in this paper have been made in both system configurations.

To summarise these comparisons, Table 1 shows the lowest cost policies for different combination of DAW capability in the two sources. The comparison has been performed with four different evaluation criteria: system overhead, system overhead combined with staleness, system overhead combined with response time, and system overhead combined with staleness and response time.

Table 1. The lowest cost policies for different criteria and source capabilities

Sources	SO	SO+Z	SO+RT	All
Both sources DAW	P_I-aux-I_I-I_I	O_I-aux-I_I-I_I	P_I-aux-I_I-I_I	I_I-aux-I_I-I_I
One source DAW	P_R-aux-P_I-P_R	O_R-aux-I_I-O_R	P_R-aux-P_I-P_R	I_I-aux-I_I-I_I
No source DAW	P_R-aux-P_R-O_R	O_R-aux-I_R-I_R	P_R-aux-P_R-O_R	O_R-aux-O_R-O_R

First of all, we note that all three timings, and both recomputed and incremental polices are used. There is great variation in integrator policy and supporting view policies. Periodic policies are common when staleness is not included in the criteria. When staleness is considered, immediate policies dominate. It should be noted that immediate supporting view policies requires sources to actively notify the client that changes have been committed (i.e. the source has to be CHAC). As few existing sources provide CHAC, this requirement limits the chance to use such policies. In such cases on-demand supporting view policies seem to be the best alternative.

It is notable that all policies use auxiliary views. The cost of maintaining these views is included in all cases, but not the additional storage space.

All of the above observations give indications concerning the types of policy that may be useful. By looking at the highest cost policies it may be possible to identify some policy types which are less useful. Table 2 shows the highest cost policies for the same scenarios as Table 1.

Table 2. The highest cost policies for different criteria and source capabilities

Sources	SO	SO+Z	SO+RT	All
Both sources DAW	P_R-noAux-O_R-O_R	P_R-aux-P_I-P_R	O_R-noAux-O_R-O_R	P_R-aux-P_I-P_R
One source DAW	P_R-aux-O_R-O_R	P_R-aux-P_R-P_R	O_R-aux-O_R-O_R	P_R-aux-P_R-P_R
No source DAW	P_I-noAux-O_I-O_I	P_R-aux-P_I-P_R	O_I-noAux-O_I-O_I	P_R-aux-P_I-P_R

We note that the worst policies use incremental supporting view policies when the sources are not DAW and recompute when they are DAW. When staleness is included in the criteria, it is not beneficial to have periodic policies both in the integrator and for supporting views. An explanation of this is that periodic supporting view policy is asynchronous with source changes and will add a staleness penalty - of a full period in the worst case. A periodic integrator policy is asynchronous with the supporting view policies and will, in addition, add a full period to staleness. This illustrates that it is important to make wrapper activity (which is responsible for supporting view policies) consistent with integrator activity. If a source is not CHAC, it may be possible to emulate an immediate policy by periodic polling. If the integrator in turn maintains the view periodically this may give inferior performance. As an example, the maintenance solution described in [24] suggests that changes should be eagerly propagated to the integrator to be available when maintenance is initiated (periodically). The rationale for this is to reduce maintenance delay, but unless the sources are CHAC this will lead to unnecessarily high data staleness. Moreover, system overhead is still not reduced compared with, for example, a periodic integrator policy combined with on-demand supporting view policies.

The comparisons above have been based on the total join view cost. These are derived by combining the costs of maintaining supporting views and maintaining the join view. Join view staleness is computed from: the time a result is returned, the source states used in the result, and the state changes in the sources. The worst case staleness of the two sources is used. The experimental log presents the individual cost for wrappers, integrator, and worst case staleness for the two sources. Table 3 shows an example for the policy I_I-aux-I_I-I_I when the DAW capability of the sources is varied.

Table 3. The cost components for a join policy when DAW is varied

XML source DAW	Rel. source DAW	XML SO	Rel. SO	Integr. SO	Total SO	XML Z	Rel. Z	Total Z
Yes	Yes	0.3	1.5	0.2	1.9	0.1	0.9	0.9
Yes	No	0.3	13.1	0.2	13.6	0	13.4	13.4
No	Yes	5.8	1.5	0.2	7.5	5.4	0.7	5.4
No	No	7.3	14.6	0.2	21.9	9.7	13.9	13.9

These experiments were conducted in the Solaris environment, where the two sources were very different. What is important is that the cost for a supporting view is relatively unaffected[5] by the properties of the other source. This means that the supporting view analysis can be considered in isolation to some extent and that our previous work on policy selection can be applied. We have actually run experiments for single source view with the same characteristics as the

---

[5] Only when both sources are non-DAW can we note a slight increase in the system overhead. As both wrappers are located in the integrator environment in this configuration, a possible explanation is that this effect is caused by network congestion.

supporting views. The results showed that the cost for these single source views actually corresponded with the components shown in Table 3. It is interesting to note that the staleness value for a join view is determined by the worst case staleness for the supporting views. This implies that the supporting view policies cannot be chosen in isolation. If, for example, a periodic policy is used in one wrapper (for example due to missing CHAC capability) this will give a relatively high staleness, and it may be pointless to use immediate propagation of changes from the other source.

To conclude, it is apparent that all policy timings are useful for join view policies. The requirement on quality of service and the characteristics of sources may vary, which implies that many different policies may be optimal. The timing for wrapper and integrator cannot be selected independently as some combinations may give sub-optimal performance with respect to view staleness. This is the case, for example, when one wrapper is propagating changes that are not needed immediately by the integrator. Support is needed for selecting an appropriate policy, and the results presented indicate that our previous work on single source views can be used to analyse supporting view costs.

5.2   Analysing the Choice between Incremental and Recompute

For a single source view, we have shown [10] that the choice between incremental and recompute may depend on the presence of DAW capability in the source. The comparison presented in the previous section shows that both recomputed and incremental policies can give the lowest cost for a join view as well. In some situations the lowest cost policy uses incremental supporting view policies for auxiliary views and recomputes the join. This makes the selection even more complex. Note that in the comparison above the join is computed using an efficient hash-based algorithm. If the join predicate involves more complex operations (such as data transformation and cleaning) then a nested loop join may be the only alternative. We conducted a set of experiments to analyse the choice between incremental and recompute.

Table 4 shows the system overhead for an incremental and a recomputed policy for combinations of join techniques and DAW capability in sources.

Table 4. The system cost (s.) for a recomputed and an incremental policy for different DAW capability and join technique scenarios

Join Technique	Source DAW	P_I-aux-O_I-O_I	P_R-aux-O_R-O_R
Hash	Both DAW	0.9	3.6
Hash	One DAW	1.8	3.6
Hash	No DAW	4.2	4.1
Nested loop	Both DAW	1.5	7.1
Nested loop	One DAW	2.5	7.1
Nested loop	No DAW	4.2	7.1

For these two policies it is clear that the incremental policy is superior for all situations except when the joining is hash-based and no source is DAW. In such a case the cost of the recomputed policy is comparable to the incremental policy. On inspection, the detailed logs from the experiments revealed that the integrator cost (i.e. to recompute the nested loop, once the auxiliary view has been updated) was approximately 3 seconds. This compares with 0.1 seconds for hash-based recompute. The implication is that when join processing is expensive then incremental policies are generally to be preferred, irrespective of DAW capability. When joining is low cost, on the other hand, it may be beneficial to recompute a join using auxiliary views and use a supporting view policy that matches the DAW capability of each source.

5.3 Analysing Auxiliary Views

We saw in Table 1 that all low cost policies used auxiliary views. Considering the amount of work that has been invested in devising algorithms to ensure consistency when auxiliary views are not used, it is interesting to analyse how policy cost depends on auxiliary views and SAW capability. Table 5 shows the cost of two immediate incremental policies with and without auxiliary views when the SAW and DAW capabilities are varied. Joining is hash-based in both situations.

Table 5. The system cost (s.) for incremental policies with and without auxiliary views for different DAW and SAW capability scenarios

Source DAW	Source SAW	I_I-aux-I_I-I_I	I_I-noAux-I_I-I_I
Both DAW	Both SAW	0.5	1.3
Both DAW	One SAW	0.6	6.9
Both DAW	No SAW	0.5	13.1
No DAW	Both SAW	15.0	17.0
No DAW	One SAW	15.0	23.0
No DAW	No SAW	15.2	29.1

Using auxiliary views gives better performance irrespective of the DAW and SAW capabilities of the sources. We have not implemented any algorithms to ensure consistency when no auxiliary views are used. If strong consistency is required these algorithms will further increase the cost of I_I-noAux-I_I-I_I. In other words, using auxiliary views will always give a lower cost and often offer a better quality of service in terms of consistency.

Another observation is that the absence of SAW makes the policy not using auxiliary views significantly more expensive than the other policy. It may even be better to use a recomputed policy in such cases. The cost of I_R-aux-I_R-I_R for the same situation is 15.0 (irrespective of DAW and SAW).

To conclude, if storage overhead in the client is not critical we claim that policies keeping auxiliary views are always to be preferred. This implies that the algorithms suggested for ensuring strong consistency will not be needed. These algorithms are designed for views not using auxiliary views

6   Conclusions

In this paper we have presented a performance evaluation of maintenance policies for an externally materialised multi-source view. The choice of policy is affected by many factors such as the set of possible policies, the evaluation criteria used, and the capabilities provided by sources. We have shown that there are a large number of possible policy combinations for a binary join view. Each source can use a separate policy to propagate the required fraction (supporting view), and the joining can be done with various policies. It is also possible to store the supporting views in the integrator (we refer to these as auxiliary views) to avoid sending join queries to sources. If auxiliary views are not used for incremental policies then the degree of support to handle join queries impacts on policy performance.

We have analysed the performance of 84 policies and found that many of these gave optimal performance under certain conditions. The capability of each source will affect the performance of each supporting view. This implies that it is not possible to handle sources collectively. In some situations it is, for example, advantageous to use incremental maintenance for one supporting view and recompute for the other. At the same time it is important to coordinate supporting view policies with integrator policies. The view staleness is most complex as the join view will have its staleness determined by the worst case staleness of the supporting views. A naive maintenance solution where wrappers monitor sources by periodic polling, and the integrator performs the joining periodically, will be the worst possible policy with respect to staleness. From the presented experiments it is possible to make some general observations. First of all, recomputed policies are less useful than incremental policies. If the join processing is costly (e.g. nested loop) or if the sources provides deltas it is always better to maintain the view incrementally. Secondly, auxiliary views are always to prefer unless storage limitations makes them impossible to use.

Most work on externally materialised views has been conducted in a data warehouse context. It should be noted that this is not the only application area. In today's Internet-based environments information is commonly retrieved from autonomous sources. The data may be stored in clients to increase availability and query performance. One such example involves biological data, which is produced and published by various universities, labs and organisations and is used by numerous clients. If data from several sources needs to be combined this may require complex and expensive computations. This is, for example, the case when protein sequences from one source are classified using regular expressions from another source[7]. Our work shows that even if the data is updated infrequently, and the data sources provide no change detection capabilities, incremental methods are to be preferred.

There are many aspects that remain to be studied with respect to externally materialised views. We have concentrated on join views in this work. It remains to explore how other operations affect the results presented. This includes set operations (union, difference, division) and aggregates. Another issue is how operations over more than two sources should be handled, for example, n-ary joins. The experiments presented have been conducted in an isolated environment with synthetically generated data. It would be valuable to analyse a real data integration scenario under realistic network conditions. Furthermore it should be relatively straightforward to extend our testbed to handle dynamic changing of policies. This would enable adaptive policy selection in which actual performance statistics are used in policy selection.

In ongoing work we have extended our single source framework for policy selection to handle join view policies [9]. The single source cost model has been useful for modelling supporting view policies which means only the join cost has been added. Based on extensive analysis and the performance evaluation presented in this paper, we have proposed a set of heuristics [12] and shown that these give good selections.

Finally, it is interesting to note that the majority of research effort on external view maintenance has been concentrated on producing algorithms for the consistent maintenance of views when no auxiliary information is maintained. In the evaluation presented in this paper it is clear that such policies will perform less well than those using auxiliary views, irrespective of the support provided by sources. Although work on consistent view maintenance may be theoretically challenging, it is our belief that it is not the most critical problem for the research community to address with respect to externally materialised view maintenance.

References

1. S. Abiteboul, J. McHugh, M. Rys, V. Vassalos, and J.L. Wiener, *Incremental maintenance for materialized views over semistructured data*, VLDB'98, Proceedings of 24rd International Conference on Very Large Data Bases, August 24–27, 1998, New York City, New York, USA (A. Gupta, O. Shmueli, and J. Widom, eds.), 1998, pp. 38–49.

2. D. Agrawal, A. El Abbadi, A.K. Singh, and T. Yurek, *Efficient view maintenance at data warehouses*, SIGMOD 1997, Proceedings ACM SIGMOD International Conference on Management of Data, May 13–15, 1997, Tucson, Arizona, USA (J. Peckham, ed.), 1997, pp. 417–427.

3. M. Akhtar Ali, Alvaro A. A. Fernandes, and Norman W. Paton, *Incremental maintenance of materialized OQL views*, Proceedings of the third ACM international workshop on Data warehousing and OLAP, Washington, USA, 2000, pp. 41–48.

4. M. Akhtar Ali, Norman W. Paton, and Alvaro A. A. Fernandes, *An experimental performance evaluation of incremental materialized view maintenance in object databases*, Data Warehousing and Knowledge Discovery, Third International Conference, DaWaK 2001, Munich, Germany, September 5–7, 2001, Proceedings, 2001, pp. 240–253.

5. J.A. Blakeley, P-Å. Larson, and F.W. Tompa, *Efficiently updating materialized views*, Proceedings of the 1986 ACM SIGMOD International Conference on Management of Data, Washington, D.C., May 28–30, 1986 (C. Zaniolo, ed.), 1986, pp. 61–71.

6. L.S. Colby, A. Kawaguchi, D.F. Lieuwen, I.S. Mumick, and K.A. Ross, *Supporting multiple view maintenance policies*, SIGMOD 1997, Proceedings ACM SIGMOD International Conference on Management of Data, May 13–15, 1997, Tucson, Arizona, USA (J. Peckham, ed.), 1997, pp. 405–416.
7. H. Engström and K. Asthorsson, *A data warehouse approach to maintenance of integrated biological data*, Workshop on BioInformatics held in conjunction with the 19th International Conference on Data Engineering (ICDE'03) Bangalore, India, March 4, 2003, On-line proceedings, 14p., 2003.
8. H. Engström, S. Chakravarthy, and B. Lings, *A user-centric view of data warehouse maintenance issues*, Advances in Databases, 17th British National Conferenc on Databases, BNCOD 17, Exeter, UK, July 3–5, 2000, Proceedings (B. Lings and K.G. Jeffery, eds.), Lecture Notes in Computer Science, vol. 1832, Springer, 2000, pp. 68–80.
9. _____, *Data integration in heterogeneous environments: Multi-source policies, cost model, and implementation*, Tech. report, University of Skövde, Sweden, 2002.
10. _____, *Implementation and comparative evaluation of maintenance policies in a data warehouse environment*, Advances in Databases, 19th British National Conference on Databases, BNCOD 19, Sheffield, UK, July 17–19, 2002, Proceedings (B. Eaglestone, S. North, and A. Poulovassilis, eds.), Lecture Notes in Computer Science, vol. 2405, Springer, 2002, pp. 90–102.
11. _____, *A systematic approach to selecting maintenance policies in a data warehouse environment*, Advances in Database Technology - EDBT 2002, 8th International Conference on Extending Database Technology, Prague, Czech Republic, March 25–27, Proceedings (C.S. Jensen, K.G. Jeffery, J. Pokorný, S. Saltenis, E. Bertino, K. Böhm, and M. Jarke, eds.), Lecture Notes in Computer Science, vol. 2287, Springer, 2002, pp. 317–335.
12. _____, *A heuristic for refresh policy selection in heterogeneous environments*, 19th International Conference on Data Engineering, Bangalore, India, March 5–8, 2003, Proceedings, 2003, pp. 674–676.
13. A. Gupta, H. V. Jagadish, and I. S. Mumick, *Data integration using self-maintainable views*, Advances in Database Technology - EDBT'96, 5th International Conference on Extending Database Technology, Avignon, France, March 25–29, 1996, Proceedings, 1996, pp. 140–144.
14. A. Gupta and I. S. Mumick, *Maintenance of materialized views: Problems, techniques, and applications*, IEEE Data Engineering Bulletin **18** (1995), no. 2, 3–18.
15. A. Gupta, I.S. Mumick, and V. S. Subrahmanian, *Maintaining views incrementally*, Proceedings of the 1993 ACM SIGMOD International Conference on Management of Data, Washington, D.C., May 26–28, 1993 (P. Buneman and S. Jajodia, eds.), 1993, pp. 157–166.
16. E.N. Hanson, *A performance analysis of view materialization strategies*, Proceedings of the Association for Computing Machinery Special Interest Group on Management of Data 1987 Annual Conference, San Francisco, California, May 27–29, 1987 (U. Dayal and I.L. Traiger, eds.), 1987, pp. 440–453.
17. R. Hull and G. Zhou, *A framework for supporting data integration using the materialized and virtual approaches*, Proceedings of the 1996 ACM SIGMOD International Conference on Management of Data, Montreal, Quebec, Canada, June 4–6, 1996 (H.V. Jagadish and I.S. Mumick, eds.), 1996, pp. 481–492.
18. _____, *Towards the study of performance trade-offs between materialized and virtual integrated views*, Proceedings of the Workshop on Materialized Views: Techniques and Applications (VIEWS'96), Montreal, Canada, 1996, pp. 91–102.

19. D. Quass, A. Gupta, I.S. Mumick, and J. Widom, *Making views self-maintainable for data warehousing*, Proceedings of the Fourth International Conference on Parallel and Distributed Information Systems, December 18–20, 1996, Miami Beach, Florida, USA, 1996, pp. 158–169.
20. N. Roussopoulos, *Materialized views and data warehouses*, SIGMOD Record **27** (1998), no. 1, 21–26.
21. J. Srivastava and D. Rotem, *Analytical modeling of materialized view maintenance*, Proceedings of the Seventh ACM SIGACT-SIGMOD-SIGART Symposium on Principles of Database Systems, March 21–23, 1988, Austin, Texas, 1988, pp. 126–134.
22. M. Staudt and M. Jarke, *Incremental maintenance of externally materialized views*, VLDB'96, Proceedings of 22th International Conference on Very Large Data Bases, September 3–6, 1996, Mumbai (Bombay), India (T.M. Vijayaraman, A.P. Buchmann, C. Mohan, and N.L. Sarda, eds.), 1996, pp. 75–86.
23. A.S. Varde and E.A. Rundensteiner, *MEDWRAP: Consistent view maintenance over distributed multi-relation sources*, Database and Expert Systems Applications, 13th International Conference, DEXA 2002, Aix-en-Provence, France, September 2–6, 2002, Proceedings (A. Hameurlain, R. Cicchetti, and R. Traunmüller, eds.), 2002.
24. A. Vavouras, S. Gatziu, and K. R. Dittrich, *The SIRIUS approach for refreshing data warehouses incrementally*, Datenbanksysteme in Büro, Technik und Wissenschaft (BTW), GI-Fachtagung, Freiburg, 1.–3. März 1999, Proceedings (Alejandro P. Buchmann, ed.), Informatik Aktuell, 1999, pp. 80–96.
25. H. Wang, M.E. Orlowska, and W. Liang, *Efficient refreshment of materialized views with multiple sources*, Proceedings of the 1999 ACM CIKM International Conference on Information and Knowledge Management, Kansas City, Missouri, USA, November 2–6, 1999, 1999, pp. 375–382.
26. X. Zhang, L. Ding, and E.A. Rundensteiner, *PVM: Parallel view maintenance under concurrent data updates of distributed sources*, Data Warehousing and Knowledge Discovery, Third International Conference, DaWaK 2001, Munich, Germany, September 5–7, 2001, Proceedings (Y. Kambayashi, W. Winiwarter, and M. Arikawa, eds.), 2001.
27. Y. Zhuge, *Incremental maintenance of consistent data warehouses*, Ph.D. thesis, Stanford University, USA, 1999.
28. Y. Zhuge, H. Garcia-Molina, J. Hammer, and J. Widom, *View maintenance in a warehousing environment*, Proceedings of the 1995 ACM SIGMOD International Conference on Management of Data, San Jose, California, May 22-25, 1995 (M.J. Carey and D.A. Schneider, eds.), 1995, pp. 316–327.
29. Y. Zhuge, H. Garcia-Molina, and J.L. Wiener, *The Strobe algorithms for multi-source warehouse consistency*, Proceedings of the Fourth International Conference on Parallel and Distributed Information Systems, December 18-20, 1996, Miami Beach, Florida, USA, 1996, pp. 146–157.

A   Appendix

This appendix contains a sample of the results of the TMID experiments. For full details the reader is referred to [9]. Table 6 shows the result of an experiment where all join policies were used for the same configuration (Solaris environment where both sources are DAW). The policies are arranged according to their total cost (All). For each policy the SO, SO+Z, and SO+RT cost is also shown.

Table 6. The comparison of all policies in a Solaris environment where both sources are DAW

Policy	SO	SO+Z	SO+RT	All	Policy	SO	SO+Z	SO+RT	All
O_I-aux-O_I-O_I	0.9	1.1	1.6	1.7	I_R-aux-I_R-P_I	6.5	34.3	6.5	34.3
O_R-aux-O_I-O_I	1.0	1.5	1.7	2.2	P_I-aux-P_I-P_I	0.8	35.8	0.9	35.9
O_R-aux-I_I-O_I	1.1	1.6	1.7	2.3	P_R-aux-I_R-O_I	6.0	37.5	6.0	37.6
I_I-aux-I_I-I_I	1.9	2.7	1.9	2.8	P_I-aux-P_I-O_I	0.9	37.6	0.9	37.6
O_I-aux-I_I-I_I	1.8	2.7	2.0	2.8	O_R-aux-P_R-O_I	6.2	37.3	6.9	38.0
O_I-aux-O_I-I_I	1.9	2.7	2.3	3.1	P_I-aux-I_I-P_I	0.9	38.1	0.9	38.2
I_R-aux-I_I-I_I	2.2	3.1	2.2	3.1	I_R-aux-P_I-P_R	11.4	38.9	11.5	39.0
O_R-aux-I_I-I_I	1.9	3.0	2.2	3.3	O_R-aux-P_I-P_R	11.0	38.8	11.3	39.1
I_I-noAux-I_I-I_I	5.9	6.7	5.9	6.8	O_I-noAux-P_I-P_I	4.9	35.4	8.7	39.2
O_R-aux-I_R-O_I	6.0	11.2	6.7	11.9	P_R-aux-I_I-P_I	0.9	39.4	0.9	39.4
O_I-noAux-I_I-I_I	5.9	11.4	9.8	15.3	O_I-noAux-O_I-P_I	4.8	35.8	8.5	39.6
O_I-noAux-O_I-I_I	5.9	11.5	9.9	15.5	O_R-aux-I_R-O_R	18.3	30.6	28.3	40.7
O_I-noAux-O_I-O_I	5.8	11.7	10.8	16.7	O_I-noAux-P_I-I_I	5.9	37.4	9.8	41.2
O_R-aux-I_I-I_R	11.8	21.7	12.1	22.0	P_R-aux-I_I-O_R	11.0	44.3	11.1	44.4
P_I-aux-I_I-I_I	1.8	22.1	1.9	22.2	O_R-aux-I_I-P_R	11.0	44.6	11.3	44.9
O_I-aux-O_I-P_I	0.9	22.3	1.3	22.7	P_I-noAux-P_I-O_I	5.8	45.3	5.8	45.4
O_I-aux-I_I-P_I	0.9	23.3	1.1	23.5	P_R-aux-O_I-O_R	11.0	46.1	11.0	46.2
I_R-aux-I_I-I_R	12.4	24.3	12.4	24.3	O_R-noAux-O_R-O_R	22.8	35.1	34.1	46.4
P_R-aux-I_I-I_I	1.9	25.9	2.0	26.0	O_R-aux-P_I-O_R	11.1	36.9	20.7	46.5
I_R-aux-I_I-P_I	1.4	26.0	1.4	26.1	P_R-aux-I_R-I_R	18.4	47.2	18.4	47.2
P_R-aux-I_I-O_I	1.0	26.3	1.0	26.3	I_R-aux-P_R-P_R	17.3	47.6	17.3	47.7
I_I-aux-P_I-P_I	1.0	26.5	1.1	26.6	I_R-aux-I_I-P_R	11.3	47.6	11.4	47.7
P_I-aux-I_I-O_I	0.9	27.2	0.9	27.2	P_I-noAux-P_I-I_I	5.7	47.8	5.7	47.8
I_I-aux-I_I-P_I	1.0	27.7	1.0	27.7	O_R-aux-O_R-O_R	23.2	36.9	34.6	48.4
P_I-aux-O_I-O_I	0.9	27.7	1.0	27.8	P_R-aux-P_R-O_I	6.2	49.1	6.2	49.1
O_R-aux-I_I-P_I	1.0	27.7	1.3	28.0	I_R-aux-I_R-P_R	19.1	49.7	19.2	49.7
O_I-aux-P_I-P_I	0.9	28.0	1.1	28.1	P_R-aux-I_I-I_R	11.8	50.8	11.9	50.9
O_R-aux-P_I-O_I	1.0	27.6	1.7	28.3	P_R-aux-P_I-O_R	11.3	50.9	11.3	51.0
P_R-aux-P_I-O_I	1.0	28.5	1.0	28.5	P_I-noAux-P_I-P_I	5.0	51.4	5.0	51.4
P_R-aux-O_I-O_I	1.0	28.6	1.0	28.7	O_R-aux-P_R-P_R	21.5	51.5	21.9	51.9
I_R-aux-P_I-P_I	1.4	29.0	1.4	29.1	O_R-aux-I_R-P_R	18.2	51.8	18.5	52.2
O_R-aux-P_I-P_I	1.0	29.6	1.2	29.9	P_R-aux-I_I-P_R	11.2	52.2	11.2	52.3
O_R-aux-I_R-I_R	18.4	30.0	18.7	30.4	P_R-aux-I_R-O_R	18.7	55.9	18.8	56.0
I_R-aux-I_R-I_R	19.1	30.9	19.2	30.9	P_R-aux-P_I-P_I	0.9	56.0	1.0	56.1
I_I-noAux-I_I-P_I	5.0	31.2	5.0	31.3	P_R-aux-I_R-P_I	6.1	56.2	6.1	56.3
O_R-aux-I_I-O_R	11.1	21.7	20.7	31.3	P_R-noAux-O_R-O_R	22.7	58.7	22.8	58.7
O_R-aux-O_I-O_R	11.0	21.9	20.5	31.5	P_R-aux-P_I-P_R	10.9	59.1	11.0	59.2
P_I-noAux-O_I-O_I	5.8	31.6	5.9	31.6	P_R-aux-P_R-O_R	16.6	60.1	16.7	60.2
O_R-aux-I_R-P_I	6.0	31.4	6.3	31.7	O_R-aux-P_R-O_R	18.3	51.5	28.4	61.6
I_I-noAux-P_I-P_I	5.1	32.3	5.1	32.3	P_R-aux-O_R-O_R	23.1	61.7	23.2	61.8
P_I-noAux-O_I-I_I	5.9	32.8	5.9	32.8	P_R-aux-P_R-P_R	21.6	66.0	21.7	66.0
P_I-noAux-I_I-I_I	6.1	33.2	6.1	33.3	P_R-aux-I_R-P_R	18.1	72.1	18.2	72.1

Database Schema Transformation Optimisation Techniques for the AutoMed System

Nerissa Tong

Department of Computing, Imperial College,
180 Queen's Gate, London SW7 2BZ, United Kingdom
nnyt98@doc.ic.ac.uk

Abstract. AutoMed is a database integration system that is designed to support the integration of schemas expressed in a variety of high-level conceptual modelling languages. It is based on the idea of expressing transformations of schemas as a sequence of primitive transformation steps, each of which is a bi-directional mapping between schemas. To become an efficient schema integration system in practice, where the number and size of schemas involved in the integration may be very large, the amount of time spent on the evaluation of transformations must be reduced to a minimal level. It is also important that the integrity of a set of transformations is maintained during the process of transformation optimisation. This paper discusses a new representation of schema transformations which facilitates the verification of the well-formedness of transformation sequences, and the optimisation of transformation sequences.

1   Introduction

A major task in database integration is the generation of a global schema from a collection of local source schemas of existing databases. There are three main approaches to database integration, namely *global as view (GAV)*, *local as view (LAV)*, and *both as view (BAV)* [12].

In GAV, the constructs in the global schema are defined as views over source local schemas. The popularity of this approach, which is adopted by a number of database integration systems such as TSIMMIS [6], InterViso [15], and Garlic [14], can be attributed to its simplicity of implementation. Source schemas are integrated by a set of view definitions which contain predefined query plans that describe the location and retrieval method of the required data. Query planning is made simple and efficient in this approach, however it suffers from one major drawback – when new schemas are added to the system or existing schemas are modified, all corresponding query templates will have to be rewritten.

In LAV, local schema constructs in data sources are defined as views over the global schema. Some systems adopting the LAV approach include Infomaster [5], Information Manifold [8], and Agora [9]. Query plans are computed at the time queries are submitted to the system. This approach offers greater flexibility over the GAV approach in changes in the number or contents of local schemas because

A. James, B. Lings, M. Younas (Eds.): BNCOD 2003, LNCS 2712, pp. 157–171, 2003.

in LAV, the changes can be handled without affecting existing view definitions. The drawbacks of the LAV approach are that, (1) query processing is much more complex than in GAV, and (2) if the contents of the global schema changes, modification is then required for all the views that contain in their definition the changed global schema constructs.

In BAV, bi-directional mappings between schemas are used for transforming schemas and thus it supports evolution of both global and local schemas [11]. It is also possible to automatically derive GAV and LAV views from BAV views. Section 2 discusses the *AutoMed* [13] framework which adopts the BAV approach. More detailed discussion on the conversion of GAV and LAV into BAV views and vice versa can be found in [12]. The flexibility of the BAV approach allows transformations to be manipulated for optimisation purposes. Section 3 describes new techniques we have developed for the optimisation of transformation sequences. Section 4 concludes the paper with some remarks on the possible extension in the applicability of our optimisation techniques.

2   The AutoMed Framework

The AutoMed framework supports the integration of schemas that are expressed in different data modelling languages. The use of a high-level data model as the *Common Data Model (CDM)* in the global schema makes it very complicated to map constructs of local schemas, which possibly use different data models, with one another. This is because, typically, high-level models provide a richer set of modelling constructs, and hence a concept may be represented in a number of ways. To avoid this complication, the AutoMed framework uses the *Hypergraph Data Model (HDM)* [13], a low-level hypergraph-based data model, as the CDM.

The constructs contained in the HDM are *Node*, *Edge*, and *Constraint*. An HDM schema S is then a triple containing a set of *Nodes*, a set of *Edges*, and a set of *Constraints* — $S = \langle Nodes, Edges, Constraints \rangle$. *Nodes* and *Edges* have a *scheme* and *Constraints* are boolean-valued queries over S. The scheme of a node is $\langle\langle N \rangle\rangle$, where N is the name of the node. The scheme of an edge is $\langle\langle E, N_1, \ldots, N_n \rangle\rangle$, where E is the name of the edge and $N_1, \ldots, N_n$ are the nodes connected by E.[1] A set of mappings between higher-level model constructs and HDM constructs is defined. A set of *primitive transformations* has been defined to transform HDM models. The operators of these transformations include add, delete and rename for semantically equivalent schemas, extend and contract for semantically overlapping (non-equivalent) schemas, and id for use only in the implementation of the AutoMed system.[2] By using the mappings between constructs of different models, schemas and transformations can be translated

---

[1] It is optional to give an edge a name: where an edge is not given a name, its scheme will be $\langle\langle \_, N_1, \ldots, N_n \rangle\rangle$.

[2] The id transformations are special transformations that are used only in the implementation of the AutoMed system. They are used for mapping Java object references that point to two semantically equivalent constructs. More details on id transformations can be found in [3].

from one modelling language to another. Table 1 shows some of the primitive transformations available for transforming ER models and their corresponding transformations expressed in the HDM.

Table 1. Example primitive transformations

ER transformations	HDM transformations
$\mathsf{addEnt}(\langle\!\langle\!\langle N\rangle\!\rangle\!\rangle,q)$	$\mathsf{addNode}(\langle\!\langle\!\langle N\rangle\!\rangle\!\rangle,q)$
$\mathsf{addAtt}(\langle\!\langle\!\langle N, A\rangle\!\rangle\!\rangle,q)$	$\mathsf{addNode}(\langle\!\langle N : A\rangle\!\rangle, \{Y \mid \langle X, Y\rangle \in q\}),$
	$\mathsf{addEdge}(\langle\!\langle\!\langle \_, N, N : A\rangle\!\rangle\!\rangle,q)$
$\mathsf{addRel}(\langle\!\langle\!\langle R, N_1, \ldots, N_n\rangle\!\rangle\!\rangle,q)$	$\mathsf{addEdge}(\langle\!\langle\!\langle R, N_1, \ldots, N_n\rangle\!\rangle\!\rangle,q)$
$\mathsf{addGen}(\langle\!\langle\!\langle G, N, N_1,\ldots, N_n\rangle\!\rangle\!\rangle)$	$\mathsf{addCons}(N_1 \subseteq N), \ldots, \mathsf{addCons}(N_n \subseteq N)$

In AutoMed [1] two schemas S_1 and S_2 are transformed into each other by *incrementally* applying to them a set of primitive transformations. This set of transformations forms the *pathway* between S_1 and S_2. A distinguishing feature of the AutoMed approach is that transformations are *automatically reversible*, i.e., transformations are bi-directional, thus pathways are also bi-directional. This is achieved by embedding in each transformation the *extent* of the construct created or removed by the transformation. The extent is expressed as a query q, as shown in Table 1, which defines how the data associated with the new/removed construct can be derived from other existing constructs in the original schema. Note that some transformations do not contain q. This means that the new/removed construct cannot be derived from existing constructs in the original schema. The reader is referred to [10] for a more detailed discussion on the AutoMed transformations and its current state of implementation [3,2]. Table 2 shows some example ER transformations t and their reversed form $\bar{t}$. The reversibility of transformations enables automatic translation of queries posed on any schema into appropriate queries on a particular target schema, as long as there exists a pathway between the schemas.

Table 2. Reversibility of ER transformations

$t : S_x \to S_y$	$\bar{t} : S_y \to S_x$
$\mathsf{addEnt}(\langle\!\langle\!\langle N\rangle\!\rangle\!\rangle,q)$	$\mathsf{deleteEnt}(\langle\!\langle\!\langle N\rangle\!\rangle\!\rangle,q)$
$\mathsf{addAtt}(\langle\!\langle N, A\rangle\!\rangle,q)$	$\mathsf{deleteAtt}(\langle\!\langle N, A\rangle\!\rangle,q)$
$\mathsf{deleteEnt}(\langle\!\langle\!\langle N\rangle\!\rangle\!\rangle,q)$	$\mathsf{addEnt}(\langle\!\langle\!\langle N\rangle\!\rangle\!\rangle,q)$
$\mathsf{deleteAtt}(\langle\!\langle N, A\rangle\!\rangle,q)$	$\mathsf{addAtt}(\langle\!\langle N, A\rangle\!\rangle,q)$

To illustrate how schemas are transformed, Figure 1 shows three source ER schemas S_1, S_2 and S_3, and their global schema S_g. In the figure, rectangular boxes, circles, diamonds and hexagons respectively denote entities, attributes, relationships and generalisation hierarchies; key attributes are underlined and nullable attributes are suffixed by #.

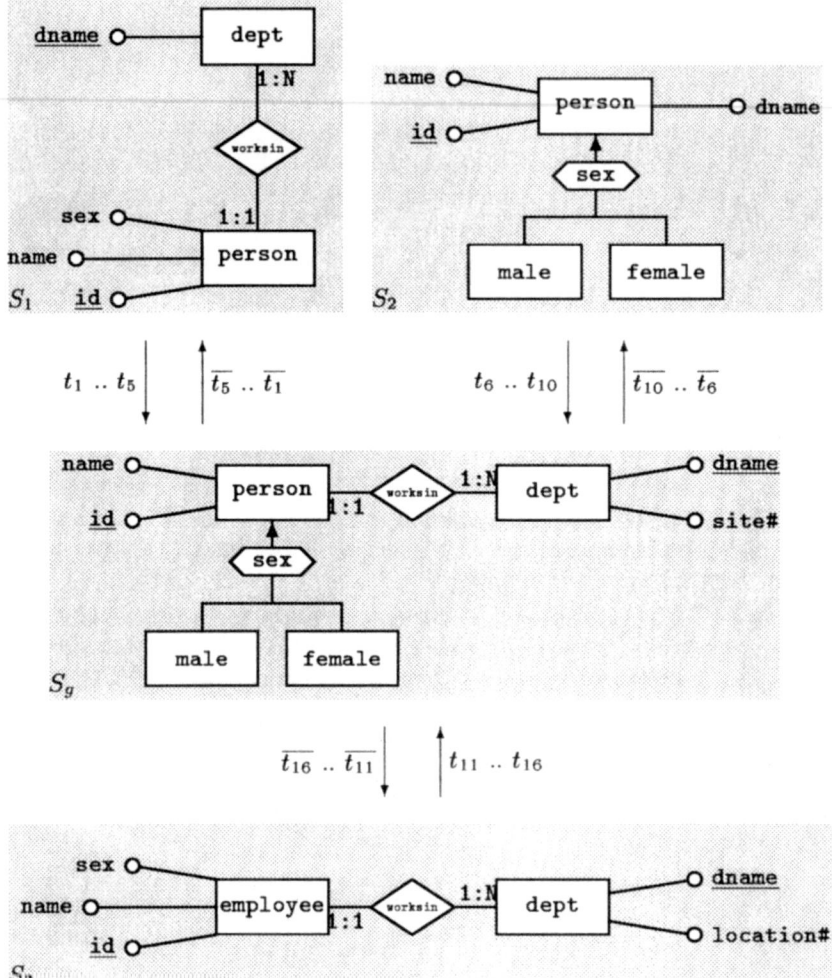

Fig. 1. Example ER schemas

The pathway from S_1 to S_g, denoted $TP_{S_1 \to S_g}$, is shown below.[3] The last value in the scheme of attributes is one of key, null and notnull, which respectively represents primary key, nullable and non-nullable attributes.

---

[3] Note that for transformation t_3, because an ER generalization is translated down into a constraint in the HDM, and constraints do not have an extent, so a query is not required for the addGen transformation. More details can be found in [10, pg. 104].

$\mathsf{TP}_{S_1 \to S_g}$:

t_1 addEnt($\langle\!\langle$male$\rangle\!\rangle$, $\{\mathsf{X} \mid \langle\mathsf{X},'\,\mathsf{m}'\rangle \in \langle\!\langle$person,sex,notnull$\rangle\!\rangle\}$)

t_2 addEnt($\langle\!\langle$female$\rangle\!\rangle$, $\{\mathsf{X} \mid \langle\mathsf{X},'\,\mathsf{f}'\rangle \in \langle\!\langle$person,sex,notnull$\rangle\!\rangle\}$)

t_3 addGen($\langle\!\langle$sex,person,male,female$\rangle\!\rangle$)

t_4 deleteAtt($\langle\!\langle$person,sex,notnull$\rangle\!\rangle$,

$\qquad\qquad \{\mathsf{X},\mathsf{Y} \mid \mathsf{X} \in \langle\!\langle$male$\rangle\!\rangle \wedge \mathsf{Y} =' \mathsf{m}' \vee \mathsf{X} \in \langle\!\langle$female$\rangle\!\rangle \wedge \mathsf{Y} =' \mathsf{f}'\}$)

t_5 extendAtt($\langle\!\langle$dept,site,null$\rangle\!\rangle$)

Reversing each of the transformations and their order in $TP_{S_1 \to S_g}$ gives us the pathway from S_g back to S_1.

$\mathsf{TP}_{S_g \to S_1}$:

$\overline{t_5}$ contractAtt($\langle\!\langle$dept,site,null$\rangle\!\rangle$)

$\overline{t_4}$ addAtt($\langle\!\langle$person,sex,notnull$\rangle\!\rangle$,

$\qquad\qquad \{\mathsf{X},\mathsf{Y} \mid \mathsf{X} \in \langle\!\langle$male$\rangle\!\rangle \wedge \mathsf{Y} =' \mathsf{m}' \vee \mathsf{X} \in \langle\!\langle$female$\rangle\!\rangle \wedge \mathsf{Y} =' \mathsf{f}'\}$)

$\overline{t_3}$ deleteGen($\langle\!\langle$sex,person,male,female$\rangle\!\rangle$)

$\overline{t_2}$ deleteEnt($\langle\!\langle$female$\rangle\!\rangle$, $\{\mathsf{X} \mid \langle\mathsf{X},'\,\mathsf{f}'\rangle \in \langle\!\langle$person,sex,notnull$\rangle\!\rangle\}$)

$\overline{t_1}$ deleteEnt($\langle\!\langle$male$\rangle\!\rangle$, $\{\mathsf{X} \mid \langle\mathsf{X},'\,\mathsf{m}'\rangle \in \langle\!\langle$person,sex,notnull$\rangle\!\rangle\}$)

Pathways $TP_{S_2 \to S_g}$ and $TP_{S_3 \to S_g}$ are shown below. Their reverse, i.e., $TP_{S_g \to S_2}$ and $TP_{S_g \to S_3}$ are derived in a similar fashion as for $TP_{S_1 \to S_g}$.

$\mathsf{TP}_{S_2 \to S_g}$:

t_6 addEnt($\langle\!\langle$dept$\rangle\!\rangle$, $\{\mathsf{X} \mid \langle\_,\mathsf{X}\rangle \in \langle\!\langle$person,dname,notnull$\rangle\!\rangle\}$)

t_7 addAtt($\langle\!\langle$dept,dname,key$\rangle\!\rangle$, $\{\mathsf{X},\mathsf{X} \mid \langle\_,\mathsf{X}\rangle \in \langle\!\langle$person,dname,notnull$\rangle\!\rangle\}$)

t_8 extendAtt($\langle\!\langle$dept,site,null$\rangle\!\rangle$)

t_9 addRel($\langle\!\langle$worksin,person,dept,1:1,1:N$\rangle\!\rangle$, $\{\mathsf{X},\mathsf{Y} \mid \langle\mathsf{X},\mathsf{Y}\rangle \in \langle\!\langle$person,dname,notnull$\rangle\!\rangle\}$

t_{10} deleteAtt($\langle\!\langle$person,dname,notnull$\rangle\!\rangle$,

$\qquad\qquad \{\mathsf{X},\mathsf{Y} \mid \langle\_,\mathsf{X},\mathsf{Y}\rangle \in \langle\!\langle$worksin,person,dept,1:1,1:N$\rangle\!\rangle\}$

$\mathsf{TP}_{S_g \to S_2}$:

$\overline{t_{10}}$ addAtt($\langle\!\langle$person,dname,notnull$\rangle\!\rangle$,

$\qquad\qquad \{\mathsf{X},\mathsf{Y} \mid \langle\_,\mathsf{X},\mathsf{Y}\rangle \in \langle\!\langle$worksin,person,dept,1:1,1:N$\rangle\!\rangle\}$

$\overline{t_9}$ deleteRel($\langle\!\langle$worksin,person,dept,1:1,1:N$\rangle\!\rangle$,

$\qquad\qquad \{\mathsf{X},\mathsf{Y} \mid \langle\mathsf{X},\mathsf{Y}\rangle \in \langle\!\langle$person,dname,notnull$\rangle\!\rangle\}$

$\overline{t_8}$ contractAtt($\langle\!\langle$dept,site,null$\rangle\!\rangle$)

$\overline{t_7}$ deleteAtt($\langle\!\langle$dept,dname,key$\rangle\!\rangle$, $\{\mathsf{X},\mathsf{X} \mid \langle\_,\mathsf{X}\rangle \in \langle\!\langle$person,dname,notnull$\rangle\!\rangle\}$)

$\overline{t_6}$ deleteEnt($\langle\!\langle$dept$\rangle\!\rangle$, $\{\mathsf{X} \mid \langle\_,\mathsf{X}\rangle \in \langle\!\langle$person,dname,notnull$\rangle\!\rangle\}$)

$\mathsf{TP}_{S_3 \to S_g}$:

t_{11} renameEnt($\langle\!\langle$employee$\rangle\!\rangle$, $\langle\!\langle$person$\rangle\!\rangle$)

t_{12} renameAtt($\langle\!\langle$dept,location,null$\rangle\!\rangle$, $\langle\!\langle$dept,site,null$\rangle\!\rangle$)

t_{13} addEnt($\langle\!\langle$male$\rangle\!\rangle$, $\{\mathsf{X} \mid \langle\mathsf{X},'\,\mathsf{m}'\rangle \in \langle\!\langle$person,sex,notnull$\rangle\!\rangle\}$)

t_{14} addEnt($\langle\!\langle$female$\rangle\!\rangle$, $\{\mathsf{X} \mid \langle\mathsf{X},'\,\mathsf{f}'\rangle \in \langle\!\langle$person,sex,notnull$\rangle\!\rangle\}$)

t_{15} addGen($\langle\!\langle$sex,person,male,female$\rangle\!\rangle$)

t_{16} deleteAtt($\langle\!\langle$person,sex,notnull$\rangle\!\rangle$,

$\qquad\qquad \{\mathsf{X},\mathsf{Y} \mid \mathsf{X} \in \langle\!\langle$male$\rangle\!\rangle \wedge \mathsf{Y} =' \mathsf{m}' \vee \mathsf{X} \in \langle\!\langle$female$\rangle\!\rangle \wedge \mathsf{Y} =' \mathsf{f}'\}$)

$\mathsf{TP}_{S_g \to S_3}$:

$\overline{t_{16}}$ addAtt($\langle\!\langle$person,sex,notnull$\rangle\!\rangle$,

$\qquad\qquad \{\mathsf{X},\mathsf{Y} \mid \mathsf{X} \in \langle\!\langle$male$\rangle\!\rangle \wedge \mathsf{Y} =' \mathsf{m}' \vee \mathsf{X} \in \langle\!\langle$female$\rangle\!\rangle \wedge \mathsf{Y} =' \mathsf{f}'\}$)

$\overline{t_{15}}$ deleteGen($\langle\!\langle$sex,person,male,female$\rangle\!\rangle$)

$\overline{t_{14}}$ deleteEnt($\langle\!\langle$female$\rangle\!\rangle$, $\{\mathsf{X} \mid \langle\mathsf{X},'\,\mathsf{f}'\rangle \in \langle\!\langle$person,sex,notnull$\rangle\!\rangle\}$)

$\overline{t_{13}}$ deleteEnt($\langle\!\langle$male$\rangle\!\rangle$, $\{\mathsf{X} \mid \langle\mathsf{X},'\,\mathsf{m}'\rangle \in \langle\!\langle$person,sex,notnull$\rangle\!\rangle\}$)

$\overline{t_{12}}$ renameAtt($\langle\!\langle$dept,site,null$\rangle\!\rangle$, $\langle\!\langle$dept,location,null$\rangle\!\rangle$)

$\overline{t_{11}}$ renameEnt($\langle\!\langle$person$\rangle\!\rangle$, $\langle\!\langle$employee$\rangle\!\rangle$)

3 Optimising Transformation Pathways

The transformations in Section 2 are specific to the ER model. In this section, the focus is on the general operation types of transformations. For example, an add transformation in this section refers to all the add-type transformations including addEnt, addRel, etc., for the ER model, addNode and addEdge, etc., for the HDM, and all other add$X$ for other data models, where X is a construct of a particular data model.

A pathway may contain redundancy as the number and size of schemas grow in a network of schemas interconnected by pathways. The aim of developing transformation optimisation techniques [11] is to detect such redundancy, and rebuild the pathway with the redundant transformations removed, so as to make the evaluation of transformations, and hence the materialization of intentional schemas, more efficient.

We have developed a formal representation of transformation called the *Transformation Manipulation Language (TML)* that can be used for detecting any redundancy in pathways, as well as validating their well-formedness.

3.1 Semantics of Transformations and a Transformation Manipulation Language

The TML is designed to represent transformations in a form suitable for the analysis of the schema constructs that are created, deleted or are required to be present or absent for the transformation to be correct. In the definitions that follow, we require a function sc which, given a query or a schema construct, determines all the schema constructs that must exist for the query or schema construct to be valid.

The function $sc(P)$, where P is a schema construct, is a recursive function that returns the union of P itself, plus $sc(p_1) \cup sc(p_2) \cup \ldots \cup sc(p_n)$, where p_i are the constructs in the scheme of P.

$$sc(\langle\!\langle p, p_1, p_2, \ldots, p_n \rangle\!\rangle) = \langle\!\langle p, p_1, p_2, \ldots, p_n \rangle\!\rangle \cup sc(p_1) \cup sc(p_2) \cup \ldots \cup sc(p_n)$$

For example, $sc(\langle\!\langle \mathsf{w,p,d} \rangle\!\rangle) = \{\langle\!\langle \mathsf{w,p,d} \rangle\!\rangle, \langle\!\langle \mathsf{p} \rangle\!\rangle, \langle\!\langle \mathsf{d} \rangle\!\rangle\}$. Table 3 shows the properties of the $sc(P)$ function.

Table 3. Properties of the $sc(P)$ function

$sc(P_i \cup \ldots \cup P_j) = sc(P_i) \cup \ldots \cup sc(P_j)$
$sc(\emptyset) \qquad\qquad = \emptyset$

The TML notation formalises a transformation t_i transforming a schema S_i to a schema S_{i+1} as having four *conditions* a_i^+, b_i^-, c_i^+ and d_i^-:

- The positive precondition a_i^+ is the set of constructs that t_i implies must be present in S_i. It comprises those constructs that are present in the query of the transformation (given by $sc(q)$) together with any constructs implied as being present by the construct c:

$t_i \in \{\mathsf{add}(c,q), \mathsf{extend}(c,q)\} \rightarrow a_i^+ = (sc(c) - c) \cup sc(q)$

$t_i \in \{\mathsf{delete}(c,q), \mathsf{contract}(c,q), \mathsf{rename}(c,c'), \mathsf{id}(c,c')\} \rightarrow a_i^+ = sc(c) \cup sc(q)$

- The negative precondition b_i^- is the set of constructs that t_i implies must not be present in S_i. It comprises those constructs which the transformation will add to the schema, and thus must not already be present:

$t_i \in \{\mathsf{add}(c,q), \mathsf{extend}(c,q), \mathsf{rename}(c',c), \mathsf{id}(c',c)\} \rightarrow b_i^- = c$

$t_i \in \{\mathsf{delete}(c,q), \mathsf{contract}(c,q)\} \rightarrow b_i^- = \emptyset$

- The positive postcondition c_i^+ is the set of constructs that t_i implies must be present in S_{i+1}, and is derived in the same way as $\overline{a_i^+}$ (*i.e.* the positive precondition of $\overline{t_i}$):

$t_i \in \{\mathsf{add}(c,q), \mathsf{extend}(c,q), \mathsf{rename}(c',c), \mathsf{id}(c',c)\} \rightarrow c_i^+ = sc(c) \cup sc(q)$

$t_i \in \{\mathsf{delete}(c,q), \mathsf{contract}(c,q)\} \rightarrow c_i^+ = (sc(c) - c) \cup sc(q)$

- The negative postcondition d_i^- is the set of constructs that t_i implies must not be present in S_{i+1}, and is derived in the same way as $\overline{b_i^-}$:

$t_i \in \{\mathsf{delete}(c,q), \mathsf{contract}(c,q), \mathsf{rename}(c,c'), \mathsf{id}(c,c')\} \rightarrow d_i^- = c,$

$t_i \in \{\mathsf{add}(c,q), \mathsf{extend}(c,q)\} \rightarrow d_i^- = \emptyset$

Example 1 shows the add and extend transformations and their corresponding TML representation. To save space, the constructs in Figure 1 are abbreviated as shown in Table 4.

Example 1.

$TML(t_7) = t_7 : [\langle\!\langle \mathsf{d}\rangle\!\rangle \langle\!\langle \mathsf{p}\rangle\!\rangle \langle\!\langle \mathsf{p,dn}\rangle\!\rangle^+, \langle\!\langle \mathsf{d,dn}\rangle\!\rangle^-, \langle\!\langle \mathsf{d}\rangle\!\rangle \langle\!\langle \mathsf{p}\rangle\!\rangle \langle\!\langle \mathsf{p,dn}\rangle\!\rangle \langle\!\langle \mathsf{d,dn}\rangle\!\rangle^+, \emptyset]$

$TML(t_5) = t_5 : [\langle\!\langle \mathsf{d}\rangle\!\rangle^+, \langle\!\langle \mathsf{d,s}\rangle\!\rangle^-, \langle\!\langle \mathsf{d}\rangle\!\rangle \langle\!\langle \mathsf{d,s}\rangle\!\rangle^+, \emptyset]$

Table 4. Abbreviations used for the scheme of constructs in examples

Abbreviation	Scheme	Abbreviation	Scheme
$\langle\!\langle \mathsf{p}\rangle\!\rangle$	$\langle\!\langle \mathsf{person}\rangle\!\rangle$	$\langle\!\langle \mathsf{w,p,d}\rangle\!\rangle$	$\langle\!\langle \mathsf{worksin,person,dept,1{:}1,1{:}N}\rangle\!\rangle$
$\langle\!\langle \mathsf{p,dn}\rangle\!\rangle$	$\langle\!\langle \mathsf{person,dname,notnull}\rangle\!\rangle$	$\langle\!\langle \mathsf{s,p,m,f}\rangle\!\rangle$	$\langle\!\langle \mathsf{sex,person,male,female}\rangle\!\rangle$
$\langle\!\langle \mathsf{p,s}\rangle\!\rangle$	$\langle\!\langle \mathsf{person,sex,notnull}\rangle\!\rangle$	$\langle\!\langle \mathsf{d}\rangle\!\rangle$	$\langle\!\langle \mathsf{dept}\rangle\!\rangle$
$\langle\!\langle \mathsf{m}\rangle\!\rangle$	$\langle\!\langle \mathsf{male}\rangle\!\rangle$	$\langle\!\langle \mathsf{d,dn}\rangle\!\rangle$	$\langle\!\langle \mathsf{dept,dname,key}\rangle\!\rangle$
$\langle\!\langle \mathsf{f}\rangle\!\rangle$	$\langle\!\langle \mathsf{female}\rangle\!\rangle$	$\langle\!\langle \mathsf{d,s}\rangle\!\rangle$	$\langle\!\langle \mathsf{dept,site,null}\rangle\!\rangle$
$\langle\!\langle \mathsf{e}\rangle\!\rangle$	$\langle\!\langle \mathsf{employee}\rangle\!\rangle$	$\langle\!\langle \mathsf{d,l}\rangle\!\rangle$	$\langle\!\langle \mathsf{dept,location,null}\rangle\!\rangle$

Example 2 shows the delete and contract transformations and their corresponding TML representation and Example 3 shows the rename transformation and its corresponding TML representation.

Example 2.

$TML(\overline{t_6}) = \overline{t_6} : [\langle\!\langle \mathsf{d}\rangle\!\rangle \langle\!\langle \mathsf{p}\rangle\!\rangle \langle\!\langle \mathsf{p,dn}\rangle\!\rangle^+, \emptyset, \langle\!\langle \mathsf{p}\rangle\!\rangle \langle\!\langle \mathsf{p,dn}\rangle\!\rangle^+, \langle\!\langle \mathsf{d}\rangle\!\rangle^-]$

$TML(\overline{t_5}) = \overline{t_5} : [\langle\!\langle \mathsf{d}\rangle\!\rangle \langle\!\langle \mathsf{d,s}\rangle\!\rangle^+, \emptyset, \langle\!\langle \mathsf{d}\rangle\!\rangle^+, \langle\!\langle \mathsf{d,s}\rangle\!\rangle^-]$

Example 3.
$$TML(t_{11}) = t_{11} : [\langle\!\langle\mathsf{e}\rangle\!\rangle^+, \langle\!\langle\mathsf{p}\rangle\!\rangle^-, \langle\!\langle\mathsf{p}\rangle\!\rangle^+, \langle\!\langle\mathsf{e}\rangle\!\rangle^-]$$

3.2   Properties of the TML

There are three types of transformations, namely *insertion-only, removal-only* and *insertion-removal* transformations. add and extend are insertion-only transformations as they insert a single construct into a schema. The delete and contract transformations are removal-only as they remove a single construct from a schema. rename and id are insertion-removal transformations where they insert a construct into a schema and at the same time remove another construct from that schema. In the TML, a transformation t_i can be deduced as an insertion-only transformation if $d_i^- = \emptyset$ because insertion-only transformations do not require in their postconditions the absence of any constructs. Similarly, t_i is a removal-only transformation if $b_i^- = \emptyset$ because removal-only transformations do not require in their preconditions the absence of any constructs. An insertion-removal transformation will have the property $(b_i^- \neq \emptyset \wedge d_i^- \neq \emptyset)$. The construct inserted by a transformation t_i can be found in b_i^- and the construct removed by t_i can be found in d_i^-.

3.3   Rules for Optimisation

We can verify whether or not a pathway is well-formed by expressing the transformation steps in the TML. Provided that the pathway is well-formed, we can determine when the order of two transformations can be rearranged, when they can be simplified, and when they are redundant and hence can be removed from the pathway. In this section, TP refers to the pathway containing transformations t_m to t_n, denoted $TP_{m,n}$, as shown below.
$$TP_{m,n} = [t_m : [a_m^+, b_m^-, c_m^+, d_m^-], t_{m+1} : [a_{m+1}^+, b_{m+1}^-, c_{m+1}^+, d_{m+1}^-], \ldots,$$
$$t_n : [a_n^+, b_n^-, c_n^+, d_n^-]]$$
The set of rules discussed include the well-formedness rules (for verifying whether or not TP is well-formed), the reordering rules (for checking whether or not two transformations can be reordered), and the optimisation rules (for detecting redundant and partially redundant transformations). A *TP must be verified as well-formed before* any optimisation rules can be applied and its well-formedness is maintained after the application of any optimisation rules.

Well-Formed Transformation Pathways. A pathway TP from schema S_m to S_n is said to be *well-formed* if for each transformation $t_i : S_i \rightarrow S_{i+1}$ within it:

- The only difference between the schema constructs in S_{i+1} and S_i is those constructs specifically changed by transformation t_i, implying that $S_{i+1} = (S_i \cup c_i^+) - d_i^-$ and $S_i = (S_{i+1} \cup a_i^+) - b_i^-$
- The constructs required by t_i are in the schemas, implying that $a_i^+ \subseteq S_i$, $b_i^- \cap S_i = \emptyset$, $c_i^+ \subseteq S_{i+1}$ and $d_i^- \cap S_{i+1} = \emptyset$

The rule for verifying the well-formedness of a pathway, wf, which captures the definition discussed above, is given below. The first wf rule applies recursively to each transformation in the pathway. When there is no more transformation, the second wf rule is used to verify that applying all the transformations in the pathway to S_m results in a schema that is equal to S_n, both in terms of the content of the schema constructs in each schema and the extent of the schemas. Note that the wf rule may be used in two different ways. Firstly, given a schema S_m representing a data source and a pathway TP, we can derive the structure and the extent of the resultant schema S_n. Secondly, if both S_m and S_n are existing schemas representing two data sources, the wf rule may be used to verify that TP contains the transformations that correctly transforms S_m into S_n.

$$wf(S_m, S_n, [t_m, t_{m+1}, \ldots, t_{n-1}]) \leftarrow a_m^+ \subseteq S_m \wedge b_m^- \cap S_m = \emptyset \wedge$$
$$wf((S_m \cup c_m^+) - d_m^-, S_n, [t_{m+1}, \ldots, t_{n-1}])$$
$$wf(S_m, S_n, []) \leftarrow S_m = S_n \wedge Ext(S_m) = Ext(S_n)$$

Reordering Transformations. Because the rules for detecting redundant and partially redundant transformations *only* apply to adjacent transformations, the order of transformations in a pathway may need to be altered during the detection of any possible redundancy, so that a transformation may be moved and paired up with any other transformations in the pathway. Moving a transformation t_i to pair up with t_j in TP involves recursively reordering t_i with the next transformation in TP until the target index is reached. For example, moving t_i in TP so that it precedes t_j involves reordering t_i with t_{i+1}, if successful, then t_i with t_{i+2}, etc., until the new index of t_i in TP is one less than the index of t_j.

To rearrange the order of two adjacent transformations t_i and t_{i+1} in a well-formed $TP = [t_m, \ldots, t_i, t_{i+1}, \ldots, t_n]$, we must first ensure that (i) t_{i+1} does not contain in its preconditions a constraint that is satisfied by the postconditions of t_i. That is, if t_{i+1} requires construct P to exist, i.e., $P \in a_{i+1}^+$, then P must not have been inserted by t_i, i.e., $P \notin b_i^-$. If t_{i+1} requires construct P not to exist, i.e., $P \in b_{i+1}^-$, then P must not have been removed by t_i, i.e., $P \notin d_i^-$. Assuming the reordering has taken place, TP would now look like $TP' = [t_m, \ldots, t_{i-1}, t_{i+1}, t_i, t_{i+2}, \ldots, t_n]$. For TP' to be well-formed, the conditions that (ii) the postconditions of t_{i+1} do not conflict with the preconditions of t_i must hold. That is, if $P \in c_{i+1}^+$, then $P \notin b_i^-$ must hold, and if $P \in d_{i+1}^-$, it must be true that $P \notin a_i^+$. Also, (iii) the postconditions of t_{i-1} must not conflict with the preconditions of t_{i+1}, which is now positioned next to t_{i-1}. Similarly, (iv) the postconditions of t_i must not conflict with the preconditions of t_{i+2}. All the reordering rules are listed below, in the order they were described.

$$(i) \quad \begin{aligned} b_i^- \cap a_{i+1}^+ = \emptyset \\ d_i^- \cap b_{i+1}^- = \emptyset \end{aligned} \qquad (iii) \quad \left. \begin{aligned} c_{i-1}^+ \cap b_{i+1}^- = \emptyset \\ d_{i-1}^- \cap a_{i+1}^+ = \emptyset \end{aligned} \right\} \text{ if } i > m$$

$$(ii) \quad \begin{aligned} c_{i+1}^+ \cap b_i^- = \emptyset \\ d_{i+1}^- \cap a_i^+ = \emptyset \end{aligned} \qquad (iv) \quad \left. \begin{aligned} c_i^+ \cap b_{i+2}^- = \emptyset \\ d_i^- \cap a_{i+2}^+ = \emptyset \end{aligned} \right\} \text{ if } i < n - 1$$

Example 4. Determining whether or not the order of transformations t_8 and t_9 in $TP_{S_2 \to S_g}$ can be swapped:

$$TML(t_8, t_9) = t_8 : [\langle\!\langle \mathsf{d} \rangle\!\rangle^+, \langle\!\langle \mathsf{d,s} \rangle\!\rangle^-, \langle\!\langle \mathsf{d} \rangle\!\rangle \langle\!\langle \mathsf{d,s} \rangle\!\rangle^+, \emptyset],$$
$$t_9 : [\langle\!\langle \mathsf{p} \rangle\!\rangle \langle\!\langle \mathsf{d} \rangle\!\rangle \langle\!\langle \mathsf{p,dn} \rangle\!\rangle^+, \langle\!\langle \mathsf{w,p,d} \rangle\!\rangle^-, \langle\!\langle \mathsf{p} \rangle\!\rangle \langle\!\langle \mathsf{d} \rangle\!\rangle \langle\!\langle \mathsf{p,dn} \rangle\!\rangle \langle\!\langle \mathsf{w,p,d} \rangle\!\rangle^+, \emptyset]$$

Because all the rules for order rearrangement evaluate to $\emptyset$, we can conclude that the order of t_8 and t_9 can be reversed without affecting the overall result of all the transformations in the pathway. The reader is referred to [16] for details of the evaluation of these rules.

Detecting Redundant Transformations. Two transformations t_i and t_{i+1}, that are adjacent to each other in a well-formed TP, are *redundant* if t_i is the reverse of t_{i+1}, i.e., $t_i = \overline{t_{i+1}}$ and vice versa, and the constructs being transformed by t_i and t_{i+1} have *the same extent*. In this case, the state of the resultant schema after applying all the transformations in TP is the same whether or not both t_i and t_{i+1} are applied. In the TML terms, two transformations t_i and t_{i+1} are redundant if the following holds:

$$(a_i^+ = c_{i+1}^+) \wedge (b_i^- = d_{i+1}^-) \wedge (c_i^+ = a_{i+1}^+) \wedge (d_i^- = b_{i+1}^-) \wedge$$
$$Ext(c_i^+ \oplus a_i^+) = Ext(c_{i+1}^+ \oplus a_{i+1}^+)$$

where $(x \oplus y) = (x-y) \cup (y-x)$, which serves to determine all the constructs added or deleted by the pair of transformations. This rule qualifies two transformations as redundant if they add/extend and then delete/contract (in either order) the same construct, providing their associated queries result in the same extent. In fact, the check on the extent is unnecessary if the transformations are a pair of add/delete in either order because add and delete imply the insertion and removal of *all* the data instances associated with the construct of the transformation. As for cases where an extend or contract is one of the transformations in the pair, a check on the extent of the construct must be carried out to ensure the transformations are indeed dealing with the same construct.

Example 5. Determining whether or not t_2 and $\overline{t_{14}}$ are redundant (assuming verification has already been done that t_2 and $\overline{t_{14}}$ can be reordered so that they are adjacent to each other):

$$TML(t_2, \overline{t_{14}}) = t_2 : [\langle\!\langle \mathsf{p} \rangle\!\rangle \langle\!\langle \mathsf{p,s} \rangle\!\rangle^+, \langle\!\langle \mathsf{f} \rangle\!\rangle^-, \langle\!\langle \mathsf{p} \rangle\!\rangle \langle\!\langle \mathsf{p,s} \rangle\!\rangle \langle\!\langle \mathsf{f} \rangle\!\rangle^+, \emptyset],$$
$$\overline{t_{14}} : [\langle\!\langle \mathsf{f} \rangle\!\rangle \langle\!\langle \mathsf{p} \rangle\!\rangle \langle\!\langle \mathsf{p,s} \rangle\!\rangle^+, \emptyset, \langle\!\langle \mathsf{p} \rangle\!\rangle \langle\!\langle \mathsf{p,s} \rangle\!\rangle^+, \langle\!\langle \mathsf{f} \rangle\!\rangle^-]$$

Because all the conditions for redundant transformations are satisfied, we can conclude that t_2 and $\overline{t_{14}}$ are redundant.

Detecting Partially Redundant Transformations. Two adjacent transformations, t_i and t_{i+1}, are *partially redundant* if they satisfy the condition that (i) either the positive precondition of t_i is the same as the positive postcondition of t_{i+1}, or the negative precondition of t_i is the same as the negative postcondition of t_{i+1}. If either of these conditions is met, it is obvious that there is a certain level of overlap or redundancy in the effects of t_i and t_{i+1}. Partially redundant transformations must also satisfy the condition that (ii) what t_i removes is not what t_{i+1} requires to be absent in its preconditions. This is because the construct c inserted by t_{i+1} may not have the same semantics as the construct c removed by t_i, therefore, we cannot treat them as the same construct. On the other hand, if t_i inserts a construct c which is required to be present in the positive precondition of t_{i+1}, because of the adjacency of t_i and t_{i+1}, c refers to the same construct and hence the operation on c in t_{i+1} may be simplified with that in t_i. However, if t_{i+1} is a remove-only type transformation and removes c, we cannot optimise t_i and t_{i+1} because they are not redundant transformations (refuted by rule (i)). Thus, (iii) partially redundant transformations are also required not to be a pair of insert-only transformation followed by a remove-only transformation. These three rules for partially redundant transformations are shown below.

(i) $a_i^+ = c_{i+1}^+ \oplus b_i^- = d_{i+1}^-$, where $\oplus$ is the exclusive-or operator

(ii) $d_i^- \cap b_{i+1}^- = \emptyset$

(iii) $\neg(d_i^- = \emptyset \wedge b_{i+1}^- = \emptyset)$

The simplified transformation of two partially redundant transformations t_i and t_{i+1} can be derived by evaluating the transformation that represents the combined effect of t_i and t_{i+1}. Example 6 shows the optimisation of a pair of partially redundant transformations t_5 and $\overline{t_{12}}$.

Example 6. Optimising partially redundant transformations t_5 and $\overline{t_{12}}$ (assuming verification has already been done that t_5 and $\overline{t_{12}}$ can be reordered so that they are adjacent to each other):

$$TML(t_5,\overline{t_{12}}) = t_5 : [\langle\!\langle \mathsf{d}\rangle\!\rangle^+, \langle\!\langle \mathsf{d,s}\rangle\!\rangle^-, \langle\!\langle \mathsf{d}\rangle\!\rangle\langle\!\langle \mathsf{d,s}\rangle\!\rangle^+, \emptyset],$$
$$\overline{t_{12}} : [\langle\!\langle \mathsf{d}\rangle\!\rangle\langle\!\langle \mathsf{d,s}\rangle\!\rangle^+, \langle\!\langle \mathsf{d,l}\rangle\!\rangle^-, \langle\!\langle \mathsf{d}\rangle\!\rangle\langle\!\langle \mathsf{d,l}\rangle\!\rangle^+, \langle\!\langle \mathsf{d,s}\rangle\!\rangle^-]$$

t_5 and $\overline{t_{12}}$ can be optimised because they satisfy the three rules for partially redundant transformations. Evaluating the effects of t_5 and $\overline{t_{12}}$ results in $t_{sim} : [\langle\!\langle \mathsf{d}\rangle\!\rangle^+, \langle\!\langle \mathsf{d,l}\rangle\!\rangle^-, \langle\!\langle \mathsf{d}\rangle\!\rangle\langle\!\langle \mathsf{d,l}\rangle\!\rangle^+, \emptyset]$, which represents the primitive transformation $\mathsf{extendAtt}(\langle\!\langle \mathsf{d,l}\rangle\!\rangle)$. The reader is referred to [16] for full details of the evaluation.

Table 5 shows all possible transformation pairs, t_x followed by t_y, that can be optimised using the techniques discussed in this section. By replacing **add** with **extend** and **delete** with **contract**, this table also applies to the **extend** and **contract** transformations.

Representing Composite Transformations. The results shown in Table 5 are derived by examining the effect of a transformation pair. The effect of a transformation is the construct added/deleted by the transformation. The effect of a composite transformation consisting of two transformations can be found by evaluating the *aggregate insertion, aggregate removal, net insertion,* and *net*

Table 5. Summary of optimisable transformations

	t_y		
	add(c,q)	delete(c,q)	rename(c,c')
add(c,q)	NWF	[]	add(c',q)
t_x delete(c,q)	[]	NWF	NWF
rename(c',c)	NWF	delete(c',q)	[]
rename(c'',c)	NWF	delete(c'',q)	rename(c'',c')

NWF = Not well-formed, [] = removal of transformations

removal of the pair of transformations. The aggregate insertion made by transformations t_m, t_n is the union of all the constructs inserted by t_m, t_n, i.e., $b_m^- \cup b_n^-$. The aggregate removal made by transformations t_m, t_n is the union of all the constructs removed by t_m, t_n, i.e., $d_m^- \cup d_n^-$. The net insertion made by t_m, t_n is their aggregate insertion minus their aggregate removal, and their net removal is their aggregate removal minus their aggregate insertion.

The resulting simplified transformation t_{sim} which shows the net effect of t_m, t_n will have as its positive precondition what t_m, t_n require to be present before any transformation is executed. However, some positive preconditions of t_m may be removed by t_n, therefore, their existence and the existence of the constructs they imply (given by sc(aggregate removal)) is not required by t_{sim}. However, the constructs in the net removal of t_m, t_n must be present before t_{sim} can be applied. Also, constructs whose existence is implied by the constructs belonging to the net insertion set must also be present in the positive precondition of t_{sim}. Since what is contained in b_i^- is the construct to be inserted by t_i, t_{sim} will have as its negative precondition the net insertion of t_m, t_n. After the execution of t_{sim}, what remains present in the resulting schema would be all the constructs that exist before t_{sim} is applied, plus the net insertion of t_m, t_n, minus the net removal of t_m, t_n. Finally, the negative postcondition of t_{sim} will contain the net removal of t_m, t_n. The evaluation of t_{sim} is summarized in Table 6.

Table 6. Representing composite transformation t_{sim}

Aggregate insertion of t_m, t_n	$b_m^- \cup b_n^-$
Aggregate removal of t_m, t_n	$d_m^- \cup d_n^-$
Net insertion of t_m, t_n	aggregate insertion - aggregate removal
Net removal of t_m, t_n	aggregate removal - aggregate insertion
Simplified transformation t_{sim} representing the composite transformgtion t_m, t_n	$a_{sim}^+ = (a_m^+ \cup a_n^+) - sc(\text{aggregate removal})$ $\cup\ sc(\text{net removal})$ $\cup\ (sc(\text{net insertion}) - \text{net insertion})$
	$b_{sim}^- = \text{net insertion}$
	$c_{sim}^+ = a_{sim}^+ \cup \text{net insertion} - \text{net removal}$
	$d_{sim}^- = \text{net removal}$

3.4   An Optimisation Example

This section shows how optimisation techniques discussed in this paper can be applied to cut down on the number of transformations in a pathway. Example 7 illustrates the optimisation of $TP_{S_1 \to S_3}$.

Example 7. Optimising $TP_{S_1 \to S_3}$:

$TP_{S_1 \to S_3}$:

t_1 addEnt($\langle\!\langle\!\langle m\rangle\!\rangle\!\rangle, \{X \mid \langle X,' m'\rangle \in \langle\!\langle p, s\rangle\!\rangle\}$)

t_2 addEnt($\langle\!\langle\!\langle f\rangle\!\rangle\!\rangle, \{X \mid \langle X,' f'\rangle \in \langle\!\langle p, s\rangle\!\rangle\}$)

t_3 addGen($\langle\!\langle\!\langle s, p, m, f\rangle\!\rangle\!\rangle$)

t_4 deleteAtt($\langle\!\langle p, s\rangle\!\rangle, \{X, Y \mid X \in \langle\!\langle\!\langle m\rangle\!\rangle\!\rangle \wedge Y =' m' \vee X \in \langle\!\langle f\rangle\!\rangle \wedge Y =' f'\}$)

t_5 extendAtt($\langle\!\langle\!\langle d, s\rangle\!\rangle\!\rangle$)

$\overline{t_{16}}$ addAtt($\langle\!\langle p, s\rangle\!\rangle, \{X, Y \mid X \in \langle\!\langle\!\langle m\rangle\!\rangle\!\rangle \wedge Y =' m' \vee X \in \langle\!\langle f\rangle\!\rangle \wedge Y =' f'\}$)

$\overline{t_{15}}$ deleteGen($\langle\!\langle\!\langle s, p, m, f\rangle\!\rangle\!\rangle$)

$\overline{t_{14}}$ deleteEnt($\langle\!\langle\!\langle f\rangle\!\rangle\!\rangle, \{X \mid \langle X,' f'\rangle \in \langle\!\langle p, s\rangle\!\rangle\}$)

$\overline{t_{13}}$ deleteEnt($\langle\!\langle\!\langle m\rangle\!\rangle\!\rangle, \{X \mid \langle X,' m'\rangle \in \langle\!\langle p, s\rangle\!\rangle\}$)

$\overline{t_{12}}$ renameAtt($\langle\!\langle d, s\rangle\!\rangle, \langle\!\langle d, l\rangle\!\rangle$)

$\overline{t_{11}}$ renameEnt($\langle\!\langle\!\langle p\rangle\!\rangle\!\rangle, \langle\!\langle\!\langle e\rangle\!\rangle\!\rangle$)

The above pathway is formed by joining $TP_{S_1 \to S_g}$ and $TP_{S_g \to S_3}$. First t_4 and t_5 are reordered. Since t_4 and $\overline{t_{16}}$ are redundant, they are removed from the pathway. We apply the same optimisation to transformation pairs t_3 and $\overline{t_{15}}$, t_2 and $\overline{t_{14}}$, and t_1 and $\overline{t_{13}}$. By now, the number of transformations in the pathway has dramatically decreased as shown in $TP'_{S_1 \to S_3}$ in Table 7. We further optimise t_5 and $\overline{t_{12}}$ to form t_{17} as extendAtt($\langle\!\langle\!\langle dept, location, null\rangle\!\rangle\!\rangle$) as shown in Example 6. The final optimised pathway $TP''_{S_1 \to S_3}$ is shown in Table 7.

Table 7. Optimising $TP_{S_1 \to S_g}$

$TP'_{S_1 \to S_3}$:	$TP''_{S_1 \to S_3}$:
t_5 extendAtt($\langle\!\langle\!\langle d, s\rangle\!\rangle\!\rangle$)	
t_{12} renameAtt($\langle\!\langle d, s\rangle\!\rangle, \langle\!\langle d, l\rangle\!\rangle$)	t_{17} extendAtt($\langle\!\langle\!\langle d, l\rangle\!\rangle\!\rangle$)
t_{11} renameEnt($\langle\!\langle\!\langle p\rangle\!\rangle\!\rangle, \langle\!\langle\!\langle e\rangle\!\rangle\!\rangle$)	t_{11} renameEnt($\langle\!\langle\!\langle p\rangle\!\rangle\!\rangle, \langle\!\langle\!\langle e\rangle\!\rangle\!\rangle$)

4   Conclusion

We have discussed in this paper the AutoMed integration system which adopts the BAV approach and techniques for optimising transformations in this system. We have looked at how transformations can be expressed in the TML, and shown how TML rules can be applied for pathway optimisation. A transformation pathway optimisation tool using the TML has been implemented in the AutoMed project. This tool, which is currently fully functional, is being optimised for more speedy performance. An evaluation of performance gain by using the TML techniques is also scheduled to be carried out.

The use of the TML can also be extended to automatically detect any possible needs for repairing the global schema [11] in the face of evolving source schemas. An initial idea of how this could be achieved is to periodically scan all the pathways connected to the global schema. If a removal of a particular construct is found in each and every of the pathways, which means this construct has now become obsolete, then this construct should be removed from the global schema to give a more updated reflection of the changes in its connected sources. The techniques on using the TML to resolve some of the issues raised by schema evolution will be investigated in the near future.

While the study of using techniques on database schema optimisation as a way to increase the efficiency in schema integration and query processing receives considerable attention [7,18], the study of optimisation focused solely on transformations is a rather new topic. It is our intention to develop the TML as a general transformation manipulation language that can be used by other schema transformation formalisms. Generally speaking, the TML is applicable with other schema transformation languages, so long as these languages clearly indicate the pre- and postconditions of the transformations and the associations between new and existing constructs. The possibility of using the TML with other transformation languages described in [4,7,17] will be investigated.

References

1. The AutoMed Project.
   http://www.doc.ic.ac.uk/automed.
2. M. Boyd, P.J. McBrien, and N. Tong. The automed schema integration repository. *Proceedings of BNCOD02*, 2405:42–45, 2002.
3. M. Boyd and N. Tong. The automed repositories and api. Technical report, Dept. of Computing, Imperial College, 2001.
4. Susan B. Davidson and Anthony Kosky. WOL: A language for database transformations and constraints. In *ICDE*, pages 55–65, 1997.
5. Oliver M. Duschka and Michael R. Genesereth. Infomaster – An Information Integration Tool. In *Proceedings of the International Workshop on Intelligent Information Integration*, Freiburg, Germany, September 1997.
6. H. Garcia-Molina, Y. Papakonstantinou, D. Quass, A. Rajaraman, Y. Sagiv, J. Ullman, V. Vassalos, and J.Widom. The TSIMMIS approach to mediation: Data models and languages. *Journal on Intelligent Information Systems*, 8(2):117–132, 1997.
7. T.A. Halpin and H.A. Proper. Database schema transformation and optimization. In *Proceedings of OOER'95*, volume 1021 of *LNCS*, pages 191–203, 1995.
8. Thomas Kirk, Alon Y. Levy, Y. Sagiv, and Divesh Srivastava. The Information Manifold. *AAAI Spring Symp. on Information Gathering*, 1995.
9. I. Manolescu, D. Florescu, and D. Kossmann. Answering XML queries on heterogeneous data sources. In *Proc. of VLDB2001*, pages 241–250, 2001.
10. P.J. McBrien and A. Poulovassilis. Automatic migration and wrapping of database applications — a schema transformation approach. In *Proceedings of ER99*, volume 1728 of *LNCS*, pages 96–113. Springer-Verlag, 1999.

11. P.J. McBrien and A. Poulovassilis. Schema evolution in heterogeneous database architectures, a schema transformation approach. In *Proc. of CAiSE2002*, volume 2348 of *LNCS*, pages 484–499. Springer-Verlag, 2002.
12. P.J. McBrien and A. Poulovassilis. Data integration by bi-directional schema transformation rules. In *Proceedings of ICDE03*. IEEE, 2003.
13. A. Poulovassilis and P.J. McBrien. A general formal framework for schema transformation. *Data and Knowledge Engineering*, 28(1):47–71, 1998.
14. M.T. Roth and P. Schwarz. Don't scrap it, wrap it! A wrapper architecture for data sources. In *Proceedings of the 23rd VLDB Conference*, pages 266–275, Athens, Greece, 1997.
15. M. Templeton, H.Henley, E.Maros, and D.J. Van Buer. InterViso: Dealing with the complexity of federated database access. *The VLDB Journal*, 4(2):287–317, April 1995.
16. N. Tong. Database schema transformation optimisation techniques for the automed system. Technical report, AutoMed Project, http://www.doc.ic.ac.uk/automed/, 2002.
17. Markus Tresch and Marc H. Scholl. Schema transformation processors for federated objectbases. In C. Moon Song and Hideto Ikeda, editors, *3rd Int. Symposium on Database Systems for Advanced Applications*, Daejon, Korea, 1993. World Scientific Press, Singapore.
18. Patrick van Bommel. Experiences with EDO: An evolutionary database optimizer. *Data Knowledge Engineering*, 13(3):243–263, 1994.

Using Similarity-Based Operations for Resolving Data-Level Conflicts

Eike Schallehn and Kai-Uwe Sattler

Department of Computer Science, University of Magdeburg,
P.O. Box 4120, D-39106 Magdeburg, Germany
{eike|kus}@iti.cs.uni-magdeburg.de

Abstract. Dealing with discrepancies in data is still a big challenge in data integration systems. The problem occurs both during eliminating duplicates from
semantic overlapping sources as well as during combining complementary data
from different sources. Though using SQL operations like grouping and join
seems to be a viable way, they fail if the attribute values of the potential duplicates or related tuples are not equal but only similar by certain criteria. As
a solution to this problem, we present in this paper similarity-based variants of
grouping and join operators. The extended grouping operator produces groups
of similar tuples, the extended join combines tuples satisfying a given similarity
condition. We describe the semantics of these operators, discuss efficient implementations for the edit distance similarity and present evaluation results. Finally,
we give examples how the operators can be used in given application scenarios.

1 Introduction

In the past few years, there has been a great amount of work on data integration. This
includes the integration of information from diverse sources in the Internet, the integration of enterprise data in support of decision-making using data warehouses, and
preparing data from various sources for data mining. Some of the major problems in
this context – besides overcoming structural conflicts – are related to overcoming conflicts and inconsistencies on the data level. This includes the elimination of duplicate
data objects caused by semantic overlapping of some sources, as well as establishing a
relationship between complementary data from these sources. The implementation of
associated operations has a significant difference to usual data management operations:
only in some rare cases can we rely on equality of attributes. Instead we have to deal
with discrepancies in data objects representing the same or related real-world objects
which may exist due to input errors or simply due to the autonomy of the sources.
Furthermore, the amount of data to be processed in integration scenarios can be equal
to, or even greater than that from a single source, so, efficiency of the implementation
becomes a critical issue.

Duplicate elimination is a sub-task of data cleaning that comprises further tasks for
improving data quality like transformation, outlier detection etc. Assuming SQL-based
integration systems, the natural choice for duplicate elimination is the **group by** operator using the key attributes of the tuples in combination with aggregate functions
for reconciling divergent non-key attribute values. However, this approach is limited to

A. James, B. Lings, M. Younas (Eds.): BNCOD 2003, LNCS 2712, pp. 172–189, 2003.

equality of the key attributes – if no unique key exists or the keys contain differences, tuples representing the same real-world object will be assigned to different groups and cannot be identified as equivalent tuples. The same is true for linking complementary data, which in a SQL system would be done based on equality by the `join` operator.

In this paper we address these problems and present similarity-based operators for joining and grouping based on previous work. We extend our earlier work by giving clear semantics of the operators, describing the implementation and evaluating optimization techniques. Both operators are based on extended concepts for similarity-based predicates. Major concerns are the new requirements resulting from the characteristics of similarity relationships, most of all atransitivity, and support for the efficient processing of similarity predicates.

The operators have not necessarily to be provided as a language extension, though we did this in our own query engine and use this syntax for illustration purposes. Instead it also can be implemented by utilizing extension mechanisms which are offered by today's DBMS. The implementation and the evaluation results described in this paper are based on table functions available in Oracle8i.

The remainder of this paper is organized as follows. After a discussion of related work in Section 2, we describe the characteristics and requirements of similarity predicates useful in data integration in Section 3. The proposed similarity operators are defined with respect to their semantics in Section 4. In Section 5 we describe strategies for an efficient implementation of these operators focusing on edit distances similarity measures. Results of our evaluation are given in Section 6. Finally, in Section 7 we present several aspects of the application of the similarity operations. Section 8 concludes the paper and points out ongoing work.

2   Related Work

The concepts described in this paper are intended to be used in data integration and cleaning scenarios. Related topics are from this field and similarity-based data operations, as well as from the field of analytical data processing.

Closely related to similarity-based operations is the integration of probabilistic concepts in data management. In [3] Dey et. al. propose an extended relational model and algebra supporting probabilistic aspects. Fuhr describes a probabilistic Datalog in [6]. Especially, for data integration issues and the aforementioned problems probabilistic approaches were verified and yielded useful results, as described by Tseng et. al. in [22]. The WHIRL system and language described in [2] by Cohen is based on Fuhr's work and uses text-based similarity and logic-based data access as known from Datalog to integrate data from heterogeneous sources. Cohen describes an efficient algorithm to compute the top scoring matches of a ranked result set. The implementation of the similarity predicate uses inverted indexes common in the field of information retrieval. A general framework for similarity joins for predicates on data types that can be mapped to multi-dimensional spaces is presented by Shim et. al. in [21]. The approach is based on an extended version of the kdB tree.

While efficient implementations of similarity predicates can be provided based on established index structures described above, most of the real-life applications considered in this paper require predicates for string attributes. Though there is a number of similarity measures for strings, namely the edit distance and it's derivatives, for which a good overview is given by Navarro in [18], the efficient implementation for large data sets is a current research topic. In [9] Gravano et. al. present an approach for similarity-based joins on string attributes using an efficient pre-selection of q-grams for optimization. In short, the approach is based on down-sizing the data sets on which a similarity predicate is evaluated by first doing an equality-based join on substrings of fixed length q. Though our approach is not limited to string based predicates, we implemented an edit distance string similarity predicate using a trie as an index structure based on results by Shang and Merret described in [20] for evaluation purposes.

A major focus of our work is the problem of duplicate detection. This problem was discussed extensively in various research areas like database and information system integration [25, 14], data cleaning [1, 7], information dissemination [24], and others. Early approaches were merely based on the equality of attribute values or derived values. Newer research results deal with advanced requirements of real-life systems, where identification very often is only possible based on similarity. Those approaches include special algorithms [16, 11], the application of methods known from the area of data mining and even machine learning [13].

An overview of problems related to entity identification is given in [12]. In [14] Lim et. al. describe an equality based approach, include an overview of other approaches and list requirements for the entity identification process. Monge and Elkan describe an efficient algorithm that identifies similar tuples based on a distance measure and builds transitive clusters in [17]. In [7] Galhardas et. al. propose a framework for data cleaning as a SQL extension and macro-operators to support among other data cleaning issues duplicate elimination by similarity-based clustering. The similarity relationship is expressed by language constructs, and furthermore, clustering strategies to deal with transitivity conflicts are proposed. Luján-Mora and Palomar propose a centroid method for clustering in [15]. Furthermore, they describe common discrepancies in string representations and derive a useful set of pre-processing steps and extended distance measures combining edit distance on a token-level and similarity of token sets. In [11] Hernández et. al. propose the sliding window approach for similarity-based duplicate identification where a neighborhood conserving key can be derived and describe efficient implementations.

The importance of extended concepts for grouping and aggregation in information integration is emphasized by Hellerstein et. al. in [10]. In particular, user-defined aggregation (UDA) were proposed in SQL3 and are now supported by several commercial database systems, e.g. Oracle, IBM DB2, Informix. In [23] the SQL-AG system for specifying UDA is presented, that translates to C code. A more recent version of this approach called AXL is described in [23] and its usage in data mining is discussed.

3   Similarity Measures

Similarity based operators like the similarity join and the similarity-based grouping discussed here are based on similarity measures for attribute values and their logical combination. Other operators requiring concepts of similarity include for instance nearest neighbour queries and attribute similarity selections. These concepts currently find their way into commercial data management solutions, or are the topic of ongoing research. This section discusses useful similarity measures, their characteristics and requirements for common applications.

3.1   Basic Similarity Predicates

We use the following basic terms of similarity measures: let x and y be objects in a given universe of discourse U, a similarity measure is a function $sim(x,y) \to [0,1]$. Alternatively a distance measure $d(x,y) \to \mathbb{R}$ can be used. The latter can be transformed to a similarity measure, for instance using the simple transformation $sim(x,y) = 1 - \frac{d(x,y)}{max}$, where max is the maximum difference between objects in U, if applicable. This transformation implies a normalization, though other normalizations of distances within a given range are conceivable. A binary similarity predicate $SIM(x,y) \subseteq U^2$, meaning "y is similar to x", can for instance be derived from a similarity or distance measure using thresholds $t \in [0,1]$ or $k \in \mathbb{R}$ like $SIM(x,y) \Leftrightarrow sim(x,y) \geq t$ or $SIM(x,y) \Leftrightarrow d(x,y) \leq k$. SIM is in most cases considered as a reflexive, symmetric and atransitive relation.

While a number of approaches to describe similarity stemming from areas like information retrieval, multimedia data management or case-based reasoning exist, one of the major problems of expressing similarity within sets of structured data is, that the concept of similarity is in most cases highly dependent on the given application domain. Therefore, we describe basic similarity measures for common data types and ways of using these as primitives for combination to derive measures suitable for real life applications.

A widely used measure is the distance d of data points x,y in a metric space S, for instance the *Euclidean Distance* in an n-dimensional space. In a metric space the distance function fulfills the following conditions:

$$\forall x,y \in S \ \ d(x,y) = 0 \Leftrightarrow x = y \tag{1}$$
$$\forall x,y \in S \ \ d(x,y) = d(y,x) \tag{2}$$
$$\forall x,y,z \in S \ \ d(x,y) \leq d(x,z) + d(z,y) \tag{3}$$

Especially the symmetry and the triangular inequality of such a distance measure given in (2) and (3) provide the fundament for efficient applications, e.g. in information retrieval and data mining. To use such measures, the data objects to be compared solely consist of coordinates in a metric space, or otherwise have to be transformed to represent points in this space, e.g. extracting feature vectors from multimedia data or deriving term-based vector representations of textual data. Supported by multi-dimensional indexing, predicates on these distance measures can be used efficiently, though efficiency is limited by the number of dimensions.

Another well-studied distance measure is the *Levenshtein* or edit distance $edist(p,w)$ on string representations. Certain costs are assigned to operations like insertion, deletion or substitution of characters to transform an original pattern string p to a comparison string w, and the minimal distance is computed. For instance, assuming constant costs of 1 for the three mentioned basic operations, the edit distance of "edna" and "eden" is 2, because the smallest sets of applicable operations are {*substitute(#3, "e"), substitute(#4,"n")*} and {*insert(#3,"e"), delete(#5)*} both having two operations. Common derivates also allow a transposition operation or apply heuristic-based costs for the operations, e.g. substituting or deleting vowels is usually less expensive than operations on consonants. This distance measure fulfills the three conditions given above for distances in metric space, this way granting efficient implementations. Though the edit distance is a powerful measure to detect inconsistencies in data, for instance for applications in the field of data integration and data cleaning, it is not widely used in current data management solutions. In Sections 5 and 6 we present an efficient implementation of a similarity predicate based on edit distance used with index-based optimization through tries as proposed in [20]. Other distance measures for strings include the *Hamming distance*, allowing only substitutions, the *episode distance*, allowing only insertions, and the *longest common subsequence distance* allowing insertions and deletions. A good overview of approximate string matching is given in [18]. Similar concepts of edit distances exist for other types of data representations, e.g. special sequences like genome data, spatio-temporal data, trees and graphs in general.

Textual and numerical data, the latter including the special case of 1-dimensional data and the difference as a distance measure plus widely used index structures like B-trees, is covered by the approaches introduced so far. A similarity measure for categorical data can be defined, if the categories can be mapped to a simple partial order, a metric space as described above, or a graph representing categories and their relationships. Distance measures for nodes in graphs are not discussed here, but it is worth mentioning that for graphs, as well as for sets, meaningful distance measures can be defined, that do not fulfill the criteria of symmetry and the triangular inequality.

3.2   Complex and Application-Specific Similarity

So far we have discussed similarity measures applicable to atomic or homogeneously structured data types independently of a special application scenario. In real-life scenarios the expression of similarity has to deal with additional aspects to improve efficiency and the results of similarity based operations.

Complex similarity conditions: Similarity-based operators have to process tuples or more complex objects. The description of similarity between two of those objects may consist of a combination of more than one similarity predicate for an attribute and may use different similarity measures on them, e.g., for information on paintings in a database we can use the edit distance on artist names and the distance of vector representations for descriptions of the pictures contents.

Application-specific similarity measures: The semantics of values to be compared in given applications is known, which allows the usage of more precise similarity measures based on domain knowledge. Though we could use the edit distance to compare names of persons, we achieve better results if the similarity measure would consider that "Andy Warhol", "A. Warhol" and "Warhol, Andy" most likely refer to the same person.

By using similarity predicates as described above we can simply build *complex similarity conditions* by applying the logical operators $\wedge$, $\vee$ and $\neg$. As an alternative, a fuzzy logic can be applied to similarity measures directly, as proposed for instance in [2]. To reach the level of expressiveness we gain by specifying thresholds as part of every similarity predicate in the former approach, the concept of weighting the desired impact of every similarity measure would have to be added to the latter. An efficient evaluation of a complex similarity condition consisting of similarity predicates is described in Section 5.

Application-specific similarity measures and predicates can be defined in terms of user-defined functions as supported in most database systems. As an example consider a function $distName(x,y)$ that takes into account the various conventions for writing names as described above. The algorithm can remove special characters, tokenize the string, find first letter matches and finally apply $edist(token1, token2)$ on candidate tokens, that possibly represent the last name, to take care of typos or inconsistent spelling of names.

Efficiency, one of the major problems of user-defined similarity, is discussed more detailed in Section 5. The general strategy would be to conjunctively combine the user-defined similarity predicates with index-supported equality or similarity predicates for pre-selection purposes. Asymmetric similarity measures are not considered here, so symmetry remains a requirement that has to be granted by the user-defined measure.

Existing operations in the relational algebra base largely on equivalence relations established through the equality of attribute values. To integrate with these concepts an equivalence relation can be derived from an atransitive similarity predicate SIM. Because establishing this equivalence relation is not our major focus here, throughout this paper we use the simple strategy of constructing an equivalence relation SIM_{EQ} by building the *transitive closure* $SIM_{EQ} := SIM^+$, i.e. a partition of the universe of discourse U is a maximal set of objects that are similar either directly or indirectly. Especially related to entity identification, centroid or density-based clustering techniques proved to be useful strategies for dealing with atransitivity and provide a high level of accuracy, as for instance described in [15] and [17].

4   Semantics of the Similarity Operators

In this section we describe the semantics of our similarity-based operators as extensions of the standard relational algebra. We assume the following basic notations: let R be a relation with the schema $S = \{A_1, \ldots, A_m\}$, $t^R \in R$ is a tuple from the relation R and $t^R(A_i)$ denotes the value of attribute A_i of the tuple t^R.

The core concept for similarity-based operations is a *similarity condition*. It expresses whether two tuples are similar in terms of their attribute values. Because we define our operators as an extension of the standard relational algebra, we do not deal with probabilities in conditions – by using a similarity threshold we can always rely on boolean values for such conditions. Hence, a similarity condition $<sim\_cond>$ is a conjunction of predicates:

$$<sim\_cond> = \bigwedge_{i=1}^{m} <sim\_pred> (A_i)$$

where <sim_pred> denotes an atomic predicate which could be either *eq* or a "similarity predicate" like with an associated threshold or any other similarity predicate as discussed in Section 3.

Similarity join. Based on the similarity condition introduced above the semantics of the similarity join between two relations R_1 and R_2 can be described in a straightforward way. For a given similarity condition <sim_cond> we denote the set of all attributes referenced in this expression as

$$\widetilde{S} = \{A_i \mid A_i \text{ is referenced in } <sim\_cond>\}$$

and S_i as the set of all attributes from relation R_i. Then, it holds

$$
\begin{aligned}
R_1 \bowtie_{<sim\_cond>} R_2 = \{t \mid \ & \exists t_1 \in R_1 : t_1(S_1 - \widetilde{S}) = t(S_1 - \widetilde{S}) \wedge \\
& \exists t_2 \in R_2 : t_1(S_2 - \widetilde{S}) = t(S_2 - \widetilde{S}) \wedge \\
& <sim\_cond> (t_1, t_2) = \mathbf{true}\}
\end{aligned}
$$

This simply means, a pair of tuples from the relations R_1 and R_2 appears in the result of the join operation if the similarity condition is fulfilled for these two tuples.

Similarity grouping. For defining the semantics of the grouping operator we rely on the algebra operator for standard grouping as presented in database textbooks [5]:

$$<grouping\_attrs> \mathcal{F}[<aggr\_func\_list>](R)$$

Here <grouping_attrs> is a list of attributes used for grouping relation R, <aggr_func_list> denotes a list of aggregate functions (e.g., count, avg, min, max etc.) conveyed by an attribute of relation R. For simplification, we assume that the name of an aggregated column is derived by concatenating the attribute name and the name of the function. An aggregate function f is a function returning a value $v \in \text{Dom}$ for a multi-set of values $v_1, \dots v_m \in \text{Dom}$:

$$f(\{\!\!\{v_1, \dots, v_m\}\!\!\}) = v$$

where Dom denotes an arbitrary domain of either numeric or alphanumeric values and the brackets $\{\!\!\{ \dots \}\!\!\}$ are used for multi-sets. We extend this equality-based grouping operator $\mathcal{F}$ with regard to the grouping criteria by allowing an similarity condition and call this new operator Γ:

$$<sim\_cond> \Gamma[<aggr\_func\_list>](R)$$

This operator again has a list of aggregate functions <aggr_func_list> with the same meaning as above. However, the grouping criteria <sim_cond> is now a similarity conjunction as introduced above. The result of Γ is a relation R' where the schema consists of all the attributes referenced in <sim_cond> accompanied with *eq* and the attributes named after the aggregates as described above. The relation R' is obtained by the concatenation of the two operators γ and ψ which reflect the two steps of grouping and aggregation. The first operator $\gamma_{<sim\_cond>}(R) = G$ produces a set of groups $G = \{G_1,\ldots,G_m\}$ from an input relation R. Each group is a non-empty set of tuples with the same schema as R. Furthermore, all tuples t_i^G of a group G are transitively similar to each other regarding the similarity condition $<sim\_cond>$:

$$\forall G \in G : \forall t_i^G, t_j^G \in G : t_j^G \in tsim_{<sim\_cond>}(t_i^G)$$

where $tsim_{<sim\_cond>}(t)$ denotes the set of all tuples which are in the transitive closure of the tuple t with regard to sim_cond:

$$tsim_{<sim\_cond>}(t) = \{t' \mid sim\_cond(t,t') = \textbf{true} \vee$$
$$\exists t'' \in tsim_{<sim\_cond>}(t) : sim\_cond(t',t'') = \textbf{true}\}$$

and no tuple is similar to any other tuple of other groups

$$\forall G_i, G_j \in G, i \neq j : \forall t_k^{G_i} \in G_i \; \nexists t_l^{G_j} \in G_j :$$
$$sim\_cond(t_k^{G_i}, t_l^{G_j}) = \textbf{true}$$

The second operator $\psi_{A_1,\ldots,A_l,<aggr\_func\_list>}(G) = R'$ reconciles (i.e., merges) the tuples from each group and produces exactly one tuple for each group of G according to the given aggregate functions. Thus, it holds $\forall G \in G$ with $G = \{t_1^G,\ldots,t_n^G\}$ there is one and only one tuple $t^{R'} \in R'$ with

$$\forall i = 1 \ldots l : t^{R'}(A_i) = t_1^G(A_i) = t_2^G(A_i) = \cdots = t_n^G(A_i)$$

where $A_1,\ldots,A_l$ are attributes referred by the eq predicates of the approximation condition, (i.e., for these attributes all tuples have the same value) and

$$\forall j = l+1 \ldots m-l : t^{R'}(A_j) = f_{j-l}(\{\!|t_1^G(A_j),\ldots,t_n^G(A_j)|\!\})$$

where $f_1,\ldots,f_m$ are aggregate functions from $<aggr\_func\_list>$. Based on these two operators we can finally define the Γ operator for similarity-based grouping as follows:

$$_{<sim\_cond>}\Gamma[<aggr\_func\_list>](R) = \psi_{A_1,\ldots,A_l,<aggr\_func\_list>}(\gamma_{<sim\_cond>}(R))$$

where $A_1,\ldots,A_l$ are again attributes referenced by the eq predicates in $<sim\_cond>$.

5   Implementation and Optimization

In this section we outline our implementation of the similarity-based operators introduced in the previous sections. For an efficient realization dedicated plan operators are required, which implement the semantics described above. That means for instance for the similarity join, even if one formulates a query as follows

```
select *
from r1, r2
where edist(r1.title, r2.title) < 2
```

the similarity join implementation exploiting special index support has to be chosen by the query optimizer instead of computing the Cartesian product followed by a selection. In case of the similarity grouping a simple user-defined function is not sufficient as grouping function, because during similarity grouping the group membership is not determined by one or more of the tuple values but depends on already created groups. In addition, processing a tuple can be conveyed by merging existing groups.

Thus, we describe in the following the implementation of these two plan operators SIMJOIN and SIMGROUPING and assume, that the query optimizer is able to recognize the necessity of applying these operators during generating the query plan. This could be supported by appropriate query language extensions, e.g. for the similarity join like

```
select *
from r1 similarity join r2
     on edist(r1.title, r2.title) threshold 0.9
```

where **threshold** specifies the maximum allowed value for the normalized edit distance. For the similarity grouping this could be formulated as follows:

```
select *
from r1
group by similarity on edist(title) threshold 0.9
```

Currently, for our implementation we focus on edit distances as the primary similarity measure. For this purpose, we have adopted the approach proposed in [20] of using a trie in combination with a dynamic programming algorithm for computing the edit distance. The main idea is to traverse the trie containing the string values of all already processed tuples in depth-first order, trying to find a match with the search pattern, i.e., the attribute value of the currently processed tuple. Due to the usage of the edit distance, we must not stop the traversal directly after a found mismatch. Instead an edit operation (insert, remove or replace a character) is applied and the search is continued. Only after exceeding the given threshold, we can stop the traversal and go back to the next subtrie. Hence, the threshold is used for cutting off sub-tries containing strings not similar to the pattern. In addition, the effort for computing the dynamic programming tables required for determining the edit distance can be reduced, because all strings in one subtree share a common prefix and therefore the same edit distance. We omit further details of this algorithm and refer instead to the original work. In our implementation of the previously introduced operators tries are created on the fly for each grouping attribute or join predicate which appears together with an edit distance predicate.

5.1   Similarity Join

The implementation of a similarity join outlined in this section is quite straightforward, only differing in their usage of similarity predicates as join conditions. Like for conventional join operators index support for predicates can be exploited to improve performance by reducing the number of pairwise comparisons. However, the different predicates of a similarity expression require different kinds of index structures:

Algorithm 1: *Processing a tuple from join relation R_1 during similarity join*

Globals

Conjunctive join condition $c = p_1 \wedge \ldots \wedge p_n$

Set of indexes $I_{p_i}, 1 \leq i \leq n$ on join relation R_2
      for index supported predicates

Mapping table *tid_tid* for matching tuples

Procedure processTuple(Tuple *t*)
    begin
        for all index supported equality predicates p_i
            set of tuples $s_{conj} := indexScan(I_{p_i}, t(A_{p_i}))$
        end for
        for all index supported similarity predicates p_i
            $s_{conj} := s_{conj} \cap indexScan(I_{p_i}, t(A_{p_i}), k_{p_i})$
        end for
        for all tuples $t_l \in s_{conj}$
            boolean *similar* := **true**
            for all non-index supported predicates p_i
                similar := *similar*$\wedge$
                    $evaluate(p_i, k_{p_i}, t(A_{p_i}), t_l(A_{p_i}))$
                if not *similar* **break**
            end for
            if similar insert (t, t_l) in *tid_tid*
        end for
    end

- For equality predicates $eq(A_i)$ common index structures like hash tables or B-trees can be utilized.
- Numeric approximation predicates like $diff_k(A_i)$ can be easily supported by storing the minimum and maximum value of the attribute for each group.
- For string similarity based on edit distances $edist(A_i)$ tries are a viable index structure, as previously introduced.
- For the other similarity predicates discussed in Section 3 index support is given, for instance through multi-dimensional indexes like R-trees and its derivates on data mapped to a metric space.

Given such index structures a join algorithm can be implemented taking care of the various kinds of indexes. In Algorithm 1 a binary join for two relations R_1 and R_2 is shown, assuming that indexes for relation R_2 either exist or were built on the fly in a previous processing step. The result of this algorithm is a table of matching tuples for usage described later on. Alternatively, result tuples can be produced for pipelined query processing directly at this point. The notations I_{p_i} and k_{p_i} refer to the index on predicate p_i and the specified threshold, respectively. A_{p_i} refers to the involved attribute.

As a side note, more complex similarity conditions could easily be supported by adding disjunctions. The similarity condition c can be transformed to disjunctive normal form. For all conjunctions of $c = \bigvee_{i=1}^{m} conj_i$ the s_{conj_i} are computed and the set of relevant groups would be $s_{disj} = \bigcup_{i=1}^{m} s_{conj_i}$.

5.2   Similarity-Based Grouping

Like the join operator, the similarity-based grouping operator is based on the efficient evaluation of similarity predicates, but in addition has to deal with problems arising from the atransitivity of similarity relations. The goal of a grouping operator is to assign every tuple to a group. A naive implementation of the similarity-based operator would work as follows:

1. Iterate over the input set and process each tuple by evaluating the similarity condition with all previously processed tuples. Because these tuples were already assigned to groups, the result of this step is a set of groups.
2. If the result set is empty, a new group is created, otherwise the conflict is resolved by merging the groups according to the transitive closure strategy.

Other grouping strategies, like for instance density-based clustering, may in contrast require more rigid similarity relations between tuples in a group. In case of any conflict with a found group or between more than one found groups, existing groups would be split and maybe not considered during further processing. This behavior can be utilized to provide pipelined processing of the operator.

Obviously, the previously described naive implementation would lead to $O(n^2)$ time complexity for an input set of size n. Similar to processing a similarity join we assume that there are index-supported predicates for equality and similarity, and in addition, predicates like user-defined similarity predicates, that can not be supported by indexes. An according Algorithm was implemented and is described in detail in [19].

5.3   Implementation Using Oracle8i

Implementing the described similarity operators in a SQL DBMS as native plan operators supporting the typical iterator interface [8] requires significant modifications to the database engine and therefore access to the source code. So, in order to add these operators to a commercial system the available programming interfaces and extensibility mechanisms should be used instead. Most modern DBMS support so-called table functions which can return tables of tuples, in some systems also in a pipelined fashion. In this way, our operators can be implemented as table functions consuming the tuples of a query, performing the appropriate similarity operation and returning the result table. For example, a table function sim_join implementing Algorithm 1 and expecting two cursor parameters for the input relations and the similarity join condition could be used as follows:

```
select *
from table (sim_join (cursor(select * from data1),
                cursor(select * from data2),
                'edist (data1.title, data2.title) < 2'))
```

However, a problem of using table functions for implementing query operators are the strong typing restrictions: for the table functions a return type has always to be specified that prevents to use the same function for different input relations.

As one possible solution we have implemented table functions using and returning structures containing generic tuple identifiers (e.g., Oracle's `rowid`). So, the SIM-GROUPING function produces a tuple of tuple identifier / group identifier pairs, where the group identifier is an artificial identifier generated by the operator. Based on this, the result type `gid_tid_table` of the table function is defined as follows:

```
create type gid_tid_t as object gid int, tid int);
create type gid_tid_table is table of gid_tid_t;
```

Using a grouping function `sim_grouping` a query can be written as the following query:

```
select ...
from table(sim_grouping (
        cursor (select rowid, * from raw_data),
        'edist(title) < 2'))) as gt,
     raw_data
where raw_data.tid = gt.tid
group by gt.gid
```

This approach allows to implement the function in a generic way, i.e., without any assumption on the input relation. In order to apply aggregation or reconciliation to the actual attribute values of the tuples, they are retrieved using a join with the original relation, whereas the grouping is performed based on the artificial group identifiers produced by the grouping operator.

In the same way, the SIMJOIN operator was implemented as a table functions returning pairs of tuple identifiers that fulfill the similarity condition and are used to join with the original data.

6 Evaluation

The similarity-based grouping and join operators described in Section 4 were implemented as part of our own query engine and, alternatively, using the extensibility interfaces of the commercial database management system Oracle as outlined in Section 5. For evaluation purposes the latter implementation was used. The test environment was a PC system with a Pentium III (500 MHz) CPU running Linux and Oracle 8i. The extended operators and predicates were implemented using C++. All test results refer to our implementation of the string similarity predicate based on the edit distance and supported by a trie index. A non-index implementation of the predicate is provided for comparison. Indexes are currently created on the fly and maintained in main memory only during operator processing time, which appears to be a reasonable approach considering the targeted data integration scenarios. The related performance impact is discussed below.

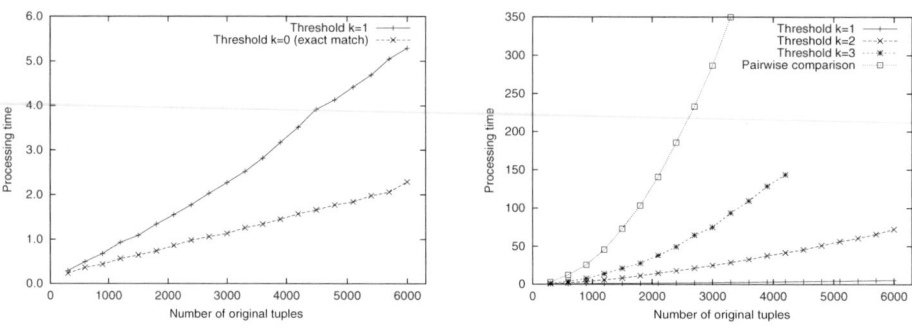

Fig. 1. Grouping with threshold $k = 0$ and $k = 1$ **Fig. 2.** Grouping with varying thresholds $k \geq 1$

For the grouping operator test runs separate data sets containing random strings were created according to the grade of similarity to be detected, i.e. for one original tuple between 0 and 3 copies were created that fulfilled the similarity condition of the test query. The test query consisted of an edit distance predicate on only one tuple. Using the edit distance with all operations having a fixed cost of 1 and a edit distance threshold k on an attribute, each duplicate tuple had between 0 and k deletions, insertions or transpositions. As the number of copies and the numbers of applied operations on the string attributes were equally distributed, for n original tuples the total size of the data set to be processed was approximately $3 * n$ with an average distance of $\frac{k}{2}$ among the tuples to be detected as similar.

Grouping based on an exact matching ($k = 0$) has the expected complexity of $O(n)$, which results from the necessary iteration over the input set and the trie lookup in each step, which for an exact match requires average word-length comparisons, i.e. can be considered $O(1)$. This conforms to equality based grouping with hash table support. For a growing threshold the number of comparisons, i.e. the number of trie nodes to be visited, grows. This effect can be seen in Figure 1, where the complexity for $k = 1$ appears to be somewhat worse than linear, but still reasonably efficient.

Actually, the complexity grows quickly for greater thresholds, as larger regions of the trie have to be covered. The dynamic programming approach of the similarity search ensures that even for the worst case each node is visited only once, which results in equal complexity as pairwise similarity comparison, not considering the cost for index maintenance etc. The currently used main memory implementation of the trie causes a constant overhead per insertion. Hence, the $O(n^2)$ represents the upper bound of the complexity for a rising threshold k, just like $O(n)$ is the lower bound. For growing thresholds the curve moves between these extremes with growing curvature. This is a very basic observation that applies to similarity based operations like similarity-based joins and selections as well, the latter providing the reason for these considerations having a complexity between $O(1)$ and $O(n)$. The corresponding test results are shown in Figure 2.

The previous test results were presented merely to make a general statement about the efficiency of the similarity-based grouping operator. An interesting question in real

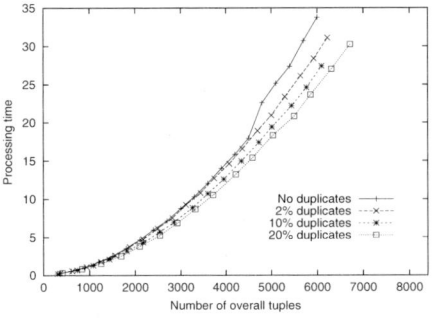
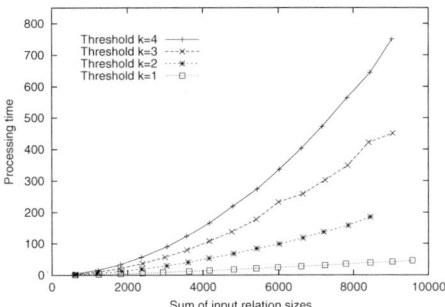

Fig. 3. Grouping with varying percentage of duplicates in the test data sets

Fig. 4. Results for varying thresholds $k \geq 1$ for a similarity join

life scenarios would be, how the operator performs on varying ratios of duplicates in the tested data set. In Figure 3 the dependency between the percentage of duplicates and the required processing time is given for the threshold $k = 2$. While the relative time complexity remains, the absolute processing time decreases for higher percentages of detectable duplicates. Obviously, and just as expected, using a similarity measure is more efficient, if there actually is similarity to detect. Otherwise, searching the trie along diverging paths represents an overhead that will not yield any results.

We received similar results for the described implementation of a similarity join. The test scenario consisted of two relations R_1 and R_2, with a random number of linked tuples, i.e. for each tuple in R_1 there were between 0 and 3 linked records in R_2 and the join attribute values were within a maximum edit distance. The results are shown in Figure 4. As the implementation of the join operation is similar to the grouping operation the complexity is between $O(n)$ and $O(n^2)$ depending on the edit distance threshold.

7   Applications

As described before, the problem of duplicate elimination in databases or during integration of various sources can be solved by applying the similarity-based grouping operations. Using an appropriate similarity predicate (see below for a discussion) potential redundant objects can be identified. However, applying a suitable similarity predicate is only the first step towards "clean" data: From each group of tuples a representative object has to be chosen. This merging or reconciliation step is usually performed in SQL using aggregate functions. But, in the simplest case of the builtin aggregates one is able only to compute minimum, maximum, average etc. from numeric values. As an enhancement modern DBMS provide support for user-defined aggregation functions (UDA) which allow to implement application-specific reconciliation functions. However, these UDAs are still too restricted for reconciliation because they support only one column as parameter. Here, the problem is to choose or compute a merged value from a set of possible discrepant values without looking at any other columns. We can mitigate this problem by allowing more than one parameter or by passing a structured value as parameter to the function.

In particular for reconciliation purposes we have defined a set of such enhanced aggregate functions including the following:

- pick_where_eq (v, col) returns the value of column col of the first tuple, where the value of v is true, i.e., $\neq 0$. In case of a group consisting of only one tuple, the value of this tuple is returned independently of the value of v.
- pick_where_min (v, col) returns the value of column col of the tuple, where v is minimal for the entire relation or group, respectively.
- pick_where_max (v, col) returns the value of column col of the tuple, where v is maximal.
- to_array (col) produces an array containing all values from column col.

With the help of these functions several reconciliation policies can easily be implemented, one of them illustrated in the following example. We assume that the final value for column col of each group has to be taken from the tuple containing the most current date, which is represented as column m_date:

```
select max(m_date), pick_where_max(m_date, col), ...
from data
group by ...
```

Another application-specific question is, how to specify the similarity predicate, consisting of the similarity or distance measure itself and the threshold. If the chosen threshold has such a major impact on the efficiency of similarity-based operations, as described in Section 6, the question is how to specify a threshold to meet requirements regarding efficiency and accuracy. Actually, this adds complexity to the well studied problem of over- and under-identification, i.e. falsely qualified duplicates. Information about the distance or similarity distribution can be used for deciding about a meaningful threshold, as well as for refining user-defined similarity predicates. Distance distributions usually conform to some natural distribution, according to the specific application, data types and semantics. Inconsistencies, such as duplicates, cause anomalies in the distribution, e.g. local minima or points of extreme curvature.

Figure 5(a) shows a result for a sample consisting of approximately 1.600 titles starting with an "E" from integrated sources of data on cultural assets. Nevertheless, drawing the conclusion of setting the edit distance threshold to receive a useful similarity predicate would lead to a great number of falsely identified tuples. For short titles there would be too many matches, and longer titles often do not match this way, because the length increases the number of typos etc.

Better results can be achieved by applying a relative edit distance $rdist(x,y) = 1 - \frac{edist(x,y)}{max(x.length, y.length)}$ as a similarity measure as introduced in section 3. The algorithm introduced in section 5 can easily be adjusted to this relative distance. Figure 5(b) shows the distribution of relative edit distances in the previously mentioned example relation. Using the first global minimum around 0.8 as a threshold, and analyzing matches in this area shows that it provides a good ratio of very few over- and under-identified tuples. A successive adjustment of similarity predicates using information from analytical data processing is also of interest for the creation of user-defined similarity predicates.

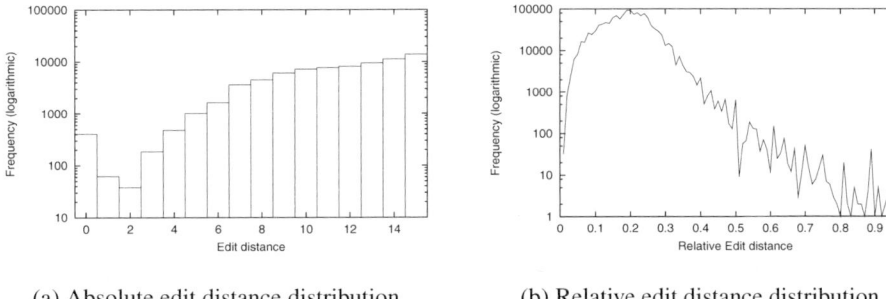

(a) Absolute edit distance distribution   (b) Relative edit distance distribution

Fig. 5. Edit distance distributions in an integrated and sampled data set

8   Conclusions

In this paper we presented database operators for finding related data and identifying duplicates based on user-specific similarity criteria. The main application area of our work is the integration of heterogeneous data where the likelihood of occurrence of data objects representing related or the same real-world objects though containing discrepant values is rather high. Intended as an extended grouping operation and by combining it with aggregation functions for merging/reconciling groups of conflicting values our grouping operator fits well into the relational algebra framework and the SQL query processing model. In a similar way, an extended join operator takes similarity predicates used for both operators into consideration. These operators can be utilized in ad-hoc queries as part of more complex data integration and cleaning tasks.

Furthermore, we have shown that efficient implementations have to deal with specific index support depending on the applied similarity measure. For one of the most useful measures for string similarity (particularly for shorter strings) we have presented a trie-based implementation. The evaluation results illustrate the benefit of this approach even for relatively large datasets. Though we focused in this paper primarily on the edit distance measure, the algorithm for similarity grouping is able to exploit any kind of index support.

A still open issue is the question how to find and specify appropriate similarity criteria. In certain cases, basic similarity measures like the edit distance are probably not sufficient. As described in Section 3, application-specific similarity measures implementing domain heuristics (e.g. permutation of first name and last name) based on basic edit distances is often a viable approach. However, choosing the right thresholds and combinations of predicates during the design phase of an integrated system often requires several trial-and-error cycles. This process can be supported by analytical processing steps as shown in Section 7 and the corresponding tools. Such tools should allow an interactive investigation of analytical results as well corresponding samples from the data level, and are part of our information fusion workbench [4]. Providing the similarity-based operators as query primitives instead of dedicated application tools simplifies this and opens the opportunity for optimization.

References

1. D. Calvanese, G. de Giacomo, M. Lenzerini, D. Nardi, and R. Rosati. A principled approach to data integration and reconciliation in data warehousing. In *Proceedings of the International Workshop on Design and Management of Data Warehouses (DMDW'99), Heidelberg, Germany*, 1999.

2. W. Cohen. Integration of heterogeneous databases without common domains using queries based on textual similarity. In L. M. Haas and A. Tiwary, editors, *SIGMOD 1998, Proceedings ACM SIGMOD International Conference on Management of Data, June 2-4, 1998, Seattle, Washington, USA*, pages 201–212. ACM Press, 1998.

3. D. Dey and S. Sarkar. A probabilistic relational model and algebra. *ACM Transactions on Database Systems*, 21(3):339–369, September 1996.

4. Oliver Dunemann, Ingolf Geist, Roland Jesse, Kai-Uwe Sattler, and Andreas Stephanik. A Database-Supported Workbench for Information Fusion: InFuse. In Christian S. Jensen, Keith G. Jeffery, Jaroslav Pokorný, Simonas Saltenis, Elisa Bertino, Klemens Böhm, and Matthias Jarke, editors, *Advances in Database Technology - EDBT 2002, 8th International Conference on Extending Database Technology, Prague, Czech Republic, March 25-27, Proceedings*, volume 2287 of *Lecture Notes in Computer Science*, pages 756 – 758. Springer, 2002.

5. R. Elmasri and S. B. Navathe. *Fundamentals of Database Systems*. Benjamin/Cummings, Redwood City, CA, 2 edition, 1994.

6. N. Fuhr. Probabilistic datalog – A logic for powerful retrieval methods. In *Proceedings of the Eighteenth Annual International ACM SIGIR Conference on Research and Development in Information Retrieval*, Retrieval Logic, pages 282–290, 1995.

7. H. Galhardas, D. Florescu, D. Shasha, and E. Simon. AJAX: an extensible data cleaning tool. In Weidong Chen, Jeffery Naughton, and Philip A. Bernstein, editors, *Proceedings of the 2000 ACM SIGMOD International Conference on Management of Data, Dallas, Texas*, volume 29(2), pages 590–590, 2000.

8. G. Graefe. Query Evaluation Techniques For Large Databases. *ACM Computing Surveys*, 25(2):73–170, 1993.

9. L. Gravano, P. G. Ipeirotis, H. V. Jagadish, N. Koudas, S. Muthukrishnan, and D. Srivastava. Approximate string joins in a database (almost) for free. In *Proceedings of the 27th International Conference on Very Large Data Bases(VLDB '01)*, pages 491–500, Orlando, September 2001. Morgan Kaufmann.

10. J. M. Hellerstein, M. Stonebraker, and R. Caccia. Independent, Open Enterprise Data Integration. *IEEE Data Engineering Bulletin*, 22(1):43–49, 1999.

11. M. A. Hernández and S. J. Stolfo. The merge/purge problem for large databases. In Michael J. Carey and Donovan A. Schneider, editors, *Proceedings of the 1995 ACM SIGMOD International Conference on Management of Data*, pages 127–138, San Jose, California, 22–25 May 1995.

12. W. Kent. The breakdown of the information model in multi-database systems. *SIGMOD Record*, 20(4):10–15, December 1991.

13. Wen-Syan Li. Knowledge gathering and matching in heterogeneous databases. In *AAAI Spring Symposium on Information Gathering*, 1995.

14. E.-P. Lim, J. Srivastava, S. Prabhakar, and J. Richardson. Entity identification in database integration. In *International Conference on Data Engineering*, pages 294–301, Los Alamitos, Ca., USA, April 1993. IEEE Computer Society Press.

15. Sergio Luján-Mora and Manuel Palomar. Reducing Inconsistency in Integrating Data from Different Sources. In M. Adiba, C. Collet, and B.P. Desai, editors, *Proc. of Int. Database Engineering and Applications Symposium (IDEAS 2001)*, pages 219–228, Grenoble, France, 2001. IEEE Computer Society.

16. A. E. Monge and C. P. Elkan. The field matching problem: Algorithms and applications. In Evangelos Simoudis, Jia Wei Han, and Usama Fayyad, editors, *Proceedings of the Second International Conference on Knowledge Discovery and Data Mining (KDD-96)*, page 267. AAAI Press, 1996.

17. A. E. Monge and C. P. Elkan. An efficient domain-independent algorithm for detecting approximately duplicate database records. In *Proceedings of the Workshop on Research Issues on Data Mining and Knowledge Discovery (DMKD'97)*, 1997.

18. Gonzalo Navarro. A guided tour to approximate string matching. *ACM Computing Surveys*, 33(1):31–88, 2001.

19. E. Schallehn, K. Sattler, and G. Saake. Extensible grouping and aggregation for data reconciliation. In *Proc. 4th Int. Workshop on Engineering Federated Information Systems, EFIS'01, Berlin, Germany*, 2001.

20. H. Shang and T. H. Merrett. Tries for approximate string matching. *IEEE Transactions on Knowledge and Data Engineering*, 8(4):540–547, 1996.

21. K. Shim, R. Srikant, and R. Agrawal. High-dimensional similarity joins. In *Proceedings of the 13th International Conference on Data Engineering (ICDE'97)*, pages 301–313, Washington - Brussels - Tokyo, April 1997. IEEE.

22. F. Tseng, A. Chen, and W. Yang. A probabilistic approach to query processing in heterogeneous database systems. In *Proceedings of the 2nd International Workshop on Research Issues on Data Engineering: Transaction and Query Processing*, pages 176–183, 1992.

23. H. Wang and C. Zaniolo. Using sql to build new aggregates and extenders for object- relational systems. In A. El Abbadi, M.L. Brodie, S. Chakravarthy, U. Dayal, N. Kamel, G. Schlageter, and K.-Y. Whang, editors, *Proc. of 26th Int. Conf. on Very Large Data Bases (VLDB'00), Cairo, Egypt*, pages 166–175. Morgan Kaufmann, 2000.

24. T. W. Yan and H. Garcia-Molina. Duplicate removal in information dissemination. In *Proceedings of the 21st International Conference on Very Large Data Bases (VLDB '95)*, pages 66–77, San Francisco, Ca., USA, September 1995. Morgan Kaufmann Publishers, Inc.

25. G. Zhou, R. Hull, R. King, and J. Franchitti. Using object matching and materialization to integrate heterogeneous databases. In *Proc. of 3rd Intl. Conf. on Cooperative Information Systems (CoopIS-95), Vienna, Austria*, 1995.

ProSQL: A Prototyping Tool for SQL Temporal Language Extensions

James Green and Roger Johnson

School of Computer Science, Birkbeck, University of London,
Malet Street, London WC1E 7HX, UK.
JamesGreen@liberata.com , r.johnson@dcs.bbk.ac.uk

Abstract. This paper describes ProSQL, a novel prototyping tool to support the development of extensions to SQL. ProSQL provides a simple way to prototype the features of a proposed extension and thus provide a proof of concept. Further, it provides proposers and reviewers of extensions with a clearer view of their positive and negative features. The approach adopted has been to build a wrapper around an existing database management system, in this case Microsoft Access, and to provide a collection of interfaces with which a designer can define extensions to the basic relational database.

1 Introduction

This paper describes ProSQL, a novel prototyping tool to support the development of extensions to SQL. The work has been carried out in the context of temporal extensions to SQL but the authors believe that the approach adopted can be readily applied to a wide range of other potential extensions to SQL.

Many temporal extensions to SQL have been proposed although few have been implemented. In studying temporal extensions it became clear to the authors of this paper that claims were being made about their ease of use and productivity which had often not been substantiated by controlled experiments.

The approach adopted has been to build a wrapper around an existing database management system, in this case Microsoft Access, and to provide a collection of interfaces with which a designer can define extensions to the basic relational database. The facilities include new data types, new comparison operators as well as temporal features. The authors recognize that there are limitations to the range of language extensions that can be implemented in this way. However, their experience suggests that the range is sufficiently large to make this approach useful for language developers and HCI researchers.

2 Motivation

The starting point for this research was the authors' previous work in extending SQL to handle spatio-temporal data by means of intervals. Assumptions have been made in

A. James, B. Lings, M. Younas (Eds.): BNCOD 2003, LNCS 2712, pp. 190–197, 2003.

the literature about the ease of use of temporal extensions [16]. Conceptual models have been presented which are claimed to be more intuitive to the user [17, 5].

The authors of this paper have a long term concern with assessing the usability of SQL extensions. Though a formal definition of usability does not exist there is a general agreement on its constituent parts [20]. These are best described as efficiency, effectiveness and satisfaction. Efficiency can be determined by speed of learning and accuracy; effectiveness by memorability and rate of errors whereas satisfaction is a subjective measure.

Designers of temporal extensions have only built implementations that support their own extension and have used them primarily to demonstrate feasibility [14] and to evaluate their extension in isolation [5]. In addition, gaining access to many of these extensions by independent researchers is not possible and, as the interfaces inevitably differ anyway, comparative analysis of extensions using their own implementation is not possible as the difference in the interface would invalidate the result [2,21].

This has provided the motivation for developing ProSQL, a prototyping tool for SQL extensions that can support a basic simulation of a range of different SQL extensions. The application allows the user to define extensions and their associated operations thus providing a tool that can be used in usability tests and other experiments at an early stage in the design without incurring the time penalties and associated development costs of a full implementation. It also eliminates the problems associated with different interface behaviour and shows that a basic simulation of a range of SQL extensions can be achieved relatively easily.

3 Previous Work

So far as the authors are aware Pro SQL is the first attempt to build a prototyping tool to support the development of extensions to SQL in this way. ProSQL offers a simple standard interface to a range of potential SQL extensions which support comparative studies between competing alternatives.

Since the implementation of a common interface for the languages being compared is beyond the scope of most usability researchers, the great majority of experiments have used paper and pen tests. These have been shown to be effective [10,11, 19]. However, Yen and Scammel found the use of an interface could yield different results to pen and paper although their experiment compared a text based language, SQL, with a graphical one, QBE [21].

Tests using query language interfaces have also been used in previous experiments [21, 3]. Prototype applications have been used in usability tests of database query languages [6]. However, these experiments were undertaken when the languages were already commercially available and, therefore, too late to influence SQL design materially.

The purpose of most SQL extension implementations appears limited to demonstrating feasibility. While they allow users to experience the language no reports of systematic testing appear in the literature.

4   Application

The definition of an SQL extension involves a sequence of relatively straightforward steps. First the extension has to be named. Once this is done the new data types, a test database, predicates and their mappings to the underlying SQL are defined followed by the specification of an extension's functions and mapping them to those built in to the underlying database. (If a required base function does not exist it has to be programmed before it can be mapped to an extension's function.). At any stage in the extensions definition the researcher can define and populate databases and use them to test their extension definition.

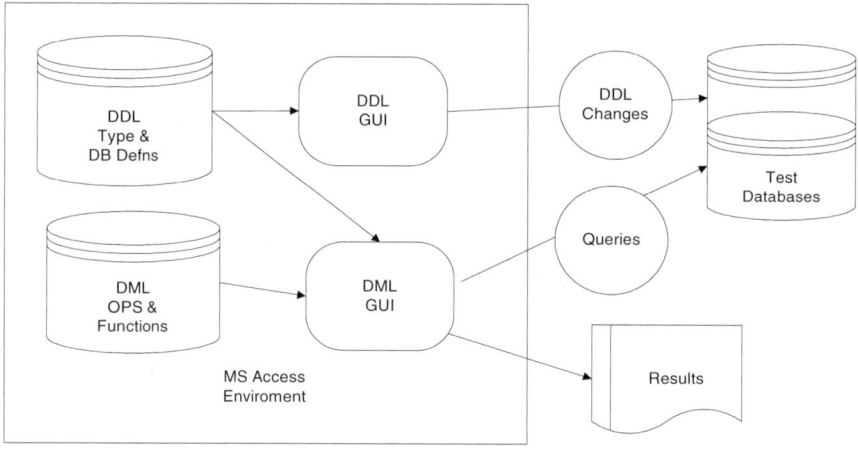

Fig. 1. ProSQL Architecture

The prototyping tool has been developed using an approach similar to that of other implementations of query language extensions using a two tiered system. In this approach, the base layer is a conventional RDBMS [18, 15]. The actual RDBMS used by ProSQL is Microsoft ACCESS. The benefit of using this is that it is cheap, widely used and does not need any specialist DBA skills to maintain it. The emphasis is on the production of a tool that can be easily installed and used without requiring additional specialist knowledge to maintain it or extra software to use it. This approach suffers from some of the problems described in [15] as the simulation of an extension using a wrapper has a detrimental affect on performance.

The outer layer is a wrapper that forms the interface with the user and maps the extension's view of a query to one that can be processed by the underlying RDBMS. It provides support for a data definition language (DDL), a data manipulation language (DML) and uses a set of system catalogues to support non-atomic data types, SQL extensions and operations.

The SQL language can be divided into three sub languages which are the data definition language (DDL), data manipulation language (DML) and data control language (DCL). Each of these will now be described in turn.

4.1 Support for a DDL

The DDL is a GUI application used to define databases, normal, valid time period and event tables and support for tuple time stamping, attribute time stamping (ATS) and explicitly defined period attributes. When a database and its relation schemes are defined it is not bound to a specific extension recorded in the RDBMS. The user selects the extension that is used when they want to query a database. The failure to bind a database to a given extension is not the result of an oversight. Query languages that provide support for the same relational model, data types and tables can be used on the same database structure in an experimental situation.

4.2 Definition of New Non Atomic Data Type

Before an extension's language can be modeled its base types must be available to the application. This includes its non-atomic data type. All the sub types of a generic domain like an interval, for example DATE INTERVAL, INTEGER INTERVAL, have to be declared separately, which renders their definition simple but relatively tedious. New data types are declared using a collection of atomic types supported by the underlying RDBMS, along with a character string for each element of the type that can be appended to an attributes name. This is used to identify part of the data type in the base RDBMS storage system.

The structure used above to map a statement belonging to an extension to an equivalent structure supported by the underlying RDBMS is typical of the approach used throughout the application as it usually allows a set of simple procedures to be used to construct the mapped statements.

4.3 Database Definition

The next step in the definition of an extension is the definition of a database whose relations utilise the extension's novel data types and relation's properties and it provides a test database when the extension is being defined.

Relations are defined using the GUI displayed in *Figure 2* which is used to declare a relation's name and its properties. As an extension to SQL can be derived from a uni-sorted or multi-sorted relational model or incorporate ATS a relation can have a number of properties including implicit temporal attributes and be in NFNF. Support for NFNF relations is limited as it can only support one level of nesting for attribute time stamped values because of limitations of MS Access.

4.4 Support for a DML

Once data types have been declared and a test database configured the user then defines additional predicate operators and functions using the DML. A GUI application that is separate from the DDL provides support for the DML and allows the user to define different SQL extensions, their associated operations and functions. It should be noted that the DML only provides functionality for general queries and cannot be used to UPDATE, DELETE or INSERT data as a data entry screen is provided that performs these functions and, in general, evaluation of query languages focuses on data retrieval. To declare an extension the user first names it and, after doing so, is allowed to define the operators and functions associated with it. This is done in two stages. The user first declares a name for an operator, states whether or not it is a unary or binary operation and the data types that can be used. They have to be declared in the order they are used in the operation with the data type for the left side being declared first. The final stage is the definition of a set of operations that allows the operator to be converted to a set of valid SQL statements of the base RDBMS. An extension can be developed incrementally which permits the user to test the extension as each operator is defined.

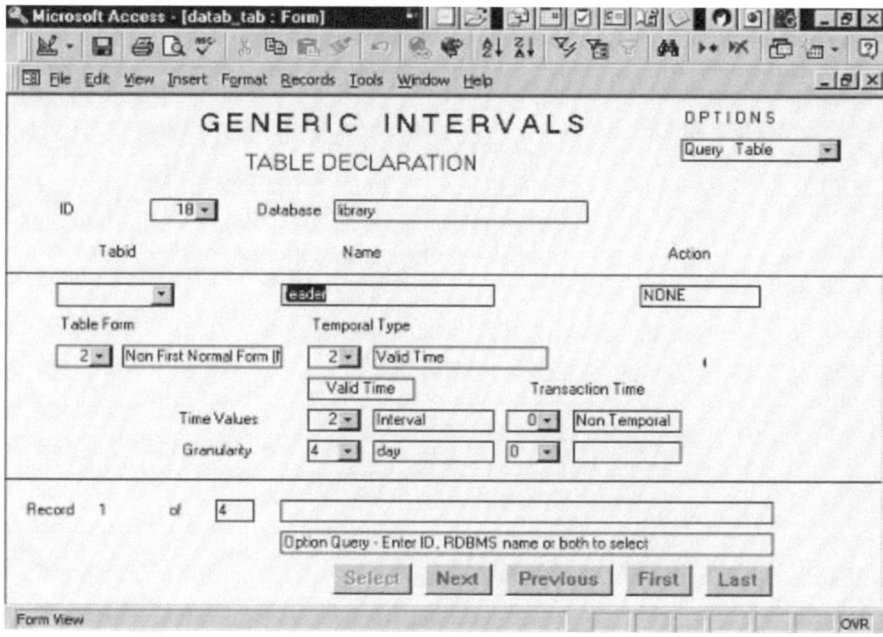

Fig. 2. Data Entry Screen for Base Table Definition

4.5 Definition of Operations

As stated before new data types are declared using a collection of atomic data types that are supported by the underlying RDBMS. When a new data type is declared part of the declaration is the definition of a name that can be appended to the attribute names used in the relation scheme. To define a suitable mapping to the RDBMS' SQL for a non atomic data type's operator the name of the data type's element used on the left hand side is declared first, followed by a theta predicate and the name of data type's element used on the right hand side. The user also has to declare where in the sequence of mappings the definition occurs and the boolean operation (AND, OR) that follows the mapping. The user continues adding mapping data until the definition is complete.

4.6 Definition of Functions

The base RDBMS used in this application allows functions defined in a database to be included in an SQL statement. This makes the inclusion of functions on data types that do not depend on grouping or involve some other operation on tuples relatively easy to implement. Support for functions or processes like coalescence that form a fundamental part of an extension are more difficult to model and are described later.

To add a function that can be used in an extension's SQL, first define the function in the database supporting the DML. If the function's arguments include a new data type, such as a DATETIME interval, the parameters specified in the actual definition of the base types of which it is made up, are used by the functions' processes.

4.7 Definitions of Functions on Relations

Functions and processes that change the values in the tuple require more consideration. For the temporal and interval extensions such functions are coalescence, FOLD and UNFOLD and NORMALIZE ON. Much of the functionality required to achieve valid time coalescence and FOLD and UNFOLD can be managed using relatively simple processes and the use of temporary tables. (It should be remembered that the prototype is being used to evaluate language extensions not to devise algorithms that improve processing speed so simple procedures are more than sufficient). To see how processes on tuples can be incorporated consider the SQL statements in *Figure 3*.

(A) SEQUENCED VALIDTIME   (B) INSERT INTO XYZ
     SELECT A,B,C   SELECT * FROM TABLEA
     FROM TABLEA

(C) SELECT A,B,C,PERIOD1
     FROM TABLEA
     REFORMAT AS UNFOLD PERIOD1

Fig. 3. Queries with a prepended or appended statement to a SELECT .. FROM .. WHERE

Queries A, B and C are similar in that the projection on TABLEA can be executed first and the processing required to achieve the statement SEQUENCED VALIDTIME in (A), INSERT INTO XYZ in (B) or UNFOLD PERIOD1 can be done afterwards. It is evident from (A) that some additions to the projection will have to be made first before the base query is executed and the processes required to achieve coalescence are run. Again these functions, or the elements that make up the users view of the function, have to be defined first. This information can be held in the system catalogs as illustrated in the tables above.

The inclusion of system catalogs in a conventional RDBMS is well known. Copying that approach has resulted in an RDBMS being used to develop an application that performs basic support for a number of SQL extensions using a single user interface.

4.8 Limitations

To date the majority of work has concentrated on firstly implementing temporal extensions to SQL and secondly implementing extensions to include the generic interval data type. The working application is currently restricted to these data domains although testing of other generic processes continues. It is hoped to develop other generic extensions in the near future as opportunity allows. The authors believe that a substantial range of interesting extensions can be readily modeled although some inherent limitations of MS Access, such as support for only one level of nesting, would probably make a full NFNF impossible.

5   Conclusions

ProSQL is a novel tool for prototyping extensions to SQL. The prototyping tool has been used to define SQL extensions for ATSQL, TSQL and IXSQL in a few days. It has successfully executed queries on databases using attribute time stamping, valid time state tables and schemas using generic interval data types.

Early evaluation of a language or extension is desirable as the results could have a positive influence on the language's evolution. ProSQL allows the user to define an emulation of one or more language extensions without rigidly tying the definition to specific lexical terms. The researcher can experiment with the lexical forms used in a query language extension, perform usability tests, undertake case studies for a range of proposals or use it to evalaute interface characteristics for a proposed extension.

The approach adopted has been to build a wrapper around an existing database management system, in this case Microsoft Access, which allow a designer to define extensions to the basic relational database. The facilities include new data types, new comparison operators as well as temporal features. While there are limitations to the range of language extensions that can be implemented in this way, the authors experience suggests that the range is sufficiently large and flexible to make this approach useful for language developers and HCI researchers.

References

1.   Blackwell, A. F. Metacognitive Theories of Visual Programming. Proceedings IEEE Symposium of Visual Languages, 1996, Pages 240–246.
2.   Chan, H. C. Wei, K. K, An empirical study on end users' update performance for different abstraction levels. Int. J. Human –Computer Studies (1994) Vol 4, Pages 309–328
3.   Davis, J. S, Usability of SQL and menus for database query. Int. J. Man-Machine Studies, 1989, Pages 447–455
4.   ORES: Towards The First Generation of Temporal DBMS Valid Time SQL. University Of Athens, Agricultural University of Athens, 1994

5. Goralwalla, I. A., Tansel A. U., Ozsu, M. T, Experimenting with Temporal Relational Databases. CIKM 95, Pages 296–303
6. Greene, S. L, Devlin, S.J, Cannata, P. E, Gomez, L.M. No IFS, ANDS, or ORS: A Study of database querying. Int. J. Man-Machine Studies (1990), Vol. 32, Pages 303–326
7. Jarke, M, Turner, J, Stohr, E.A, Vassiliou Y, White, N.H, Michielsen, K. A Field Evaluation of Natural Language for Data Retrieval., IEEE Transactions on Software Engineering, Vol. SE-11, 1985 Pages 97–114
8. Lorentzos, N. A, Mitsopoulos, Y. G. SQL Extension for Interval Data., IEE Transactions on Knowledge and Data Engineering, Vol. 9, No. 3, 1997
9. Rumbaugh, J, Blaha, M, Premerlani, W, Eddy, F, Lorensen, W. Object-Oriented Modeling and Design. Prentice Hall International Editions.
10. Reisner, P, Boyce, R.F, Chamberlain, D.D. Human Factors Evaulation of Two Database Query Langugaes- Square and Sequel., Proceedings of National Computer Conference (1975), Pages 447–452
11. Reisner, P. Use of Psychological Experimentation as and Aid to Development of a Query Language. IEEE Transactions on Software Engineering, Vol. SE-3, No. 3, 1997, Pages 218–229
12. Human Factors Studies of Database Query Languages: A Survey and Assessment. Computing Surveys, Vol 13, No. 1, 1981
13. Shneiderman, B. Improving Human Factors Aspect of Database Interactions. ACM Transactions on Database Systems, Vol 3., No. 4, 1978, Pages 417–439
14. Snodgrass, R T. The Temporal Query Language TQUEL. ACM Transactions on Database Systems, Vol. 12, No. 2, 1987
15. Stonebraker, M, Brown, P, Object Relational DBMSs – The Next Great Wave. Morgan Kaufman Publishers,
16. Snodgrass, R. T, Bohlen, M. H, Jensen, C. S., Steiner, A. Transitioning Temporal Support in TSQL2 to SQL3. Time Centre Technical Report, TR-9, 1997
17. Toman, D. Point vs. Interval based Query Languages for Temporal Databases. PODS 1996, Pages 58–67
18. Torp, K, Jensen, C. S, Snodgrass, R. T, Stratum Approaches to Temporal DBM Implementation, IDEAS Cardiff, 1998
19. Welty, C, Stemple, D.W, Human Factors Comparison of Procedural and Non Procedural Query Language. ACM Transactions. on Database Systems Vol. 6, No.4, 1981 Pages 626–649
20. van Welie, M, van der Veer, G, Eliens, A. Breaking Down Usability. Human Computer Interaction – INTERACT 99, 1999, Pages 613–620
21. Yi-Miin Yen, M, Scammel, R. W. A Human Factors Experimental Comparison of SQL and QBE. IEEE Transactions on Software Engineering, Vol. 19, No. 4, 1993, Pages 390–409

MVMBS: A Multiple Views Supporting Multiple Behaviours System for Interoperable Object-Oriented Database Systems

M.B. Al-Mourad[1], W.A. Gray[2], and N.J. Fiddian[2]

[1] Aston University, Computer Science Dept., B4 7ET UK
m.b.al-mourad@aston.ac.uk
[2] Cardiff University, Computer Science Dept., CF24 3XF, UK
{w.a.gray, n.j.fiddian}@cs.cf.ac.uk

Abstract. This paper addresses the problem of integrating object-oriented local database schemas by creating several tailored global views using multiple structures and behaviours which fully match user requirements. Different users have different needs for integrating databases, and even the same user might want to integrate the same data in a variety of ways and/or include different behaviours to satisfy different tasks in an organisation. Supporting the global views with multiple behaviour, when possible saves effort, cost and time where the investment made in developing them can be exploited again by the original owner of these behaviours and also by new users in the interoperation context. We describe the theoretical framework we are using in the construction of the (MVMBS) *Multiple Views supporting Multiple Behaviours System*. MVMBS offers the potential for users to work in terms of integrated and customised global views supported by multiple behaviours.

1 Introduction

The architectures of *Multidatabase Systems* (MDBS) range from tightly coupled to loosely coupled [1], and they employ static [2,3] or dynamic [4,5] views in accessing data from multiple databases. The emphasis of these systems has traditionally been placed on the structural aspects of data integration. Even though the use of an *Object-Oriented* (OO) data model as the canonical data model for database integration has been widely favoured [6], attention to behavioural aspects of such models has been ignored [7]. OO MDBSs generally do not present object methods other than those implementing generic query and transaction facilities to a global user, in spite of the fact that component databases may have implemented application-specific methods with their local objects. Reuse or sharing of these methods by other users in a MDBS environment saves effort, cost and time where the investment made in developing them can be exploited again by the original owner of these methods and also by new users in the interoperation context. We suggest that interoperability between a set of heterogeneous OO databases is best achieved by building several tailored global

A. James, B. Lings, M. Younas (Eds.): BNCOD 2003, LNCS 2712, pp. 198–206, 2003.

views supporting multiple behaviours to fully meet user requirements and this allows local conflicts to be resolved in various ways. These views are built by MVMBS and defined in terms of *virtual classes* and *materialisation rules*; they are created by applying a set of semantically-rich integration operators to local database schemas represented in the ODMG standard. The operators comprise a language we call the *Multiple Views supporting Multiple Behaviours Language* (MVMBL). To build such views and to facilitate the use of MVMBL we require identification of semantic relationships between object types in different databases and resolution of schematic differences between these related object types. MVMBS uses both structural and behavioural characteristics of objects to detect object semantic similarity in *Object-Oriented Database* (OODB) schemas.

2   The Object Model

Real-world entities are modelled as a set of objects (O). An object $o_i \in O$ consists of *structure properties* (attributes of the object) and *behaviour properties* (the methods that can be executed on or by the object). We will refer to the attributes and behaviours of an object as *object properties* [8] and together they identify the object's *Type*. Each object has an *object identifier* (OID). Objects that have the same properties (Type) are grouped into sets called classes C. A class $c \in C$ has a unique class name, Properties(c), Type(c), and a set of instances Ext(c). Formally, Properties(c)={A, M}, where:

- A is the set of all attributes of class c: $A = \{a_1 : D_1, ..., a_n : D_n\}$; where D_i $(i = 1, n)$ is the type of attribute a_i.
- M is the set of all methods of class c: $M = \{m_1, m_2, ..., m_j\}$; where m_i $(i = 1, j)$ is the signature of method i and has the form: Name $(Arg_1 : T_1, ..., Arg_k : T_k) \rightarrow (R_1 : S_1, ..., R_p : S_p)$ where Name is the method name; Arg_i is an input parameter and T_i is the type of $Arg_i((i = 1, k)$, k$\geq$ 0); and R_j is a return value and S_j its type $((j = 1, p)$, p$\geq$ 0).

The domain of each method is a cross-product of the domains of its result values: $\text{dom}(m) \subseteq \{\times_{i=1,p} dom(R_p)\}$ and the domain of c is: $\text{dom}(c) \subseteq \{\times_{i=1,n} dom(a_i)\}$ $\times \{(\times_{i=1,j} dom(m_j)\}$. For two classes c_1 and $c_2 \in$ C: we call c_1 a *subset* of c_2, denoted as $(c_1 \subseteq c_2)$, if and only if: $((\forall o \in O$ and $o \in c_1) \Rightarrow o \in c_2)$. We call c_1 a *subtype* of c_2, denoted as $(c_1 \preceq c_2)$, if and only if: Properties$(c_1) \supseteq$ Properties(c_2) and $(\forall p \in$ Properties$(c_2) \Rightarrow dom_{c_2}(p) \subseteq dom_{c_1}(p))$. We will call c_1 a *subclass* of c_2, denoted by $(c_1$ is a $c_2)$, if and only if $(c_1 \subseteq c_2)$ and $(c_1 \preceq c_2)$.

3   Sharing Behaviour – Scope and Requirements

Let us consider the classes EMPLOYEE and WORKER in DB1 and DB2, respectively (Fig. 1). Assume that both classes are semantically related and ideal for integration by merging into a global class GLOBAL-EMPLOYEE (see section 5.7) where its extension is the union of both EMPLOYEE and WORKER extensions

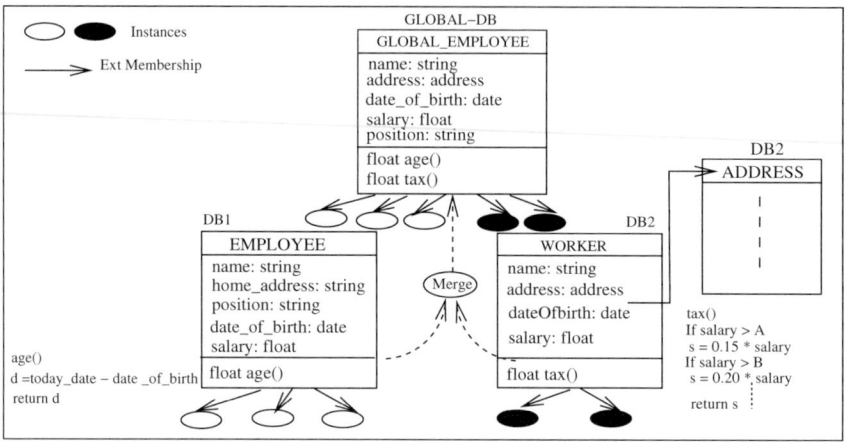

Fig. 1. Method property requirements

[3]. Typically, reusing the tax() method defined in local class WORKER at the global level offers an additional feature to the global users. So they can share this method by applying it to instances derived from the EMPLOYEE class in DB1 as well as instances derived from class WORKER in DB2 . From the previous example we can differentiate between two different meanings, *reusing* and *sharing* behaviour at the global level. Reusing behaviour is the ability to use the behaviour defined in a component database class on instances of this class but at global schema level. In contrast, sharing behaviour is the ability to use the same behaviour but on instances belonging to other component database classes.

3.1 Semantic Requirements for Reusing and Sharing Behaviour in MDBS

We found that sharing behaviour at the global level implies three basic semantic requirements: *property, property assertion validity* and *property value validity* requirements. For the sake of space limitations we will briefly describe the property requirement alone as it is fundamental to this paper, and the reader is invited to review [9] for fuller details. The global class that wishes to reuse or share a method should ensure the properties required by the method in order to perform its functionality. For example, the method (tax) in WORKER requires the data represented in an attribute (salary) in order to perform its functionality, which is calculating employee income tax based on salary. The global class GLOBAL_EMPLOYEE (which is a merger of both classes in the global schema) must have the attribute salary in order to share the salary method defined in the WORKER class. Formally: for semantically related classes c_1 and c_2 in DB1 and DB2 respectively, with: Properties(c_1)={$A1, M1$} and Properties(c_2)={$A2, M2$} Let us have m $\in M_1$ a method available in the class c_1 and the global user would like to reuse this method on the global class G_c that is an integration of the classes c_1 and c_2 by applying one of the integration operators (see section 5.7). We define the function MethodProperties(m,c) which returns a set of properties (Properties(c*)) from class c that is required by the method m in order to perform its functionality: MethodProperties(m,c) = Properties(c*) = {A*,M*} $\subseteq$ Properties(c). Assuming that c is an integration of c_1 and c_2, we can formally recognise three cases:

- If MethodProperties(m,c) $\subseteq$ {Properties(c_1) $\cap$ Properties(c_2)} and dom(m) $\subseteq$ (dom(c_1) $\cup$ dom(c_2)) this means the method m is applicable on instances retrieved from both class c_1 and class c_2. This corresponds to both Reusing and Sharing at the same time.
- If ((MethodProperties(m,c) $\subseteq$ Properties(c_1) and dom(m) $\subseteq$ dom(c_1)) and (MethodProperties(m,c) $\not\subseteq$ Properties(c_2) or dom(m) $\not\subseteq$ dom(c_2))). The method m is applicable only on instances retrieved from class c_1 (Ext(c_1)), and corresponds to Reusing only.
- If ((MethodProperties(m,c) $\subseteq$ Properties(c_2) and dom(m) $\subseteq$ dom(c_2)) and (MethodProperties(m,c) $\not\subseteq$ Properties(c_1) or dom(m) $\not\subseteq$ dom(c_1))). The method m is applicable only to instances retrieved from class c_2 (Ext(c_2)), and corresponds to Reusing only.

4   Detection of Semantic Relationships

In our research we assume that two classes are *Semantically Related* when they have corresponding intended *Real World Semantics* (RWS) for some universe of discourse, and *Semantically Incompatible* when they are not semantically related; where the real-world semantics of a class C, RWS(C), is defined as the set of objects in the real world in C's database schema definition. As we cannot depend on the extension of classes in reality, we adopt class properties as the basis for class comparison, assuming that the properties represent the intended meaning of the classes. To detect whether two classes are similar, we designed a heuristic module *Class Similarity Detector* (CSD) that quantifies the measure of similarity between two classes according to a hierarchical aggregation of similar properties. If the measure exceeds or equals a certain threshold (which can be altered by the user), then we can consider the two classes to be similar. The result of CSD application is presented to the user for review and response in two respects. He/She has to: 1) accept, reject, or modify the heuristic result, solving any conflict that may be found; 2) determine what type of relationship exists between these classes (i.e. equivalent, overlap, inclusion, disjoint). The following equation is used to determine whether two classes c_1, c_2 from two databases are similar or not:

$$\sum_{i=1}^{n} F_i(c_1, c_2) \times W_i \geq Threshold \qquad (1) \qquad where:$$

- F_i are the similarity functions and their result is a value in [0,1].
- W_i are the function similarity weights given by the user, and $\sum_{i=1}^{n} W_i = 1$.
- The threshold is a value in [0,1].

Each function's similarity weight can be altered and the user may assign a higher weight for a function that he feels is more efficient or important than other functions. We call each function a factor:

- Class Name Similarity Factor (CNSF): see (Fig. 2) for values:
- Class Property Similarity Factor (CPSF): to detect whether two properties (attributes or methods) are similar or not we consider the name and type of each property.

$$CPSF = \frac{No.\ of\ equivalent\ properties}{Average\ No.\ of\ properties\ in\ both\ classes}$$

Two properties are considered as equivalent if the *Property Similarity* (PS) factor exceeds or equals a threshold value, where PS is calculated by the following equation:

$$PS = \begin{cases} 0 & if\,PNS \times W_{PNS} = 0 \\ PNS \times W_{PNS} + PTS \times W_{PTS} & otherwise \end{cases}$$

PNS is the *Property Name Similarity* factor and PTS is the *Property Type Similarity* factor. W_{PNS} and W_{PTS} are the weights for PNS and PTS which are determined by the values in (Fig. 2):

Factors \ Values	1	0.5	0
CNSF PNS PTS	If they are the same name	If they have minor splelling differences/ or they are synonyms (based on WordNet thesaurus)	if they are different names

Fig. 2. Factor Values

Two types are considered compatible if they are both members of a certain type set (e.g. long/short integers). If the types are non-primitive objects (i.e. user defined classes), CSD is re-consulted to detect the similarity of these types.

- Class Behaviour Similarity Factor (CBSF): this considers the shareable behaviours from both classes c_1, c_2. We consider the behaviours m_i from class c_1 where $m_i \in c_1$ and can be shared by class c_2 (if MethodProperties(m_i,c_2)? is true); likewise for behaviours m_j from class c_2 that can be shared by class c_1.

$$CBSF = \frac{ShareableMeth(c_1)\ +\ ShareableMeth(c_2)}{No.\ of\ methods\ in\ both\ classes}$$

where ShareableMeth(c) is the number of shareable methods in a class c.

If the value of CBSF is high, this means that both classes c_1 and c_2 have similar behaviours and therefore this factor adds a further valuable aspect to the process of class similarity detection.

5   Overview of MVMBS Architecture

MVMBS is a semi-automatic knowledge based schema meta-integration tool (see Fig. 3). It is directed by an inference engine using a real world data modelling framework based on an OO modelling methodology, which uses a knowledge base consisting of schema facts and predefined integration rules supplemented by information generated during the MVMBS integration process or elicited interactively from the global schema designer. The roles of the major software modules are explained in the following sub-sections.

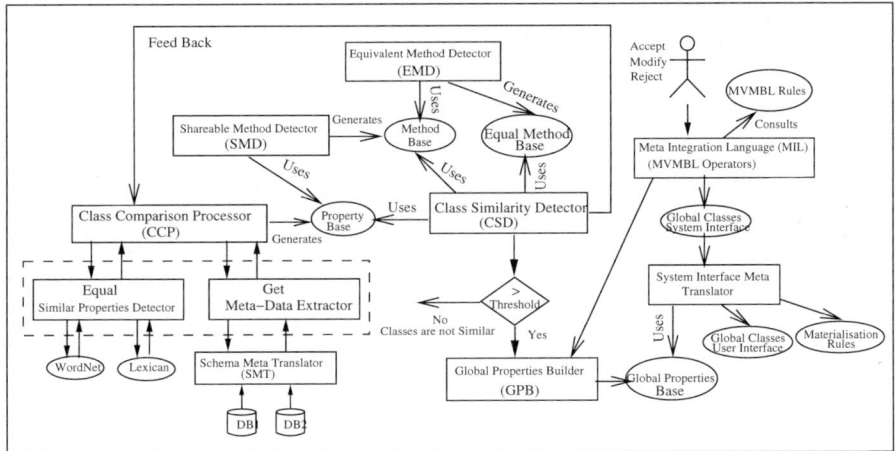

Fig. 3. MVMBS architecture

5.1   Schema Meta Translator (SMT)

Existing data and schemas do not have to be modified unnecessarily. This is assisted by the SMT, which by interpretation of local database schemas transforms them into their representation in the MVMBS *Internal Intermediate Data Model* (IIDM) which is compliant with the ODMG data model. Also, the local schemas' behaviours are mined in this process to extract the properties required by each method. The properties of each method (name, type, arguments, argument types) are stored in the MVMBS IIDM (see the example in Fig. 4 (A)).

5.2   MVMBS Internal Intermediate Data Model (IIDM)

The MVMBS IIDM is created by a knowledge based modelling system. It creates an object model of the schema based on the ODMG standard. This knowledge base consists of facts that represent the meta-data extracted from the component databases' schemas during the schema translation phases. Each fact captures the meta-data that belongs to one class and is represented in a Prolog frame.

5.3   Class Comparison Processor (CCP)

This module compares two classes by using various aspects of their meta-data. It scans the meta-data of the classes to detect potentially similar properties and stores its findings as Prolog facts in the *Property Meta Knowledge Base* (property base). This comparison is done in two phases, namely:

Phase 1: compares the names and types of all attributes in both classes and generates facts that represent potentially similar or corresponding properties.

Phase 2: If CCP fails to detect a correspondence for an attribute in phase 1, it compares the name of this attribute with the names of the methods in the other class. If the attribute and a method name are found to be similar, CCP stores the result in a Prolog fact. If no corresponding property is found for a property or a method, a *null* value is assigned to the second property. CCP uses two auxiliary modules: *Equal* (Similar Properties Detector) which detects whether two properties are similar, and *Get* (Meta-data Extractor) which contains a number of functions designed to obtain the meta-data required by CCP.

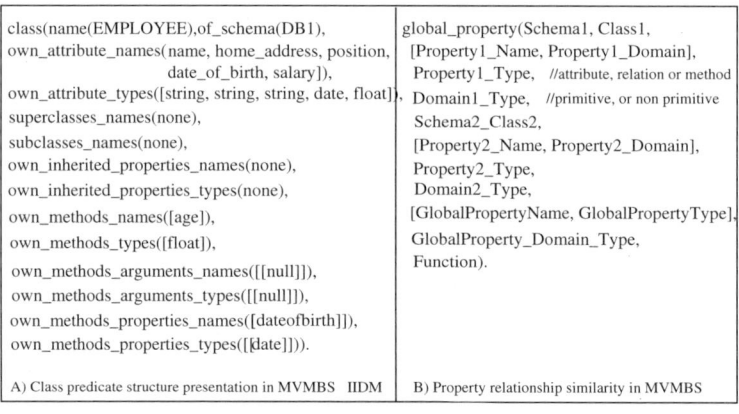

Fig. 4. Example of facts in MVMBS IIDM

5.4   Shareable Method Detector (SMD)

SMD investigates the possibility of reusing the methods of the compared classes based on the algorithm in section 3. The output of this module is stored in the *Methods Meta Knowledge Base* (method base) which holds a fact about the method in each class and expresses whether this method is usable by the corresponding class or not.

5.5   Equivalent Method Detector (EMD)

EMD investigates potentially equivalent methods. It assumes that two methods from the compared classes are semantically equivalent, if the following conditions are fulfilled: 1) Both methods have similar names and types. 2) Both methods have the same property requirements (facts from the *method base* and *property base* are used for this purpose). 3)Both methods are detected as reusable by corresponding classes. The output of this module is stored in the *Equivalent Methods Meta Knowledge Base* (equal-method base) which holds facts about potentially equivalent methods.

5.6   Class Similarity Detector (CSD)

CSD determines whether two classes are similar and consequently mergeable. The result of CSD is presented to the user in the form of rich facts (see Fig. 4 (B)). The last slot is occupied by a function. If there is any conflict between the correspondence properties, the user must provide a function to resolve this conflict. After user approval, all facts are stored in the *Global Properties Meta Knowledge Base* (global property base).

5.7   Meta Integration Language (MIL)

Once CSD finishes its operation, the user is able to start the integration process. MIL performs the integration via MVMBL operators (Union, Merge, Intersect and Include), see Fig. 5 and [10] for fuller details.

Operator	Semantics	Extension Ext(Gc)	Properties(Gc)	ShareableMeth(Gc)
Merge(c1,c2)	merges two classes into one global class	Ext(c1) U Ext(c2)	Prop(c1) U Prop(c2)	ShareableMeth(c1) U ShareableMeth(c2)
Union(c1,c2)	generates a superclass for two local classes	Ext(c1) U Ext(c2)	Prop(c1) $\cap$ Prop(c2)	ShareableMeth(c1) U ShareableMeth(c2)
Intersect(c1,c2)	generates a common subclass	Ext(c1)$\cap$ Ext(c2)	Prop(c1) U Prop(c2)	Meth(c1) U Meth(c2)
Include(c)	imports a single class	Ext(c)	Prop(c)	Meth(c)

Fig. 5. Summary of MVMBL operators

5.8   Global Class Materialisation Rules

The instances of the generated virtual classes are derived from their corresponding local ones. This is done by possibly aggregating several local instances where the same instance may have heterogeneous representations in different databases. Specifying the rules that derive the global class instances and reconciling heterogeneous representations is the task of the set of materialisation rules that augments each global view. MVMBS generates such rule sets automatically as a result of applying one of the MVMBL operators. When a query is posed against a global class, the query processor uses its corresponding materialisation rules to decompose the global query into local sub-queries. The following is the general syntax of an MVMBS rule, which is an upgraded version of [11]:

Rule<name> on retrieve to <virtual class properties>, apply <virtual class methods>
do instead: retrieve <local corresponding properties>, apply <local corresponding methods>
where <condition> // the condition under which the rule is executed.

References

1. Sheth, A.P., Larson, J.A.: Federated database systems for managing distributed, heterogeneous and autonomous databases. ACM Computing Surveys (1990)
2. Dayal, U., Hwang, H.: View definition and generalization for database integration in a multidatabase system. IEEE Transactions on Software Engineering **SE-10** (1984) 628–645
3. Motro., A.: Superviews: Virtual integration of multiple databases. IEEE Transactions on Software Engineering **SE-13** (1987) 785–798
4. Litwin, W.: O*sql: A language for object oriented multidatabase interoperability. In Hsiao, D.K., Neuhold, E.J., Sacks-Davis, R., eds.: Interoperable Database Systems (DS-5) (A-25), North Holland (1993)
5. Gingras, F., Lakshmanan, L.V.S.: nd-sel: A multi-dimensional language for interoperability and olap. Proc. 24th International Conference on Very Large Data Bases (1998) 134–145
6. Garcia-Solaco, M., Saltor, F., Castellanos, M.: Semantic heterogeneity in multi-database systems. In Bukhres, O.A., Elmagarmid, A.K., eds.: Object-Oriented Multidatabase Systems, A Solution for Advanced Applications. Prentice-Hall (1996)
7. James, A., Salem, M.: Classification and resolution of behavioural conflicts in federated information systems. 4th Int'l Workshop Engineering Federated Information Systems (EFIS2001) (2001) TU Berlin, Germany.
8. Castano, S., Antonellis, V.D., Gugini, M.G.: Conceptual schema analysis: Techniques and applications. ACM Transactions on Database Systems **23** (1998)
9. Mourad, M.B.A., Gray, W.A., Fiddian, N.J.: Semantic requirements for sharing behaviours in federated object-oriented database systems, Ukraine (2001)
10. Mourad, M.B.A., Gray, W.A., Fiddian, N.J.: Detecting object semantic similarity by using structural and behavioural semantics. In: Proc. 5th World Multiconference on Systemics, Cybernetics and Informatics, Orlando, USA (2001)
11. Stonebraker, M., Rowe, L.A., Hirohama, M.: The implementation of POSTGRES. IEEE Transactions on Knowledge and Data Engineering **2** (1990) 125–142

Efficient Filtering of Composite Events

Annika Hinze

Institute of Computer Science
Freie Universität Berlin,Germany
hinze@inf.fu-berlin.de

Abstract. Event Notification Services (ENS) are used in various applications such as remote monitoring and control, stock tickers, traffic control, or facility management. The performance issues of the filtering of primitive events has been widely studied. However, for a growing number of applications, the rapid notification about the occurrence of composite events is an important issue. Currently, the detection of composite events requires a second filtering step after the identification of the primitive components. In this paper, we propose a single-step method for the filtering of composite events. The method has been implemented and tested within our ENS prototype CompAS. Using our method, the filter response time for composite events is significantly reduced. Additionally, the overall performance of the event filtering has been improved.

1 Introduction

Event Notification Services (*ENS*) are used in various applications such as traffic control and remote monitoring project control. They have gained increasing attention in the past few years. Several systems have been implemented, such as Siena [4], Le Subscribe [17], or Ready [11]. An event notification service informs its users about new events that occurred on providers' sites. Events could be, for example, the change of a web-page, a new temperature value, or the occurrence of a traffic jam. Users define their interest in events by means of *profiles*. A user profile defines a periodically-evaluated query (similar to a search query). Users may be interested in primitive (atomic) events, their time and order of occurrence, and in composite events, which are formed by temporal combinations of events. An example for a composite event is the crossing of a certain temperature threshold after an experiment has been started in a laboratory.

After having studied efficient filtering of primitive events [12], this paper concentrates on the filtering of composite events. Composite events are formed by temporally combined primitive events. The filtering of composite events is based on the detection and filtering of their primitive components. The response time for a composite event is the time between the occurrence of the last event contributing to the composition and the user notification. To the best of our knowledge, all existing methods for composite event detection consist of two steps: In a first step, the primitive profiles are evaluated and in a second step, the composite profiles are identified. Thus, the composite event is detected in a separate step after the filtering of primitive events. In this paper, we propose a new method for filtering of composite events that integrates the detection of composite events into the detection of primitive events: After the filtering of a primitive event, its

A. James, B. Lings, M. Younas (Eds.): BNCOD 2003, LNCS 2712, pp. 207–225, 2003.

contribution to a composite event is tested. In that way, the composite event is detected successively. No additional step is required for the identification of the composite event after the last contributing primitive event has been detected. The identification of the composite event after the primitive event is accelerated and the overall filtering time is reduced.

This paper is organized as follows: Section 2 gives an overview of necessary background information. Then, we analyze typical methods for the filtering of composite events in Section 3. In Section 4, we introduce our approach of combined filtering of primitive and composite events. We present and discuss the results of a performance analysis of our prototype implementation in Section 5.

2   Background

This section is devoted to our context of study. It first describes our running example from the field of computer-aided facility management (CAFM). Then, the basic event-related concepts are introduced.

2.1   Application Scenario: Remote Monitoring

Remote monitoring and control applications in commercial buildings are an important domain for the employment of event notifications. Examples are monitoring of single factories, powerplants, and facilities. Let us consider a surveillance system for several buildings that monitors lighting, heating, air conditioning, and sun protection (e.g., the OWL system [3]). Such a service aims at the improvement of security, energy saving, and flexibility, and at the reduction of service costs.

A number of sensors are located within each of the monitored buildings. The surveillance system monitors the status of these sensor readings. In case of emergency, the systems reacts, e.g., by sending notification to a technician or by triggering an automatic emergency program. The system controls the building by monitoring the sensors: Some sensors send status information on a regular basis to the system. Other sensors send only critical events, i.e., if the status values cross a predefined threshold. A third group of sensors passively collects data and is to be observed by the system.

Often, the building's technicians and service personnel are interested in certain combinations of events. The following examples demonstrate user profiles in a facility management system:

P1   The air-condition technician is to be notified if the temperature in the offices crosses a given threshold during the night.

P2   The service personnel is to be notified if a sensor does not send data for more than half an hour.

P3   The chemical technician is to be notified if in a laboratory, concurrently, the temperature is too low and the humidity too high.

P4   The security personnel is to be notified if at an office first a window is broken and then the presence detector sends a signal.

These profile examples describe profiles with human-oriented time requirements, but other examples with stronger demands towards the response time are conceivable, e.g., for safety in a chemical laboratory. Typically, surveillance or facility management systems may have of the order of 10^4 profiles and an event frequency of 10^3 events per second for each controlled building.

2.2   Concepts: Events, Profiles, and Notifications

A monitored system consists of a number of objects of interest, e.g. real world objects such as offices or laboratories, or logical objects such as time. Objects have certain states, defined by their properties, e.g., the temperature of a room.

Definition 1 (Event). *An event (or event instance) is the occurrence of a state transition of an object of interest at a certain point in time.*

In contrast to states, events have no duration. Events may be state changes in databases, signals in message systems, or real-world events such as the departures and arrivals of vehicles. Within an event notification system, events are reported as event messages describing the event. Within this paper, we do not explicitly distinguish events from their reporting messages.

We consider *primitive events* and *composite events*, which are formed by combining primitive events. We further distinguish two kinds of primitive events: *time events* and *content events*. Time events describe the occurrence of a certain point in time (e.g., 5 o'clock). Content events involve changes of object states in general (e.g., the temperature of a room). In this paper, we use the (attribute,value) pair notation for primitive event examples, for instance: $e_{laboratory} = event(room\_number = 273, temperature = 35°C, timestamp =14:22:03.456)$.

Definition 2 (Profile). *A profile is a query that is periodically evaluated by the event notification system against incoming events.*

A simple example profile is $p_{temp} = profile(temperature < 10 °C)$. The stream of incoming events at an event notification service is called history, or *trace* of events.

We distinguish *event instances* from *event classes*: an event class is specified by a query while an event instance relates to the actual occurrence of an event. We will simply use the term *events* whenever the distinction is clear from the context.

Definition 3 (Event Class). *An event class is a set of event instances that share certain properties, e.g., attribute values. These properties are described by a query. Then an event class is the set of all event instances for which the query evaluates to true.*

Note that user profiles define event classes, e.g., all event instances regarding the temperature. Even though instances of the same event class share some properties (e.g., temperature of a sensor), they may differ in other event attributes (e.g., location). Events (instances) are denoted by lower Latin e with indices, i.e., $e_1, e_2, \ldots$, while event classes are denoted by upper Latin E with indices, i.e., $E_1, E_2, \ldots$. The fact that an event e_i is an instance of an event class E_j is denoted *membership*, i.e., $e_i \in E_j$.

Definition 4 (Composite Event). *Composite event instances are formed by temporal combinations of event instances.*

Note that our notion of composite events differs from Gehani [8], where a composite event is a set of the events it is formed of.

The definition of composite events requires temporal operators and additional parameters for the handling of duplicate events, for details see [13]. Composite event operators are, e.g., sequence $(E_1; E_2)_t$, conjunction $((E_1, E_2)_t$, disjunction $(E_1 | E_2)$, and negation $(\overline{E_1})_t$. For example, a *sequence* $(E_1; E_2)_t$ occurs when first $e_1 \in E_1$ and then $e_2 \in E_2$ occurs. The parameter t defines in the profile the maximal temporal distance between the events. The time of the sequence event instance $e_3 := (e_1; e_2)$ is equal to the time of e_2: $t(e_3) := t(e_2)$. Additionally to the description of the component events and the temporal restriction, profiles referring to composite events can contain predicates regarding the composite event attributes. For example, the predicate $E_1.temperature == E_2.temperature$ could be defined for two temperature events. This additional conditions are called binding predicates.

Definition 5 (Duplicate). *Duplicates of events are event instances that belong to the same event class.*

Duplicates could be, e.g., all temperature events regarding laboratory 273, but also all temperature events in the building referring to the same temperature value.

For profiles regarding composite events, the handling of duplicate events has to be defined. For example, the air-condition technician is to be notified only once per night about the high temperature, at the first occurrence. On the other hand, the service personnel is to be informed about every occurrence of a failing sensor.

Two parameters carry the information about the user's preferences for the duplicate handling:

1. *Event instance selection* defines for each event, whether the user is interested in all, the first, last, or n^{th} event instance in a sequence of duplicate events.
2. *Event instance consumption* defines for each composite event, whether the event instances participate in only one pair of event instances or in several pairs.

For the event instance consumption, consider the profile defined by the chemical technician: within 30 minutes the temperature reaches a peak for three times while the humidity crosses the threshold but once. Only one notification needs to be sent. Similarly, the security personnel is not interested in all people entering a room after a broken window was signaled, but only the first one.

3   Methods for Composite Event Filtering

Several proposals have been made for the filtering of composite events. We distinguish approaches using automata (e.g., Ode [7]), petri nets (e.g., Samos [6], Eve [9]), or trees (e.g., Ready [11], GEM [16]). Here, we do not consider the specific conditions of distributed event filtering.

Example 1. Let us consider a composite event profile for the sequence of two events within a time span T: $E_T = (E_1; E_2)_T$. The steps for the detection of the composite event depend on the method used. Figure 1 displays simplified structures for detecting the composite event instance of E_T using the different methods described in this section.

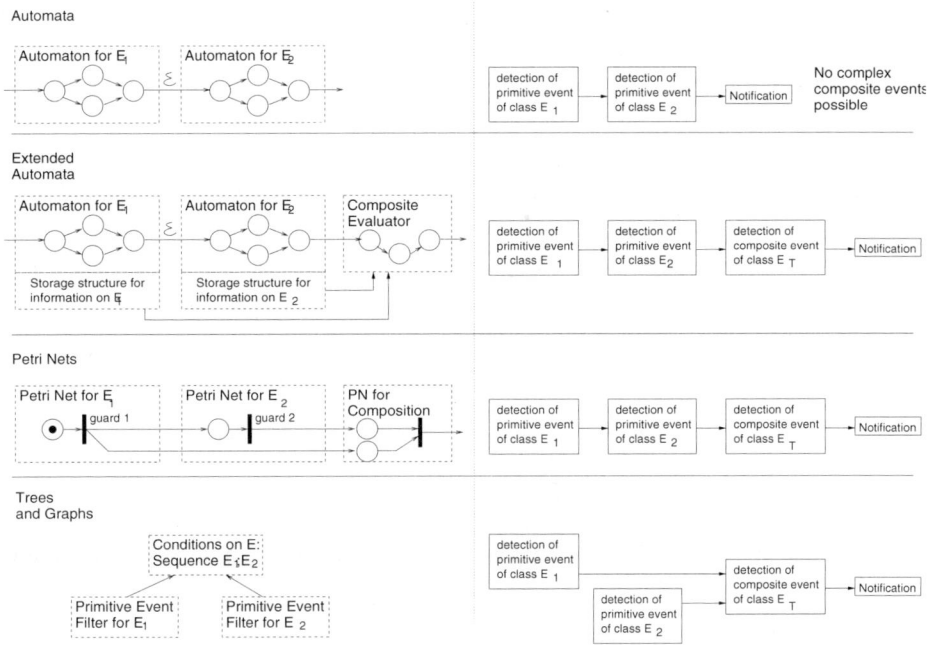

Fig. 1. Methods for detection of composite events

Automata. Composite event expressions are similar to regular expressions if they are not parameterized. Using this observation, it is possible to implement event expressions using finite automata. The first approach for using automata has been made in the Compose system of Ode [8], an active database system. The history of events provides the sequence of input symbols to the automaton implementing the event expression. The automaton input are the primitive event components from the corresponding composite event as they occur in the history. If the automaton enters an accepting state after the input of a primitive event, then the composite event implemented by the automaton is said to occur at the time of this primitive event.

Automata are not sufficient if binding predicates have to be supported. The automata have to be extended with a data structure for storing the additional event information of the primitive events from the time of their occurrence to the time at which the composite event is detected. This extension is shown in the second row in Figure 1.

Petri Nets. Petri nets are used in several event-based systems to support the detection of complex events that are composed of parameterized primitive events, for example in the active database system SAMOS [6], and the monitoring system HiFi [2]. In a Petri Net created for a profile regarding a composite event, the input places refer to primitive events, and the output places model the composite event. Each new profile describing a composite event causes the creation of the appropriate Petri Net. The incremental detection of composite events is described by the position of the markings in the petri net. The firing of the transition depends on the input tokens and the positive evaluation of the transition guards. The occurrence of the composite event is signaled as soon as the last element of a given sequence order is marked. Petri Net based composite event detection is shown in the third row in Figure 1.

Matching Trees. Another approach to implement composite event filters are matching trees that are constructed from profiles describing composite event structures. This method has been used in Ready [11] and Yeast [15]. The primitive event parts are the leaves of the matching tree, composites are the parent nodes in the tree hierarchy, as shown in the fourth row in Figure 1. Parent nodes are responsible for maintaining binding information, which represents information for matched events, such as mapping of event variables and successfully matching event instances. Binding information is updated by child nodes on every match and is passed to the parent nodes. Parent nodes perform further filtering. A composite event is detected if the root node is reached and the respective event data are successfully filtered in the root node. Then context-related information and binding information (e.g. the subscriber) is passed to the notification component. Note that in tree-based composite filtering, components of a composite event may be filtered unnecessarily, e.g., the second event of a sequence is filtered even though the first event of the sequence did not occur.

Graphs. An approach very similar to the tree-based one described above is the graph-based detection of composite events. Here, each composite event is represented by a directed acyclic graph (DAG), where nodes are event descriptions and edges represent event composition, see also the fourth row in Figure 1. Nodes are marked with references to respective event occurrences. After event detection, parent nodes are informed and checked for consumption recursively. References to events are stored until consumption is possible. In addition to event composition edges, nodes are accompanied with rule objects that are fired after the corresponding event occurred. Graph-based composite detection is implemented in Sentinel [5] and Eve [9].

The processing time of a composite event is the time between the occurrence of the last necessary primitive event to fulfill the composition until the notification is sent. Thus, the response time for composite events is the time to identify the (last) primitive event and the time to identify the appropriate composite events. We extend our Example 1 as follows:

Example 2. For the profile describing the set of composite events $E_T = (E_1; E_2)_T$ as before, we now consider an exemplary trace: $tr = \langle e_1, e_2, e_3, e_4, e_5, e_6, e_7 \rangle$ with $\{e_3, e_4, e_6\} \in E_1$ and $\{e_1, e_2, e_5, e_7\} \in E_2$. We are interested in all matching composite events. Figure 2 shows the event filtering using the different methods described above. We do not show the filtering of each incoming event but only depict the filter efforts contributing to the composite event. The events e_3 and e_4 do not form a composition with e_5, because the temporal distance is larger than T. Only the event instances e_6 and e_7 match our composite profile.

Composite event filtering based on trees or graphs considers each matching primitive event, regardless of their order or temporal distance. This results in a high number of unnecessary filter operations.

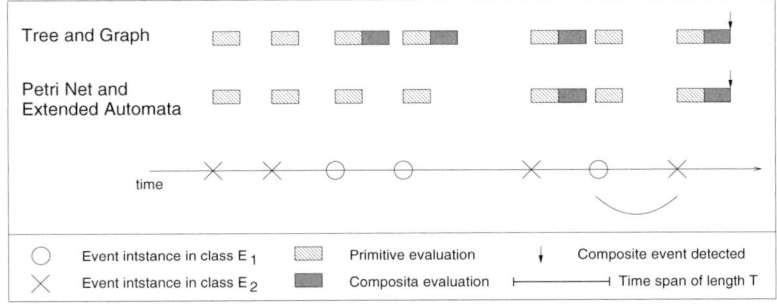

Fig. 2. Composite event detection for exemplary trace as described in Example 2

Composite event filtering based on Petri Nets or extended automata considers only matching primitive events that are in the desired order. Matching of temporal conditions is performed during the composition phase. Unnecessary filter operations are performed for non-matching composites.

All approaches for filtering of composite events applicable to parameterized composite events (i.e., all but simple automata) have in common, that two steps are necessary to identity composite events: The detection of primitive events followed by the evaluation of the composite binding predicates.

In the next section, we propose our method to identify the composite event within the single step of detecting the contributing primitive events.

4   Composite Event Detection in a Single Step

We use the idea of partial evaluation [14]: Primitive profiles contributing to composite ones are evaluated only if they potentially contribute to a composite event. For example, for the sequence of events $(E_x; E_y)$, first only the E_x-profile is evaluated. The E_y-profile is included into the evaluation process only after an event e_x did occur.

We further illustrate the idea of composite filtering in a single step by explaining the differences to the two-step filtering. For doing that, we consider the following three example profiles:

- User A: $E_A = E_1$ (profile regarding primitive events)
- User B: $E_B = (E_1; E_2)_T$ (profile regarding composite events as in P4 in Section 2.1 and Example 2)
- User C: $E_C = E_2$ (profile regarding primitive events)

Figure 3 shows the principle of *composite event detection in two steps* for these three profiles: The triangle represents the primitive event pool. The pool contains all profiles regarding primitive events. Each incoming primitive event has to be filtered against all profiles in that pool, e.g., using the efficient tree-based algorithm [1,10,12]. Users with profiles regarding primitive events (i.e., users A and C) are notified after the detection of

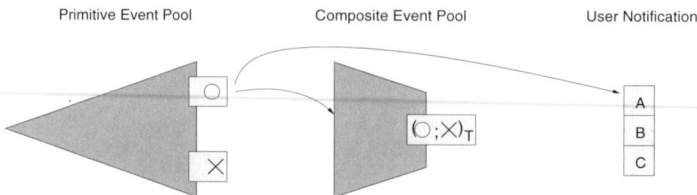

(a) Situation after occurrence of event $\circ \in E_1$

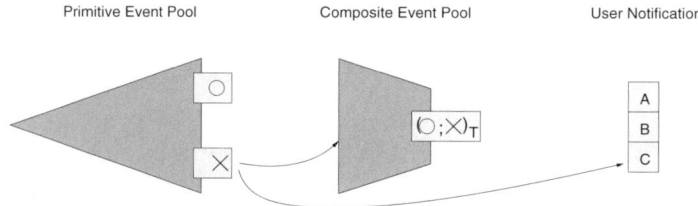

(b) Situation after occurrence of event $\times \in E_2$

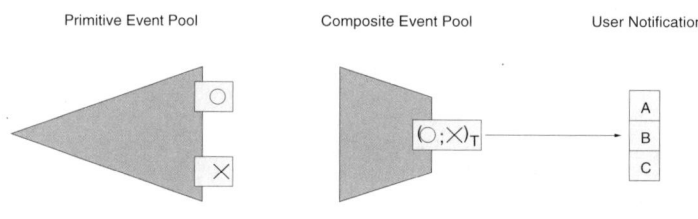

(c) Composite event filtering

Fig. 3. Composite event detection using two-step methods

these events. This detection of the primitive events is the first step in the event detection mechanism.

The results of the primitive filtering serve as input for the composite filtering (events $e_1 = \circ$ and $e_2 = \times$ in the Figures 3(a) and 3(b)). The profiles regarding composites are stored in the composite pool, represented by the square in Figure 3. The incoming primitive events are assigned to the composite profiles. If all contributing events for a certain composite did occur, the composite event is signaled to the interested users (user B in Figure 3(c)). If the time-span between the primitive events is larger than T, the composite profile is not matched, and the detected primitive events are dismissed. Figure 4 shows the principle of *composite event detection in a single step*: The primitive event pool and a temporal pool are required, the composite pool is not used. After the detection of a primitive event, the interested users are notified (user A in Figure 4(a)).

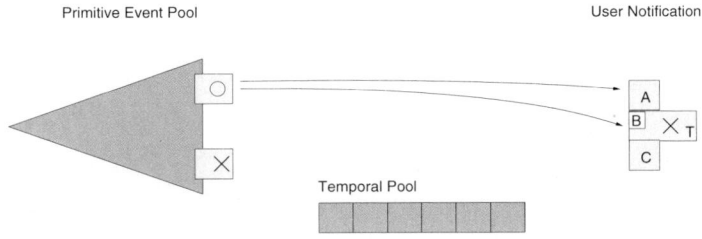

(a) Situation after occurrence of event $\circ \in E_1$ at time $t1$

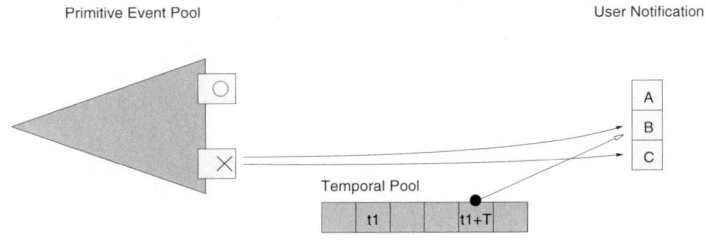

(b) Situation after occurrence of event $\times \in E_2$

Fig. 4. Composite event detection using our single-step method

For storing the information about composite profiles, auxiliary profiles are created. Instead of notifications to interested users, an internal notification regarding the auxiliary profile is created. This notification triggers the insertion of the remaining composite part into the primitive profile pool.[1]

Consider the auxiliary profile for the composite profile of user B: an internal auxiliary user is notified about the occurrence of the partial composite event (see Figure 4(a)). The auxiliary profiles for the internal user carry the information about the composite profile as well as the information about its partial evaluation.

In Figure 4(b), after the detection of event $\circ$, the profile for event $\times$ has been inserted into the pool. For the observation of the maximal time span T, a reference is inserted into the temporal pool - an auxiliary terminator. Terminator references cause the removal of the referenced profile from the pool. The temporal terminator in Figure 4(b) causes the removal of the profile for user B at time $t1 + T$, where $t1$ is the time of the primitive event $\circ$.

After the match of the final primitive event within the composite profile, the notification to the user is sent. Using the single step method, the notification about the composite does not suffer additional delays due to additional filtering of binding information for the composition.

---

[1] The remaining parts of profiles can be identified, for example, by analyzing the respective Petri Net for the composite profile.

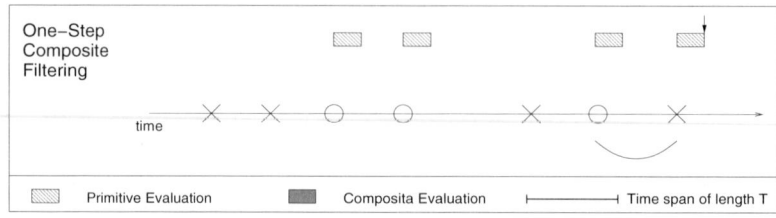

Fig. 5. Composite event detection for exemplary trace as described in Example 3

In analogy to the example for the two-step approach (see Example 2), we discuss the composite evaluation for an exemplary trace in the following example.

Example 3. We consider the profile describing the set of composite events $E_T = (E_1; E_2)_T$ and the exemplary trace $tr = \langle e_1, e_2, e_3, e_4, e_5, e_6, e_7 \rangle$ with $e_1, e_2, e_5, e_7 \in E_1$ and $e_3, e_4, e_6 \in E_2$. Figure 5 shows the single-step filtering for that trace. Again, we only depict the filter efforts contributing to the composite event.

Only those primitive events are evaluated that contribute to the composite event. Additionally, the composite event is detected earlier. Few unnecessary filter operations are performed for non-matching composites.

As we can clearly see in Figure 5, the filtering costs of the one-step method are less than the costs of the two-step methods (cf. Figure 2).

Temporal Operators for Composite Events. In our example, we have shown the single-step filtering for a simple temporal sequence. The principle can be translated for the other temporal composition operators conjunction, disjunction, selection, and negation, see Table 1. Here, for each temporal operator, we give the filter procedure that implements the respective single-step method. The filter procedure is defined both graphically and by description. In the graphics, we show the order of insertions into the profile and temporal pool. For example, the temporal disjunction $E_1 \| E_2$ requires the insertion of both the profiles regarding E_1 and E_2; after the detection of either event instances in E_1 or E_2, a notification is sent. For the negation, terminator references are required: At starting time of the profile, a temporal profile is inserted that triggers a notification after the time span t_1. If an event instance of E_1 occurs within that time span, the temporal profile is removed and no notification is sent. Different from the sequence handling, here the auxiliary terminator is attached to the primitive profile for the event in question. The temporal restriction provides the accepting reference to the user to be notified.

Parameterized Composite Events. Profiles regarding composite events can also carry additional parameters, as briefly introduced in Section 2. These parameters can also be supported in the single-step approach, see Table 2.

The parameter for event instance detection influences which of the duplicated partial events is stored. For example, for the *first* event in the duplicate list, the auxiliary profile refers to the remainder of the composite profile. For the *last* event, two auxiliary profiles have to be created: One that refers to the remainder of the composite profile (in case

Table 1. Profile handling for various composite operators using our single-step algorithm

Operator	Filter Procedure
Temporal Sequence e.g. $(E_1; E_2)_{t1}$	$E_1 \longrightarrow E_2 \longrightarrow$ notif[$(E_1; E_2)_{t1}$] $t_{e1} + t1$ insert profile E_1, after $e_1 \in E_1$ insert profile E_2 and time profile $t_{e1} + t1$ with terminator to profile E_2
Temporal Conjunction e.g. $(E_1, E_2)_{t1}$	$E_1 \longrightarrow E_2$ $t_{e1} + t1$ $E_2 \longrightarrow E_1 \longrightarrow$ notif[$(E_1, E_2)_{t1}$] $t_{e2} + t1$ insert profiles E_1 and E_2, after $e_1 \in E_1$ insert profile E_2 and time profile $t_{e1} + t1$ with terminator to profile E_2, react on $e_2 \in E_2$ respectively
Temporal Disjunction e.g. $(E_1\|E_2)$	$E_1 \longrightarrow$ notif[$(E_1\| E_2)$] $E_2 \longrightarrow$ notif[$(E_1\| E_2)$] insert profiles E_1 and E_2, notify after $e_1 \in E_1$ or $e_2 \in E_2$
Negation e.g. $(\overline{E_1})$	E_1 $t_{start} + t1 \longrightarrow$ notif[$\overline{E_1}$] insert profile E_1 with an terminator to the time profile $t_{start} + t1$, notify after matching time profile, each A starts the process anew
Selection e.g. $(E_1^{[i]})$	E_1 [1] [2] ..... [i-1] notif[$E^{[i]}$] E_1 E_1 insert profile E_1, after $e_1 \in E_1$ insert profile E_1, notify after the $i^{th} e_1 \in E_1$

Legend: A $\longrightarrow$ B: after event A insert profile B   A $\bullet\!\!-\!\!\triangleright$ B: after event A remove profile B

there is only a single event instance), and another one that refers, again, to the already matched partial profile (to detect the duplicates).

The parameter for event consumption influences how long partially matching events have to be stored. We distinguish three modi: remove after match, hold after match, and reapply filter after remove. For example, for remove after match mode, the partially matching events are deleted after the composite has been found (i.e., only *unique event pairs* are detected). For the hold after match mode, the auxiliary profiles for the remainder

Table 2. Profile handling for various composite parameters using our single-step algorithm

Parameter	Filter Procedure
All Duplicates e.g. regarding E_1	$E_1 \longrightarrow$ notif[E_1] do not remove profiles after match
First Duplicate e.g. first $e_1 \in E_1$	$E_1 \longrightarrow$ notif[E_1] remove profile after match
Last Duplicate e.g. first $e_1 \in E_1$ before $e_2 \in E_2$	$E_1 \longleftarrow$ $\downarrow$ $E_2 \longrightarrow$ notif[E_1] keep updating event information until last event instance
All Pairs e.g. of $(E_1; E_2)_{t1}$	$E_1 \longrightarrow E_2 \longrightarrow$ notif[$(E_1; E_2)_{t1}$] t_{e1} +t1 do not remove profiles after match
Unique Pairs e.g. of $(E_1; E_2)_{t1}$	$E_1 \longrightarrow E_2 \longrightarrow$ notif[$(E_1; E_2)_{t1}$] t_{e1} +t1 remove composite event information after after match

Legend: A $\longrightarrow$ B: after event A insert profile B   A $\bullet\!\!-\!\!\rhd$ B: after event A remove profile B

of the composite profile remain in the system (i.e., *all event instance combinations* are detected).

5 Performance Evaluation

In this section, the response times of the different filter methods for composite events are evaluated. We discuss selected results of the tests performed on our prototypical implementation. Additionally, we introduce implementation variants for the single-step method and discuss their influence on the response time.

5.1 Performance Tests and Discussion

The test implementation of the one-step method is based on our event notification system CompAS that has been developed within the project MediAS [18] at the Freie Universität Berlin. The filter component of our system is based on a modified Gough-algorithm for the filtering of primitive events [12]. For the filtering of composite events, we implemented the tree-based algorithm as used, e.g., in the ENS Ready [11].

Performance tests of composite events underly several parameters, e.g., the composite operator, the operator parameters, the time between the parts of the composite event (composition distance), and the number of events and profiles.

For the performance, we measure the overall response time per event or per composite event. The response time of composite events is the time between the occurrence of the last contributing event and the time the user notification is sent.

We discuss selected test results obtained with our prototypical implementation. Several combinations of parameters have been tested. For brevity, we restrict the presentation to profiles regarding simple event sequences of two events $(A; Z)$ without temporal restrictions. The events are posted to the filtering mechanism as continuous stream, such that the additional delay due to event frequencies is not considered here.

We used events and profiles with one integer attribute and the attribute domain $[-100.000; 100.000]$. To eliminate the influence of profile overlapping, only distinct profiles have been defined.

For both, the two-step and the one-step method, we tested the following parameter settings:

1. The first event instance within a group of duplicate events is selected, subsequent instances of the same event class are ignored. If no duplicate event instances occur, as in most of our tests, the results for selecting the first event instance equal those for all instances and for the last event.
2. For the event composition, two opposite versions have been tested: single unique pairs and all pairs. For single unique pairs, the first occurring pair triggers a notification, afterwards the profile is removed. For all pairs, every possible combination of event instances triggers a notification.

Response time depending on composition order. First, we evaluate the influence of the composition order on response time. We show the test results for 10,000 profiles regarding composite events and 10,000 starting events (distinct A-events). For our tests, we formed g groups of e_x events with an e_y event at the end of each of the groups. Within each group, first come $10,000/g$ e_x events and then one e_y event that closes the group. Figure 6 shows the influence of this event grouping on the response time.

We see that the overall response time for each event directly depends on the number of groups, i.e., on the number of interleaving e_y-events. In the two step method, each E_y profile carries a list of matching E_x-profiles. The complete list has to be checked after each e_y-event. In the one-step method the E_y is only inserted after the occurrences of e_x events. Additionally, the E_y carries only references to those E_x-profiles that match events that already occurred.

Response time depending on number of profiles. We evaluated the influence of the number of profiles on the response time. We show the results for sequences in a single group of events and for sequences in 1,000 groups of events.

Figure 7(a) and 7(b) show the response time per event (measured in milliseconds) using the one-step and two-step methods for two different parameter settings.

For the case of events in a single group (Figure 7(a)), both methods using all events are faster than the methods using only unique matches. For the unique matches, the profiles are removed after the matches, causing maintenance costs.

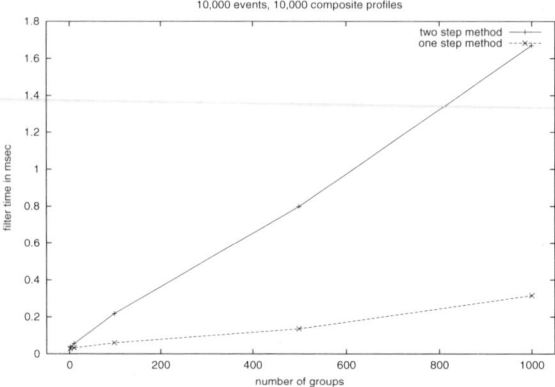

Fig. 6. Influence of composition order (event grouping

The one-step method with profile removal is faster than the two-step method with profile removal. In the first method, the profiles regarding the e_x-events are removed directly after the e_x-events have been detected. In the two-step method, all profiles are only removed at the end of the event detection, i.e., after the e_y-event. Therefore, the performance benefit due to a smaller profile pool applies to the one-step method, but does not affect the two-step method.

The one-step method without removal is faster than the two-step method without removal. For the first method, less profiles are stored in the profile pool, i.e., less profiles have to be evaluated. Additionally, the number composite profiles to be checked in each step (in the composite pool or as auxiliary profiles) is lower for one-step.

In all four graphs, the filter time increases linearly depending on the number of composite profiles between 0 and 10,000 profiles. In that interval, each of the profiles is matched by exactly one event pair. For more than 10,000 profiles, an increasing number of profiles remains unmatched. For the methods without profile removal, a flattened logarithmical increase can be measured – the influence of the binary search on the profile values. For the methods with removal, the removal costs have a major influence on the response time.

In Figure 7(b), the effects already observed in Figure 7(a) are overlayed with the influence of the event grouping as shown in Figure 6. The influence of interleaving events (grouping) is strongest in the two-step method.

Response time depending on profile cardinality. In Figure 8, the response times for different profile cardinalities are shown. The profile cardinality for a set of sequence-profiles $(E_x; E_y)$ describes the number of distinct profiles for E_x and E_y. This cardinality is shown at the x-axis of the diagrams in Figures 8(a) and 8(b).

Figure 8(a) shows the overall response time for 30.000 events, for the one-step and two-step methods. The filter time of the one-step method is in most cases less than the filter tim for the two-step method. Only for the extreme case of one event starting off 30.000 sequences, the response time is equal.

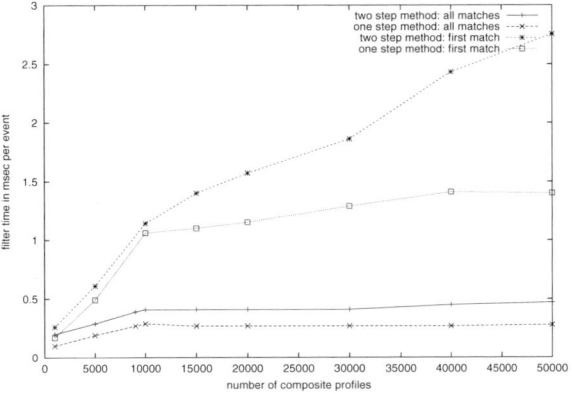

(a) Events structured in 1 event-group

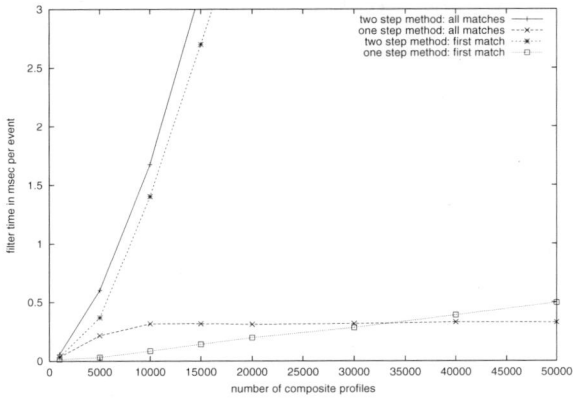

(b) Events structured in 1,000 event-groups

Fig. 7. Response time depending on number of profiles

Figure 8(b) shows the composition times for the same experiments. Two values are shown for each test: the overall time needed for composing events and the additional time required after the last contributing event. As argued earlier, the latter defines, together with the primitive filter time for the last event, the response time of composite events. As composition time for the one-step approach, we measured the time for the handling of auxiliary profiles. The composition time for the one-step method is shorter than that for the two-step method. The additional response time for the composite events due to a composition step is zero.

We argued, that for the efficiency analysis of composite event filtering only the response time of the last contributing event has to be considered. We have shown in our analysis that the one-step method efficiently minimizes this response time for composite events to zero. Additionally, the overhead of unnecessary profile filtering is reduced - the overall performance increases.

5.2   Implementation Variants

For the implementation of the single-step method, several variations are conceivable, which may lead to different performance results depending on the profile and event

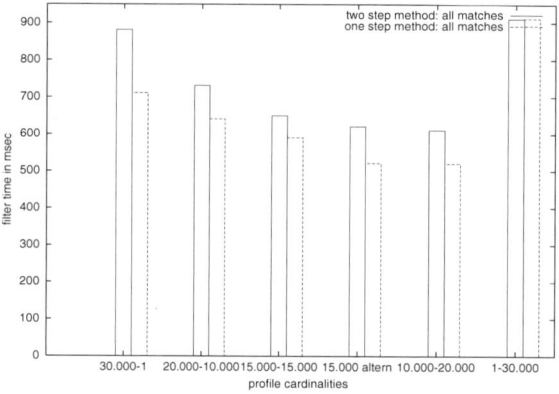

(a) Overall response time

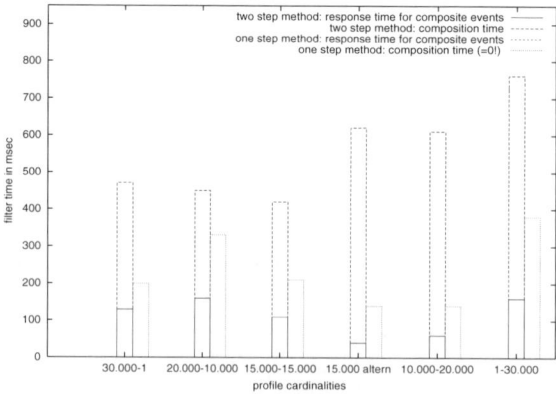

(b) Composition time

Fig. 8. Response time depending on profile cardinality

distributions. Here, we briefly introduce the variations and discuss their consequences for the filter performance.

1. Dynamically handle primitive profiles: This approach corresponds directly to the algorithm introduced in the previous section. For the composite profiles, the partial and auxiliary profiles are dynamically inserted into and deleted from the primitive-profile pool. If the same profile has already been defined by a different user, then the information is already in the pool and only references to the users have to be added. If the profiles do not overlap to a large extent, this approach requires a filter algorithm that supports frequent changes to the profile pool for adding and deleting profiles.

2. Mark/unmark primitive profiles: Another approach is the insertion of all partial and auxiliary profiles at once, marking them for use and unmark if the profiles are not used. The links referring to the profile owners have to be removed or unmarked as well.

   Response time is expected to be slightly higher than in the first approach, since the markings have to be checked in each filtering step. If the profiles do not overlap, this approach requires minor changes to the profile pool, but the pool is larger. More disc space may be used.

3. Store primitive profiles, only reference handling: The third approach requires the fewest changes to the profile pool: All partial and auxiliary profiles are inserted at once. Active profiles have references to the respective users, inactive profiles have no users assigned. Inserting and deleting of profiles results in inserting or deleting (or marking and unmarking) of references.

   The disk usage is similar to the one in the second approach. If the profiles do not overlap, the response time is expected to be slower than in the other approaches: All profiles have to be checked, also the ones without a reference to a user.

For all three approaches, the references could be inserted/removed or only marked/unmarked. The second and the third approach are especially feasible for profile sets with a large overlap. Then, almost all profiles do reference to some users; inserting or deleting profiles results in changes to references.

6   Summary

In this paper, we presented an one-step algorithm for the filtering of composite events. Current implementations use two-step algorithms that perform unnecessary filter operations. Our algorithm takes advantage of the idea of partial evaluation: only those profiles are evaluated that may directly contribute to a composite profile. Only few unnecessary filter operations are performed.

After the general introduction of our one-step algorithm, we presented methods for the handling of profiles that use different composition operators. Additionally, we discussed profile handling under various composition parameters.

We implemented both a two-step method and our one-step algorithm within our ENS prototype CompAS. In extensive performance tests, we have shown that our one-step method significantly reduces the response times for composite events with the effect that a composite event is detected as fast as a primitive event. Additionally, the overall filter performance has been improved.

Additionally, CompAS is extended into a distributed event notification system for facility management systems to improve scalability. The system is designed for easy adaptation to changing application requirements and differently structured event sources.

Acknowledgements. We wish to thank the other members of the database group at the FU Berlin for their helpful comments on our approach. We are especially grateful to Steven König and Sven Bittner for the implementation.

References

1. M. Aguilera, R. Strom, D. Sturman, M. Astley, and T. Chandra. Matching events in a content-based subscription system. In *Proceddings of SIGMOD Principles of Distributed Computing*, 1999.
2. E. S. Al-Shaer, H. M. Abdel-Wahab, and K. Maly. Hifi: A new monitoring architecture for distributed systems management. In *International Conference on Distributed Computing Systems*, 1999.
3. Bernd Bruegge, Ralf Pfleghar, and Thomas Reicher. Owl: An object-oriented framework for intelligent home and office applications. In *Proceedings of the Second International Workshop on Cooperative Buildings (CoBuild99)*, 1999.
4. A. Carzaniga, D. S. Rosenblum, and A. L Wolf. Design and evaluation of a wide-area event notification service. *ACM Transactions on Computer Systems*, 19(3):332–383, August 2001.
5. S. Chakravarthy and D. Mishra. Snoop: An expressive event specification language for active databases. Technical Report UF-CIS-TR-93-007, University of Florida, Gainesville, Department of Computer and Information Sciences, March 1993.
6. S. Gatziu and K. R. Dittrich. SAMOS: An Active Object-Oriented Database System. *IEEE Quarterly Bulletin on Data Engineering, Special Issue on Active Databases*, 15(1-4):23–26, December 1992.
7. N. Gehani and H. Jagadish. Ode as an active database: Constraints and triggers. In *Proceedings of the Seventeenth International Conference on Very Large Databases (VLDB)*, 1991.
8. N. H. Gehani, H. V. Jagadish, and O. Shmueli. Composite event specification in active databases: Model & implementation. In *Proceedings of the 18th International Conference on Very Large Data Bases*, 1992.
9. A. Geppert and D. Tombros. Event-based distributed workflow execution with EVE. Technical Report ifi-96.05, University Zurich, Computer Science Department, 20, 1996.
10. K. J. Gough and G. Smith. Efficient Recognition of Events in a Distributed System. In *Proceedings of the Australasian Computer Science Conference ACSC-18*, 1995.
11. R. E. Gruber, B. Krishnamurthy, and E. Panagos. The achitecture of the READY event notification service. In *Proceedings of the 19th IEEE International Conference on Distributed Computing Systems Middleware Workshop*, 1999.
12. A. Hinze and S. Bittner. Efficient distribution-based event filtering. In *22nd International Conference on Distributed Computing Systems (ICDCS- 2002), Workshops: 1st International Workshop on Distributed Event-Based Systems(DEBS)*, IEEE Computer Socienty, 2002.
13. A. Hinze and A. Voisard. A parameterized algebra for event notification services. In *Proceedings of the 9th International Symposium on Temporal Representation and Reasoning (TIME 2002)*, 2002.

14. N. Jones, C. Gomard, and P. Sestoft. *Partial Evaluation and Automatic Program Generation*. Prentice Hall, 1993.
15. B. Krishnamurthy and D. S. Rosenblum. Yeast: A general purpose event-action system. *Transactions on Software Engineering*, 21(10), October 1995.
16. M. Mansouri-Samani and M. Sloman. GEM: A generalised event monitoring language for distributed systems. *IEE/IOP/BSC Distributed Engineering Journal*, 4(2), Feb 1997.
17. J. Pereira, F. Fabret, H. Jacobsen, F. Llirbat, R. Preotiuc-Prieto, K. Ross, and D. Shasha. LeSubscribe: Publish and subscribe on the web at extreme speed. In *Proceedings of the ACM SIGMOD Conference*, 2001.
18. Project MediAS: Efficient Internet-wide Notification on Composite Events. Project Homepage: http://page.inf.fu-berlin.de/~hinze/projects/project_medias.html.

Multilevel Secure Rules and Its Impact on the Design of Active Database Systems

Indrakshi Ray

Colorado State University, Fort Collins, CO 80523
iray@cs.colostate.edu

Abstract. The event-condition-action paradigm (also known as *triggers* or *rules*) gives a database "active" capabilities – the ability to react automatically to changes in the database or in the environment. One potential use of this technology is in the area of multilevel secure (MLS) data processing, such as, military, where the subjects and objects are classified into different security levels and mandatory access control rules govern who has access to what. Unfortunately, not much work has been done in the area of multilevel secure active database system. In this paper we define the structure of MLS rules and identify what effects these rules have on the execution semantics of an active database system. Such knowledge is essential before developing a multilevel secure active database system.

1 Introduction

Traditional database management system are *passive*: the database system executes commands when requested by the user or application program. However, there are many applications where this passive behavior is inadequate. Consider for example, a financial application: whenever the price of stock for a company falls below a given threshold, the user must sell his corresponding stocks. One solution is to add monitoring mechanisms in the application programs modifying the stock prices that will alert the user to such changes. Incorporating monitoring mechanisms in all the relevant application programs is non trivial. The alternate option is to poll periodically and check the stock prices. Polling too frequently incurs a performance penalty; polling too infrequently may result in not getting the desirable functionalities. A better solution is to use active databases.

Active databases move the reactive behavior from the application into the database. This reactive capability is provided by *triggers* also known as *event-condition-action rules* or simply *rules*. In other words, triggers give active databases the capability to monitor and react to specific circumstances that are relevant to an application. An active database system must provide trigger processing capabilities in addition to providing all the functionalities of a passive database system.

One potential use of this technology is in the area of secure data processing, such as, the military which uses an underlying multilevel secure (MLS) database. A multilevel secure database system is characterized by having a partially ordered set of security levels (the ordering relation is referred to as the dominance relation); all the database objects and the operations (transactions) on the database objects have security levels associated with them. Mandatory access control policies determine which transactions can access which objects. The idea is that information can flow from the dominated level to the dominating level but not in the other direction.

A. James, B. Lings, M. Younas (Eds.): BNCOD 2003, LNCS 2712, pp. 226–244, 2003.

To the best of our knowledge, the only work in providing active capabilities to an MLS database is done by Smith et al. [33]. Smith's work is based on the MLS relational model that supports polyinstantiation. Since this relational model is not widely prevalent, the MLS active database system proposed by Smith is not used either. The absence of a suitable MLS active database limits the potential use of active technology to applications that use an MLS database as the underlying database. This paper aims at filling this gap.

Providing reactive capabilities in a MLS database system has two components. First, we must provide a knowledge model for triggers. The knowledge model will specify what kinds of rules can be supported, what can be said about these rules, and how can the rules be classified into security levels. Next, we must provide an execution model for the triggers. The execution model will specify the runtime strategies for rule execution. The execution model must ensure that no illegal information flow occurs because of the execution of triggers.

This paper has two contributions. Our first contribution is that we focus on the knowledge model of an MLS active database system. Specifically, we show how to define an MLS rule, and how to assign security levels to such rules. Our second contribution illustrates the different execution models in existing active database systems, and the impact our MLS rules have on these execution models. Specifically, we identify those choices in execution model that can be supported without violating the MLS constraints. This knowledge is essential before developing an MLS active database system.

The rest of the paper is organized as follows. Section 2 briefly describes the underlying MLS model on which our work is based. Section 3 proposes the knowledge model of an MLS active database system. Section 4 identifies the impact our knowledge model has on the execution model. Section 5 describes the possible architectures for an MLS active database. Section 6 describes the relevant related work in this area. Section 7 concludes the paper with some pointers to future directions.

2   Our Model of an MLS Database

A database system is composed of database objects. At any given time, the *database state* is determined by the values of the objects in the database. A change in the value of a database object changes the state. Users are responsible for submitting transactions and application programs that are to be executed on the database. A *transaction* is an operation on a database state. An *application program* may or may not perform an operation on the database state. Execution of a transaction or application program may cause the database to change state.

An MLS database is associated with a security structure that is a partial order, $(\mathbf{L}, <)$. $\mathbf{L}$ is a set of security levels, and $<$ is the dominance relation between levels. If $L_1 < L_2$, then L_2 is said to strictly dominate L_1 and L_1 is said to be strictly dominated by L_2. If $L_1 = L_2$, then the two levels are said to be equal. $L_1 < L_2$ or $L_1 = L_2$ is denoted by $L_1 \leq L_2$. If $L_1 \leq L_2$, then L_2 is said to dominate L_1 and L_1 is said to be dominated by L_2. Two levels L_1 and L_2 are said to be incomparable if neither $L_1 \leq L_2$ nor $L_2 \leq L_1$. We assume the existence of a level U, that corresponds to the level unclassified or public knowledge. The level U is the greatest lower bound of all the levels in $\mathbf{L}$. Any data object classified at level U is accessible to all the users of the database.

Each database object $x \in \mathbf{D}$ is associated with exactly one security level which we denote as $L(x)$ where $L(x) \in \mathbf{L}$. (The function L maps entities to security levels.) We assume that the security level of an object remains fixed for the entire lifetime of the object.

The users of the system are cleared to the different security levels. We denote the security clearance of user U_i by $L(U_i)$. Consider a military setting consisting of four security levels: *top-secret* (TS), *secret* (S), *confidential* (C) and *unclassified* (U) (where $U < C < S < TS$). The user Jane Doe has the security clearance of *top-secret*. That is, $L(JaneDoe) = TS$. Each user has one or more principals associated with him. The number of principals associated with the user depends on his security clearance; it equals the number of levels dominated by the user's security clearance. In our example Jane Doe has four principals: $JaneDoe.TS$, $JaneDoe.S$, $JaneDoe.C$ and $JaneDoe.U$. At each session, the user logs in as one of the principals. All processes that the user initiates in that session inherit security level of the corresponding principal.

Each transaction T_i is associated with exactly one security level. The level of the transaction remains fixed for the entire duration of the transaction. The security level of the transaction is the level of the principal who has submitted the transaction. For example, if Jane Doe logs in as $JaneDoe.S$, all transactions initiated by Jane Doe will have the level *secret* (S).

We require a transaction T_i to obey the simple security property and the restricted $\star$-property [3] that are given below.

1. A transaction T_i with $L(T_i) = C$ may read a database object x only if $L(x) \leq C$.
2. A transaction T_i with $L(T_i) = C$ may write a database object x only if $L(x) = C$.

Property 1 is the simple security property. This property places a restriction on the objects that a transaction can read. A transaction can read an object only if the level of the transaction dominates the level of the object. For example, a *secret* level transaction can read *secret* and *unclassified* documents but not *top-secret* documents. Property 2 describes the restricted $\star$-property. This property places a restriction on the objects that a transaction can write. By virtue of this property, a transaction can write to database objects that are at its own level. To prohibit a transaction from passing information from the dominating level to the dominated level, a transaction at a dominating level is not allowed to write to the objects at the dominated level. For example, if a *top-secret* level transaction is allowed to write an *unclassified* document, then the transaction may pass along *top-secret* level information to the *unclassified* document. For integrity reasons, a transaction is not allowed to write to objects at the dominating level. For example, an *unclassified* transaction can corrupt a *top-secret* level document by writing incorrect information.

We give the formal definition of an MLS transaction below.

Definition 1. [MLS Transaction] *An MLS transaction T_i is a set of read and write operations on database objects which are preceded by the command* begin *and followed by the command* abort *or* commit. *The transaction T_i is associated with security level $L(T_i)$ where $L(T_i) \in \mathbf{L}$; it accesses database objects in accordance with the simple security and the restricted $\star$-property.*

We use the term application program in a more general manner.

Definition 2. [MLS Application Program] *An MLS application program A_i is a set of operations submitted by the user – the operations may or may not access the database objects. An application program A_i that accesses the database objects is associated with security level $L(A_i)$, where $L(A_i) \in \mathbf{L}$; it accesses database objects according to the rules specified by the simple security and the restricted $\star$-property.*

3   Rules in an MLS Active Database

In addition to transactions and application programs, an active database system also has *rules*. A rule is specified by three components: *event, condition* and *action*. An event causes a rule to be triggered. Active database systems have mechanisms that monitors the database to check whether an event has occurred. If an event associated with a rule occurs, the rule's condition is evaluated. If the rule's condition evaluates to true, then the rule's action is scheduled for execution. The details of rule execution are considerably more complex than this simple description. We elaborate on the details of rule execution in Section 4.

A rule is a database object on which we allow the following operations.

1. Create – this operation allows a new rule to be created.
2. Delete – this operation allows an existing rule to be deleted.
3. Update – this operation allows an existing rule to be modified.
4. Enable – this operation allows an existing rule to be enabled. Only enabled rules can be triggered.
5. Disable – this operation allows an existing rule to be disabled. A disabled rule cannot be triggered.
6. View – this operation allows an existing rule to be viewed.

Like other database objects in an MLS database, rules are also associated with security levels. Each rule R_j is created by some principal, say P, and it inherits the security level of the principal that created it, that is, $L(R_j) = L(P)$. Creation, deletion, modification, disabling, enabling of the rule corresponds to writing of the rule object. Hence, by the restricted $\star$-property these operations can be performed only by transactions or applications whose security level is the same as that of the rule. Viewing the rule corresponds to a read operation of the rule object. Thus, the view operation can be performed by transactions or applications whose security levels dominate the level of the rule.

Next, we give the formal definition of an MLS rule.

Definition 3. [MLS Rule] *An MLS rule R_j is defined as a triple $< e_j, c_j, a_j >$ where e_j is the event that causes the rule to be triggered, c_j is the condition that is checked when the rule is triggered and a_j is the action that is executed when the rule is triggered. The MLS rule R_j is associated with exactly one security level which we denote by $L(R_j)$ where $L(R_j) \in \mathbf{L}$. The operations allowed on rules obey the mandatory restrictions specified by the simple security and the restricted $\star$-property.*

Before describing how the security level of a rule is related to the levels of its components (that is, events, conditions and actions), we must describe the components of a rule in more details.

3.1   Events in an MLS Active Database Systems

Event specifies what causes the rule to be triggered. Possible events that can be supported in an active database system are

1. Data modification/retrieval events – the event is raised by an operation (insert, update, delete, access) on some database object.
2. Transaction event – the event is raised by some transaction command (e.g. begin, abort, commit etc.).
3. Application-defined event – the application program may signal the occurrence of an event.
4. Temporal events – events are raised at some point in time. Temporal events may be absolute (e.g., 25th December, 2002) or relative (e.g. 15 minutes after x occurs).
5. External events – the event is occurring outside the database (e.g. the sensor recording temperature goes above 100 degrees Celsius).

Events can further be classified into primitive and composite events.

– Primitive event – the event cannot be divided into subparts.
– Composite event – the event is raised by some combination of primitive events.

For example, inserting a tuple in $Employee$ relation is a primitive event. Two hours after a tuple has been inserted in $Employee$ relation is a composite event.

A composite event is constructed using two or more primitive events connected by an event operator. Any composite event e can be denoted as follows.

$$e = e_1 \ op_1 \ e_2 \ op_2 \ldots \ e_n$$

where $e_1, e_2, \ldots, e_n$ are the primitive events making up the composite event E, and $op_1, op_2, \ldots op_{n-1}$ are the event operators. Event operators can be logical event operators ($\vee, \wedge$, etc.), sequence operators (;), or temporal composition operators ($after, between$, etc.).

Assigning Security Levels to Events.   First, we discuss how to assign security levels to primitive events.

Security Level associated with Data Modification/Retrieval Event: The event e has the same security level as the operation O that caused it, that is, $L(e) = L(O)$. If this operation O is performed by some transaction T, then the level of O is the same as the level of T.

Security level associated with the Transaction Event: The event E has the same security level of the transaction T that caused it, that is, $L(e) = L(T)$.

Security Level associated with Application-Defined Event: The event e has the same security level as the level at which the application A that generated it is executing, that is, $L(e) = L(A)$.

Security Level associated with Temporal Event: An absolute temporal event e is observable by any body and so its security level is public, that is, $L(e) = U$. A relative temporal event is a composite event. The manner in which the level of composite event is calculated is given below.

Security Level associated with External Event: The level of the event e is the greatest lower bound of the security clearances of the users $U_1, U_2, \ldots, U_n$ who can observe this external event e, that is, $L(e) = glb(L(U_1), L(U_2), \ldots, L(U_n))$ (where $L(U_i)$ denotes the security clearance of user U_i).

An event like the outside air temperature is 110 degrees Fahrenheit, is observable by all users and so its level is public. Whereas, an event like the sensor reading from a military satellite that can be observed only by *top-secret* personnel, will have a security level of *top-secret*.

Now we discuss how to assign security levels to composite events.

Security Levels associated with Composite Event: Consider the composite event E given by, $e = e_1 \ op_1 \ e_2 \ op_2 \ldots \ e_n$, where e is composed of primitive events e_1, $e_2, \ldots, e_n$. The security level of the composite event e is the least upper bound of the levels of the primitive events $e_1, e_2, \ldots, e_n$ composing it, that is, $L(e) = lub(L(e_1), L(e_2), \ldots, L(e_n))$.

3.2 Conditions in an MLS Active Database System

In an active database, when a rule has been triggered *condition* specifies the additional conditions that must be checked before the action can be executed. If the condition part of the rule evaluates to true, then the action is executed. Possible conditions in a rule are

1. Database predicates – the condition might be a predicate on the database state (average salary of employees greater than 50000).
2. Database queries – the condition might be a query on the database state. If the query returns some results, the condition is said to be satisfied. If the query fails to return any result, the condition is not satisfied.
3. Application procedures – the condition may be a specified as a call to an application procedure (example, *max_exceeded()*) which may or may not access the database.

Assigning Security Levels to Condition. Checking a condition involves reading database objects associated with the condition. We define the level of a condition c, denoted by $L(c)$, as follows: It is the least upper bound of all the data that is accessed by the condition. That is, $L(c) = lub(L(D_1), L(D_2), L(D_3), \ldots, L(D_n))$ where $D_1, D_2, \ldots, D_n$ are the data objects accessed by condition c.

3.3 Actions in an MLS Active Database System

When the rule is triggered and its condition evaluates to true, the action of the rule must be executed. Possible actions in an MLS active database include

1. Data modification/retrieval operation – the action of the rule causes a data operation (insert, update, delete, access).
2. Transaction operation – the action of the rule causes a transaction operation (e.g. abort).

3. Application-defined operation – the action causes some procedure in an application to be executed.
4. External operation – the action causes some external operations (e.g. informing the user).

Some active database languages allow a rule to specify multiple actions. Usually these actions are ordered which allows them to be executed sequentially.

Assigning Security Levels to Actions. This is how we assign security levels for the actions.

Security Level associated with Data Modification/Retrieval Action: The action has the same level as the operation it causes, that is, $L(a) = L(O)$.

Security Level associated with Transaction Operation: The action a has the same level as the transaction T, that is, $L(a) = L(T)$.

Security Level associated with Application-defined Operation: The action a has the same level as the application process A, that is $L(a) = L(A)$.

Security Level associated with External Operation: In this case, the action is viewed by external observers. The level of the action must be lower than or equal to the security clearances of all the users viewing the action. The level of action a is the greatest lower bound of the security clearances of the users U_1, U_2, ..., U_n who can observe this operation, that is, $L(a) = glb(L(U_1), L(U_2), \ldots, L(U_n))$ where $L(U_1), L(U_2), \ldots, L(U_n)$ are the security clearances associated with users U_1, U_2, ..., U_n respectively.

Security Level of Action composed of Multiple Constituents: Consider a rule $R = < e, c, a >$ where the action a is composed of multiple actions, $a_1, a_2, \ldots, a_k$. To keep our model simple, we require that the level of all the actions must be the same. That is, $L(a_1) = L(a_2) = \ldots = L(a_k)$.

3.4   Relationship of Security Levels Associated with a Rule

The following illustrates the relationship of the level of the rule R_j with the levels of the constituent event e_j, the condition c_j and the action a_j.

1. $L(e_j) \leq L(R_j)$
2. $L(c_j) \leq L(R_j)$
3. $L(a_j) = L(R_j)$

Item 1 states that a rule may be triggered by an event whose level is dominated by the level of the rule. Item 2 states that a rule may require checking conditions at the dominated level before it can be fired. Item 3 states that a rule can take an action only at its own level.

In a secure environment it might be necessary for dominating levels to monitor suspicious events taking place at some dominated level and take some precautionary action; hence the need for $L(e_j) \leq L(R_j)$. Moreover, $L(e_j) \not> L(R_j)$ ensures that a dominating event does not trigger a dominated rule and create a covert channel. The same reasoning applies for condition c_j; thus, the rule R_j might check conditions involving dominated level data (that is, $L(c_j) \leq L(R_j)$), but not data at the dominated levels ($L(c_j) \not> L(R_j)$). The level of the action is the same as the level of the rule, that is, $L(a_j) = L(R_j)$. Since $L(a_j) \not< L(R_j)$, a rule at the dominating level cannot result in an action at the dominated level and create a covert channel[1]. Also, since $L(a_j) \not> L(R_j)$, a rule at the dominated level while executing its action cannot corrupt data at the dominating level.

4   Execution Model

The execution model of an active database specifies how the active database behaves at run-time. The execution model will depend on the underlying DBMS. At this point, we do not wish to commit to any particular DBMS. Hence, we do not propose a detailed execution model for an MLS active database system. Instead, we identify the issues that need to be addressed before developing an execution model.

Irrespective of the execution model used, the following activities (as outlined by Paton et al. [29]) are involved during rule execution. When or how these activities are carried out constitute the details of the execution model.

Event Detection Phase – refers to the detection of an event occurrence caused by an event source.

Triggering Phase – triggers the rules corresponding to the events produced. The association of a rule with its event occurrence is termed rule instantiation.

Evaluation Phase – evaluates the condition of the triggered rules. The conflict set is formed which is made up of all the rule instantiations whose conditions evaluate to true.

Scheduling Phase – chooses which rule will be processed from the conflict set.

Execution Phase – carries out the actions of the chosen rule instantiation.

Next, we investigate each component of the execution model and identify what effect, if any, our MLS rules have on these components.

4.1   Rule Processing Granularity

The granularity of rule processing indicates at which instances rules can be processed. Widom and Ceri [38] have identified four kinds of granularity:

1. Always – rules may be processed at any point in time,
2. Smallest database operations – for example, insertion, deletion, update or fetch of a single tuple.
3. Data manipulation statements – for example, at the end of every SQL statement where a statement inserts, deletes, updates, or fetches numerous tuples.
4. Transaction boundaries.

---

[1] Path of illegal information flow based on monitoring the usage of system resources.

Kinds of Granularity in an MLS Active Database. In our model, an event at the dominated level can trigger a rule at the dominating level. Since the event may have been generated by a transaction or an application program, we do not want the dominated transaction to be suspended for the execution of a dominating rule and introduce the possibility of a timing channel. A timing channel arises between a dominating level and a dominated level when the dominating level can vary the amount of time required to complete a task to signal information to the dominated level. Thus, the first three kinds of rule processing granularity enumerated above cannot be supported in an MLS Active Database. The only viable rule processing granularity is the fourth item, that is, transaction processing boundaries.

4.2   Conflict Resolution and Rule Priorities

In sequential processing, at any given time, only one rule is chosen for execution. However, in an active database system many rules may be triggered at the same time. This may happen because of several reasons: (i) several rules specify the same triggering event, (ii) the rule processing granularity is coarse – many events are triggered before the rules are processed, (iii) rules that are triggered but not chosen for execution remain triggered.

In such a scenario, conflict resolution specifies how the rule to be executed can be chosen. Some conflict resolution strategies are

1. a rule may be chosen arbitrarily,
2. a rule may be chosen based on static properties – time of rule creation or the data on which rules are defined,
3. a rule may be chosen based on dynamic properties – most recently fired rule,
4. a rule may be chosen based on priorities that are specified during rule definition. Priorities are specified by ordering the set of rules, by declaring relative priorities between each pair of rules, or by assigning numeric priorities.

Conflict Resolution and Rule Priorities in an MLS Active Data base. We can specify any of the conflict resolution policies enumerated above for rules having the same security level. However, if there are rules belonging to different security levels, the conflict resolution policy must always favor the dominated rule. This is because delaying a rule at the dominated level because of the execution of a rule at the dominating level may give rise to a timing channel.

In a multilevel secure active database system we can also specify priorities, but the requirement is that no dominating rule must have a higher priority than a dominated rule. Thus, if priorities are specified by ordering the set of rules, then all rules at dominated levels must be ordered before any rule at the dominating level.

If numeric priorities are to be specified, one approach is to make the priority specification have two parts: one for the security level and the other for the number. For rules having different security levels, the dominated rules will get preference over the dominating rules. For rules having the same security level, the number will decide which rule is chosen for execution.

Note that if dominated rules always get more preference than dominating rules, then the dominating rules might suffer from starvation. One solution is to allocate fixed time slots for each level. Suppose there are two levels: Low and $High$, where $Low < High$. We allocate the time slot $< T_1, T_2 >$ for rules at level Low, the slot $< T_2, T_3 >$ for rules at level $High$, $< T_3, T_4 >$ for rules at level Low etc. The problem with this approach is that if there are no $High$ rules for execution at $< T_2, T_3 >$, then processor time gets wasted. To minimize wasting computational resource, a better approach would be to study the processor requirements of the rules at different levels and then divide the time slots accordingly.

4.3   Sequential versus Concurrent Execution

In sequential rule processing only one rule is executed at a time. If multiple rules are triggered, the conflict resolution strategy decides which rule should be executed. An alternate approach to sequential rule execution is concurrent execution. Concurrent rule execution provides a better performance than sequential execution. There can be two kinds of concurrent rule execution:

1. inter-rule concurrency – a rule is executed as one atomic transaction.
2. intra-rule concurrency – rules are divided into parts and each of these part is executed as an atomic transactions. In other words, these parts are executed concurrently.

We can, of course, have systems that allow both the above options.

In inter-rule concurrency, each rule R_j generates a transaction T_j at the same level. In intra-rule concurrency, each rule R_j generates two transactions at its own level: T_{cj} (for evaluating the rule's condition) and T_{aj} (for executing the rule's action). Note that, we need to ensure that T_{aj} commits only after T_{cj} commits and returns a true value.

Concurrent Execution in an MLS Active Database. Both inter-rule and intra-rule concurrency can be supported in an MLS active database system. Each rule in such a scenario generates one or more transactions at its own level. Since rules at different levels generate transactions at different levels, these transactions must be executed concurrently. The concurrency control algorithms must ensure that no illegal information flow occurs due to the execution of rules. Multilevel secure concurrency control algorithms [2] can be used in such a scenario.

4.4   Coupling Modes

Coupling modes are specified which dictate when a triggered transaction is processed relative to the triggering transaction.

We need to specify when the condition will be evaluated relative to the triggering event. We also need to specify when the action will be executed relative to condition evaluation. Each of these can be specified using coupling modes.

Coupling Modes between Event and Condition. There are three basic kinds of coupling modes between event and condition.

1. Immediate Coupling Mode between Event and Condition – The rule's condition is evaluated as soon as the event has occurred as a part of the triggering transaction.
2. Deferred Coupling Mode between Event and Condition – The rule's condition is evaluated after the triggering transaction has completed all its operation, but before it has been committed.
3. Detached Coupling Mode between Event and Condition – The rule's condition is evaluated in a different transaction than the triggering one.

Coupling Mode between Event and Condition in an MLS Active Database
Let the triggering transaction be denoted as T_i and the triggered rule be denoted as R_j. If $L(T_i) < L(R_j)$ and the coupling mode between event and condition is immediate or deferred then this may give rise to a timing channel – by manipulating the time taken to execute the triggered rule, information may be transmitted from the level $L(R_j)$ to level $L(T_i)$. In other words, the immediate and deferred mode can be supported for cases where $L(R_j) = L(T_i)$. When $L(R_j) \neq L(T_i)$, the immediate and deferred modes cause a breach of security.

The detached coupling mode, however, can be supported safely in all cases. The detached coupling mode also provides more concurrency than the immediate or deferred mode. This is because in immediate or deferred mode the triggered rule and the triggering transaction execute as one large transaction and hence this large transaction takes more time to complete; this in turn delays the transactions that are waiting to lock items that are locked by this large transaction. In detached coupling mode the triggered rule is executed as a separate transaction and the performance problem associated with one large transaction does not arise.

Coupling Modes between Condition and Action. Coupling modes can also be used to specify when the rule's action takes place relative to condition evaluation. Here also three modes are specified.

1. Immediate Coupling Mode between Condition and Action – The rule's action is executed immediately after condition evaluation.
2. Deferred Coupling Mode between Condition and Action – The rule's action is executed as a part of the same transaction as the condition evaluation, but not necessarily immediately.
3. Detached Coupling Mode between Condition and Action – The rule's action and the rule's condition evaluation are executed as two different transactions.

Coupling Mode between Condition and Action in an MLS Active Database
Since the level of the transaction evaluating the rule's condition is the same as the level of the transaction executing the rule's action, all the above modes can be supported in a multilevel secure active database system. However, in detached coupling mode we can take advantage of the intra-rule concurrency because the rule's action execution and condition evaluation are two separate transactions.

4.5   Iterative versus Recursive Algorithms

Often times the condition evaluation or action execution of a rule signals events which in turn trigger other rules. In such a scenario, how should the rule processing proceed? There are two choices:

1. recursive rule processing – the original condition evaluation or action execution is suspended and any immediate rules triggered by the (condition evaluation or action execution) event are chosen for execution,
2. iterative rule processing – the original rule proceeds to completion after which other rules are chosen for execution.

Iterative vs. Recursive Algorithms in an MLS Active Database. Recursive rule processing can be supported only if the triggering rule and the triggered rule have the same security level. Recursive rule processing may introduce timing channels if the triggered rule and the triggering rule belong to different security levels. This happens because the dominated triggering rule is suspended to allow for the completion of the dominating triggered rule – the dominating rule can manipulate the time taken to complete and convey information to the dominated rule. Iterative rule processing, on the other hand, does not suffer from this security breach and can safely be supported in an MLS Active Database System.

4.6   Error Handling

An error may occur while a rule is being processed. Widom and Ceri [38] elaborates on why an error may be generated during rule processing. Their reasons include (i) data required by a rule for condition evaluation or action execution has been deleted, (ii) authorization privileges required for rule condition evaluation or action execution have been revoked, (iii) a rule's condition or action reveals an error condition, (iv) the number of rules processed exceeds the systems limits, (v) concurrent execution of transaction creates a deadlock, or (vi) a system generated interrupt or error occurs.

Once an error occurs during rule processing, the question is how is the error handled. There are various options for handling the error.

1. Abort the transaction responsible for the event that in turn triggered the rule.
2. Ignore the rule that caused the error and continue processing.
3. Backtrack to the state when rule processing started and either restart rule processing or continue with the transaction.
4. Adopt a contingency plan that attempts to recover from the error state.

Error Handling in an MLS Active Database System. All the above options can be supported for cases where the level of the rule is the same as the level of the transaction. However, if the level of the triggering transaction is dominated by the level of the rule, then option 1 cannot be supported because aborting a dominated level transaction because of an error in a dominating rule constitutes a covert channel. In such a scenario option 4 may be the best one.

5   Architecture

The architecture of an active database system will depend on the knowledge model and execution model of the active database system. In general, there are two approaches to building active database systems. One is the layered approach where the active database components are built on top of an existing passive database system. The alternate approach is of a built-in architecture where active database components become a part of the database itself. The layered approach is easier to construct than the built-in one, but it is not as efficient as the built-in one.

5.1   Architecture for an MLS Active Database System

In a multilevel secure active database system the built-in approach is preferred. The main reason for this preference is performance. Also, for the layered approach we need an existing efficient multilevel secure database as an underlying database which is not widely available.

As mentioned previously, the actual architecture of an MLS active database system will depend on the knowledge and execution model. However, we do describe an architecture at a very abstract level of an MLS active database system (refer to figure 1). This will give an idea of the extra components that must be supported for processing MLS rules. The principal components are depicted by rectangles and the data stores are depicted by ellipses.

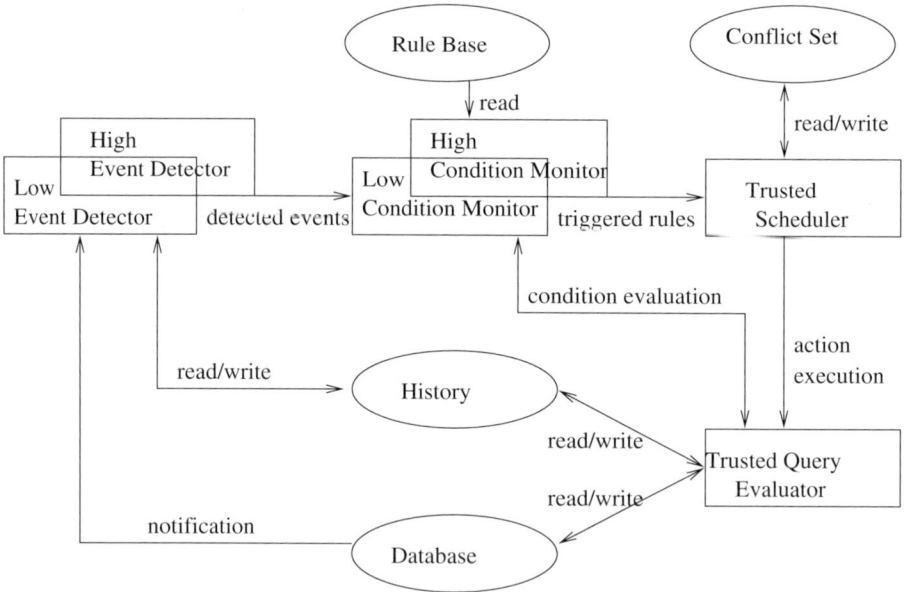

Fig. 1. A High-Level Architecture for Processing MLS Rules

The main components are:

1. Event Detector at Level l_i – This is responsible for detecting events at level l_i. Note that, event detector at level l_i can detect events at all levels that are dominated by l_i. The database notifies the event detector al level l_i about all primitive events occurring at levels dominated by l_i. Composite events are constructed using the knowledge about incoming primitive events and past events obtained from the history.
2. Condition monitor at Level l_i[2] – This is responsible for evaluating the conditions of rules that are triggered by the events detected by the event detector l_i. The condition monitor sends a request to the query evaluator to evaluate the condition. On the basis of the response from the query evaluator, the condition monitor decides which rules are triggered. These rules are then sent to the scheduler.
3. Trusted Scheduler – This is responsible for scheduling which rule is to be executed. Since the scheduler accesses rules at different levels, it must be a trusted component.
4. Trusted Query Evaluator – This is responsible for executing database actions and queries. We have shown the query evaluator to be a trusted component because it is responsible for executing database operations at all levels. In real world, the query evaluator will have several components, some of which are trusted and others which are not.

The above is a very abstract view of rule processing. Each of these components will be composed of sub-components and how these sub-components are connected will constitute the low-level architecture of the MLS active database system.

6   Related Work

6.1   Related Work in Multilevel Secure Active Databases

Very little work appears in the area of multilevel secure active databases. The major work in this area is by Smith and Winslett [33]. The authors show how an MLS relational model can be extended to incorporate active capabilities. The underlying MLS relational model supports polyinstantiation: that is, all MLS entities in this model can exist at multiple security levels simultaneously. An MLS rule being an MLS entity can also exist at multiple security levels. The main difference with our work is that this work is based on the polyinstantiation model.

6.2   Related Work in Expert Systems

Morgenstern [26] considers the problem of covert channels in deductive databases that are subject to mandatory security requirements. Berson and Lunt [4] describe the problems that must be solved in incorporating mandatory security requirements in a product rule system. Garvey and Lunt [14] extend an MLS object-oriented database system with

---

[2] We can have a single event detector and condition monitor instead of having event detectors and condition monitors for each of the security levels. However, this would require a trusted event detector and a trusted condition monitor. Developing trusted components requires considerable effort. Hence, we choose to have event detectors and condition monitors for each security level.

productions rules. Expert system rules differ from active database rules. Expert system rules are executed upon an explicit request for information; active database rules are executed as side effects. Expert system rules are used for inferencing – the order of rule execution is not important. This is not so with active databases. Both forward chaining and backward chaining rules are supported in an expert system. Active databases, on the other hand, support only forward chaining rules.

6.3   Related Work in Active Databases

Many work has been performed in the area of active databases. We will only describe a few of these works. Most of these work differ in the knowledge model and execution model. Some of these active databases use a relational model as an underlying database and others use an object-oriented one.

Most commercial systems support some form of triggering mechanisms. Some of the prototypes based on the relational model are Starburst [37], Ariel [17], POSTGRES [35]. Starburst rule system is quite conservative – supports a limited set of facilities. The most important feature of Starburst is its set-based execution model. Whenever an event that is of importance to some rule takes place, the event is logged in a transition table. At rule assertion points, this transition table is checked and the net-effect of all the logged events is taken into consideration before firing a rule. The POSTGRES project included a number of extensions to the relational model – providing active capabilities is one such extension. POSTGRES supports immediate rule processing and does not support the deferred modes. Ariel supports both ECA and condition-action rules. This has important consequences for the implementation of the rule processing system.

Notable among the object-oriented models are HiPAC [24,30], NAOS [10], Chimera [8], Ode [1] , SAMOS [15], Sentinel [9] and REACH [7]. HiPAC is one of the earlier projects in active database systems and they have contributed to many of the pioneering ideas: coupling modes, composite events, parallel execution of triggered rules in the form of subtransactions, to name a few. Also, this project identified real-time applications that can benefit from active database systems. NAOS is an active rule system for the O_2 commercial OODB database. However, NAOS has been implemented as a part of kernel of O_2. The NAOS execution model supports depth-first, recursive processing of immediate rules and breadth-first iterative processing of deferred rules. SAMOS provides active capabilities to the ObjectStore commercial OODB. The most significant feature of SAMOS is the event detector, the semantics of which is based on petri nets. The event language is also expressive and allows the specification of composite events. Sentinel and REACH extends the C++ based OpenOODB system from Texas Instruments with active capabilities. Chimera builds upon a deductive object-oriented database system.

6.4   Related Work in Multilevel Secure Databases

A large number of works also appears in multilevel secure database system. Majority of these works [11,12,13,16,18,19,20,21,31,32,34] are in the area of relational database systems and some [5,6,19,22,25,27,36] are in the area of object oriented database systems.

In a multilevel relational database system the data are classified into different security levels, and the users are associated with different security clearances. An important issue is the granularity at which the data can be classified. There are four possibilities: the data may be classified (i) at the element level, (ii) at the attribute level, (iii) at the tuple level, or (iv) at the relation level. A relation in which the data has been classified as above is a multilevel relation.

Most of the work differ in the way they solve integrity and polyinstantiation problems. Entity integrity ensures that no user sees a null value for the primary key of a relation. Unless, no action is taken, entity integrity would be violated when a user with a low clearance sees null for the cases where the primary key of a tuple is classified at a level higher than the user. One solution is that all the primary key elements be classified at the same level. The other solution is that the primary keys should be as low as any other elements in the tuple. Referential integrity requires that a tuple of low security level cannot reference a tuple of a high security level because the referenced tuple would appear to be non existent to users with low clearance.

There are three kinds of polyinstantiation [12]. A polyinstantiated relation [36] occurs when two subjects at different security levels try to create a relation of the same name. A polyinstantiated tuple occurs when a user inserts a tuple that has the same primary key value as an existing tuple at the higher level. A polyinstantiated element [23] is created if a user updates an element in a tuple which appears to be null (because the element has a higher security classification than the user).

A lot of work appears in the area of multilevel secure object oriented databases. Some of these work [5,25,36] consider single-level objects: each object is assigned a security level and this security level applies to all the properties and the methods of this object. The main advantage of this approach is its simplicity. The security kernel remains small so that it can be efficiently verified. The disadvantage is that in real-world there is a need for multilevel objects (where the different attributes of an object may be associated with different security levels) which cannot be adequately modeled.

The alternate approach is of supporting multilevel objects. The main problem of supporting multilevel object is that the security kernel becomes complex. Verifying the trusted security kernel becomes a difficult task. To keep the security kernel simple, researchers [5,6] have proposed the idea of decomposing multilevel objects into single-level ones and storing them as single-level objects. In such cases, mechanisms are developed that ensure that the users get the multi-level view of the object, even though they are stored as single-level ones.

Many security models pertaining to object-oriented database systems have been proposed. The notable ones are the Jajodia-Kogan filter model [19], SORION model [36], Millen-Lunt model [25] and the SODA model [22]. Olivier et al. [28] identify security issues and properties that are relevant to the modeling and implementation of a secure object-oriented database system.

7   Conclusion and Future Work

The absence of a multilevel secure active database limits the applicability of active technologies to applications that use an underlying MLS database system. Our work is a first step towards fulfilling this gap. We have identified what kinds of rules can be supported and how these rules can be classified into security levels. Next, we have identified what impact these rules have on the rule execution semantics. In many cases it turns out that some features of active databases cannot be supported without introducing illegal information flow. We have not based our work on any relational or object-oriented models; our observations, therefore, will be useful to developers of any MLS active database system.

A lot of work remains to be done. The next step will be to finalize on the rule execution semantics. Consider, for example, iterative versus recursive rule processing. For an MLS active database there are two possibilities: (i) support only iterative rule processing or (ii) support iterative as well as recursive rule processing and limit recursive rule processing to rules having the same security level. Option (ii) offers more flexibility but is more complicated and potentially more time consuming. Note that, we need to study the kinds of applications that will be executed on MLS active database systems before finalizing on the rule execution semantics.

Once the rule execution semantics have been finalized we will develop a detailed architecture for an MLS active database system. The detailed architecture will identify the rule processing components and their interactions with the underlying MLS database. This will also provide guidelines as to which of these components must be trusted. The final step is to implement each of these components such that rule processing can be performed in a secure and efficient manner.

References

1. R. Agarwal and N. Gehani. Ode (Object database and environment): The language and the data model. In *Proceedings of the ACM-SIGMOD International Conference on Management of Data*, pages 36–45, Portland, OR, May 1989.
2. V. Atluri, S. Jajodia, T.F̃. Keefe, C. McCollum, and R. Mukkamala. Multilevel Secure Transaction Processing: Status and Prospects. In P. Samarati and R.S̃. Sandhu, editors, *Database Security X: Status and Prospects*, chapter 6, pages 79–98. Chapman & Hall, 1997.
3. D. E. Bell and L. J. LaPadula. Secure computer system: Unified exposition and multics interpretation. Technical Report MTR-2997, MITRE Corporation, Bedford, MA, July 1975.
4. T. A. Berson and T. F. Lunt. Multilevel Security for Knowledge-Based Systems. In *Proceedings of the IEEE Symposium on Research in Security and Privacy*, pages 235–242, Oakland, CA, April 1987.
5. E. Bertino and S. Jajodia. Modeling Multilevel Entities using Single Level Objects. In *Proceedings of the Third International Conference on Deductive and Object-Oriented Databases*, volume 760 of *Lecture Notes in Computer Science*, pages 416–428, Phoenix, AZ, December 1993. Springer-Verlag.
6. N. Boulahia-Cuppens, F. Cuppens, A. Gabillon, and K. Yazdanian. Virtual View Model to Design a Secure Object-Oriented Database. In *Proceedings of the National Computer Security Conference*, pages 66–76, Baltimore, MD, October 1994.
7. A.P. Buchman, H. Branding, T. Kundrass, and J. Zimmermann. REACH: A REal-time ACtive and Heterogeneous Mediator System. *Bulletin of the IEEE Technical Committee on Data Engineering*, 15(4), December 1992.
8. S. Ceri and R. Manthey. Consolidated specification of Chimera, the conceptual interface of idea. Technical Report IDEA.DD.2P.004, Politecnico di Milano, Milan, Italy, June 1993.

9. S. Chakravarthy, E. Hanson, and S.Y.W. Su. Active data/knowledge base research at the University of Florida. *Bulletin of the IEEE Technical Committee on Data Engineering*, 15(4):35–39, December 1992.

10. C. Collet, T. Coupaye, and T. Svensen. NAOS– efficient and modular reactive capabilities in an object-oriented database system. In *Proceedings of the Twentieth International Conference on Very Large Databases*, pages 132–143, Santiago, Chile, 1994.

11. O. Costich and J. McDermott. A multilevel transaction problem for multilevel secure database system and its solution for the replicated architecture. In *Proceedings of the IEEE Symposium on Research in Security and Privacy*, pages 192–203, Oakland, CA, May 1992.

12. D. Denning and T. F. Lunt. A multilevel relational data model. In *Proceedings of the IEEE Symposium on Research in Security and Privacy*, pages 220–234, Oakland, CA, May 1987.

13. P. A. Dwyer, G. D. Gelatis, and M. B. Thuraisingham. Multilevel security in database management systems. *Computers and Security*, 6(3):252–260, June 1987.

14. T. D. Garvey and T. F. Lunt. Multilevel Security for Knowledge-Based Systems. In *Proceedings of the Sixth Computer Security Applications Conference*, pages 148–159, Tucson, AZ, December 1990.

15. S. Gatziu, A. Geppert, and K. R. Dittrich. Integrating active concepts into an object-oriented database system. In *Proceedings of the Third International Workshop on Database Programming Languages*, Nafplion, Greece, August 1991.

16. J. T. Haigh, R. C. O'Brien, and D. J. Thomsen. The LDV Secure Relational DBMS Model. In S. Jajodia and C.E. Landwehr, editors, *Database Security IV: Status and Prospects*, pages 265–279. Elsevier Science Publishers B.V. (North-Holland), 1991.

17. E. Hanson. Rule condition testing and action execution in Ariel. In *Proceedings of the ACM SIGMOD International Conference on Management of Data*, pages 49–58, San Diego, CA, June 1992.

18. D. K. Hsiao, M. J. Kohler, and S. W. Stround. Query Modifications as Means of Controlling Access to Multilevel Secure Databases. In S. Jajodia and C.E. Landwehr, editors, *Database Security IV: Status and Prospects*, pages 221–240. Elsevier Science Publishers B.V. (North-Holland), 1991.

19. S. Jajodia and B. Kogan. Transaction Processing in Multilevel Secure Databases using Replicated Architecture. In *Proceedings of the IEEE Symposium on Research in Security and Privacy*, pages 360–368, Oakland, CA, May 1990.

20. S. Jajodia and R. Sandhu. Polyinstantiation Integrity in Multilevel elations Revisited. In S. Jajodia and C.E. Landwehr, editors, *Database Security IV: Status and Prospects*, pages 297–307. Elsevier Science Publishers B.V. (North-Holland), 1991.

21. S. Jajodia and R. Sandhu. Toward a Multilevel Relational Data Model. In *Proceedings of the ACM SIGMOD International Conference on Management of Data*, pages 50–59, Denver, CO, 1991.

22. T. F. Keefe, W. T. Tsai, and M. B. Thuraisingham. A Multilevel Security Model for Object-Oriented Systems. In *Proceedings of the National Computer Security Conference*, pages 1–9, Baltimore, MD, October 1988.

23. T. F. Lunt and E. B. Fernandez. Database Security. *SIGMOD Record*, 19(4):90–97, December 1990.

24. D.R. McCarthy and U. Dayal. The architecture of an active database management system. In *Proceedings of the ACM-SIGMOD International Conference on Management of Data*, pages 215–224, Portland, OR, May 1989.

25. J. K. Millen and T.F. Lunt. Security for Object-Oriented Database Systems . In *Proceedings of the IEEE Symposium on Research in Security and Privacy*, pages 260–272, Oakland, CA, May 1992.

26. M. Morgenstern. Security and Inference in Multilevel Database and Knowledge-Base Systems. In *Proceedings of the ACM SIGMOD International Conference on Management of Data*, pages 357–373, San Francisco, CA, May 1987.

27. M. Morgenstern. A Security Moddel for Multilevel Object with Bidirectional Relationship. In S. Jajodia and C.E. Landwehr, editors, *Database Security IV: Status and Prospects*, pages 53–71. Elsevier Science Publishers B.V. (North-Holland), 1991.

28. M.S. Olivier and S. H. Von Solms. A Taxonomy for Secure Object-Oriented Databases. *ACM Transactions on Database Systems*, 19(1):3–46, March 1993.

29. N.W. Paton and O. Diaz. Active Database Systems. *ACM Computing Surveys*, 31(1):63–103, 1999.

30. A. Rosenthal, S. Chakravarthy, B. Blaustein, and J. Blakeley. Situation monitoring for active databases. In *Proceedings of the Fifteenth International Conference On Very Large Databases*, pages 455–464, Amsterdam, The Netherlands, August 1989.

31. R. Sandhu and S. Jajodia. Referential Integrity in Multilevel Secure Databases. In *Proceedings of the National Computer Security Conference*, pages 39–52, Baltimore, MD, September 1993.

32. L. M. Schlipper, J. Filsinger, and V. M. Doshi. A Multilevel Secure Database Management System Benchmark. In *Proceedings of the National Computer Security Conference*, pages 399–408, Baltimore, MD, October 1992.

33. K. Smith and M. Winslett. Multilevel secure rules: Integrating the multilevel and the active data model. Technical Report UIUCDCS-R-92-1732, University of Illinois, Urbana-Champaign, IL, March 1992.

34. P. D. Stachour and M. B. Thuraisingham. Design of LDV: A Multilevel Secure Relational Database Management System. *IEEE Transactions on Knowledge and Data Engineering*, 2(3):190–209, June 1990.

35. M. Stonebraker and G. Kemnitz. The POSTGRES Next-Generation Database Management System. *Communications of the ACM*, 34(10):78–92, October 1991.

36. M. B. Thuraisingham. Mandatory Security in Object-Oriented Database Systems. In *Proceedings of the International Conference on Object-Oriented Programming Systems, Languages and Applications*, pages 203–210, New Orleans, LA, October 1989.

37. J. Widom. The Starburst Rule System: Language Design, Implementation and Application. *Bulletin of the IEEE Technical Committee on Data Engineering*, 15(4):15–18, December 1992.

38. J. Widom and S. Ceri. *Active Database Systems Triggers and Rules For Advanced Database Processing*. Morgan Kaufmann, San Francisco, CA, 1996.

Using the Compliant Systems Architecture to Deliver Flexible Policies within Two-Phase Commit

Diana Howard, Henry Detmold, Katrina Falkner, and David Munro

School of Computer Science
The University of Adelaide
Adelaide 5005, Australia
{diana, henry, katrina, dave}@cs.adelaide.edu.au

Abstract. The compliant systems architecture (CSA) is a structuring methodology for constructing software systems that exhibit strict separation of policy and mechanism. Components of an instantiated CSA adapt to their environment under application control. This ability to evolve allows a single system to provide optimal support for arbitrary applications through flexible policy specification. Applications may determine their preferred level of participation in the specification of policy.

In a distributed database system, two-phase commit (2PC) delineates a family of algorithms governed by policies that affect different performance, overhead and recovery characteristics. Whilst the literature describes many different algorithms, a given implementation employs a particular subset of policy choices. Consequently applications are captive to decisions made by the underlying system and are unable to exploit domain-specific knowledge. This paper outlines an instantiation of a distributed CSA and illustrates how it delivers flexibility within 2PC.

1 Introduction

System architectures are designed to support applications; they provide an abstraction over the underlying computer hardware. Their role is to facilitate application performance, where possible metrics include execution time, throughput and the provision of some particular functionality. To fulfil this role, systems require policy and mechanism. Policies comprise strategies to achieve particular goals, whereas mechanisms implement these strategies.

Traditional architectures are characterised by their rigid structure and the tight encapsulation of policy and mechanism into static layers. Whilst this abstraction technique has well-known benefits, it limits policy and mechanism cooperation to that within individual layers. Furthermore, since policy is determined within system levels, application-level code has only indirect and limited control. Policy and mechanism designs for conventional systems are derived from simulation and benchmarking of sample applications. Combinations of policies and mechanisms that yield the best average performance across a majority of samples are adopted and set in concrete. An application whose behaviour does not

A. James, B. Lings, M. Younas (Eds.): BNCOD 2003, LNCS 2712, pp. 245–252, 2003.

match the average case must engage in a process of *policy subversion*, attempting to coerce the system's policies to meet the application's distinct requirements. Not only do conventional architectures fail to support different policy needs, but they preclude applications from effecting any real alternatives.

Previous attempts to overcome the failings of conventional architectures include modern microkernels and adaptive systems. The former, exemplified by the Exokernel [1], isolate mechanisms to the kernel and implement policies as user-level libraries. Whilst applications may select the most appropriate policy by choosing the corresponding library, control ends at this point. Adaptive systems collate details of past and present system behaviour to determine future policy. Recent research has produced a variety of adaptive systems in a range of contexts including distributed databases [2], [3], [4]. Such examples typically address only a single element of the overall system, such as replication or distributed commit, and support limited, pre-determined options within that area. Adaptive systems are ineffective in the face of phase changes because they operate incrementally.

In contrast, all components of a CSA can modify their behaviour based on the current environment and application preferences [5]. A complete separation of policy from mechanism underpins this concept of compliance. The segregation is observed at every level of system design and incorporates information passing across all architectural layers. The controlled exposure of policy allows applications to exploit and mould the system by directing policy choices dynamically. The principal benefit of this approach is that individual applications can obtain optimal support from a single system. The capacity for applications to describe their unique requirements potentially leads to simpler semantics and improved performance. Moreover, the extent to which applications concern themselves with questions of policy is itself a matter of policy and as such is determined by the application.

In building a CSA instantiation of a distributed database, there are many components whose policies can profitably be placed under application control. Distributed commit is an important exemplar due to the degree to which application characteristics effect commit performance and hence overall throughput [6]. There is a wealth of atomic commit protocols with differing performance trade-offs and atomicity guarantees. The major family of commit algorithms descends from the 2PC protocol [7] and offers various optimisations based on different behavioural assumptions [8], [9], [10]. For applications concerned with network resources, linear 2PC [7] reduces the message overhead; whereas decentralised 2PC [11] is more appropriate when overall delay is the dominant factor. Similarly, presumed commit [12] may outperform the standard 2PC protocol for update transactions with a sufficient degree of distribution [6].

The major contribution of this work is to demonstrate how these application-dependent choices may be specified flexibly and dynamically using a CSA. This paper describes the key tenets of the architecture, as instantiated in a distributed database context. A worked example fleshes out the capacity for applications to control policy choices within 2PC. This process reveals where the algorithm relies on policy decisions, how applications may interpose their own policy and to what advantage.

2   The Compliant Systems Architecture

The generic CSA is a structuring methodology that defines systems in terms of operational abstractions or components; a formal treatment of this architecture is presented in [5]. To instantiate a CSA, decisions must be made regarding:

- The operational abstractions in the architecture and their relationships.
- Possible layering within each operational abstraction.
- The set of system functions amenable to application control.
- How to specify policy information.
- How to pass system information between components and system functions.

These issues capture the requirements of a flexible architecture and how policies and mechanisms will be separated and exposed.

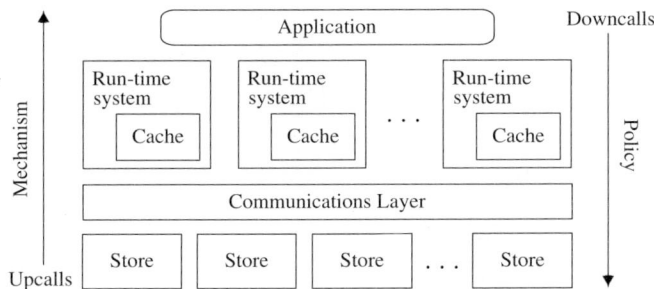

Fig. 1. An exemplar CSA instantiation

Figure 1 illustrates an instantiation of the distributed CSA framework, that consists of four distinct architectural layers. The application layer views the remaining layers as a unified system through a single logical address space. The second operational abstraction comprises a set of virtual machines, one per node in the system. Each virtual machine is further decomposed into a run-time system and a local cache. The communications layer facilitates communication between the virtual machines. A collection of object stores constitutes the fourth layer and provides orthogonally persistent storage.

The instantiation described above is implemented in a compliant language system called ProcessBase [5]. ProcessBase is strongly typed and supports first class procedures and types, structural reflection and a flexible transaction system. Existing research with ProcessBase has investigated how application control may be implemented with respect to scheduling, concurrency control and distributed shared memory [13]. Current work is concerned with delivering flexible policy choices in regard to distribution transparency.

In general, core mechanism exists at each level of the architecture; policy to control a particular mechanism may exist at any higher level. Mechanism is invoked through a downcall, allowing information about policy to be shared with a lower layer. Policy information can be requested through an upcall which exists as a form of control interrupt, triggering the execution of policy code written at the application level. Upcalls allow information about mechanism to be shared with higher levels. Unlike conventional interrupts, upcalls are able to pass information back when control returns to the lower level. Upcalls and downcalls that pass information between components at the same level are called lateral calls; these correspond to conventional function calls.

The definition of mechanism is static; mechanisms are the core activities that define the services available to the application. For example, primitives include the reading or writing of an object to or from a stable store, or the sending of a communications message. The addition of compliant components requires the identification of any further mechanism and the integration of this mechanism into the appropriate layer. Policy is dynamic and uses the mechanisms provided to reach its goal. Mechanism can, in turn, invoke policy to receive direction.

When exploring compliance in a practical setting, a pragmatic limit must be placed on the available mechanisms. This CSA instance supports dynamic policy specification at the topmost layer only. Mechanism at all lower layers must perform upcalls to this layer in order to receive policy direction.

3   Application to Two-Phase Commit

To implement two-phase commit in a compliant fashion it is necessary to identify what constitutes mechanism and policy. The purpose of a distributed commit algorithm is to maintain the atomicity of a transaction executed across multiple sites; hence, mechanism is defined as the actual commit or abort process and policy as those decisions made to determine whether a transaction commits or aborts.

The standard presentation of 2PC is delineated in Figure 2. Each process involved in a given transaction acts as a participant in the commit protocol, with a distinguished process taking on the role of coordinator. Note that the coordinator's first write is non-forced and the decision to commit requires a unanimous vote in the affirmative. Participants only execute their second phase if they vote in favour of commit in the first.

Mechanisms are required at the run-time system, communications and store levels to perform low level operations at the request of a higher-level policy. The core mechanisms required in this scenario are the abilities to read and write records to the store and for processes to communicate with each other.

Invocation of the commit protocol occurs when an application finishes issuing the operations involved in a transaction. In existing distributed database systems, this state is made known to the underlying transaction manager through an instruction issued by the application; this is the point where application control ceases. Figure 3 delineates our design for distributed commit processing in

```
Phase 1                          Phase 1
(1) Send prepare to all          (1) Receive prepare
    participants                 (2) Vote
(2) Write prepare to log         (3) Write vote to log
                                 (4) Send vote to coordinator
Phase 2
(3) Wait for all votes           Phase 2
(4) Decide                       (5) Wait for decision
(5) Write decision to log        (6) Write decision to log
(6) Send decision to all         (7) Send acknowledgement
    participants                     to coordinator
```

Fig. 2. The standard 2PC protocol, decomposed into the roles of coordinator (left) and participant (right)

the ProcessBase architecture. Applications signal their readiness to complete a transaction by invoking a downcall. Application control does not end here, however, because the implementation of 2PC incorporates upcalls that invoke policy code to modify or optimise the existing algorithm. These upcalls may pass directly to the application or to application-level modules, such as the commit and concurrency managers. Note that these particular modules belong to the same conceptual layer; upcalls and downcalls between the two are lateral.

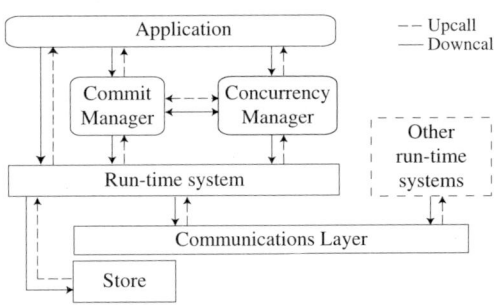

Fig. 3. Policy interactions for 2PC in terms of upcalls and downcalls

3.1 Policy Identification

The previous sections have identified the operational abstractions in ProcessBase and its methods for passing system information between components. It now remains to derive the set of policies that should fall under application control in a compliant transaction system. Policies considered here include the addition of time-outs, how to decide and how to recover from node failures.

Time-Outs. A common modification to the standard specification of 2PC is to introduce time-outs whenever processes block for messages. This situation arises for both the coordinator and participants at the start of their second phases. Via an upcall, an application can detect blocked processes and take appropriate action. For standard 2PC the alternative to blocking the coordinator is to abort the transaction. For some styles of real-time transactions this may be desirable [3]. However, this is, of course, a matter of policy. The same application in other circumstances may prefer the possibility of a protracted commit to a speedy abort. Participants that time-out can bypass a slow, or failed, coordinator. This policy results in a cooperative 2PC [9] where participants attempt to learn the final transaction status from each other.

Applications are free to determine policy on a per coordinator and per participant basis. Control is achieved by the run-time system invoking an upcall to the commit module at step (3) of the coordinator's algorithm and at step (5) of the participant's. A still finer degree of control is obtained when applications choose, through the same process, the period necessary to trigger a time-out. In this situation, the relevant upcall returns the desired time-frame.

When policy determines that participating processes can time-out, a new mechanism is required to enable these processes to communicate as per the cooperative 2PC variant. These communication details are possessed by the coordinator and can be distributed to the remaining processes via another upcall.

Deciding. According to the standard 2PC description and the isolation requirement of ACID transactions, a coordinator decides to commit a transaction only when each participant votes in favour of the commit. Whilst this represents an integral part of the algorithm, it is an important policy decision. The idea that weakened atomicity guarantees are sometimes appropriate is not new. Commercial database systems rarely employ the full ACID transaction model because it is too restrictive for applications. However these systems still provide a fixed model of atomicity that precludes flexible control over the degree of relaxation.

To incorporate a decision-making policy, the coordinator invokes an upcall in step (4), passing the participants' votes as parameters. The application's policy decision may be based on majority- or priority-based rules and have the capacity to override local decisions to abort. In this scenario all participants must wait for the agreed decision. Alternatively, the policy may delay the transaction commit while it repeats operations sent to nodes that intend to abort. Application input is necessary here because the semantics of "repeating operations" is entirely application-dependent. Clearly, these policies alter the semantics of 2PC but in a structured manner that introduces a level of flexibility over previous work.

Similarly, a voting upcall determines how each process votes in step (2) of the participant algorithm. Time-outs can identify when real-time constraints require processes to vote for a transaction abort. More interestingly, execution of the upcall involves lateral calls with the concurrency manager to determine whether the latter detected conflicts in the process' operations. Conflicts are the principal reason why participants vote to abort transactions. The concurrency module performs conflict detection via its own set of policies and mechanisms.

These lateral calls mean that an application's domain-specific knowledge can be applied to determine the voting response to conflict.

Recovery. Many variations on 2PC focus on optimisations for the case when the coordinator fails before writing a decision to the stable log [8], [12]; an upcall can also determine the appropriate behaviour here. Presumed abort is obtained by directing the coordinator to abort and inform participants of this decision only when polled by these processes. When the upcall causes the coordinator to automatically send its abort decision to the participants the algorithm corresponds to presumed commit. A third policy option is for the upcall to repeat the voting phase to ascertain the original decision. This may be appropriate for "important" transactions where nodes are "reasonably" reliable and the overhead of repeating phase one outweighs the consequences of aborting a potentially committable transaction. This policy may be revoked when the coordinator reaches a certain failure rate. The recovery process has ramifications for the number and timing of forced writes within a 2PC. For instance, presumed commit relies on the presence of participant lists in the stable log.

Summary. This discussion covers just a few aspects of flexible policy specification in the realm of two-phase commit. The same techniques will produce compliant communication patterns that encompass decentralised and linear 2PC. Moreover, the policies explored above are not restricted to 2PC but can be easily extended to other distributed commit techniques, such as three-phase commit. ProcessBase's capacity for evolution means that these policy options do not have to be incorporated at the point of system or application design but may be developed as their use becomes appropriate.

4   Related Work

Database systems that support adaptive commit protocols have a similar aim to this work: to provide more suitable commit algorithms on a per-application basis. Soparkar *et.al* [3] describe a framework in which atomicity semantics may be relaxed when the system detects sufficient workload to threaten real-time requirements. This study agrees that an application may derive real benefit from the use of particular commit protocols. However the proposed system limits the choice of protocol to standard 2PC or a single variety of relaxed commit based on compensating transactions. The model fails to identify how the underlying implementation would change policies, let alone how an application can apply its knowledge to control the commit model employed for a given transaction.

Panadiwal and Goscinski [2] present an implementation of a client-server based transaction service in which the commit protocol is adaptive in that it may select write-ahead logging or shadow paging to maintain records on stable storage. This work demonstrates the relationship between data storage strategies and the performance of commit processing but does not address how applications may specialise the storage policy to derive a more efficient commit protocol.

5   Conclusion and Future Directions

The compliant systems architecture (CSA) is a methodology for facilitating application control of system components. In a distributed database setting, one such component is the commit protocol used to ensure transaction atomicity. ProcessBase is a distributed instantiation of the CSA and supports high-level policy specification. The contribution of this work is a demonstration of how this system and the CSA framework provides flexible policies for distributed commit processing and two-phase commit in particular.

The current instance of the ProcessBase architecture supports application-level compliance, providing a pragmatic environment for tractable experimentation. Future research avenues include the detailed design and implementation of those policies and mechanisms identified in Section 3. This will lay the groundwork for an investigation into optimal policy choices for a range of database applications and the measurement of this framework's effectiveness.

References

1. Engler, D., Kaashoek, M., O'Toole, J.: Exokernel: An Operating System Architecture for Application-Level Resource Management. In: Proc. of the 15th ACM Sym. on Operating Systems Principles. (1995) 251–266
2. Panadiwal, R., Goscinski, A.: A High Performance and Adaptive Commit Protocol for a Distributed Environment. ACM SIGOPS Operating Systems Review **30** (1996) 52–58
3. Soparkar, N., Levy, E., Korth, H., Silberschatz, A.: Adaptive Commitment for Real-Time Distributed Transactions. CS-TR 92-15, University of Texas (1992)
4. Wolfson, O., Jajodia, S., Huang, Y.: An Adaptive Data Replication Algorithm. ACM Trans. on Database Systems **22** (1997) 255–314
5. Morrison, R., Balasubramaniam, D., Greenwood, M., Kirby, G., Mayes, K., Munro, D., Warboys, B.: A Compliant Persistent Architecture. Software – Practice & Experience **30** (2000) 363–386
6. Gupta, R., Haritsa, J., Ramamritham, K.: Revisiting Commit Processing in Distributed Database Systems. ACM SIGMOD Record **26** (1997) 486–497
7. Gray, J.: Notes on Database Operating Systems. In: Operating Systems: An Advanced Course. Volume 66 of LNCS. Springer-Verlag (1978) 393–481
8. Al-Houmaily, Y.: Commit Processing in Distributed Database Systems and in Heterogeneous Multidatabase Systems. PhD thesis, University of Pittsburgh (1997)
9. LeLann, G.: Error Recovery. In: Distributed Systems: Architecture and Implementation. Volume 105 of LNCS. Springer-Verlag (1981) 371–376
10. Stonebraker, M.: Concurrency Control and Consistency of Multiple Data in Distributed INGRES. IEEE Trans. on Software Engineering **5** (1979) 188–194
11. Skeen, D.: Nonblocking Commit Protocols. In: Proc. of the ACM SIGMOD Int. Conf. on Management of Data. (1981) 133–142
12. Mohan, C., Lindsay, B.: Efficient Commit Protocols for the Tree of Processes Model of Distributed Transactions. In: Proc. of the 2nd ACM Sym. on Principles of Distributed Computing. (1983) 76–88
13. Falkner, K., Detmold, H., Munro, D., Olds, T.: Towards Compliant Distributed Shared Memory. In: 4th Int. Workshop on Software Distributed Shared Memory. (2002) 305–310

A Concurrent $\mathbf{B}^{link}$-Tree Algorithm Using a Cooperative Locking Protocol*

Sung-Chae Lim[1], Joonseon Ahn[2], and Myoung Ho Kim[3]

[1] WST Lab., Korea Wisenut Inc., Yangjae-dong, Seocho-gu, Seoul, 137-130, Korea,
sclim@dbserver.kaist.ac.kr
[2] Hankuk Aviation University, Hwajundong, Koyang, Kyounggido 412-791, Korea
jsahn@mail.hangkong.ac.kr
[3] Korea Advanced Institute of Science and Technology 373-1, Kusung-dong,
Yusung-gu, Taejon, 305-701, Korea, mhkim@dbserver.kaist.ac.kr

Abstract. We present a new concurrent B^{link}-tree algorithm that provides a concurrent tree restructuring mechanism for handling underflow nodes as well as overflow nodes. Our algorithm does not require any lock for downward searching and preserves bottom-up tree restructuring without deadlock. To this end, we develop a new locking mechanism for inserters and deleters and a node update rule that preserves the semantical tree consistency during tree restructuring. Our analytical experiment shows that the overhead of additional disk I/O is acceptable.

1 Introduction

While various index structures have been proposed for high performance transaction processing, B-tree indexing has been typically used by many commercial database systems [1]. Therefore, many concurrent B-tree algorithms have been proposed to deal with concurrent accesses to B-trees efficiently [2,3,4,5,6,7,8,9].

Among the concurrent B-tree algorithms, it has been indicated that the B^{link}-tree [3,5,6] which provides non-blocked downward searching and bottom-up node splitting is among the best choices considering transaction throughput [13,14]. However, they have no concurrent mechanism for restructuring underflow nodes. When underflow nodes cannot be handled, B-trees become sparse, which leads to the degradation of performance [10,11]. In [6], underflow nodes are restructured by a background mode process that retrieves all the tree nodes. This method suffers from heavy retrieval cost and tree compaction time.

In this paper, we propose a concurrent B^{link}-tree algorithm that can handle underflow nodes concurrently. We first present a new locking protocol which provides a deadlock-free locking sequence to updaters competing for lock grants on the same nodes. Also, we provide a node update rule for key transfer and

---

* This research was supported by IRC (Internet Information Retrieval Research Center) in Hankuk Aviation University. IRC is a Kyounggi-Province Regional Research Center designed by Korea Science and Engineering Foundation and Ministry of Science & Technology.

A. James, B. Lings, M. Younas (Eds.): BNCOD 2003, LNCS 2712, pp. 253–260, 2003.

node merging to guarantee concurrent search operations to access nodes that are under restructuring and maintain the consistency of B-trees [7,9].

The rest of this paper is organized as follows. Section 2 revisits the problem of B^{link}-tree concurrency control (CC). In Section 3, we present a new algorithm for the concurrent access to B^{link}-trees. Section 4 describes the node update rule for deleters. Section 5 proves deadlock-freeness of our algorithm and Section 6 addresses performance issues. Finally, Section 7 gives a conclusion.

2   Preliminaries

2.1   Backgrounds on B^{link}-Tree Concurrency Control

B^{link}-tree is a modification of the B-tree such that sibling nodes at each level are linked from the left to the right [3,6]. An internal node with n index entries has the format $< p_1, k_1, \ldots, k_{n-1}, p_n, k_{max}, siblinglink >$. $siblinglink$ points to the right sibling. p_i points to the subtree having keys k such that $k_{i-1} < k \le k_i$, where $k_n = k_{max}$. In leaf nodes, p_i points to the record with key value k_i.

If an inserter makes a node overflow, the inserter moves the right-half portion of the node to a new node, updates the sibling links and k_{max} of the two nodes and inserts a new index entry into the parent node [5]. If a process arrives at a node searching for a target key greater than k_{max} of the node, which means the node has been split, the reader moves to the next node by following the sibling link. In this way, search operations can execute concurrently with node splits not requesting any locks. This non-blocked downward search improves the concurrency of B-trees and reduces the CPU cost for locking operations [13,14].

2.2   The Basic Idea of the Proposed B^{link}-Tree CC Algorithm

In B^{link}-tree, multiple updaters, each of which is an inserter or a deleter, may get to their target leaf nodes following the same path. Handling underflow nodes needs to exclusively access their parent and sibling nodes to transfer index entries or merge half-full nodes. Also, handling overflow nodes needs to exclusively access their parent nodes. Therefore, multiple updaters restructuring the same nodes can cause deadlock.

In our locking protocol, we use two kinds of locks, the X mode and IX mode locks. The X lock is not compatible with any lock, while the IX lock is compatible with itself[12]. At the lock grant time of an IX lock, the function for lock request returns a value, Shared or Alone. If there exist other IX-lock holders on the node, Shared is returned. Otherwise, Alone is returned.

A lock holder can change the kinds of its locks. If a process P holding an X lock on a node N requests a conversion to an IX lock, IX lock is immediately granted to P. Also, IX lock is granted to other processes that have been blocked requesting IX locks for N if such processes exist. If P holding an IX lock on a node N requests a conversion to an X lock, P has the highest priority to hold an X lock on the node. If there were other IX-lock holders on the node, P is inserted to the waiting queue. Otherwise, P is granted the X lock immediately.

---

procedure search_for_leaf(*kvalue, Leaf*) /* read the leaf with a key value of *kvalue* */
begin
    Ptr ← the pointer to the root node; *Height* ← the height of the tree;
    while (*Height* > 1) **do** /* pass down internal nodes */
        Read the node pointed to by *Ptr* into a local memory node, *N*;
        while (*kvalue* > *N*.largest_key) **do**   /* The node was split */
            Ptr ← *N*.siblinglink;
            Read the node pointed to by *Ptr* into the memory area *N* again;
        endwhile
        Ptr ← the pointer to the next child node; /* search down to the child level */
        Decrease variable *Height* by 1;
    endwhile
    get_node(*Ptr, kvalue, Leaf ,Lockmode*); /* lock and read the leaf node */
end.
procedure get_node(*Ptr, kv, Node, Lockmode*)
begin
    State ← lock(*Ptr, Lockmode*); /* lock node *Ptr* with a given lock mode, *Lockmode* */
    label1: Read the node pointed to by *Ptr* into the local memory node, *Node*;
    if (*kv* > *Node*.largest_key) **then**
        unlock(*Ptr*); *Ptr* ← *Node*.siblinglink; *State* ← lock(*Ptr, Lockmode*);
        goto label1;
    endif
end.

Fig. 1. The algorithm for procedures search_for_leaf() and get_node()

Our locking protocol is based on lock stratification and lock cooperation. The former defines a rule which prevents deadlocks associated with nodes at multiple levels. The rule forces an updater which locks both a parent and child nodes to have an X lock for the parent and IX locks for the child. When a deleter observes that a sibling node to be restructured already has been locked by another updater, it follows lock cooperation, which prevents deadlocks associated with nodes at the same level and keeps trees consistent not losing any update.

3   The Proposed B^{link}-Tree CC Algorithm

3.1   The Key Search Algorithm

Fig. 1 shows procedures for key search. In our algorithm, all processes use the procedure search_for_leaf() for their downward searching. Arriving at a leaf node, they calls get_node() to lock and read the node having a given key value. If an IX lock is requested, lock() returns Shared or Alone at the lock grant time. Otherwise, its return value has no meaning. In the procedures search_for_leaf() and get_node(), examining the largest key and chasing along sibling links are necessary because the node can be split from overflow right before the arrival.

3.2   Algorithm for Inserting a New Index Entry

The insertion algorithm performed by an inserter is as follows:

(1) Search the target leaf node and lock it in X mode; then, insert an index.
(2) Unless the node overflows, write the node and exit after releasing the lock. Otherwise, go to the next step.
(3) Create a new node and lock the new node in IX mode.
(4) Perform a half-splitting by using the newly created node, and then convert the X lock on the overflow node to IX mode.
(5) X Lock and read the parent node by using get_node(). Then, release IX locks on the half-splitting nodes.
(6) Insert an index entry pointing to the new node into the parent node. If the parent node does not overflow, write it and exit after releasing all the locks. Otherwise, go to step (3) for key insertion into the parent node.

In step (4), the X lock is converted to an IX lock to observe the lock stratification rule. Unlike [5], we retain locks on the half-splitting nodes until an X lock is granted on the parent node. Otherwise, a deleter may delete one of the half-splitting nodes for node merging while the inserter is blocked.

3.3   Algorithm for Deleting an Index Entry

The deletion of an index entry is performed as follows.

(1) Search the target leaf node and lock it in X mode; then, delete the index.
(2) Unless the node underflows, write the node and exit after releasing the lock. Otherwise, go to the next step.
(3) Convert the X lock on the underflow node to IX mode. Then, X lock and read the parent node by using get_node().
(4) Choose a sibling for key transfer (or node merging) and IX lock the node.
(5) If the lock request on the sibling returns Alone, update nodes according to the steps described in Section 4. Otherwise, i.e., if the return value is Shared, follow the lock cooperation procedure given in the next subsection.

3.4   Lock Cooperation

If IX locks are shared between a deleter and an updater, we call such case a cooperation demanding situation (CDS). Only deleters can detect CDS when they receive Shared from the IX lock request for a sibling node. To enable deleters to deal with CDS, we use a *state* field in each node. When a deleter makes a node N underflow and subsequently detects a CDS on the left(or right) sibling of N, it sets the *state* field in N to LS(or RS). Otherwise, the *state* field is NULL.

Suppose a deleter Pd making node N underflow detects a CDS on the left sibling Ns on which an updater P1 holds an IX lock. Then Pd checks the *state* field in Ns. We describe the actions by Pd and P1 based on the two categories.

(a) If Ns has value RS, it means that P1 is a deleter which already detected a CDS on Pd and thus has a completely overlapped scope with Pd. In this case, Pd terminate after releasing all its locks and P1 completes tree restructuring.

(b) Otherwise, it can be one of three cases: (i) P1 is an inserter, (ii) P1 is a deleter that will detect a CDS on N, or (iii) P1 is a deleter that does not use N for tree restructuring. For all cases, Pd releases the X lock on the parent node after setting *state* of N with LS and suspends until P1 releases its lock on Ns by converting the IX lock on Ns to X mode. Then, Pd will resume tree restructuring after P1 performs its actions described below. In cases of (i) and (iii) P1 completes its tree restructuring after acquiring the X lock on the parent node. In (ii), P1 will later detect the completely overlapped situation with Pd, and hence will leave the tree as Pd does in (a).

In case of a CDS on a right sibling, the same rules can be applied analogously. The followings are steps for lock cooperation by Pd that detects a CDS on Ns.

(1) If Ns.*siblinglink* is not N, which means that Ns has been split, place a new IX lock on the node pointed to by Ns.*siblinglink* and release the IX lock on Ns; the newly locked node is regarded as Ns from now on.

(2) If the *state* field in Ns indicates a completely overlapped situation(i.e., the *state* field is LS(RS) and Ns is the right (left) sibling), then write N into the disk and exit after releasing all the locks; otherwise, go to the next step.

(3) Set N.*state* to LS or RS appropriately, and then write N into the disk.

(4) Release the X lock on the parent node and then request lock conversion on Ns from IX mode to X mode (self blocking).

(5) Convert the X lock on Ns to IX mode, then lock and read the parent Np of N. At this point, Ns may not be a correct sibling. For instance, an inserter may split the parent and make N and Ns have different parents.

(6) Check N and Ns are adjacent in Np. If Ns is a correct sibling, read Ns and restructure the three nodes N, Ns and Np following the update rule described in Section 4. Otherwise, Pd releases the IX lock on Ns and goes to step (4) of the deletion algorithm in Section 3.3. Note that lock cooperation is a part of step (5) of the deletion algorithm in Section 3.3.

4   Restructuring an Underflow Node

Suppose a deleter P has locked and read nodes N, Ns and Np using the procedure in Section 3.3. Here, N is an underflow node, Ns is a sibling of N and Np is their parent. Currently, P is the unique process that can update these nodes.

4.1   Transferring the Index Entries

If Ns has sufficient index entries, P moves some index entries of Ns to N. This is straightforward when Ns is the left sibling. That is, some rightmost index entries in Ns are inserted into N and these index entries are deleted from Ns, and then Np is properly updated. We should be careful when Ns is the right sibling and leftmost index entries in Ns are deleted because such deletion may spoil other search operations which use the pointer to Ns. Therefore, we create a new node which stores the remaining entries of Ns and replace Ns with the new node.

(1) Create a new node Nnew and write the right portion of entries in Ns into Nnew. Nnew contains those entries of Ns which are not transferred to N.
(2) Write the left entry of Ns into N and update N.*siblinglink* to point to Nnew.
(3) Update the maximum key value for N in Np so that it reflects the index transfer to N and replace the pointer to Ns with the pointer to Nnew.
(4) Update the first pointer of Ns to point to N and mark Ns invalid so that any process arriving at this node can follow the pointer to N.
(5) Release all the locks and exit.

The invalidated node needs to be kept temporarily for processes that have the pointer to Ns by reading the old value of its parent node.

4.2   Merging the Half-Full Nodes

Unless Ns has sufficient index entries, node merging is performed. In node merging, we always transfer entries in a right sibling Nr into a left sibling Nl.

(1) All the index entries of Nr are inserted into Nl and the sibling link of Nl are updated with that of Nr. And we set the *state* field of Nl with **NULL**.
(2) The pointer to Nr and the old maximum value of Nl in Np are deleted. The previous maximum value of Nr becomes that of Nl.
(3) Nr becomes invalidated as in the case of the leftward key transfer.
(4) If Np underflows, P performs (3) of the algorithm in Section 3.3 after releasing locks on Nl and Nr. Otherwise, P releases all its locks and exits.

5   Deadlock-Freeness of the Proposed Locking Protocol

To prove deadlock freeness of our protocol, we use a lock-wait-for graph described below. When a certain updater P requests an IX or X lock for node N and is blocked due to lock conflict, we draw arcs heading for N from every node for which P already holds any lock. We remove these arcs heading for N when the lock is granted to P. For the proof, we have only to show that any cycle cannot be formed in this lock-wait-for graph using the following lemmas.

Lemma 1. *Any cycle composed of nodes at more than one level cannot be formed in the lock-wait-for graph.*

Lemma 2. *Any cycle composed of nodes at only one level cannot be formed in the lock-wait-for graph.*

The first lemma can be easily proved from the lock stratification rule. We can prove second lemma as follows. In our protocol, a process can hold only an IX lock on a node N when it requests a lock for a sibling of N. Therefore, because IX locks are compatible with IX locks, a cycle composed of nodes at the same level can be constructed from X lock requests only. Before a lock holder of N requests an X lock for a left(right) sibling of N, it always confirms that the state field of the sibling is not RS(LS) and sets the state field of N with LS(RS), holding an X lock for the parent of the two nodes. From this, we can show that any cycle composed of nodes at one level cannot be formed in the lock-wait-for graph. The complete proof is omitted here because of limited space.

6   The Performance Overview

Because a deleter which detects a CDS has to set the *state* field in the underflow node and re-read the parent node and the sibling node after the self-blocking state, our lock cooperation has the overhead of additional one page (i.e. node) write and two page reads. Because the overhead of disk I/Os may degrade the performance, we investigate how often the CDS may occur.

Let the number of nodes in a tree be N_T and suppose each update operation can exist at a certain node with the probability of $1/N_T$. When two sibling nodes are updated by two updaters, we call the updaters are adjacent. The mean number of the pairs of updaters that are adjacent is denoted by N_{adj}.

Suppose N_U number of updaters come into a tree in sequence. We define I_k such that $I_k = 1$, if the k-th updater is adjacent to one of k-1 other updaters, otherwise, $I_k = 0$. Then, the expectation of $Y_k = \sum_{i=1}^{k} I_i$ is given as follows:

$$E(Y_k) = E(\sum_{i=2}^{k} I_i) < \sum_{i=2}^{k} E(I_i|I_{i-1} = 0, \ldots, I_2 = 0) = \sum_{i=2}^{k} E(I_i|Y_{i-1} = 0) \quad (1)$$

Since $N_{adj} = E(Y_{N_U})$ and $E(I_k|Y_{k-1} = 0) = \frac{2*(k-1)}{N_T}$, we have the following.

$$N_{adj} < \sum_{k=2}^{N_U} \frac{2*(k-1)}{N_T} = \frac{N_U*(N_U-1)}{N_T}, \ N_U = 2, 3, 4, \ldots \quad (2)$$

Let each node have between $2D-1$ and D index entries and X_n be the probability that a given node has n index entries where $D \le n \le 2D-1$. Equation (3) shows X_n whose complete description can be found in [17].

$$X_n = \frac{1}{(n+1)}(H(2D) - H(D))^{-1}, \text{ where } H(D) = \sum_{i=1}^{D} 1/i \approx lnD \quad (3)$$

X_D is the probability that a deleter incurs an underflow and X_{2D-1} is the probability that an inserter incurs an overflow. Assuming that the frequencies of insertions and deletions are the same, the probability that an updater causes tree restructuring is $\frac{X_D+X_{2D-1}}{2}$. Then, the probability that a pair of adjacent updaters results in a CDS is less than $\frac{(X_D+X_{2D-1})^2}{4}$. Thus, the upper bound on the mean number of CDS occurrences N_{CDS} is driven as follows:

$$N_{CDS} < \frac{(X_D + X_{2D-1})^2}{4} * N_{adj} \approx (\frac{3}{4ln2})^2 * \frac{N_U*(N_U-1)}{N_T*(D+1)^2} \quad (4)$$

From this, we can see N_{CDS} is very small. For instance, N_{CDS} is $2.6 * 10^{-4}$ when there are 300 concurrent updaters in a B^{link}-tree with 5 M index entries.

7   Conclusion

We have presented a deadlock-free B^{link}-tree algorithm that can handle overflows and underflows concurrently while supporting non-blocked downward searches. To this end, we have developed a locking mechanism composed of lock stratification and lock cooperation and methods for restructuring underflow nodes.

Since lock cooperation requires additional disk accesses, we have analyzed the overhead based on a probability model. This shows that the overhead from the lock cooperation is acceptable.

References

1. D. Comer: The Ubiquitous B-tree. *ACM Computing Surveys,* **11(2)** (1979) 121–137
2. Bayer, R. and Schkolnick, M.: Concurrency of Operations on B-Trees. *Acta Informatica* **9** (1977) 1–21
3. Philip L. Lehman and S. Bing Yao: Efficient Locking for Concurrent Operations. *ACM Transactions on Database Systems* **6(4)** (1981) 650–670
4. Udi Manber and Richard E. Ladner: Concurrency Control In a Dynamic Search Structure. *ACM Transactions on Database Systems* **9(3)** (1984) 439–455
5. Yat-Sang Kwong and Derick Wood: A New Method for Concurrency in B-Trees. *IEEE Transactions on Software Engineering* **8(3)** (1982) 211–222
6. Yehoshua Sagiv: Concurrent Operations on B*-Tree with Overtaking. *Journal of Computer and System Science* **33(2)** (1986) 275–296
7. Shasha, D. and Goodman, N.: Concurrent Search Structure Algorithms. *ACM Transactions on Database Systems* **13(1)** (1988) 53–90
8. C. Mohan: ARIES:IM: An Efficient and High Concurrency Index Management Method Using Write-Ahead Logging. *ACM SIGMOD* **21** (1992) 371–380
9. Ragaa Ishak: Semantically Consistent Schedules for Efficient and Concurrent B-Tree Restructuring. *International Conference on Data Engineering* (1992) 184–191
10. Chendong Zou and Betty Salzberg· On-line Reorganization of Sparsely-populated B⁺-trees. *ACM SIGMOD* **25** (1996) 115–124
11. Jan Jannink: Implementing Deletion in B⁺-Trees. *ACM SIGMOD* **24** (1995) 33–38
12. Gray, J. and Reuter, A.: Transaction Processing: Concepts and Techniques. *Reading Mass* (1993) 449–490. Morgan Kaufmann Pub.
13. Johnson, T. and Shasha, D.: The Performance of Current B-Tree Algorithms. *ACM Transactions on Database Systems,* **18(1)** (1993) 51–101
14. V. Shrinivasan and Michael J. Carey: Performance of B⁺ Tree Concurrency Control Algorithms. *VLDB Journal* **2** (1993) 361–406
15. Johnson, T. and Shasha, D.: The Performance of Current B-Tree Algorithms. *ACM Transactions on Database Systems* **18(1)** (1993) 51–101
16. Jayant R. Haritsa and S. Seshadri: Real-Time Index Concurrency Control. *SIGMOD Record* **25(1)** (1996) 13–17
17. Theodore Johnson and Dennis Shasha: B-trees with Inserts and Deletes: Why Free-at-Empty is Better than Merge-at-Half. *Journal of Computer and System Science* **40** (1993) 45–76

Tools for Personalised Presentation of Information

Euan Dempster, Daniel Pacey, M. Howard Williams, Alison Cawsey,
David Marwick, and Lachlan MacKinnon

School of Mathematical and Computer Sciences, Heriot-Watt University, Riccarton,
Edinburgh EH14 4AS, UK
{euan, jdp, mhw, alison, dhm, lachlan}@macs.hw.ac.uk

Abstract. There is a growing interest in personalisation techniques due to the rapid expansion of information systems on the Internet and the increasing dependence on the latter for access to information and services. Personalisation techniques are used to present information that is relevant to the user, and in a form that suits the user or is most desirable from the point of view of the information provider. Opportunities for personalisation are arising from the recent improvements in communication and information systems and the growing links between the two. This paper discusses briefly a framework for personalisation and an initial prototype toolkit.

1 Introduction

Finding interesting and relevant information becomes more and more difficult to achieve as the Internet continues its dramatic expansion. Personalisation provides a growing set of techniques to assist in overcoming these problems.

Personalisation techniques can be loosely divided into those concerned with acquisition of information about the user, and those concerned with using that information in the production of adapted material [1]. The adaptation processes can be further clarified into filtering operations which reduce the amount of material to be presented to the user, and customisation operations which are concerned with the structure and presentation of the material.

From the point of view of the information provider, personalisation offers a means to provide information which is most relevant to the user's needs. This is particularly important if one is trying to interest the customer in buying something. One of the most widely known examples of this is the Amazon web site. Techniques for personalisation are discussed by [2] who presents a web-shopping assistant that personalises information on products. The area of tourism is another area where various forms of personalisation have been explored. An example in this area is GUIDE [3], an online tourist guide where the tourist supplies a user profile. In the medical domain personalisation is used to try and improve information communication. Some examples of personalised medical web-sites are detailed in [4]. A review of personalised systems in general is given in [5].

A. James, B. Lings, M. Younas (Eds.): BNCOD 2003, LNCS 2712, pp. 261–270, 2003.

An essential prerequisite for any form of personalisation is that there must be some information on each user that is utilised to tailor the actions performed to produce a different effect for different users. This information may be sought by interacting directly with the user and capturing the information that each user is willing to provide about themselves. In addition, it may be obtained by monitoring the user's actions when using a service and analysing the resulting information to determine where the user's interests lie. Content can be prepared for each individual user and may additionally be formatted according to the tastes of the user if aesthetic preferences have been indicated.

There are a number of existing tools incorporating user modeling. An example is Doppelgänger [6], which applies a clustering algorithm to the profiles available to it, to find similar users and to form group profiles. This is similar to stereotyping methods but regular application of the clustering procedure allows changes in individual profiles to be taken into account. Another example is GUMS - General User Modeling Systems [7] which has simple stereotype hierarchies describing stereotype members and rules describing the systems reasoning about them. At runtime, GUMS accepts and stores new facts about the user, provided by the application system, verifies the consistency of a new fact with currently held assumptions, informs the application about recognised inconsistencies and answers queries of the application concerning the currently held assumptions about the user. Other examples of existing user modeling tools include IR-NLI [8], IR-NLI II [9], UMT (User Modeling Tool) [10], TIMS [11], ELFI [12] and PROTUM (a PROlog base Tool for User Modeling) [13].

Care must be taken when using personalisation techniques, especially when dealing with information sensitive to a user, for example, the financial or medical details of a user as considered by Bental et al. [5]. Security and confidentiality issues [14] require to be explained carefully by such services to try and maintain user confidence and, if used, these details should be kept up-to-date. If information is shared with other services, externally or even internally within a large organisation, the user should again be made aware of the issues and preferably given the option to control which of their details are made available and to whom.

In this paper we discuss a framework that attempts to address the problems encountered when implementing personalised sites. These problems include conflicts between the information provider, the owner of the site and the user, relating to what is considered important or relevant information. Another problem is the lack of desire or motivation on the part of a user to supply information on themselves. There are also presentation problems, such as users browsing information from different starting points, which could result in a user starting in the middle of some information and being confused or misled because of this. Filtering and customisation can in some cases lead to information being removed which may be required later on, which can also lead to problems. We describe briefly an architecture and a Toolkit , which addresses a number of these problems and allows the rapid development of a wide range of personalised information services by non-specialised staff.

2   The Personalisation Framework

Frameworks are important because they provide a means of classifying and comparing elements in a particular problem space, leading to the development of generic solutions that can be developed to address a range of more specific problems with relative ease. Resulting applications are consistent, easy to maintain and similarly structured, due to sharing the same underlying framework [15]. Our work builds from our own previous work on frameworks - the MIPS project [16] and complements previous research in the field on frameworks and architectures for personalisation such as IMMPS [17] and a number of others [18, 19, 20, 21, 22].

The DIP project (Dynamic Information Presentation) has its primary focus on personalisation. This is broken down into the identification, selection, assembly and presentation of information for an individual user, based upon details provided either directly by the user when answering explicit questions or inferred by the system during observation of user activity. The DIP framework is based on practices and problems that are already emerging in the commercial world, placing emphasis on the personalisation of data elements from existing heterogeneous multimedia resources.

The DIP framework aims to address some of the problems associated with personalised services and to facilitate the use of different personalisation techniques in combination with one another. These techniques might be operating on behalf of different parties, some acting for the interests of the Information Provider, others for the interests of the user or even other external parties. A set of generic tools for implementing systems based on the developed framework is being developed, although additional or application-specific tools can be added later. The flexibility of the framework has to facilitate the development of new personalised services, while reducing the problems that may be encountered. A specific architecture based on this framework has been developed.

In terms of knowledge, the architecture should have access to:

- Information about users of the service in the forms of user profiles [23]. In [9], user modeling/profiling is referred to as the consideration of any kind of information that a program has about its users, to be utilised in order to increase, in a general sense, the level of human-computer interaction. They aim to improve the performance of the system by first tuning the system's external behaviour to the interaction with the user and secondly by adjusting the system's internal operation to the user's characteristics.
- Metadata details relating to the actual information that is available for use by the service and an underlying ontology to define all aspects of the service. An ontology is used to define concepts used in the system (such as metadata fields and user profile attributes). Ontological information is important in the construction of filtering and customisation rules, allowing easy extension by adding new concepts relating to the existing model, and is useful for checking values for errors.
- The actual documents, or links to external sources, containing the information that is to be personalised.

In terms of processing, the architecture should be able to:
- handle acquisition of user information from explicit and dynamic methods,

- filter information by explicit and predictive methods [24],
- customise both information and presentation details [25],
- carry out the final rendering of the service for presentation to a user [26].

The flows for the DIP architecture, shown in Fig. 1, consist of three paths:

- Process flow paths denote the flow of the information that is finally presented to the user.
- Information exchange paths track the information required to carry out personalisation. It is obtained from the user, content and knowledge bases and may be updated during processing.
- External data paths show how the documents that are not held in the content base can be added to the working data structure from sources external to the Information Providers.

The Customisation and Filtering stages can be repeated a number of times either individually or in sequence. They utilise the Content, Knowledge and User Bases where appropriate. They can be maintained independently by the Information Provider.

The result of the Customisation and Filtering stages is an updated Working Data Structure. This contains details of modifications relating to the content and presentation. This Working Data Structure will be marked up, but will still contain, or have links to, the original information to support backtracking in case of conflict problems further on in the personalisation process. When other stages are complete, the working data structure is passed to the Presentation stage, which processes the decisions and prepares the final mark-up that is presented to the User.

Documents that are not held in the Content Base can be added to the Working Data Structure from sources external to the Information Providers.

It is important to note that the process flow is distributed. Parts of the process may take place on the client device in addition to processing by agents belonging to Information Providers on their external servers.

Client processing will involve the final presentation processing and rendering of the information but may also include some last minute customisations, which can potentially take advantage of information about the user stored locally on their display device. In some cases, further information about the user may be requested upon displaying the service, which can be passed to the User Bases belonging to the participating agents assuming appropriate authorisations are allowed.

Generic operations have been identified, such as searching the metadata for particular values or transforming the structure of information that is being assembled for personalisation. These can be developed into the more abstract functionality of data handling, filtering, customisation and presentation. From this base a wide range of personalised services may be developed, from basic applications using only one or two techniques to complex services that combine them all.

3   Personalisation Toolkit

The aim of developing a personalisation Toolkit is to enable Web-site developers to create and maintain personalised services for their site using a variety of personalisation techniques. The broad range of techniques includes filtering based on rules, user groups and content, customisation of the information and presentation to suit individual users. The Toolkit makes extensive use of metadata to describe and process the information that is made available by a personalised service.

The broad structure of the Toolkit is:
- Service (required site dependent information)
- Filtering Engine
- Customisation Engine
- Output Engine
- User Interface (for operating the Interface and running services)

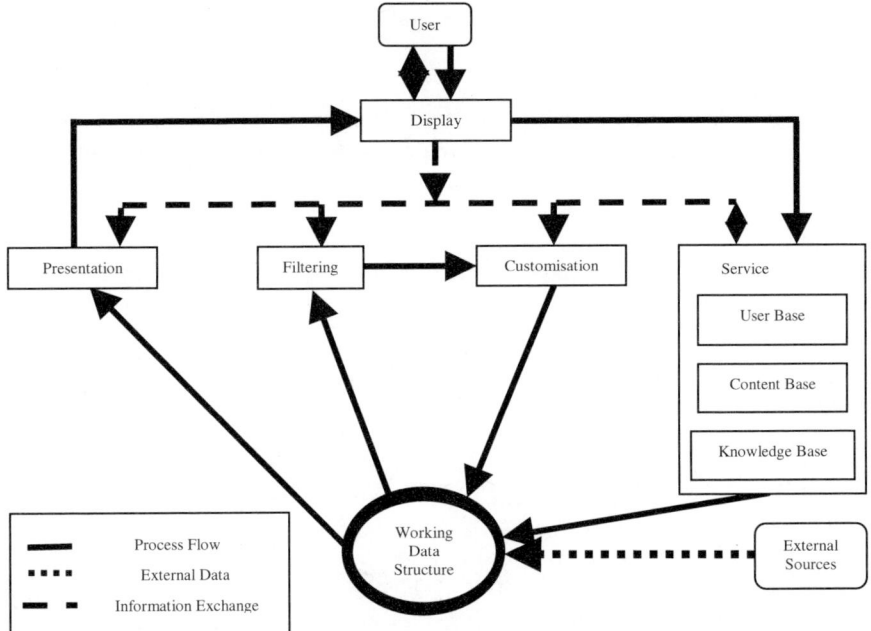

Fig. 1. Process-Flow for DIP Architecture

3.1   Service

The generic structure of the information required by a service being operated using the Toolkit has a user base, consisting of user profiles, stereotypes and user groups. There is also a content base which is made up of documents, look-up tables and multimedia content such as images, videos, etc. Lastly there is the knowledge base which contains the metadata mappings, ontology, rules and templates to be used to personalise the service.

User Base

Profiles contain the documents storing information about each user of the service. Similar to an individual document from the content base, the user profile should have a method of validation which will define what elements from the ontology mapping can be added to it to describe a user. Stereotypes and Groups are a specialised form of user profile which can be merged with an individual user profile in such a way as to make assumptions about the user and use this data in the processing of the service.

Content Base

The Content Base contains the individual documents that feature pieces of information and metadata that are stored locally for use by a service. Each document for a service should have at least an individual name and some meaningful content with some associated metadata that describes the nature of the content in relation to the service domain. Further information should easily be added to the service.

Knowledge Base

The knowledge base contains additional metadata that is mapped to internal or more usefully external content as well as metadata relating to the rules and templates that are available to the service. For example, pre-conditions for rules are stored as meta-mappings. A metadata mapping should define the name of the service for which it is used along with the path to the information to which it refers.

The ontology contains definitions that constrain the service. These definitions are a mapping of the overall ontology for personalised services that can be created using the Toolkit.

3.2 Filtering Engine

The information in the working data structure is filtered using filtering rules in the form of style-sheets which perform transformations on the working data to add content. A rule is chosen by matching pre-conditions against elements in the user profile. The rules can be modified to filter, based on different requirements by specifying different tests based on the user profile. Details of new filtering rules can be added to filter under particular circumstances, including pre-conditions that will trigger the rule.

3.3 Customisation Engine

The working data is customised using the customisation rules/style-sheets of the service. These can be modified to customise, based on different requirements, for example specifying which parts of the successfully filtered information should be displayed or determining ordering constraints on the information. Details of new customisation rules can be added, including pre-conditions that will trigger a particular style-sheet or collection of style-sheets to be used in certain situations to perform a complex sequence of customisations.

3.4 Output Engine

The working data is transformed in preparation for presentation, using the output templates. Templates are required for processing the output of information by the service. Templates are designed to interpret the changes made to working data by the rules and to prepare it for output on a specific display device (e.g., HTML browser, WAP phone). Details of new templates can be added, including pre-conditions that will trigger a particular template to be used in certain situations.

3.5 User Interface

The user-interface consists of two main sections. The first section is a developer interface which is being written to allow users to view and edit the files which are generated for each stage of the processing of a service. The second section automatically displays the output produced by a service when it is run and also displays an automatically generated user profile form, produced from the service ontology, at the start of the service. The processing engine output includes the results of filtering and customisation on the working data, plus the marked-up output (output files of other types may be used given appropriate templates for processing the output, e.g. WAP).

There is a shared section which contains specific tools that have been created to address common requirements between the different components of the Toolkit that have presented themselves during the development. These tools take a number of parameters than can be provided to describe the given context and can therefore be reused and help reduce the complexity of the individual processing engines and the Toolkit Interface.

4 Breastfeeding Prototype

One of the prototypes that has been developed is a breastfeeding site for pregnant mothers. The user fills in an initial questionnaire, to the level of completeness they are willing to offer, and then submits the form. From this questionnaire a user profile file (XML) is produced. Further processing (XSLT [27]) is applied to get that into a form suitable for the application, resulting in a profile e.g, Fig. 2.

As can be seen, the profile consists of a number of keywords which reflect the answers given by the user. These keywords include an indication of the user's response even where the requested information was not supplied. For example, for "job", noanswer means that the user did not fill in an answer to the job question and for "age", noyb means that they filled in the 'prefer not to answer' (none of your business) option for the age question.

```
- <keywords>
    <keyword name="breastfeeding">yes</keyword>
    <keyword name="numchildren">2</keyword>
    <keyword name="antinatal">yes</keyword>
    <keyword name="friend">noanswer</keyword>
    <keyword name="age">noyb</keyword>
    <keyword name="job">noanswer</keyword>
    <keyword name="caesarean">no</keyword>
    <keyword name="mothersmokes">noyb</keyword>
  </keywords>
```

Fig. 2. User Profile

The user profile is then used in a top level filtering process. At this stage we effectively have a working data file which contains the information that is or may be of interest to the user.

The next process is to customise the information to be presented to the user. This is achieved by applying stylesheets, representing rules, to the working data to identify the data that is of interest to the user, using information from the content, knowledge and user bases. This may be repeated until all customisations have been achieved. Finally, stylesheets are applied to present the information to the user in a desirable and appropriate format.

5   Conclusions

A framework has been developed which enables us to describe and categorise a range of personalisation processes. A specific architecture based on this framework has been developed and a set of tools is being realised that can be used to create personalised services incorporating a range of techniques with relative ease. The basic structure of the Toolkit was discussed.

The Toolkit consists of generic tools which operate on specific services. Thus, for each new personalised service created the same basic engines (e.g., filtering and customisation engines) are utilised to process the information for the user, although the user, knowledge and content bases used are from the service specifically designed for that web-site. This permits reuse of well defined generic tools in specialised situations and should enable the rapid creation of personalised sites by non-specialist people.

The Toolkit has so far been used to produce three prototype web-sites. These are; a health news site, a breast-feeding information site for expectant mothers and a DVD site which supplies information on all types of DVD films. A range of personalisation techniques have been incorporated into these sites.

Acknowledgements. The authors acknowledge the support received from the Engineering and Physical Science Research Council under grant reference GR/N22229/01 (Dynamic Information Presentation). They also wish to thank Dr. Jamie Inglis and Kerr Donaldson of the Health Education Board for Scotland (HEBS) for their contribution to this work.

References

1. A. Kobsa, Generic User Modeling Systems. User Modeling and User-Adapted Interaction 11(1-2), Ten Year Anniversary Issue, 49–63 (2001)
2. Ardissono, L., Goy, A., Tailoring the interaction with users in electronic shops. In Kay, J., (ed), User Modelling: Proceedings of the Seventh International Conference, UM99, Springer (1999)
3. Cheverst, K., Davies, N., Mitchell, K., Smith, P., Providing tailored (context-aware) information to city visitors. in Brusilovsky, P., Stock, O., Strapparava, C., (eds), Adaptive Hypermedia and Adaptive Web-Based Systems, 73–85. Springer (2000)
4. D. S. Bental, M. H. Williams, D. Pacey, A. J. Cawsey, L. M. McKinnon and D.H.Marwick, Dynamic personalization of Web resources for presenting healthcare information, Proc. MEDICON 2001, Croatia, June 2001, IFMBE Proceedings, 86–89 (2001)
5. Bental D., MacKinnon L., Williams H., Marwick D., Pacey D., Dempster E., Cawsey A., Dynamic Information Presentation through Web-based Personalisation and Adaptation - An Initial Review, In Joint Proccedings of HCI 2001 and IHM 2001, A Blandford, J Vanderdonckt, P Gray (Eds), pp 485–500, Springer (2001)
6. Orwant, J., Heterogeneous Learning in the Doppelgänger User Modeling System. User Modeling and User-Adapted Interaction, 4(2): 107–130 (1995)
7. Finin, Tim and David Drager, GUMS - A General User Modeling System, Proceedings of the 1986 Canadian Society for Computational Studies of Intelligence (CSCSI-86) (1986)
8. Brajnik G., Guida G. and Tasso C. Design and Experimentation of IR-NLI: An Intelligent User Interface to Bibliographic Data Bases. In L.Kerschberg (Ed.), Expert Database Systems - Proceedings From the First International Conference, The Benjamin/Cummings, Menlo Park, CA, pp. 151-162. (EDS Conference 1986, Charleston, South Carolina (1987)
9. Brajnik G., Guida G. and Tasso C. User Modelling in Intelligent Information Retrieval. Information Processing & Management, 23(4), pp. 305–320 (1987)
10. Brajnik G. and Tasso C., A Flexible Tool for Developing User Modeling Applications with Nonmonotonic Reasoning Capabilities. In E.André, R.Cohen, W.Graf, B.Kass, C.Paris, W.Wahlster (Eds.) UM92 - Third International Workshop on User Modeling – Proceedings, August 9-13 1992, DFKI – Deutsche Forschungszentrum fuer Kuenstliche Intelligenz, Kaiserslautern, FRG, pp. 42–66 (1992)
11. Strachan, L., Anderson, J., Sneesby, M., and Evans, M.. Pragmatic User Modeling in a Commercial Software System. In Jameson, A., Paris, C., and Tasso, C., eds., User Modeling: Proceedings of the Sixth International Conference, Wien, New York. Springer-Verlag, 189–200 (1997)
12. Schwab, I., A. Kobsa and I. Koychev, Learning about Users from Observation. In: Adaptive User Interfaces: Papers from the 2000 AAAI Spring Symposium. Menlo Park, CA: AAAI Press (2000)
13. H. Vergara. PROTUM: A Prolog Based Tool for User Modeling. WIS Memo 10, WG Knowledge-Based Information Systems, Department of Information Science, University of Konstanz, Germany (1994)

14. Volokh, E., Personalization and privacy. Communications of the ACM, Vol 43, Number 8, 84–88 (2000)
15. Gamma, E., Helm, R., Johnson, R., Vlissides, J., Design Patterns: Elements of Reusable Object-Oriented Software. Addison Wesley (1995)
16. Conallen, J., Modeling Web Application Architectures with UML, Communications of the ACM, October 1999, Volume 42 Issue 10 (1999)
17. Instone, K., An Information Architecture-Based Framework for Personalization Systems, position paper for the CHI 2000 workshop "Designing Interactive Systems for 1-to-1 E-commerce" (2000)
18. Kamyab, K., Charlton, P. and Mamdani, E.,An Ontological Framework to Support Affective Personalisation Services in an Open Agent. Architecture International Workshop on Affect in Interactions, Annual Conference of the EC I3 Programme, Siena (1999)
19. Kramer, J., Noronha, S. and Vergo, J., A User-Centred Design Approach to Personalization, Communications of the ACM. 43.8 (2000) 44–48 (2000)
20. Kunz T. and J. Black. "An Architecture for Adaptive Mobile Applications", In Proceedings of the 11th International Conference on Wireless Communications (Wireless'99) (1999)
21. Lei, Y., Motta, E. and Domingue, J., (2002). IIPS: an intelligent information presentation system, Proceedings of the 7th international conference on Intelligent user interfaces (2002)
22. Torre, I., Goals, Tasks and Application Domains as the Guidelines for Defining a Framework for User Modelling. User Modeling 2001, 260-264 (2001)23. Rich, E., User Modelling via Stereotypes. Cognitive Science, 3: 329–354 (1979)
23. Nicholas J. Belkin, W. Bruce C., Information Filtering and Information Retrieval: Two Sides of the Same Coin? Communications of the ACM (CACM), Volume 35, Number 12 (1992)
24. Bental D., Cawsey A.J., Jones R.B., Patient Information Systems that Tailor to the Individual, Journal of Patient Education and Counselling, 36, 171–180 (1999)
25. Ceri S., Fraternali P., Paraboschi S., Data-driven One-to-one Web Site, Generation for Data-Intensive Applications, Proc. 25th VLDB, 615–626 (1999)
26. Kay, M., XSLT 2nd Edition - Programmer's Reference, Wrox Press Ltd, Birmingham, UK, (2001)

Extracting Database Information from E-mail Messages[1]

Richard Cooper and Sajjad Ali

Computing Science, University of Glasgow, 17 Lilybank Gardens, Glasgow G12 8QQ
rich@dcs.gla.ac.uk

Abstract. We present an approach to extracting information (IE) from electronic mail messages for addition to a specific data repository. Whereas most IE systems start with a syntactic analysis of the message, our software generates possible sentence structures from the metadata and then pattern matches these structures and generates update statements which can be used to add the new data to the repository. The paper describes an initial version of a component which handles a number of kinds of sentences, and also discusses approaches to working with more complex communications.

1 Introduction

There are many mechanisms for acquiring the data needed by an information system, from freshly entering real world data to automatic data capture. Electronic communication is important in modern information processing and lies somewhere between these two extremes. Although, the messages contain data already accessible in the computer, the data is loosely structured and unlikely to fit the repository managed by the system. The work described here attempts to process electronic free text communication and extract structured data so that it can readily be added to the repository.

This project arose as part of a system for building informational websites in which pages represent single items or catalogues and each page solicits fresh information from the visitor [2]. Information is submitted by form or e-mail message to a moderator who edits and transfers the data to the repository. The first version of the system allowed the moderator to copy text from the messages to the repository and this proved helpful but cumbersome [6]. Automating the moderator's task was the major stimulus to this project, by producing a component which automatically extracts data from the messages in a form suitable for addition to the repository.

Identifying structured data from unstructured documents is referred to as *Information Extraction*. In this case, the data are found in natural language text and the structure is the schema of the repository. The component identifies linguistic structures in the message and transforms these into updates on the repository. On encountering "The author of Emma was Jane Austen.", the program turns this into the SQL command "update Book set Author = 'Jane Austen' where Title='Emma';".

---

[1] A fuller version is available as a technical report from the address above.

A. James, B. Lings, M. Younas (Eds.): BNCOD 2003, LNCS 2712, pp. 271–279, 2003.

IE systems range from those which fully parse the text to those which match key-words and ignore linguistic structures. The phases of Cardie [1] typify the former approach: text tokenising; sentence structure identification; entity relationship struc-ture extraction; anaphoric reference resolution; and template generation.

Most IE researchers try to develop adaptive systems. The Message Understanding Conferences [4] produced a series of messages to challenge the ability of contributing systems to learn to process novel syntactic structures. Adaptability is a key concept behind a recent summer school in IE [7]. Systems are intended to develop both recog-nisable syntactic structures and a knowledge base as new messages are encountered.

Our IE component does not require a full linguistic analysis, since of the enormous number and variety of natural language sentences, we are only interested in a tiny subset and are happy not to understand the rest. However, keyword matching seems insufficient and ignores the support provided by the linguistic and domain structures. Here, we take a much simpler approach which exploits the following assumptions about the restricted world within which the component must function.

1. The information discovered is restricted to that expressed by the unchanging schema of a database and so adapting the information structure is not an issue.
2. The schema structure is simple consisting of entities grouped into collections.
3. The natural language used is likely to be fairly simple and direct.

We therefore start from the repository schema and a set of templates[2] for sentences, using these to generate sentence patterns. This avoids a syntactic analysis at extraction time and provides a component which is re-usable for different languages and do-mains. The syntactic structure of the language is used in generating pattern once at start-up time for each database rather than once for each message. We are also quite happy to ignore sentences which have nothing to do with the domain.

However, in achieving this we have a number of problems to overcome:

1. There are many sentence structures which can express the same concept.
2. Most of the sentences will include anaphoric references, such as pronouns.
3. Although the database metadata is fixed, there are usually a number of alterna-tive names that could have been chosen instead of the ones actually used.

The first version of the component takes a simple minded view of some of these problems in order to demonstrate that even so, useful extraction can be achieved.

2   The Information Extraction Process

2.1   The Information Extraction Architecture

The system has three phases – schema generation, pattern generation and database update statement derivation. The component recognises sentences and displays update commands which the moderator can execute. Sentences expressing a single fact are termed *simple sentences*, but we also need to be able to deal with *compound sentences*

---

[2] In IE research, the term *template* usually means the structure in which the extracted data is returned. Here we mean an abstract form of the sentences the component can recognise.

of two kinds, ones which update entities of the same type and ones which require the update of multiple entities of different types. Figure 1 illustrates the architecture.

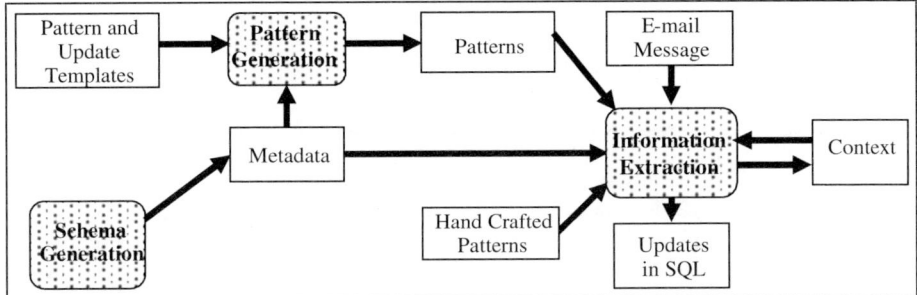

Fig. 1. An Architecture for Information Extraction to a Database

Entity	Property	Domain	0Store	DKey	0HKey	Coll	Ent	FormIn
Book	ISBN	Varchar(20)	R	v	v	v	v	v
Book	Title	Varchar(30)	R		v	v	v	v
Book	Date	Date	R				v	v
Book	Page-Length	Number2	R				v	
Book	Author	Author	R				v	v
Book	Publisher	Publisher	R				v	v
Author	ID	Number2	R	v				
Author	Name	Varchar(20)	R		v	v	v	v
Author	Nation-ality	Varchar(10)	R				v	v
Author	Birth-Date	Date	R				v	v
Author	Death-Date	Date	R				v	v
Author	Gender	Gender	R				v	v
Author	Photo-graph	Image	F				v	
Author	Writings	Book	R				v	v
Publisher	ID	Number2	X	v				
Publisher	Name	Varchar(20)	X		v	v	v	v
Publisher	Address	Varchar(50)	X			v	v	v
Publisher	Phone	Varchar(20)	X				v	v
Publisher	Publishes	Book	X				v	v

Fig. 2. A Sample Data Repository Schema

2.2   The Information Extraction Process

Step 1   Generating the Schema Structure

The data model is entity-based with a few additions[3]. Entity types have properties with domain and storage type (relational, XML or multimedia file data). Each property may appear on catalogue pages, on item pages and in information request forms. Of relevance here is the three valued simple type *Gender*, which is used to disambiguate pronouns of different genders. As an example, Figure 2 shows a schema for a web site describing published books.

Of most importance here is the treatment of keys. The model supports traditional database primary keys (called *Dkeys*), and also humanly intelligible keys (*Hkeys*), vital since the Dkey is often be artificial and unavailable to the person sending the e-mail. Even if we create an identifier for authors, visitors will communicate in terms of the name – of course, the Dkey may be an Hkey as well (e.g. ISBN). Hkeys might not be unique resulting in problems of ambiguity; and there may be more than one of them, which means that searches for the entity will use all of those properties.

The IE process starts from a collection of templates, each of which has two parts – one part for describing the structure of a group of sentences we expect to encounter and the second describing the equivalent update command we expect to generate.

Step 2   Generating the Patterns

A message contains three kinds of word: structural words ("a", "was", etc.); meta-data ("author") or their synonyms ("writer"); and data, either fresh data that the visitor is communicating or an Hkey referring to an entity. The pattern template structure distinguishes these three and pattern generation takes the template, leaves the first set of words unchanged, replaces the second set with meta-data and leaves the third as place holders. The pattern template structure is a text string made up of words including two kinds of placeholder for the metadata (surrounded by single angle brackets) for type and property names and the data for Hkey and property values (in double brackets)[3]. Here is one of the simplest examples:

Template: "The <PropName> of this <TypeName> is <<PropValue>>."

Pattern: "The date of this book is <DateValue>."

Recognised Sentence: "The date of this book is 1816."

The first version of the IE component can only deal with simple structures – essentially those whose main verb is "to be". Such sentences make simple statements relating data to metadata – e.g. "the value of this property is that data". Sentences like this are comparatively easy to deal with since they only require the replacement of placeholders with the available metadata. The steps for generating patterns are as follows.

Take each entity type in turn and each property of the entity type and replace all instances of <PropName> and <TypeName> with the appropriate names and replace all

---

[3] Thus moving from the general template to the more specific pattern and then to the exact sentence has the appearance of removing one set of brackets.

instances of <<PropValue>> and <<HkeyValue>> with placeholders for values for a property. Should there be more than one HKey property, generate one set of patterns for each. Using our example schema, "The <PropName> of <<HkeyValue>> is <<PropValue>>", will create 24 patterns (12 for *Book* – 6 properties by 2 Hkeys; 7 for *Author* since multimedia properties are excluded; and 6 for *Publisher*).

The pattern matching approach also works for compound structures such as:

Template: <<PropValue>> was the <PropName> of <<HkeyName1>> and <<HkeyName2>>.

Pattern: <authorName> was the author of <TitleValue1> and <TitleValue2>.

Recognised Sentence: Jane Austen was the author of 'Emma' and 'Persuasion.

Rather more difficult to manage are sentences which use verbs other than "to be - "Jane Austen wrote it." is equivalent to "The author was Jane Austen.", for instance. In the first version we have resorted to the unsatisfactory technique of allowing the system builder to insert hand crafted patterns and have these available alongside the automatically generated patterns. In this case, the following would be added:

"<AuthorValue> wrote it."

After the IE process, the component will now have a value for a particular property, in this case the date property. It can discover which entity the property is for, either by context in this instance or by using the Hkey if this is supplied.

Step 3   Managing the Context

This assumes that a sentence is complete in itself, but this is rarely the case. Most sentences have contextual references embedded in them – for example: "It was written by Jane Austen", so the component must use context to discover a referend before the sentence can be processed. **Pronouns** ("Its title is Emma"), **entity type names** ("The book's title is Emma."), and **implicit context** ("The title is Emma.") must be dealt with. Thus, the component has a context object with references to: the most recently mentioned entity; the most recently mentioned entity of each gender; the most recently mentioned entity of each type; and the most recently mentioned entity type.

The starting context is supplied by the page from which the e-mail is sent. The entity of an item page or the entity type of a catalogue is used to populate the context object. Thus the message might well start "The title is Emma." if the message was sent from an entity page representing a book. After a sentence has been dealt with, the context is updated with the entities mentioned in the sentence. Thus "The author of Emma was Jane Austen." updates the most recent book, author, female and neutral entity.

Step 4   Extracting the Information

The process consists of the following steps: identifying sentences; matching sentence against patterns; ignoring sentences which don't match; moderating multiple matches; and extracting the data from the matched sentence.

Extracting data from a sentence proceeds as follows. Identify entities explicitly specified by Hkey. Dereference a pronoun using one of the gender variables. Dereference a type name, using the variable of that entity type. Dereference implicit references using the most recently mentioned entity. If this is the wrong type, use the variable for the entity type which has the property names identified.

Step 5 Generating the Updates

The extraction process leaves us with the property values for one or more entities. To modify the repository to accommodate them, in the simplest case, this might mean setting a single property of a single entity. More generally, it involves creation foreign key references or setting multiple properties in multiple entities and even in creating new entities.

Extraction gives the name of the type to be updated; the names of properties to be updated; Dkey values of entities to be updated; and new property values. The update statement is generated differently depending upon the property type. The simplest SQL template is:

Update Template: **update** <TypeName> **set** <PropName$_i$> = <<PropValue$_{ij}$>>
where <DkeyName> = <<DkeyValue$_{ij}$>>;

The pattern generation process takes this template and generates an equivalent update pattern for each sentence pattern, as shown in the example below:

Pattern: The title is < TitleValue >.

Update Pattern: **update** Book **set** title = <TitleValue>   **where** ISBN = <BookDkey>;

Recognised Sentence: The title is Emma.

Update: **update** Book **set** Title = 'Emma' **where** ISBN = '0140620109';

An entity property must be found first using a program module which takes the Hkey value and returns the appropriate Dkey value for use as a foreign key with the template above.

Step 6 Generating New Entities

There are two occasions when we need to add a new entity – a new entity that the visitor is informing us about – "There is a book called Emma." – and an entity property value that turns out not be in the repository – "The author was Jane Austen.". In either case, the component turns the Hkey into a Dkey. If this fails to find a value, a new entity must be created. Then the following SQL template is used:

Insert Template: **insert into** <PropTypeName>(<DkeyName>, <HkeyName>)
values(<<DkeyValue>>, <<HkeyValue>>)

Pattern: The author is < AuthorValue >.

Insert Pattern: insert into Author(ID, Name) **values**(<IDValue>, <AuthorValue>)[4]

Now the new entity can be used as the reference of a foreign key as before.

---

[4] Note – Figure 4 shows screenshots from a previous version which used the more complex syntax involving locating the positions of the columns used by the DKey and the Hkey and filled in null values for the rest, all of which are optional.

> *"This book[1] was written by Jon Harper[2]. He[3] is also the author of the Big Guru[4].*
> *It[5] was published by JK Simth[6]. The publisher[7] address is 7 torness Street Glasgow[8].*
> *Lorain Inkster[9] wrote the book called Good Wishes[10]. She[11] was born on 25-Mar-1975[12]. "*

Fig. 3. A Typical E-mail Message

2.3   A System for Extracting Information from E-mail Messages

Messages sent to the server are held in a mail spool and the component displays a list of available messages. At any time, a message can be deleted, stored permanently or selected for IE, in which case the SQL appears in a window in which it can be edited and committed. Here is a fully worked example as processed by the first version of our system using Oracle. The message is shown in Figure 3 (typos left in).

Fig. 4. Screenshot of the Updates Generated

In this message, "*This book¹*" refers to a book entity shown on the current page and is "The Master, ISBN 012-345-68", and " *Jon Harper²*" is the author and is not in the database. The pronoun "*He³*" refers to "*Jon Harper²*" and there is another book called "*Big Guru⁴*" also written by him. "*It⁵*" refers to the book "*Big Guru⁴*" that was published by "*JK Simth⁶*" who are located at "*7, Torness Street, Glasgow⁸*". "*The publisher⁷*" refers to "*JK Simth⁶*". Similarly, "*She¹¹*" refers to "*Lorain Inkster⁹*".

Figure 4 shows the output from processing this message, leaving the context object with the most recent entity type, *Author*; most recent entity, *Lorain Inkster*; most recent gender entities, *Lorain Inkster*, *Jon Harper* and *Good Wishes*; most recent typed entities: author *Lorain Inkster*, book *Good Wishes*, publisher *JK Simth*.

3 Conclusions

We have demonstrated a pattern matching approach to Information Extraction in which the patterns are automatically generated from the metadata to accord with whichever linguistic structures we choose to recognise. The pattern matching approach is unusual in the IE world, but we can reasonably hope to be successful because we are working in an extremely restricted universe of discourse, only being interested in sentences which tell us facts that we can add to the data in our repository.

Even so, our first version is limited in the range of sentence structures we can handle. We could compensate for this with the mechanism of instructions to contributors on which sentence structures they can use. This is unsatisfactory since this is little better than providing a form, and so our plan is to rectify the major deficiencies in subsequent versions. Essentially, we have started from a simple account of language and intend to add complexity later.

The full version of the paper [3] discusses our intentions with respect to the following deficiencies in the current version:

1. Synonyms for the metadata require the addition of not only a thesaurus but also a full associative dictionary to allow us to transform nouns into verbs and so on.
2. Ambiguity arises in a variety of ways and although there will often be a need to consult the moderator for a resolution, we should be able to extend the context with a history of recent entities to help us deal with plural pronouns as well.
3. We need to extend the pattern template structure to handle subsidiary clauses.
4. We would like to evolve the schema of the repository as information comes in.
5. We need to extend our work so that the output is an update to an XML equivalent to SQL we have used so far.
6. We would like to handle attachments, integrating the work of David Kerr [5].
7. We will tackle different languages, e.g. the emerging syntax for text messaging.

Acknowledgements. The authors would like to thank Anders Hermansen, Nicola Laciok and David Kerr for early versions of this software.

References

[1]   C. Cardie, *Empirical Methods in Information Extraction*, AI Magazine, 18:4, 65–79 1997.

[2]   R.Cooper, *An Architecture for Collaboratively Assembled Moderated Information Bearing Web Sites*, Web based Collaboration, September, 2002.

[3]   R.Cooper and M.Davidson, *Managing Typed Hybrid XML and Relational Data Repositories*, Technical Report *in preparation*, 2003.

[4]   R. Gaizauskas and Y. Wilks, *Information Extraction: Beyond Document Retrieval*, Journal of Documentation, 54(1):70–105, 1998.

[5]   D. Kerr, *Incorporating Multimedia Data into a Collaborative Web Site Design Tool*, MSc Dissertation, University of Glasgow, 2001.

[6]   N. Laciok, *An XML Component for a Collaboratively Developed Website*, MSc Dissertation, University of Glasgow, 2000.

[7]   M.T. Pazienza, *Information Extraction: Towards Scalable, Adaptable Systems*, Lecture Notes in Artificial Intelligence 1714, Springer, 1999.

Author Index